MW00427725

SHOWDOWN IN MEMPHIS

Retrospective Productions
Dallas

SHOWDOWN
in memphis

An Epic Tale of the Forties

Tom Hammond

Library of Congress Catalog Card Number: 97-65479

Publisher's Cataloging in Publication Data

    Hammond, Tom
        Showdown in Memphis: an epic tale of the Forties/
      Tom Hammond
          p. cm.
      ISBN 0-9643846-4-7
      1. Football - Tennessee - Memphis - History. 2. Memphis
(Tenn.) - History. 3. Christian Brothers College (Memphis, Tenn.)
- Football - History. 4. Central High School (Memphis, Tenn.) -
Football - History. 5. Tarawa - Battle of - 1943. I. Title.
796.332'62'0976819-dc

First Edition

Photo Credits:

(HD,M/SCPL&IC): History Department, Memphis and Shelby County
Public Library and Information Center.

(A): Tom Hammond

For

Barbara Cobb Hammond, constant and supportive wife and exemplary mother of our four, whose capacity to brighten a room remains a marvel.

Yes, give me the land
That hath legends and lays
That tell of the memories
Of long-vanished days.

-Father Abram Joseph Ryan

Time present and time past
Are both perhaps present in time future,
And time future contained in time past.

Burnt Norton
-T.S. Elliot

The destruction of sentiment
leaves us not animals,
who have their own nobility,
but ruined men.

-Richard Weaver

ACKNOWLEDGEMENTS

Many people contributed stories and anecdotes – funny, heroic, exciting, dramatic, poignant and sad – that are related in this book, and I owe them a great deal of thanks for their interest and help. A significant number of them also supplied photographs that enable the reader to grasp more readily the events described and the character of the people who participated in them.

Without the friendly and untiring assistance of Dr. Jim Johnson and his staff in the History Department of the Memphis and Shelby County Public Library and Information Center in dredging up old photographs and extending other courtesies, it would not have been possible to prepare adequately the section entitled "Shapers of the Character." Many of these rare pictures could not leave the Memphis Room, and their reproduction there by accomplished photographer Beverly Hammond was a godsend. Others providing help in this regard were Brother Robert Worley at the Christian Brothers University Archives, the courteous staff at Central High School's library, the Plough Foundation and the Casey Jones Home and Railroad Museum.

Jim McWillie, Harry Woodbury, Howard Handwerker and Phil Arnoult are of an age that enables them to recall vividly pre-World War II Memphis, but only a very small part of their memories, which, undoubtedly, could provide grist for further writing, has been tapped. Jim was particularly helpful, and his enthusiasm for the project helped provide the encouragement to keep it moving; the late Frank Liberto also made a contribution. Tim Treadwell's memories of his grandmother and great-aunt shed new light on Mary Harry Treadwell and Georgia Harry, two fascinating and resourceful grande dames of the old school.

Through his book and personal correspondence and conversations, Bruce Barnes cut through the haze of hearsay and misrepresentations of previous accounts to provide a more personal and accurate portrayal of the life of his father, George "Machine Gun Kelly" Barnes, Jr.

For help in filling out the story of the Pig 'n Whistle, I am indebted to George McKelvey, Eddins Hopps, and former waiters and carhops Vernon Jackson, George Scott, Samuel Peace and, in particular, T. J. "Junior" Murray (Flopsy).

Ralph Hatley's input was important in clarifying the circumstances of the "spying incident," and his earnest desire that the event be described with taste and in a fashion that would not cause offense, has been respected. His other contributions to and interest in the book are sincerely appreciated. Burke Cranford, George Sneed, John Schaffler and Tony Evangelisti supplied details that helped portray accurately the event's inception, occurrence and culmination.

Thanks go to Howard "Bud" de Correvont of Chicago, a fine gentleman who, with alacrity and graciousness, provided anecdotes and clippings about his younger brother, the late Bill de Correvont.

In the description of the Battle of Tarawa many personal interviews were conducted with participants to supplement the published accounts. Jack Lent, Larry Wade, Eddie Owen, Bill Trero, Charles Taliaferro of Memphis, Norm Hatch (Marine Corps combat photographer who filmed the action), Aubrey Edmonds, Bill Graham and Eddie Albert gave generously of their time. Elden Beers and Harry Niehoff, who were with Medal of Honor winners William Bordelon and Alexander Bonnyman, respectively, when they were killed, told their stories, and personal information was provided about his brother by Bob Bordelon and about her father by Alexandra Bonnyman Prejean. In lengthy conversations and provision of written material, however, no one was more helpful than Edward Moore, who supplied his personal military journal and stories of Tarawa and other events. Sincere gratitude and a personal salute go out to these genuine and unselfish heroes and appreciation is also extended to Milas Henshaw, who readily assented to my using quotations of these veterans from interviews he conducted for production of his video, *Return to Tarawa*.

Of all those whose thoughtfulness and generosity supplied me with sufficient stories and photographs to help make this a book, Bill Buckles, Ray Brown and Julius Smith immediately come to mind. Others who helped in this regard are Herbert Abraham, Dr. William F. "Chubby" Andrews, Sam Angier, Bill and Joyce Bolton, Patsy (Mrs. Bill) Burke, Jack Callicott, Hall Crawford, Rebecca (Mrs. Leo) Davis, Jim "Red" Doyle, Gayden Drew, John Fox, Dr. Jack Hall, Jerry Hanover, Joe Highfill, Arvin James, Harley Jeffery, Maurice Keathley, Ed

Kallaher, Roy Key, Bob Ladd, Ambassador James T. Laney, Hal Lewis, William Neely Mallory, Jr., Don Malmo, Leslie Morgan, Mike Mosteller, Tommy Mulroy, Jack Nieman, Bob Porter, Bill Rainer, Henry Reynolds, Bill Roberds, Percy Roberts, Pat (Mrs. Elwyn) Rowan, Lou Sampson, David Steffan, Joe Steffy, Russell Swink, Ray Terry, Bill Trickett, the late Phil Turner, Judge William "Slick" Williams, Judd Williford, Mark Follis, Emmel Golden, Don Hollowell, Ira Whitley, Bill Wright and Jack Salmon, who also helped bring the book into print.

Appreciation goes out to Richard Langford who, in addition to providing encouragement throughout, helped in so many ways, and to Betty Crump McGeorge for her admirable tenacity in reading the entire manuscript and offering helpful suggestions.

The professional guidance and skills of Wendell Givens of Birmingham, Ellis Chappell of Memphis and Britt Winn of Dallas resulted in a more polished product. Wendell, who worked for the *Birmingham News* for over 40 years and is the author of *Ninety-Nine Iron*, the story of the amazing Sewanee football team of 1899, edited *Showdown in Memphis* and Ellis and Britt designed the dust jacket, while the latter also typeset, designed and laid out the book.

Note

This book focuses on the decade of the 1940s, a time with viewpoints and customs different than today. Regarding a matter of some contemporary sensitivity, I have sought to be consistent with these times in my use of the word Negro; that term, along with "colored," was widely accepted in the black community, where it was a part of many official titles and designations. Decades later the word Negro was dropped in favor of black and, subsequently, in many cases, African-American, but to use the latter in connection with the forties would be contrived and ludicrous. As Paul Fussell said in this regard in his collections of essays titled *The Boy Scout Handbook and Other Observations*: "The past is not the present: pretending it is corrupts art and thus both rots the mind and shrivels the imagination and conscience."

PREFACE

In the 1960s there was a late-night cops and robbers television program that began with a panoramic aerial view of a metropolis and a background voice matter-of-factly intoning: "There are many stories in the city; this is one of them." Through gleanings from books, old newspaper files, deteriorating scrapbooks, personal remembrances of the author and the conveyed recollections of others, this book tells many stories in the life of a unique American city. Although almost thirty biographical sketches of those prominent in the development of Memphis, Tenn., from its founding in 1819 up until the 1940s, provide insight into what shaped the city's character, this is not an attempt to construct a comprehensive history. Rather, the intent is to depict a "slice of life" of the era encompassing World War II.

The inspiration for the book originated with the events surrounding two football games played by a couple of high school teams in 1943. But, once begun, it soon was apparent that, for the benefit of the reader unfamiliar with the time and place, there was a need to embrace a larger story characterizing the city in which these events occurred.

While the somewhat yellowed and crinkled written record provides the structural framework, it has been the long-submerged tales of people and events spontaneously dredged up from the recesses of mental filing cabinets that have put flesh on the bones of the story and endowed it with whatever degree of life it may possess. Interviews and discussions with many people have emphasized how much untapped lore of the ridiculous and the sublime lies fallow in a community's reservoir of the subconscious. Ordinarily, these are akin to the blind men feeling parts of the elephant with each narrator coming up with a different version of an event involving as many colorations and nuances as there are tellers of the story. The writer must make value judgments relating to individual credibility and peripheral supporting incidents to arrive at the most accurate description. There has been very little utilization of literary license herein.

The book speaks to a time significantly different than the one we know today. Subject to alien influences, for better or worse, each generation shucks a little of the customs and manners of the preceding one, adds new trappings as it moves along and, thereupon, changes the cultural atmosphere of its locale. But this is not to imply that changing mores always proceed in a manner that is constant and virtually imperceptible. The attitudes, viewpoints and ways of doing things in Memphis probably were little changed from, say, 1900 (or earlier) to 1945, but World War II jerked the world around and set it on a different course. The Memphis of the 1950s and 1960s was substantially different than the one of the 1920s and 1930s.

Hence, while this book certainly is not a social or economic treatise, it just so happens that the focus of the story occurs at a time that could be considered a watershed of the culture constituting the first half of this century, and the players herein are a part of that time. What is set down here encapsulates a small part of a chronological period whose grain and texture was a blending of all that went before it in the city on the Fourth Chickasaw Bluff. As in an archeological dig, this little fragment of history needs to carefully be set aside so that as we unearth additional shards we will have the necessary components for a reconstruction that will help us to remember and define who we are.

CONTENTS

Kids and Things

They were children of the Great Depression, born on its eve in the span of years 1925-1928, generally too young to have been concerned with helping support the family through the lean and, sometimes, desperate years, but old enough to be affected materially by its deprivations and influenced psychologically by their elders' dreaded references to it – a time when the extended family reassembled under the same roof, some people stood in line at soup kitchens, and many relied on their feet or the streetcar and bus for transportation.

Britling's Cafeteria offered two eggs with hot biscuits and butter for ten cents, a loaf of bread was the same price, a gallon of gasoline was fifteen cents and radio was still young and television a distant dream. In the daylight hours small kids who had passed the corduroy knickers ("whistle britches") stage, building dams in gutters on rainy days and digging trenches and building forts for their toy lead soldiers, stayed active playing baseball or tackle football, king of the mountain, sliding down grassy slopes with their seats on wax-coated bread wrappers, engaging in rubbergun, snowball, mudball or rock fights, roller skating, wrestling, boxing, foot racing and riding their bicycles. Their imagination projected them back to the Crusades and they made wooden swords and decorated shields with which to liberate the Holy Land from the Turks. They built tree houses, made rubberguns out of one-by lumber and clothespins, with circles cut off auto tire inner-tubes for ammunition, and built scooters using 2X4s and old steel skate wheels. Everybody carried their marbles around in a little cloth or leather bag with a drawstring, a pocket knife was always handy for a game of mumblety-peg, and the reputed luck-bestowing capabilities of a rabbit's foot made it a necessary accouterment in a pocket or hanging from the belt. Shelby has long been considered to contain more horses per capita than any other county in the nation, so when a kid stumbled across an old horseshoe in a weedy, vacant lot or in some semi-remote area the customary practice to ward off bad luck required spitting on the shoe and throwing it over a shoulder without looking back.

The kids told knock-knock jokes and went to the corner drug store to play the pinball machine and buy Batman, Superman and Captain Marvel comic books; and they read all the Hardy Boys books while the girls devoured Nancy Drew. Initial experimentation with cigarettes or chewing tobacco invariably precipitated paroxysms of nausea and encouraged that further puffing be limited to corn silk wrapped in cigarette paper and chewing confined to either bubble gum or wads of wax with a fruit juice-like center from the drug store. Some of the kids contracted the mild skin disease impetigo and wore the purplish daubings of ammoniated mercury.

At neighborhood parks kids could stay busy all day and late into the evening playing volleyball, left field ball, pitching horseshoes, climbing around on the jungle gym and other equipment, and sneaking onto a nearby municipal golf course so early in the morning that they wouldn't have to pay the fee, or sometimes caddying for a little change; at night there usually was an adult softball league game to watch.

At Williamson Park, between Williamson and Willett just north of Poplar, boys from Sacred Heart Grammar School regularly got together for sandlot football games pitting the seventh and eighth grades. Some of the participants were Hall "Jughead" Crawford, Tommy Mulroy, Jim "Red" Doyle, Bob Wallace, Mark Follis and Roy Key. Another of the boys, who shall go unidentified, had an unusually long tongue that, on demand, he would curl back to tickle his uvula, causing him to upchuck. When he could find someone unawares, he would make a bet with them about how many RC Colas he could drink. He would down a couple, throw them up, and continue the process as many times as necessary to win the bet. At a crucial point in a ball game, when his team might need a few yards to make a first down, he would say, "Lemme run the ball," and the "Puke Play" would be called. When an unsuspecting foe moved in for a tackle the tongue would roll into action and the potential tackler would get doused, making his immediate recoil as effective as a good shoulder block and having a disarming effect on the rest of the opposition.

In the years just before World War II, many a pickup baseball game was played at the big, grassy fields next to Smith Lumber Company at Tutwiler and Avalon. But it was the tackle football games at that site, sans equipment, that attained legendary proportions. Games might start out with only a half dozen on a side, but others, ranging in age from 12 to 20, would steadily show up so that, ultimately, there could be as many as 15 players on each team. Some of the participants, in addition to those cited from Williamson Park, were Bussy Dwyer, Percy Roberts, Slick Williams, Raymond Burdick, Joe Johnson, Aubrey and Gordon White, Charlie Redders, Richard Lynch, Paul Francis, Gene Doyle, George Bland, Jack Salmon, Lamon Kelley, Johnny Nash and Al Huebner. A handful of this group went on to achieve all-star status in high school. On a couple of occasions, Kenny Holland, who was an All-Southern halfback at Central High and later a Southwestern Conference star at Arkansas, joined in the fray, and sometimes participants included boys who had played at Ole Miss or Southwestern at Memphis, a small college capable of competing against the big universities. Trees spaced about ten yards apart lined the sidewalk along Tutwiler and were used for first down markers. As the games increased in intensity, people in passing cars would stop and watch. Fortunately, other than a few bashed heads and several broken arms and legs, no catastrophic injuries ever resulted.

During the long summers in the 1930's, Memphis kids might go off to camp for a week or two, take golf, tennis or swimming lessons, or stay home and operate a coke stand. The Coca Cola Company would provide a portable, 6X6 foot framed-up stand with roof, counter, waist-high sides made of metal coke signs and a heavy wooden half-barrel for the drinks. Early each morning the delivery truck would pull up to the curb where the stand sat under a conveniently located mature sycamore tree and drop off several wooden cases containing 24, six-ounce bottles. The driver was paid eighty cents per case and each drink would be sold for a nickel, resulting in a profit of forty cents per case. Soon the iceman would arrive and, for a dime, deposit a large block in the barrel for the fledgling entrepreneur to break up with his ice pick. The Nehi driver would come with his 12-ounce bottles in various flavors, but a favorite for an active person on an especially hot day was Chase Bottling Company's 32-ounce "bellywashers," also a nickel, in orange, strawberry, grape or cream flavors.

At twilight the boys would play kick-the-can and catch lightning bugs in glass jars with perforated screw-on lids. After good dark, boys and girls would sit around in a circle in a yard or on a front porch and invent collaborative ghost stories, with each person striving to contribute a more ghastly and blood-curdling segment than the preceding narrator.

Lying in bed on school nights, they relished the time between homework completion and lights out when the radio was tuned to the fantasies of "Inner Sanctum," "Gangbusters" (hosted by the father of Desert Storm's H. Norman Schwarzkopf), "I Love a Mystery" (with the adventures of Jack, Doc and Reggie), the spooky "Hermit" and "Mr. District Attorney," or to more lighthearted fare a la Jack Benny, Edgar Bergen with Charlie McCarthy and Mortimer Snerd and "Kay Kyser and the Kollege of Musical Knowledge." Unlike the lazing, stupefying effects of television that shows and tells all, radio challenged the mind to paint mental pictures from only what the ear could discern. When it was announced on Mr. District Attorney that the cast consisted of "Len Doyle as Harrington, Vickie Vola as Miss Miller and Jay Josten in the title role," individual perceptions took over to envision, from their names and the sounds of and inflections of their voices, what they looked like, their mannerisms, how they dressed and the setting they were in. Similarly, the sound effects portraying the careening car and the inevitable metal-crunching, glass-shattering crash, the chattering of the "tommygun" on a gangster-ruled Chicago street, or the ominous midnight chiming of a grandfather clock in a darkened mansion on a windswept moor forced the listener to draw mental pictures and apply his own interpretation of the action.

The country was trying to reassert itself economically and wanted to throw off the shackles of malaise and dreariness inflicted by the Depression. It looked to the future with hope and a strong desire for a world imbued with romance and class and fabulous composers – Cole Porter, Jerome Kern, Johnny Mercer, Hoagy Carmichael, Irving Berlin, and George Gershwin, among others – provided the wonderful music that lifted spirits and sparked a dancing craze that swept the country. Coast-to-coast remote broadcasts of Big Bands from such ballrooms as Hollywood's Palladium, Chicago's Aragon and Trianon and the Glen Island Casino outside New York and chic supper clubs with names like Chez Paree, Blue Room, Cafe Rouge, Pump Room and Copacabana, enthralled eager listeners in the hinterlands. Kids would envision themselves one day being in such a fascinating milieu with a sophisticated date at their side as they regaled elegant companions with light repartee while holding their cigarette at just the right angle. Ben Burnie, "the old maestro," always would sign off with, "au revoir, a fond cheerio, a bit of a tweet-tweet, God bless you, and pleas-s-sant dre-ams."

On Saturdays, Memphis kids might ride the streetcar downtown for seven cents, attend a picture show at one of the five theaters for fifteen cents, and then indulge in a couple of Krystal hamburgers and a half pint of chocolate milk at seven cents each. At least two of these theaters were ornate affairs featuring huge lobbies with broad, curved marble staircases on each side leading up to a mezzanine and an inside balcony. The auditoriums were cavernous with twinkling stars on the celestial ceilings, from which hung stupendous chandeliers, and loges elevated along the side walls.

A movie at the Malco, formerly, and now again, the Orpheum, was a particular treat. After the main feature, a newsreel, previews of coming attractions, maybe a "short subject" featuring the Three Stooges, Our Gang/Little Rascals, or Arthur Kennedy, and an animated cartoon (whose appearance always was the occasion for loud, inane cheers), a huge organ would rise from the depths of the orchestra pit with Milton Slosser at the keyboard. As he played a dramatic introductory piece that reverberated throughout the theater, three colossal gossamer curtains, one by one, would sweep across the spacious stage and the words of a well-known old song would be flashed upon the screen. After a cheery welcome by Milton and his admonition to "watch the bouncing ball," which ping-pong-like hopped gaily from word to word in time with the music, everyone would burst heartily into song, with any self-consciousness cloaked by the anonymity of the darkness.

Fortified by the two onion-laced hamburgers, Kid Memphis' next stop likely would be the Fun Shop. Here, for the next 30 minutes to an hour, he would pick up and examine every gimcrack and gimmick available to the practical joker. Frequently advertised in magazines, the most cherished item was a "whoopie cushion," but a paucity of funds made a yen for this and most other doodads a simple exercise in curiosity; in all likelihood, he would walk out without buying a thing. A stroll down Main Street inevitably would involve an encounter with a man encased in a huge peanut shell and loping along on stilts with a happy face under a top hat and carrying a cane. And then the enticing aroma emanating from the Planters' shop, which could activate the most callous of taste buds, necessitated a visit resulting in a nickel's worth of cashew nuts and a bag of peanuts in hand to share with the squirrels in shady Court Square, where Hebe, "Goddess of Youth," in the form of a cast iron fountain in a large pool, had reigned since 1882, or in Confederate Park at the rim of the high bluff overlooking the muddy waters of the Mississippi River.

A big round street clock topping an ornate cast iron pole at the curb between Madison and Monroe indicated it was about time to board the streetcar for home. But if any change remained in Kid Memphis' pockets, the thirst whetted by the salty nuts and exploring downtown required a stop at the juice bar. This was equally as alluring as the nut shop: the oranges piled high in pyramids on the counter, the tangy scent wafting out to the sidewalk from the attendant's continuous juicing, and the enticing sight of the juice geysering up and down within big glass containers were irresistible to a dry mouth on a warm day.

As Kid Memphis got a little older, his fancies naturally turned to more diverse activities demanding a broader geographic roaming area resulting in a lengthening and increased elasticity of the familial apron strings. Not only was he traveling farther to attend school, the assemblages providing social intercourse with his peers were more distant. To a large extent, of course, the basic impetus for this was a heightened awareness of the opposite sex. He might shoot some pool and snooker with the boys and grease the streetcar tracks on the downgrade turnaround at University and Jackson on Halloween, but he also would frequent those places where girls were likely to congregate and join those formalized groups whose functions periodically placed the two sexes together in social situations, such as dances, hay rides and similar activities. Particularly during the Christmas season, open houses were enjoyable events, but by the 1940s, possibly due to the war, their popularity had waned somewhat from their heyday in the twenties and thirties when every Sunday afternoon saw several in full swing.

Over at Jimmy "Red" Doyle's house on McNeil his two older sisters had a lot of friends and sometimes 50 or 60 boys and girls would congregate there on a summer evening. Red's father was manager of Cudahy Packing Company's Memphis plant and once a week he would come home with big sacks of groceries for his family of nine and stash them in the refrigerator. This was during the Depression when food could be skimpy in some homes, so when all the visiting kids showed up Mr. Doyle would sort of stand guard in the kitchen. But the boys would conjure up ways to distract him while others sneaked in the back door and pilfered food out of the family's larder. Invariably, some of the guys would get a crap game going under the street light in front of the house and after they left Red's little sisters would scour the gutter and the grass between the curb and sidewalk looking for pennies and nickels.

Air conditioning for homes and cars was, essentially, non-existent. Some cars weren't even equipped with heaters or radios, and most people kept their houses warm by shoveling coal into their furnace in the basement. While laid up for a week in Baptist Hospital after an appendectomy at age eleven, the author got a stitch-threatening belly laugh when he received a get well card from West Kentucky Coal Company. Cooling was by attic fans and smaller portable fans. In the summer windows stayed raised around the clock, and on still mornings, just as it began to get light, those living within a two-mile radius of the zoo at Overton Park could hear distinctly the deep-chested primeval roaring of the zoo's resident celebrity, Leo, the MGM lion, and his compatriots as the keepers prepared their morning feeding. Lying there in the hazy dawn, visions of these mighty beasts stalking their prey on the African veldt entered the mind's eye. Because of Memphis' eminence as a distribution center and railroad hub, other familiar nocturnal sounds were the lonely grade crossing whistle and muted clackaty-clack of the cars rolling along as a steam engine pulled another long load out of town.

There were few clothes washers and dryers and the laundryman was a frequent visitor picking up and delivering laundry and dry cleaning. A lot of people still had ice boxes instead of refrigerators and the iceman would bring in his 25 or 50 pound "tastefree" block in a canvas bag and put it in the compartment at the top. The ice company provided a square piece of cardboard with numbers and an arrow on it to be placed in the front window so the delivery man could read from the street what size block was needed. The postman delivered twice a day and the milkman from Forest Hill or Klinke Brothers dairies also made his early rounds, sometimes in a horse-drawn wagon. Others who stopped by on a periodic basis were the piano tuner, a man who would come into the kitchen and sharpen all the knives, and the Italian organ grinder and his uniformed, trained monkey who would do flat-footed flips and proffer his little red kepi in which to receive the pennies and nickels of the small crowd that had been attracted.

Their arrival might have interrupted the housewife's rapt absorption with one of the many soap operas – such as Stella Dallas, Ma Perkins, The Romance of Helen Trent, When a Girl Marries, Backstage Wife, John's Other Wife, The Stolen Husband, and Young Widder Brown – that filled up the airwaves in the afternoon. If the "lady of the house" was out somewhere running around, the maid likely would be in the kitchen ironing and humming along with the radio emitting the sensual piano renditions and throaty vocalizations of Fats Waller or some passionate and lively gospel music accompanied by lots of exuberant hand-clapping.

When fresh produce was in season, people with small

farms on the urban fringe would travel the neighborhoods offering fruits and vegetables from horse-drawn wagons, announcing their approach by clanging a fight-ring bell or simply hollering. One wouldn't think that such a mundane occupation would be subject to hazard, but the risk was starkly illustrated one summer morning in the mid-1920s as an Italian immigrant peddled produce on his weekly trek along quiet, residential Oliver Avenue. Unbeknownst to this gentle, hard-working soul, a nefarious plot against his well-being was festering in the prank-driven mind of a ten year old boy. Knowing the day and time the peddler would come by, Reese Hammond sneaked into the attic of his two-story house and lay in wait with his BB gun. His timing was on cue; in a little while he heard the familiar refrain from down the block: "watermelons, cantaloupes, fresh okra..." Sales were good along the way, but after a few stops the horse-drawn wagon was now clopping along in front of Reese's house. The man was loudly hawking his wares and didn't hear the pellet as it smacked the horse's rump like the snap of a lion-tamer's whip:

>That horse lowered his ears, put a hump in his back and took off. The man couldn't figure out what was going on and was yelling in Italian and pulling on the reins. Oliver stopped at McLean and the horse tried to turn right at a gallop and unloaded the wagon. I think even the horse went down and got skinned up a little but, luckily, the man wasn't hurt. After he got the wagon righted and picked up what he could of his load, he finally got an idea of what had happened. He came door to door and when he got to our house Mama told him I had done it. I didn't know it, but she had seen me get the BB gun and knew I was in the attic. When Dad got home he really put the limb on me; it was the worst whipping I ever got. And then he had to pay the man for the loss of his produce.

Diphtheria, whooping cough, smallpox, typhoid fever, malaria, and particularly tuberculosis were still threats to some extent. Antibiotics to reduce ear infections didn't exist and some children underwent mastoid operations. Poliomyelitis, commonly called infantile paralysis, was a frequent summer scare. The cause wasn't known and outbreaks would sometimes force the closing of swimming pools and the cancellations of scheduled assembling of groups.

"Grass" was something cut in the spring and summer with a push mower. LSD, "crack" and heroin were unknowns. Opium was something Chinese smoked in "dens" somewhere and, although it was available on Beale Street, cocaine was some abstraction from which Cole Porter got no kick, or Sherlock Holmes did. There were no frozen foods until Birds Eye came out with its strawberries in the early forties, ice cream didn't come in 40 or 50 flavors and obesity among young and old was uncommon.

Immature and unimaginative contemporary journalistic types frequently refer to the fifties (and forties) as "an age of innocence," whatever that means. There is a certain smugness inherent in such a statement, particularly in the context in which it usually is expressed, with an implication that today's mores have attained a loftier level of sophistication and intellectuality. Only a lazy (and innocent) mind could concoct such an imperious analyzation. How, pray tell, could a people endure one or two world wars, a catastrophic economic depression, and frolic through the excesses of the "Roaring Twenties" and be categorized as "innocent?" In making comparisons between then and now we find they mainly are bound up in a differing of opinion regarding the need for assumption of personal responsibility and contemporary gullibility of acceptance of precepts that run counter to a time-honored moral code.

It was one of those crystalline and soft divinely-bestowed autumn days peculiar to the Mid-South, producing an unfathomable yearning that tugged at the gut. All life seemed swathed in a somnambulism that slowed its pace and muted its sounds. Nearing winter's gelid breath had just begun nightly forays into Memphis, leaving the tall, thick hardwoods along the Parkways, Peabody, Belvedere and neighboring streets tinged with golds and russets; in the coming weeks, eager second-graders would splash through the grounded leaves of Overton Park's virgin forest seeking ideal colorations for their classroom displays.

The gentle sun had just passed its daily zenith, but in Cecil Glass' second-floor study hall on the east side of Central High School its warming effect lingered, and the bottom sash of two of the tall windows across the back of the room were raised. George Sneed and the other 22 students in the room marked time until the bell rang.

Some actually appeared to be studying or working deliberately on some math problem with a busy pencil; others were obviously day-dreaming or drowsing. George fiddled with a geometry problem for his next class, but the angles and the sides soon lost his interest. He wasn't sure what he was going to do with his life, but he was certain geometry would play no major role in it – his thoughts turned to the upcoming football practice after school.

George heard a drawer slam shut and looked up to see Coach Cecil Glass rise from his desk with something in his hand. Glass shifted his ponderous girth around the desk and headed down the aisle toward George. "Sneed, come back here with me a minute," he said, in undertone.

George followed him to an open window overlooking the playing field at E. H. Crump Stadium where the more important high school and all the area college football games were played. He handed George a pair of field glasses. "At the far end of the stadium and across the street from it is a drugstore; look through these and tell me if you can see it clearly."

They were above and about ninety yards behind the west goalpost, so he had an unobstructed view down the field and to the drugstore. As he looked through the glasses, George wondered what was going on. He focused on the store, a tree off to the side along the street, one end of the stadium stands and back to the store. "Maybe he's trying to tell me something," he thought, and he peered intently trying to discern some writing on the plate glass windows, a sign – something! Seeing nothing of significance, he gave up.

"Yes sir, I can see it fine, very clearly," he said.

A slight smile of satisfaction creased Glass' pudgy

face. "Thank you, George," he said. He retrieved the glasses and lumbered back to his desk, leaving a bewildered George Sneed.

Thus began the initial step in a bizarre scandal that would shake the Memphis football scene to its core, involve highly-placed politicians, be the impetus for the establishment of a tradition and literally reverberate around the world when the story was printed in the overseas edition of *Stars and Stripes*.

Crump Stadium looking east from the roof of Central High School (HD, M/SCPL&IC)

BOOK ONE

Shapers of the Character

Perhaps the easiest way of making a town's acquaintance is to ascertain how the people in it work, how they love, and how they die [and how they play].

The Plague
-Albert Camus

A cotton broker on Front Street, Memphis' "Cotton Row," checks a cotton staple while classer works in the background. (Courtesy of Library of Congress)

Before investigating the purpose behind Cecil Glass' mysterious request of George Sneed, and what later transpired, it would be helpful to learn something about the city in which this event occurred. Through the years, as Memphis developed from a raw frontier village overlooking the Mississippi River to a prosperous and attractive city, who were the people that sprang from its environment and through their enterprise, ingenuity and heroics attained national prominence and helped make Memphis what it was in the 1940s? What is the setting for the story and what kind of place was it that produced the people who lived it?

In his travels from Florida through what is now the American southeast, in search of gold, in 1541 the Spanish explorer Hernando De Soto came upon the Mississippi River at or near the site of present-day Memphis. This established Spain's claim to the area drained by the great river. Joliet and Marquette's explorations in the 1660s and LaSalle's trips downriver in the 1680s provided the basis for France's claim to the Mississippi Valley and the French built Fort Assumption near the present location of the three bridges south of downtown Memphis. Continuing strong resistance from the Chickasaw Indians prohibited French attempts to solidify their position in the Valley, and they finally gave up and burned the fort in 1739.

France lost its claim to Great Britain through the Treaty of Paris ending the French and Indian War in 1763, but Spain still was a power in this part of the world. On May 30, 1795 the Spaniards moved in and built a fort on the Fourth Chickasaw Bluff, the site of Memphis. Only five months later Pinckney's Treaty recognized the area as being within the United States, but the Spanish under General Gayoso continued to occupy Fort San Fernando de las Barrancas until 1797. When they finally left, the United States quickly built Fort Adams and, shortly thereafter, Fort Pike, which later was renamed Fort Pickering.

In 1794 John Overton of Nashville acquired title, of dubious legality, to 5,000 acres in the Chickasaw Indian nation lying along the Fourth Chickasaw Bluff. But in 1818 Andrew Jackson negotiated the Chickasaw Cession which acquired for the United States all the lands between the Tennessee and Mississippi Rivers and cleared the way for Overton to develop his property. A year later Jackson and General James Winchester joined their friend in a plan to develop a town on the site. Surveyor William Lawrence laid out a town with 362 lots paralleling the river. His plan included a scenic promenade along the top of the bluff and four squares as public open spaces; of these only Court Square survives as envisioned.

The promoters had been successful in various land speculations in Middle Tennessee but, in this instance, their enthusiasm for the site exceeded the current demand and lot sales went slowly. In 1820 there was a population of only 251 whites and 103 slaves. Because of this, and the need to divest himself of all business activities prior to making a run for the federal presidency, Jackson eventually sold his interest to John McLemore, a nephew by marriage. To expedite development James Winchester sent his son Marcus to the new settlement to manage its promotion.

The fledgling town was incorporated in 1826 and named Memphis – Place of Good Abode – after the city on the Nile that had been the capital of the Old Kingdom in Egypt. Marcus Winchester became the first mayor while McLemore founded a rival town just two miles to the south, known as Fort Pickering. Both towns prospered, but McLemore's later was absorbed by Memphis.

In those early days before railroads and decent wagon roads to connect it with other towns, Memphis looked to the river for its economic sustenance and social intercourse with other areas. This wide, brown, watery highway travels over 2,300 river miles from its birthplace in Minnesota to the Head of Passes just above the Gulf of Mexico; it feeds on the Illinois, the Missouri, the Ohio, the Arkansas and Red Rivers, and scores of other lesser-known streams, and drains one and one-quarter million square miles. Debris floating by Memphis could have originated in one of the tributaries in western Montana or western Pennsylvania – or even in Canada! It ranges in width from 1,400 to 7,000 feet; in the lower valley, where Memphis is located, its normal channel approximates 3,000 feet. At Cape Girardeau, Mo. the great alluvial valley, which the river built, begins. This point was the upper end of an ancient gulf that the Mississippi gradually filled with silt, in some places as much as 700 feet deep, building a fertile valley four times as large as that of the Nile – and Memphis was strategically located to function as a distribution center for the agricultural products and vast timber resources that the valley produced. The "Father of Waters," "Big Muddy," "The Old Man" – he has a mind of his own, with his capriciousness tempered somewhat in this century by the U. S. Army Corps of Engineers. During summer's dog days he "just keeps rolling along" in his serene inexorable constancy below the Fourth Chickasaw Bluff, but when the snows melt up north and the spring rains hit the valley he can turn into a roiling, destructive beast that mocks man's pitiful attempts to control him.

As the river became a conduit for trade between the port of New Orleans and towns on its upper reaches, particularly the Ohio River, Memphis grew. There were the flatboats that floated downstream, the improved keelboats, and then the steamboats with flat bottoms and paddle wheels, rather than screw propellers, that were designed to navigate shallow waters and tricky currents and lessen the danger of getting hung up on snags caused by river debris. By 1850 there were over 1,000 of these hauling freight and passengers; some were so stylized and ornate they were called "floating palaces" and in their white, pristine glory resembled a several-tiered cake. But, while they affixed an enduring legacy of romanticism to the river, they could be dangerous to their occupants. In 1832 one exploded while tied up at the Memphis wharf killing and injuring 50 to 60 people. By 1850 more than 4,000 people had been killed or injured when boilers exploded, fires raged or a boat was wrecked on snags. Immediately after the War for Southern Independence, the steamboat *Sultana* headed north from New Orleans with a load of Union soldiers anxious to return home. It stopped off in Vicksburg and picked up another 2,000 Yankee soldiers, who had been released from prisoner of war camps, and then continued upstream. The heavily overloaded boat, with a legal capacity of 396, now had over 2,500 people aboard, putting a terrific strain on the boilers. When, on the night of April 27, 1865 seven miles above Memphis, the boilers exploded and the boat sank, an estimated 1,547 people perished, making it the worst peacetime naval disaster; the *Titanic* went down with a loss of 1,513.

All the boats helped bring prosperity to the Bluff City, but it was the flatboatmen, floating downstream with their livestock, agricultural and wood products, which they sold in New Orleans, who set the tone of boisterousness for Memphis that lingered into the early part of the Twentieth Century. Being a favorite stopover point on the trip to the Crescent City, hordes of flatboatmen would tie up their crude crafts, guided by a simple tiller and pushed over snags by poles, at the foot of the bluff and pounce on Memphis for an extended stay of riotous frolicking that resulted frequently in property damage, shootings and cuttings. In order to exert a little more control

The Robert E. Lee, one of Memphis' Lee Line steamboats. (HD, M/SCPL&IC)

over the situation, the city eventually enacted a wharfage fee. But being of independent mind, most of the boatmen had no intention of paying it. Two volunteer militia companies, the Guards and the Blues, were formed to help enforce the law. In May 1842 there were 4,000 flatboats on the river and 500 of them were tied up at Memphis at the same time. One rambunctious boatman decided to bring things to a head once and for all. He not only refused to pay his fee but threatened to assault the wharf master if he persisted in his collection attempts. The official returned with a small force of deputies to arrest the recalcitrant bully and in the ensuing scuffle the latter was killed. The irate boatmen, whose force of two thousand approximated the entire population of the town, threatened to lay waste to everything in sight, but the militia forces were called out and stood their ground and the incident died down. This was a turning point that brought to an end the more serious problems caused by the flatboatmen for twenty years, but the tenor of lawlessness and violence they had been instrumental in inculcating into the character of Memphis would persist for many decades.

In the early 1830s one of the city's aldermen was in Cincinnati on business and happened across a small used fire engine for sale. He promptly purchased it and, thereupon, Memphis acquired its first piece of fire-fighting equipment. The contraption was only three feet high, but the two long cranks, handled by eight men, had the ability to produce a strong force of water. The fire-fighting history of "Little Vigor," as it was dubbed, essentially is lost to posterity, and it is remembered more for an event in which it became an instrument for the protection of decency and morals in the community.

A group of prostitutes had moved to town and set up shop in the Chelsea area. To drum up business they began daily afternoon tours of town in a hack, whereby their activities left no misunderstanding as to the service being offered. One afternoon, dressed rather grotesquely and inebriated, the whores hired the two-horse hack of Alf Richardson, a free man of color, and proceeded to parade through town stridently advertising their wares in uncouth language. At this point, the outraged citizenry decided it had had enough of this new addition to its populace. A determined and purposeful group of them broke out Little Vigor and hauled it to the corner of

Front and Jackson Streets where a Negro washerwoman had a big tubful of suds. Into this they dumped an ample bag of lampblack and Little Vigor sucked up the concoction until its box was full. When Alf came along with his raucous load, two men held the horses while Little Vigor cut loose with a mighty blast that knocked the indecorous ladies about and drenched them a hue darker than Alf. Later, after a brief period of mutual counsel, the Chelsea whores departed the town in search of a more amiable locale in which to offer their services. One hundred years later a similar event, but one involving less drama and humor, would occur.

About this time David Crockett stopped off in Memphis to visit and party with friends on his way from his home in West Tennessee to his doom at The Alamo. Prior to losing his reelection bid for a fourth term in Congress, he had told his constituents that he would serve them to the best of his ability, but if they saw fit not to return him to Washington then they could go to Hell and he would go to Texas. After bar-hopping, a great drinking bout and marksmanship contest – with Davy using "Old Betsy" – was held on the bluff where Martyr's Park is now located.

During this era of rough and tumble lawlessness, pirates flourished both on the river and on land. In 1834 a band of river pirates, whose lair was at Shawnee Village 18 miles upriver from Memphis, ambushed a flatboat. When word of the attack reached Memphis, a hastily assembled group of vigilantes boarded a steamboat and soon cornered the pirates, who were hanged on the spot. John Murrell, termed the "Great Western Land Pirate," and his gang operated near Memphis in West Tennessee and stole slaves, horses and land and passed counterfeit money, among other things. Legend has it that when he was branded in the palm of his hand with "HT," for horse thief, he promptly bit it out and contemptuously spit it in the faces of his captors. The area also had its share of arguments that ended up being settled by duels with pistols and Bowie knives. Across the river was the little settlement of Hopefield where gamblers and other unsavory characters would go when periodically banished from Memphis; after local indignation had cooled, they would trickle back. Although they would rail and threaten when run out, their fate was better than a like group who were summarily strung up in Vicksburg.

For decades Memphis had a reputation as a squalid, ugly, odoriferous and unhealthy place to live, rife with gambling dens, bawdy houses and saloons. The alley running from Main to Front between Court and Madison was lined with so many saloons that it was known as Whiskey Chute, and it was only many years later that the name was changed to the sedate and less-colorful Park Lane. Bayou Gayoso, which ran a few blocks east of and parallel to the river and then swung west to empty into Wolf River, which, in turn, emptied into the Mississippi, became a mainly stagnant, fetid morass clogged with the discards and waste of decades. Wooden blocks used for street paving were rotting and stank to high Heaven. But lest Memphis be perceived as a garbage heap peopled only by criminals, drunkards and assorted scum from the river, there were those who believed in its future and, through their commercial enterprise and civic betterment activities, worked to enhance its cultural atmosphere.

As early as 1827 a thespian group was organized to bring theatrical entertainment to the Bluff City. In the 1830s Irish immigrant Eugene Magevney established the first school in a meeting house in Court Square. Later in the decade the Memphis Jockey Club race track was established. In 1844 flamboyant Robertson Topp, premier stock and bond salesman of his time and ubiquitous entrepreneur, in a joint venture with William Vance, built the Gayoso House hotel. Through the portals of this Memphis landmark passed such as Sam Houston, Zachary Taylor, James K. Polk, Andrew Johnson, Henry Clay, Stephen A. Douglas and many other notables. In one of his real estate enterprises Topp developed and named Beale Avenue. The menu of the Commercial Hotel offered barbecued rabbits, codfish-egg sauce, roast bear meat, calf's-head with wine sauce, current pies and calf's-foot jelly.

Robertson Topp, Memphis' first big time entrepreneur. He promoted real estate and railroad ventures. HD, M/SCPL&IC)

Beginning with modest productions in John Potter's theater in a stable, and at Hart's Saloon, traveling companies and troupes appeared in Ash's Old Memphis Theater; the Gaiety Theater presented Strakosch's Italian Opera Troupe and Edwin Booth and his Shakespearean troupe performed at Crisp's Gaeity. In 1851 P. T. Barnum brought Jenny Lind, the "Swedish Nightingale," to town for a performance at the New Memphis Theater, and the same year St. Peter's Catholic Church organized St. Agnes Academy for girls. For those who could afford them, numerous private academies and girls' "finishing schools," which attracted students even from outside Memphis, were established, but in 1848, through the efforts of Magevney and others, the city decided, for the first time, to undertake the establishment of public schools. In 1857 an historical society was started and by 1860, the year the Memphis Philharmonic Society was established, there existed Leath Orphanage, St. Peter's Orphanage, and the Memphis Medical Association. Also in 1860 a chamber of commerce was organized and the city made its first appropriations for a water works and a paid fire department. In the late 1850s a number of mercantile businesses were established by people whose names are still active or recognized by living Memphians: William R. Moore, Bernard Lowenstein and brothers, Gerber, Sessel, Gronauer and Halle.

Memphis and cotton are synonymous; the first load arrived from Fayette County, Tenn. in 1826. It's what fueled the economy. It took mules and plows and seed and rain, and then sun – lots of sun – and hoeing and picking and ginning and classing and marketing. And along the way the mules had to eat and the hoers and pickers – the slaves and sharecroppers – needed groceries. And the planters needed to finance all this until the crop was made and ginned and sold, and they got it from the factors on Front Street, Memphis' "Cotton Row." Teams of oxen hauled the white gold from West Tennessee and the Mississippi Delta, or it was ferried across the river from Arkansas. When it was moving during the fall and early winter teamsters, waiting for their cotton to be ginned, camped along the bluff and the glow of hundreds of campfires cast an eerie scene of stygian proportions. Steamboats hauled millions of bales with some so heavily loaded the decks seemed to barely be above the water.

Loading and unloading boats on the waterfront was a fascinating operation of such diverse and colorful magnitude that it frequently attracted crowds of the curious who observed the activities from the top of the bluff or from windows in the upper floors of buildings along Front Street. Boxes, sacks, barrels and bales would be piled all along the cobblestones with each conglomeration signified by an individually designed

Looking north along Cotton Row, circa 1895, a four-block section of Front Street between Beale and Monroe.(HD, M/SCPL&IC)

The steamboat T.P. Leathers enters Memphis Harbor with a reported 4,000 bales of cotton. The lower deck was actually taking water.(HD, M/SCPL&IC)

flag that identified a particular shipper or recipient. Clusters of roustabouts, working independently, would sprawl on cotton bales, or, in a secluded area amongst the bales, sip liquor with straws out of a jug while awaiting satisfactory bids for their services. Loudly hawking hot catfish, hoecakes and cookies, peddlers wended their way through the masses of humanity and piles of freight and dodged the comings and goings of the rattling, mule-drawn wagons and cotton carts, their cries occasionally submerged in the clangor of a bell or deep-throated whistle of a departing steamboat with its passengers and on-shore well-wishers waving and yelling their good-byes. After primitive negotiations and eventually accepting the shouted offer of a boat clerk, the roustabouts got to work hauling the sacks, boxes and barrels on their shoulders, breaking into song and cutting monkeyshines with shuffling little dances. "Po' rouster ain't got no home, make his livin' wid his shoulder bone." Then the rousters paired up to roll the 500 pound cotton bales up the plank to the boat, making up songs as they went, with a tough mate overseeing all from the top deck and yelling and cursing to cut down on the rousters' hijinks and keep them working steadily.

No one more epitomized the river and the steamboats, with all their attendant glamour and romance, than James

Roustabouts unloading on the Memphis waterfront, circa 1905. The Sadie Lee is in the background. (HD, M/SCPL&IC)

Lee. He grew up working on boats on the Cumberland River out of Dover, Tenn. and came to Memphis in 1856 at age forty-eight. He established the Lee Line that operated as many as 14 boats at the same time. In his younger days when a boiler exploded he waded through scalding water to save a mate who was trapped. Particularly as he grew older, the damage done to his legs made it increasingly difficult to support his weight of 300 plus pounds. After the evening meal aboard the boat, he would settle into one of his large specially built hickory and white oak chairs on the promenade deck and regale his male passengers with one or more tall tales from his vast repertoire of experiences on the river.

Respected for his knowledge of the hazards of the Mississippi and its tributaries and the capacity of his boats, Jim Lee was concerned foremost with the safety and comfort of his passengers. And his reputation for good humor and fair dealing made him a revered figure by all those whose livelihood depended on the river – particularly his crew and the roustabouts.

Years before, on the wharf at Nashville, he had succumbed to the continued pleas of a little six-year-old free Negro waif who followed him around begging to be taken aboard his boat. His name was Sam and, after awhile, he began calling himself Sam Lee. Principally as a valet, he served Jim Lee for 40 or more years and was the envy of all the other Negroes on the river. When Jim's son, Stacker, rode off to the war with Forrest at age 16, Jim sent Sam with him. When Stacker came back to Memphis he started at the bottom as fourth clerk at a dollar a day and worked his way up to captain. Diligent in his duties and loving the river like his father, he commanded the same respect and admiration that was afforded to him. But there were additional reasons. In the common parlance of today, he was somewhat of a "swinger," which captured the imagination of the roustabouts, and when Sam would gather them around and tell stories about, "Me and Mista Stack in de wah," it only increased their awe of him. James Lee, Jr., a Princeton graduate and a lawyer, joined the company in 1887 when his father's damaged legs would no longer permit him to stand. For thirty days after Jim Lee's death in January, 1889, all steamboats entering Memphis flew their flags at half-mast.

The sons and grandsons kept the Lee Line going, but the competition from the railroads was slowing killing the steamboats and when one burned or sank it was not replaced. The names of some of the boats reflected a genealogical litany of Lees: *Robert E. Lee* (not the one that raced the *Natchez;* on it the first name was abbreviated to "Robt."), *Rowena Lee*, *Rosa Lee*, *Rees Lee*, *Georgia Lee*, *James Lee*, one of the largest and fastest on the river, and *Stacker Lee*, sometimes referred to as the "Old Stack-0'-Dollars," for the money it earned.

By 1910 the Lee Line was losing money and it was liquidated in 1925, but one of the grandsons, G. Peters Lee, stayed on running four boats. By 1931 there was only one remaining, and it was too antiquated to continue running. It was sold to a company for refitting as an excursion boat. Duplicating the occasion of his grandfather's retirement, Pete Lee gave a farewell dinner party on the *Harry Lee*, the conclusion of which was noted by the sounding of the whistle that originally had been on the *James Lee*. The whistle was removed and given to Cap'n Pete and he and his guests retreated to the cobblestones to watch a Lee boat leave the Memphis wharf for the last time.

The Memphis and Charleston Railroad was completed in 1857 providing a rail line to the Atlantic Ocean and a more direct route to the cotton hungry mills of Liverpool. The burgeoning multifaceted industry provided untold thousands of jobs and was the basis for many fortunes, as the firms along Front Street provided the financing and supplies for its production and then sold it to customers around the world, becoming the world's largest inland cotton market.

Large wholesale companies in Memphis provided the tools and the hardware, the groceries, the clothing and notions and the furniture. But most of the manufactured goods were made in the North. Basically, local industry supplied only certain aspects of the local needs for manufactured products with an infinitesimal part exported to other areas. Memphis had access to the raw materials, the entreprenuership and the financing to support large industrial enterprises but it did not choose to do so. This was a phenomenon peculiar to the South, which in 1860 contributed only one-tenth of the total industrial output nationwide.

This is what editor Henry Grady of Georgia persistently railed against a couple of decades after the war. What he must have known, but obviously refused to acknowledge, was that the soul of the Southern people, despite the ultimate economic detriment, was wed to the soil and they preferred to live their lives in consonance with the isochronal rhythms of nature – as professed so eloquently by the Agrarians at Vanderbilt two generations later. On Front Street the wisps of cotton clinging to the clothes of those who classed and sold it was personal reassurance of their sacrosanct oneness with nature. And this communion carried over to the wood, the stream and the field where the gun, the rod, the horse and the dog also became instruments of participation in the periodic natural order. Because it restricted his cherished independence and removed him from association with what he best loved, the time-clock regimentation and the impersonality of the manufactured product were anathema to the Southerner. When, in the last century, lawyer, judge and local character Archibald Wright was taken to task by a friend for losing money planting cotton instead of concentrating on his profession, he chuckled and replied, "Why you oughta know I practice law jus' so I can farm."

The ante-bellum cotton economy was, of course, dependent upon slave labor. One of those who provided slaves to the planters probably was the most extraordinary man the area ever produced. He certainly has had more written about him than anyone else from Memphis. Starting from nothing, Nathan Bedford Forrest built a fortune of over one million dollars as a cotton planter and trader in land, livestock and slaves. For those slaves who passed through his market on Adams Avenue near Third Street, he had a reputation for kindness and fair treatment; he wouldn't sell to a master known for cruelty and he wouldn't permit the separation of families. For those who fell sick, he would send them to his 3,300 acre plantation in Coahoma County, Miss. where they could regain their strength on good food and exercise.

He was born in Middle Tennessee near Chapel Hill, in what was then Bedford County but now is in Marshall County. As a young boy the family moved to north Mississippi and at age sixteen, with only approximately six months of schooling, he assumed much of the support of his mother and nine younger brothers and sisters upon the death of his blacksmith father.

He came to Memphis at thirty, prospered, and was elected a city alderman. He enlisted in the Confederate Army as a private one month before his fortieth birthday and soon was raising a battalion of cavalry and helping equip it out of his own pocket. Forty-five of the slaves on his plantation served with him during the war as teamsters. He had told them, "that I was going into the army; and that if they would go with me, if we got whipped they would be free anyhow, and that if we succeeded and slavery was perpetuated, if they would act faithfully with me to the end of the war, I would set them free. Eighteen months before the war closed I was satisfied that we were going to be defeated, and I gave these forty-five men, or forty-four of them, their free papers, for fear I might get killed."

Forrest was six feet two and weighed probably about 185 pounds; forged by the hardships and rigors of the frontier, his body was lithe and strong. His lean, swarthy face had high cheekbones and his wide-set, gray-blue eyes produced a penetrating steady gaze that hinted of the intrinsic strength of mind and body. He indulged in neither liquor nor tobacco in any form. His capacity for explosive anger and prompt action was legendary, but he lacked pretense and could be gentle and patient at times, particularly with children who would prevail upon him to tell them stories.

During the war he was wounded four times, had 29 horses shot from under him and killed 30 men in hand-to-hand combat. He quipped that that tally put him one ahead. He was a commander who led into the maw of battle and with his fierceness, enormous endurance, courage and common sense, inspired ordinary men to superhuman effort and drove them and himself unmercifully. He never shirked from performing

LtGen Nathan Bedford Forrest; the "Wizard of the Saddle." Recognized as one of history's greatest cavalry commanders. (HD, M/SCPL&IC)

the most menial task alongside his men and he commanded them with such energy and absolute confidence that they feared him more than they did the enemy. As long as they lived they could reflect with pride that "I rode with Forrest" or "Old Bedford."

Despite his lack of formal education and any training whatever in military science, Forrest had the innate capacity to plan his military operations meticulously, well in advance of carrying them out. Then, during battle, he had the additional ability to analyze quickly conditions relating to terrain and troop dispositions and thereupon make necessary adjustments. When planning an operation he did not like to be disturbed and would get off to himself in deep concentration. Once, while in this process, he walked around and around a large circle with head down and hands clasped behind him, but he was bothered persistently by some thoughtless person with a problem he insisted on discussing with the General. As one would swat at a pesky insect, Forrest lashed out with his fist, knocked the man cold and kept on with his studied rounds, automatically stepping over the unconscious man as he encountered him on each circuit.

While discussing recent operations and comparing notes with Basil Duke, brother-in-law and second in command to General John Hunt Morgan, Forrest synthesized his tactical philosophy by stating: "I just get there first with the most men." Of course, most of the time his victories were achieved with forces numerically inferior to those of his opponent, and he had no reservations about dividing his troops into yet smaller units and moving them around the battlefield to strike the enemy on his flanks or in his rear. "To get there first with the most men," was referred to by Sir Frederick Maurice in a dispatch from the front in World War I and again in his book *Lee, the Soldier*: "There we have in eight words the gist of many volumes of Jomini and Clausewitz." In writing of Forrest in 1892, General Viscount Wolseley, retired leader of Britain's armed forces, remarked in analyzing his operations that his tactics "... seem as if designed by a military professor," and he commented on his remarkable fearlessness, "always to be in front of those he led," which enabled him to "find the enemy's weak point, and, having ascertained it, he forthwith went for it ..." Another Forrest tactic was to strive to put the "skeer" on his opposition and, attaining it, to keep it on through relentless pursuit of his routed foe.

At Fort Donelson, early in the war, the Confederate command was in somewhat disarray, due to three brigadier generals on the scene sharing responsibilities and confusion as to the size and disposition of the Federal forces. Forrest, a colonel at the time, objected to the decision to surrender and led his men and some others out of the fort unscathed and to safety through a deep slough in freezing temperatures. A year later, frustrated at the ineptitude and lack of aggressiveness of his commander, General Braxton Bragg, and the latter's failure to use Forrest to his maximum capabilities, he angrily quit Bragg's army and told him face to face that if their paths crossed again, "it will be at the peril of your life."

With Union troops barricaded in forts or blockhouses and his own obscured from their view by a railroad embankment or small hills, Forrest would parade the same units back and forth with bugle calls and sharp commands. The Yankees could see the flags on staffs and hear the orders being given and come to the conclusion that they were about to be attacked by overwhelming numbers when, in actuality,

Forrest frequently would have fewer troops than they. But these ruses ordinarily were convincing enough to effect a surrender without a shot being fired.

At Brice's Cross Roads, in northeast Mississippi, Forrest won his greatest victory, smashing a Union army of 8,300 with a force of about 5,000. Prior to the battle Forrest had accurately predicted how each stage of it would develop and unfold and what would be the ultimate result in each. One of his innovative, and unheard of, tactics late in the battle was to mass his artillery in the center and have it "charge right down the road," firing as they went without benefit of support from infantry or cavalry. The victory turned into a rout as the demoralized Yankees abandoned 250 supply wagons and 18 pieces of artillery and threw away anything that impeded their flight. They were pursued and harassed for half the distance along their swift 110-mile flight back to Memphis. Forrest truly put the "skeer" on them at Brice's Cross Roads. Comments by eminent military men who studied him, by those who commanded him and by those he fought against are illuminating testimonials to his greatness.

In 1914, Colonel Grenville Sevier, an American army officer stationed in England as an observer, had a chance meeting in a London bookstore with Sir Douglas Haig, who had just led the British First Corps to victory in the first Battle of Ypres. Initially not knowing the identity of the Englishman, Sevier helped him locate a book on Forrest for which he was searching. When Haig learned Sevier's father had been a good friend of Forrest and that, when a child, the Colonel himself had received riding lessons from Forrest, Haig began plying him with questions and it became apparent that he knew more about the "Wizard of the Saddle" than did Sevier. Haig made the comment that, "Officers of our British cavalry service study his campaigns and his methods. We regard him as one of the greatest, if not the greatest, of English-speaking commanders of mounted troops."

The highly respected Joseph E. Johnston, commander of Confederate forces in the western theater and under whom Forrest served, unhesitatingly named him "the greatest soldier the war produced." He added that if Forrest had had the advantages of an education, he would have been the conflict's "great central figure."

William Tecumseh Sherman, with whose operations Forrest consistently interfered by disrupting his supply lines and smashing forces sent out to intercept him, called him "that devil Forrest," who must be "hunted down and killed if it costs ten thousand lives and bankrupts the Federal treasury." But he also said that Forrest had "a genius for strategy which was original and to me incomprehensible" – meeting attack by attacking; not waiting to receive the attack of the enemy. He called him "the most remarkable man the war produced."

And then there is the legend that seems to have a life of its own, that German Field Marshall Erwin Rommel so admired Forrest's tactical abilities that he actually came to the United States in the early 1930s to study his battles at the scenes, firsthand. This premise was expanded upon in an entertaining novel a few years ago entitled, *Rommel and the Rebel*, that had the Desert Fox, after attending a garden party in Oxford, Miss., playing a nocturnal game of tennis with William Faulkner at Rowan Oak and then, with a jug of moonshine in tow, taking off with him by car in the middle of the night for a visit to the Shiloh battlefield and, a day or two later, commandeering a new motorcycle from a young redneck to bounce all over the hills and gullies of Brice's Cross Roads.

Just after dawn on June 6, 1862 almost one-fourth of Memphis' population of about 24,000 people perched on the bluff and watched the naval Battle of Memphis. With makeshift Confederate boats, some using cotton bales as armament, opposing Union gunboats and steel-nosed rams with many more guns, the fight was over before it started. The battle lasted about 90 minutes and the Federals took control of the city for the remainder of the war.* During the occupation, with the large number of troops, army contractors and wide variety of speculators that had arrived from the North, Memphis boomed and resembled a northern commercial city. The occupancy was not threatened for over two years when, at four o'clock on the foggy morning of August 21, 1864, Forrest sent about 1,500 men galloping into the city while he waited at the southern edge to coordinate the raid.

The purpose was to capture the three Yankee generals there and free Confederate soldiers and civilian sympathizers imprisoned in the Irving Block Building on Second Street near

---

* Some of the troops, looking for booty, invaded the home of the author's great-grandmother (then in her late teens) "with muddy boots, and even snatched doilies off the arms of the furniture."

Court Square. Forrest's brother, Bill, rode his horse into the lobby of the Gayoso House in search of General Hurlburt, who happened to be spending the night at the home of a colonel on his staff. The other two were alerted in time to escape, with one, General Washburn, dashing to the safety of a fortification in his nightclothes. His dress uniform was pilfered but, under a flag of truce, was sent back to him by Forrest later in the day. Subsequently, Washburn responded by sending a Confederate dress uniform to Forrest that he had the latter's Memphis tailor make up. General Hurlburt quipped that, previously, he had been relieved of command because he could not keep Forrest out of West Tennessee, whereas Washburn couldn't keep him out of his own bedroom.

At the end of the war Memphis was primed to take off economically. In 1865 contracts were let for the construction of 1,900 new houses. The biggest change in the years immediately following was in the composition of the population. Of the 22,623 residents in 1860, 11,803 were native whites; 4,159 were Irish; 3,882, Negroes; 1,412, Germans; 662, English; 120, French; 113, Scots; and 472 other foreign origin. With the war's end former slaves poured into the city from plantations in the region. Undereducated and unskilled, for the first few years they received food, shelter and monthly payments from the Freedman's Bureau. Although nearby fields needed hands to work them, as long as the dole provided minimal subsistence, supplemented by whatever else their wits, including robbery and theft, might provide, most preferred to idle away their time in the city. The charitable activities of the Bureau had only compounded the problem by making more difficult the former slaves' adjustment to an urban environment and a different economy. Whereas in 1860 Negroes comprised only 17 percent of the population, by 1870 they represented 39 percent of the residents. And the trend continued. Between 1860 and 1900 the number of whites increased from just under nineteen thousand to a little over fifty-two thousand, while the Negro population grew from a little less than four thousand to fifty thousand, to comprise 48 percent of the total.

At the close of hostilities a substantial portion of Forrest's troops prevailed upon him to go to Texas, or even Mexico, to join up with other Confederate forces to continue the fight. Fully aware of Forrest's doggedness and his native instinct to fight, Sherman even predicted that he would.

Forrest mulled over the idea but decided it would be impractical and only result in needless loss of additional life, and he felt he should serve as an example for his men. In his farewell address to them he closed by saying: "You have been good soldiers; you can be good citizens. Obey the laws, preserve your honor, and the government to which you have surrendered can afford to be and will be magnanimous."

He returned to his Coahoma County plantation and strove to reduce the indebtedness that had mounted during his absence. His once strong physique had been ravaged by his wounds and four years of almost constant physical exertion and exposure to all kinds of weather, as well as the mental stress from the responsibilities of command. At a dinner party during the war a lady asked him why his hair had turned gray while his beard had remained dark. He responded that it was possibly due to working his brains more than his jaws.

Beset by unscrupulous carpetbaggers and scalawags, hordes of aimless and restive Negroes, roving bands of bushwhacking white outlaws, and unprincipled state legislators, the South was in chaos. William G. "Parson" Brownlow, an East Tennessee Unionist, had taken over the governorship and, through various legislative enactments, pursued a course of vindictiveness toward former Confederates. Particularly significant were his efforts to disenfranchise as many of them as possible in order to enhance his voting base. In May 1866 some Negro Union soldiers, who had just been discharged at Fort Pickering, went to a local saloon to celebrate. When they came out they caused some kind of disturbance and got into an affray with two white policemen. The confrontation spread and touched off a tragic two-day riot that left 46 Negroes and two whites dead. Within a week Brownlow used this as a pretext to obtain passage of a law to remove control of local police from municipal hands in Memphis, Nashville and Chattanooga and place it in under the jurisdiction of a state board.

As lawlessness increased and depredations in many forms heightened against former Confederates, Forrest found it necessary to hire a private secretary to respond to the hundreds of letters that poured in to him enumerating illegal confiscation of property, assaults and insults, to which people were being subjected, and asking him what they should do about it. His reputation as a strong leader and decisive man of action had become known throughout the South. It was felt that the Radical Republicans were manipulating the Constitution of the United States for their own political ends, which is pretty much what the war was all about to begin with! Even the low-keyed Robert E. Lee, in January 1866, wrote to a sympathetic United States senator that "...I do not see how those responsible can tolerate it."

Several clandestine organizations were formed to counteract these problems and, although he never publicly admitted it, it is generally assumed that Forrest was recruited by the Ku Klux Klan, in late 1866 or early 1867, and agreed to head it as its Grand Wizard. The Invisible Empire was very effective in the election of 1868 and in reestablishing order and allowing people to live peacefully and conduct business, but it began to be used by some of its members and others, under its guise, to carry out acts of terror that its leadership did not countenance. Because of this, and feeling that the Klan had fulfilled its purpose, the hierarchy decided that it should be disbanded. Accordingly, it is reputed that, probably in early 1869, Forrest passed the word to the various dens that all robes, regalia and literature should be burned and the organization cease to function.

Because of his farm indebtedness and a flood that ruined a crop, Forrest pursued other business endeavors to reestablish his fortune. He helped organize and headed an insurance company for a brief period, but it was not successful. For an even shorter period he was associated with a street-paving company. His next venture was in attempting to build a railroad from Memphis to Selma, Ala. and into this project he threw all the energy and resourcefulness he had exhibited in his wartime exploits. He traveled along the proposed route obtaining commitments from towns and counties to issue bonds to help finance the line and visited other cities such as New York and Detroit in his fundraising efforts. But the untimely Franco-Prussian War had put a damper on the bond market and some of the initial subscribers dawdled on their pledges. The energy and fortitude demanded of Forrest in the promotion of the railroad, along with several acrimonious affairs with old friends resulting from it, took their toll and weakened his constitution, and the old wounds and illnesses incurred during the war reasserted themselves and he began to decline physically.

After the failure of the railroad he returned to farming, this time on President's Island at Memphis' doorstep. He approached his new enterprise with his customary enthusiasm and zeal, but he could not overcome the debilitation that steadily sapped his strength and caused him to lose weight. So that his son would not have to contend with the exigencies of a protracted legal fight after his death, he instructed his attorney to drop his suit for reimbursement of personal expenses incurred during his presidency of the Memphis and Selma Railroad. He said, "...I want to close my days at peace with all the world, as I am now at peace with my Maker." He died in the evening of October 29, 1877 in his fifty-sixth year.

He lay in state in the uniform of a Confederate lieutenant general at the home on Union Avenue of his only surviving brother, Jesse. Hordes of people flocked there to pay their respects. Included were hundreds of Negro men, women and children, more than 500 alone on the morning of the funeral, who viewed the body and said nothing that was not in praise of him. While this may seem strange to some, knowledge of Forrest's fair treatment before the war, that fact that more than forty of his slaves served with him during the war and his activities after the war wherein, upon invitation, he attended Negro festivities and, in speeches to them, encouraged them to progress in life and pledged his assistance in their so doing, had made him generally popular within their community. Thousands of people thronged in

Forrest astride "King Philip" in Forrest Park, Memphis. He and his wife are buried beneath the statue. (A)

and about the Court Street Cumberland Presbyterian Church that he had joined two years previously.

As church bells tolled and a cannon periodically was fired under the direction of one of Forrest's old battery commanders, a funeral procession almost two miles long made the trek to Elmwood Cemetery along streets lined with 20,000 people, black and white. A large mounted troop of his former cavalrymen led, followed by a brass band and lodges of the Independent Order of Odd Fellows. The pallbearers included Jefferson Davis, then in business in Memphis, and Governor James D. Porter and were followed by carriages of clergymen and a hearse drawn by four black horses. Then came the carriages of the family and all the city officials, groups of policemen and firemen, and former soldiers on foot. Many citizens also saw fit to follow the procession to the cemetery.

Lafcadio Hearn, pausing in Memphis on his way to New Orleans, observed the procession from a window of his hotel and later wrote about what he had seen and heard. To him it "seemed a strange coincidence that the funeral procession down mourning Main Street by the Gayoso House ... was passing down the very street along which Forrest's cavalry had made their desperate charge one gray morning, thirteen years before." And he noted that "soldiers who served under him never seem to tire of talking about Forrest." Years later one of his soldiers, the author George Washington Cable, noted that Forrest had the unusual capacity to take men who were "aching weary, staggering sleepy, starving hungry" and "make heroes out of common mortals."

The last male of Forrest's direct line was his great-grandson, BrigGen Nathan Bedford Forrest, III, father of three daughters. While leading a flight of twenty-six B17's in a 1943 bombing of Kiel, Germany, two of his plane's engines were knocked out by German fire. The last man to parachute out of the plane into the Baltic Sea, his body washed ashore near the German town of Wiek. The first American general to die in European combat, he is buried in Arlington National Cemetery.

After the war Memphis boomed; in the cotton season of 1870-1871, for example, 511,432 bales, worth $40 million, passed through the Memphis market. More than anyone else, the man most effective in capitalizing on this prosperity was Napoleon Hill. Called the "Merchant Prince of Memphis" he seemed to profit in virtually every enterprise in which he became involved. Like Bedford Forrest before him and Ed Crump, who came along later, he spent his youth in Marshall County, Miss., lost his father at an early age and had little formal education.

In 1850 at age twenty, two years after the discovery at Sutter's mill, he got the gold fever and, with a companion, joined a wagon train heading west. For two years they panned for gold in the Sacramento River with little success. One day, in exasperation, Hill threw his pick in the river and told his friend they were going into the grocery business. For four years they ran a store and operated a ferry across the river. Returning to Memphis with ten thousand dollars each, they opened up a store to supply the cotton planters.

As he prospered, Hill's thoughts turned to marriage. Having been born in Bolivar, Tenn., he was acquainted with a young lady there, Miss Mary Wood, who had caught his fancy. Her father was a wealthy planter and supply merchant and she was related to James K. Polk. His pursuit was successful. On the day of the wedding, dressed to the nines and his carriage pulled by six irrepressible white horses, Hill charged up the Wood's driveway and, with much ado and commotion and in a cloud of dust, ground to a stop in front of the house. Not to be outdone by Hill's theatrical exuberance, at the reception Mr. Wood presented the newlyweds with a huge tray stacked with as many shiny, silver half dollars as four big servants could carry.

In addition to buying and selling cotton and supplying groceries and farm supplies, Napoleon Hill was Front Street's first big-time cotton factor, loaning money to the planters to make their crops. By 1888 his brokerage firm was handling 100,000 bales a year and he branched out into warehousing, established a fire insurance company to cover the cotton and helped found Union Planters Bank. He also invested heavily in real estate. He paid $11,000 for a downtown lot on which he later erected a building for Goldsmith's department store for $400,000.

He built a French Renaissance mansion at the north-east corner of Third and Madison and also bought the other three corners. He spared no expense in furnishing the home, including acquiring the bedroom suite that was awarded first prize at the 1876 Centennial Exposition in Philadelphia. When his daughter left for Mrs. Sylvestre Reed's School in New York, she was accompanied by a chef to prepare special meals for her. In Hill's twilight years he would sometimes imbibe a little in late afternoon and ride the ferry back and forth across the Mississippi, possibly reflecting nostalgically on his youthful days in the West when his operation of the ferry across the Sacramento helped provide the basis for his fortune.

The story of Napoleon Hill would not be complete without mentioning his workaday ten o'clock appointments, weather permitting, with three of his cronies at Main and Madison in the 1870s and early 1880s. The comfortable assurance from having attained financial security and respected standing in the community enabled these four men to indulge themselves in assembling every morning to engage in genial repartee about whatever happened to be of current interest. The "Corner Quartet" became a familiar sight to others going about their busy routines on Main Street and their klatch grew into the status of a local institution. An artist was so intrigued that he put the scene on a large canvas.

As well as being what might be considered local "statesmen," they also were genuine "characters." David P. "Pappy" Hadden, who was to shepherd the city through a lengthy financial crisis as president of the Taxing District, after Memphis was decimated by yellow fever and surrendered its charter to the state, was a lawyer and Police Court Judge. He lived in a brick Georgian mansion with a 500-foot lawn on Rayburn Avenue. With his long legs almost touching the ground, he would arrive at the Corner Quartet's meetings astride his little mule, Hulda. The free-wheeling, humorous manner in which he conducted Police Court was viewed with disdain by some, but many came solely to be amused by the proceedings. He would slam down the gavel and shout, "The show is on," and what transpired from that point frequently took on the trappings of a minstrel show. His closing remarks were, "The performance is over. Don't be late tomorrow, there are no reserved seats."

Because many of those who appeared before him were participants in fights and cuttings resulting from crooked dice games on Beale Street, as a way of reducing the mayhem he developed a device known as the "Hadden Horn." It was a heavy-leather, bell-shaped container about seven inches high open at top and bottom. On the inside, leather thongs crossed at two points. When dice were dropped in the top they were bounced around by the thongs before landing on the table under the bell. It did not provide as much excitement and accompanying hoopla as shaking and clicking the dice in the fist, but it undoubtedly saved some lives and reduced injuries. For many years the Hadden Horn was popular across the country and available through the catalogs of gambling house suppliers.

Another member of the foursome was a tall, bony man suggesting some character out of Dickens. Judge Archibald Wright usually was attired in old-fashioned tight trousers, long black coat, open collar and a long red bandanna hand-kerchief that he called a "jim-swinger." One end was anchored in a trouser pocket while he chewed on the corner of the other end as he would walk leaning forward in a loose gait, seem-ingly unmindful of anything around him. Despite his eccen-tricities, he was respected as a jurist and served two terms on the Tennessee Supreme Court until removed by the radical Governor Brownlow in 1865. After that he practiced law for the rest of his life.

The final member of the group likely as not would come riding up in his sulky pulled by a fast trotter. An Irish immi-grant who had arrived in Memphis in 1850, Henry Montgomery had that love of horses so common to the sons of Erin. Starting as a laborer on the wharf, ten years later he owned a small telegraph system, but after the war he sold it and built a large cotton compress that made him wealthy. After being ginned (seeds removed), the loose cotton was compressed into bales weighing up to 500 pounds with a density of 35 pounds per cubic foot. Founder of the New Memphis Jockey Club in the early 1880s, he built Montgomery Park where full racing seasons were conducted until 1900; on opening day 15,000 people were in attendance.

Montgomery was a big, exuberant Irishman who loved life. With an overflow crowd on hand at the track, he would arrive with a flourish. As he approached the park in his tally-ho full of pretty girls and himself handling the reins of the four magnificent steeds pulling it at top speed, a bugler on the back step would blow a long, loud blast and then they would sweep onto the grounds to the thrilled cheers of all in attendance. In 1912 the City of Memphis bought the property as the site for the fairgrounds.

Ever on the lookout for a prank or stunt to produce a good laugh, he had a standing bet with an old drayman friend of his. Year after year each December he would send him a new, fancy, high silk hat and bet him five dollars that he could not walk through Whiskey Chute, from Main to Front, on Christmas morning without some drunk bashing the hat in. Montgomery always won the bet.

On June 12, 1882 Montgomery hosted a reception at his home for Oscar Wilde, who had that evening lectured at

Hadden's Horn in use. (HD, M/SCPL&IC)

Lubrie's Theater to a capacity crowd of 600. When Wilde had stepped off the boat in New York to begin his American lecture tour and had been asked by customs if he had anything to declare, he replied, "Only my genius." A young girl at the time, all that one of Montgomery's daughters could remember of the affair years later was, "a tall dark man with a sunflower in his lapel and a white, flabby hand." Wilde's visit was sponsored by another Irishman, Peter Tracy, known for his large, red bulbous nose. He regularly brought the great and near-great to town for performances and always heralded their arrival with explosions of bombs and fireworks, for which he was dubbed "The General." Because of this, one citizen commented that he "should have been locked up," and that "he caused more horses to run away and hurt more people than anybody or anything in town."

Another who made his way to Memphis from Marshall County and became rich was a light-skinned Negro who was born into slavery. Robert R. Church, Sr. came to the Bluff City in 1851 at age 13 to work as a dishwasher on the boats of Captain C. B. Church, who owned his people. He progressed to cook and then became a steward aboard the *Victoria*. In this position he learned how to buy supplies wholesale and taught himself to read and figure well enough to provide a basis for

entry into the business world. During the Battle of Memphis the boat was captured by the Federals, but he escaped.

Ashore, he first went to work at a livery stable and by 1865 had the wherewithal to open up a saloon. With the large number of Negroes coming to Memphis after the war, he couldn't have picked a

Robert Reed Church, Sr. The South's first Negro millionaire. (HD, M/SCPL&IC)

better time or place. Putting into practice what he had learned on the boats, he ran his business with a close eye for detail and soon was making enough money to invest in real estate, which was the cornerstone of his fortune. When the yellow fever epidemics hit in the 1870s and people fled the city and real estate values plummeted, Church stayed in Memphis and raked and scraped to purchase every piece of property he could get his hands on. He eventually owned close to 300 homes and various business properties which provided a substantial monthly rental income.

He earned the respect of the white business community and he frequently called on S. M. Neely for financial advice. After the yellow fever epidemic of 1878 bankrupted Memphis, the city surrendered its charter and became a taxing district of the state for 13 years. There was an urgent need to improve sanitary conditions and it was necessary to issue bonds to provide the financing. D. T. Porter, the first president of the taxing district, apparently thought it would be good psychology for Church to buy the first bond and, thereby, encourage white business people to follow suit; when asked, Church readily assented. And in 1901 he gave one thousand dollars to help sponsor a reunion of Confederate veterans in Memphis.

In 1899 Church acquired a 300 by 500 foot tract of land on Beale Street and built a 2,000 seat auditorium on it for use by the Negro community. The remaining land around it was landscaped for use as a park. Church became the South's first

Arch of cotton bales, with Second Street decorated for Confederate veterans reunion in 1901. (HD, M/SCPL&IC)

Negro millionaire and W. C. Handy said that he was so widely known and respected by Negroes throughout the South that his success inspired many of them to come to Memphis.

In 1906 he organized the Solvent Savings Bank and Trust Company, the first Negro-owned bank in the city, located at 329 Beale. Less than two years later, in the panic of 1907, while one local bank failed and some others were having difficulties, Church's bank stayed open and, except for tightening up on loans, conducted business as usual.

The man who started out as an illiterate slave prospered sufficiently to send his son to Yale and his daughter to Oberlin College.

On November 19, 1871, the Institute of the Brothers of the Christian Schools opened a school for boys at 282 (later renumbered 612) Adams Avenue. It occupied a building previously used by the Female Academy. Local Catholics had been trying to get the Brothers to establish a school in Memphis for some years. Legend has it that a group of Brothers who were scheduled to come to Memphis from New Orleans died in a yellow fever epidemic before they could leave the Crescent City, but when the great fire struck Chicago on October 8, 1871 and destroyed two of the Brothers' schools, some of the excess teachers were sent to Memphis the next month. Brother Maurelian, who served as president for 40 years, and three others constituted the faculty. That first year the school had an enrollment of 25.

During the yellow fever epidemics of 1873 and 1878 the Brothers took the students to a camp outside the city and all escaped the disease, including the one Brother who remained behind as caretaker for the school.*

The Institute was begun by St. John Baptist de la Salle about 1680 in Rheims, France, principally for the Christian

---

* Brother Maurelian wrote Tennessee Senator Isham G. Harris suggesting the federal government do something to curb the periodic yellow fever epidemics. Out of his suggestion developed the U.S. Public Health Service, the experimental work of Gen W. C. Gorgas and Col Joseph LePrince in Cuba and Panama that identified the mosquito as the carrier of yellow fever and enabled the building of the Panama Canal. After retiring, LePrince moved to Memphis and headed the successful effort to eliminate malaria from the South.

education of the sons of the poor and the working class of that time. The Brothers aim first at their personal sanctification; they take the usual religious vows of poverty, chastity, and obedience, but they also take a vow to persevere in their vocation and another to teach gratuitously. Since the days of de la Salle the Christian Brothers have directed elementary and high schools, boarding schools, colleges, agricultural schools, technical and trade schools, commercial schools, reform and penal institutions and houses of retreat. Their institutions have spread around the world to 90 countries.

The original building was a four-story structure suggesting the Federal style of architecture. Here, until 1915, elementary, secondary and collegiate units were conducted when, at that time, the college division was suspended. The elementary school was gradually phased out by 1923 and from that year until 1940 the school, popularly known as CBC (Christian Brothers College, High School for Boys), operated as a four-year high school. After almost 70 years at the Adams Street location, the school moved into a new facility on a spacious campus at the northeast corner of East Parkway and Central. The new classroom building was an attractive three-

Christian Brothers in Memphis. Artwork by Lafayette Ragsdale. (Courtesy of Christian Brothers High School)

story structure in Georgian style architecture. A nearby building provided housing for the Brothers and contained an underground boiler room connected by a pedestrian tunnel with the main building. In addition to the high school, a junior college was operated from 1940 to 1943 but was suspended during the remaining years of World War II. The junior college was reinstated from 1946 to 1953 when a four-year college was established.

In 1965 the high school was relocated in a new facility at 5900 Walnut Grove Road, thereby permitting the college to continue its expansion program at the Parkway campus. The college increased the number of its degree programs and is now Christian Brothers University. The high school is now referred to as "CBHS" (Christian Brothers High School), rather than "CBC" as it was known for so many years.

From 1872 to 1882 Memphis had a Mardi Gras with balls, colorful nighttime parades and all the customary hoopla attending such a festivity. One of its main purposes was to dispel the psychological malaise brought on by the war and Reconstruction. Pappy Hadden was one of the organizers of the event and also was an original member of Memphi, a "secret society," that reappeared with the inception of the Cotton Carnival in 1931.

Since its founding Memphis had periodically been beset by epidemics of smallpox, cholera, and yellow fever. In 1867, 2,500 people contracted yellow fever and 550 of these died. The same disease took the lives of 2,000 people in 1873, including that of Eugene Magevney. The city was able to recover from it, but another epidemic in 1878 was calamitous. In the intervening period, between these two in the 1870s, the city fathers had made some attempts at improving sanitary conditions, but Memphis still had the reputation, rightly or wrongly, as possibly the most unhealthful city in the nation, although New Orleans probably was worse.

Because of the flow exuding from those in the latter stages of the disease, yellow fever was called negro vomito, or black vomit, by the early Spanish who encountered it.

Although not realized at the time, the disease was transmitted by the aedes aegypti mosquito during warm weather and it raged until the first frost provided surcease. It was prevalent in the West Indies and Central America and probably was brought to Memphis by an infected person from the lower Mississippi Valley.

On August 13, 1878 Mrs. Kate Bionda, who operated a small store on the riverfront, was the first to die from the plague that was to decimate Memphis. The next day a panic-stricken populace began a great exodus that, in four days, resulted in more than half the city's population of almost 50,000 fleeing on trains, steamboats, wagons and on foot for sanctuaries they considered reasonably safe. Many never returned. In particular, a substantial segment of the German element, that contributed so much to the city, took their business and professional skills permanently to St. Louis. Of those Memphians who remained, at least 5,150 were to die, including a son of Jefferson Davis.

Mardi Gras was celebrated in Memphis from 1872 to 1882. The first parade featured floats and 3,000 costumed horsemen as 25,000 people observed. The disruptions caused by the yellow fever epidemics led to its eventual demise. (HD, M/SCPL&IC)

People literally dropped in the streets and, because of the mass emigration, there were few of substance left to minister to the sick and all business ceased. A volunteer group of young businessmen, called the Howard Association, stayed and spent over half a million dollars delivering food and medicine to the homes of the 17,600 afflicted and the destitute; ten of the 32 Howard members died. Thirteen Catholic priests and 30 nuns who stayed died. Although they were unable to cure the disease, 2,900 nurses and 111 doctors were brought in by the Howards from other cities to help; 33 of these doctors died. The Protestant clergy essentially left en masse, and the newspapers criticized them harshly for months.

As these martyrs made their rounds, the sights and sounds they encountered were almost unworldly. Like the plagues of the Middle Ages, it was thought that the disease was somehow caused by a foulness in the air or because of unsanitary conditions. Barrels of burning tar filled the air with roiling columns of black smoke, cannons were brought in from Helena, Ark. to blast the pestilence from the atmosphere, lime was so liberally sprinkled in areas of filth that it looked like snow had drifted over them and the streets and sidewalks were soaked with disinfectants and carbolic acid; dogs howled pitiably for their dead masters and hungry cows lowed to be fed, and the awful frequency of the mournful tolling bell at Elmwood Cemetery, as wagon-loads of caskets passed through its gates, was a constant reminder to the survivors of their mortality and heightened their sense of desperation. Coffins were placed in fronts of houses of the stricken and, as they made their rounds on the return, the wagon drivers collecting them cried, "Bring out your dead." Mattresses and bedclothes of the deceased were piled in the streets and burned. Frantic casket makers worked day and night and couldn't keep up with the demand, nor could the overworked grave diggers; many of the dead were left untended for days and others were placed in shallow, unmarked graves.

Doctors and nurses desperately utilized every nostrum they could imagine, to no avail. Returning to their patients the following day they might find them dead or, succumbing to the utter hopelessness of the situation and the shock of losing loved ones in such a dreadful manner, insane. Odors permeating the city were so overwhelming that many walked

Providing succor during the curse of the yellow jack, 1878. (HD, M/SCPL&IC)

around with sponges affixed to their nose or doused themselves liberally with cologne, rose water, musk or other counteracting agents.

The stranglehold of yellow jack was broken on October 19 when the first heavy frost arrived. People immediately began trickling back into the city to pick up the tenuous strands of their lives and begin anew, but irreparable damage had been done. It not only was the loss of so much of the German population, but others as well. Memphis' population in 1870 of slightly over 40,000 was exceeded only by New Orleans and St. Louis in the South and West. Atlanta was only half its size and Birmingham, Dallas and Houston were not much more than villages. By 1880 the population was only 33,592, instead of the 60,000 or more that its previous rate of growth would have generated. Although there certainly were other factors involved, one commentator attributed Atlanta's subsequent economic and population ascendancy over Memphis to the visitation to the Bluff City of a little mosquito. The catastrophic upheaval recurred the very next summer with over half the population again fleeing the city; of those remaining, 600 died.* Subsequent outbreaks of yellow fever never approached the severity of the two in the 1870s. The last deaths occurred in 1897 when 50 were stricken and 13 died. The last known case was in 1900.

The economic body blow Memphis suffered resulted in a corresponding drop in property valuation to one-half, or less, former value. Combining this with the excesses of Reconstruction and loose management of financial affairs, the city was rendered incapable of meeting its bond obligations; bankrupt, Memphis surrendered its charter in January 1879 and for the next twelve

Yellow fever victims awaiting burial in Elmwood Cemetery. (HD, M/SCPL&IC)

years became a taxing district of the state. Angered at Memphis' lack of attention to sanitation, periodic plagues, and its inability to pay its indebtedness to Wall Street, newspapers around the country trumpeted that the city should be burned to the ground and salt spread over the remains. City leaders responded with indignation and vowed to make Memphis a model of cleanliness. D. T. Porter, John Overton, Jr. and Pappy Hadden successively served as presidents of the Shelby County Taxing District and much was accomplished.

The first sanitary sewer program was begun and thirty miles were laid in 1880. Sanitation laws applying to individual properties were strictly enforced by Hadden in his role as Police Court Judge and garbage collection and street cleaning services were instituted. Being drawn from the mouth of Wolf River in a muddy, polluted unfiltered state or hauled in barrels

* In 1880, during a milder epidemic, the author's great-grandmother fled to Little Rock, "in a delicate condition," and returned with his maternal grandmother.

from nearby springs, the public water supply had always been a problem. But in 1887, while drilling a well for an ice company, Richard C. Graves discovered clear and sparkling artesian water at a depth of 354 feet. A total of 40 wells were promptly drilled providing a volume three times the demand. Since then, Memphis has had a plentiful supply of pure water.

Tombstone, Arizona calls itself "the town too tough to die," but that description is much more apt when applied to the spirit of Memphis. When the city regained its charter and Pappy Hadden retired from office, he wrote:

It is a proverb that fortune favors the brave. Evidences of solid prosperity are now to be seen on every hand. We are a busy, happy population – and, as someone has said, a smiling city that sits like a queen on the bluffs and bathes her feet in the waters of the great river that flows ceaselessly by.

Both before and after the war militia companies were popular in Memphis. Probably the best known was the Chickasaw Guards, led by Samuel T. Carnes who, in 1894, brought the first automobile into Memphis. The various companies were very competitive and watching them drill was a popular entertainment. The Chickasaw Guards won many contests on the national level and their performances raised substantial sums of money earmarked for yellow fever victims. The Guards were also active socially and had club rooms and a ballroom on the top of the Exchange Building.

Despite all its difficulties, Memphis made a remarkable recovery in the decade from 1880 to 1890 by eclipsing all other southern cities in industrial growth (mainly cottonseed and lumber). By 1900, with a population of 102,320, it again had surpassed Nashville and Atlanta and retaken its position behind St. Louis and New Orleans.

Almost since its founding, the economic engine that kept Memphis growing and prosperous had been fueled by cotton, but by 1891 the city had also become the country's fifth largest wholesale grocery market. That decade also saw the rise of the timber industry as lumbermen moved south from the depleted forests of the North and Northeast to the virgin forests of the Mississippi Valley with trees a hundred feet high and five feet thick. If one had gone up in a balloon and looked to all points of the compass, except for land cleared for cotton, the sight would have been comparable to an aerial view of Amazonas. Into the Memphis market came huge quantities of white oak, walnut, gum, hickory, ash, cypress, poplar, cotton-wood and yellow pine. Only 13 percent was used locally to convert into various wood products with the rest being sold throughout the world, some in entire trainload lots. Memphis became the world's largest hardwood lumber market, the largest supplier of persimmon golf club heads and provided hickory for skis, white oak barrels for whiskey and millions of handles for all kinds of tools.

In 1892 a railroad bridge, known as the Memphis Bridge, but later the Frisco Bridge, was built across the Mississippi River. It was the first one south of St. Louis and, because of Memphis' strategic location, it enhanced the city's importance as a distribution center. It also assisted in the continuing decline of steamboats as haulers of freight. In the 1896-1897 season, steamboats handled only seven percent of the 575,929 bales of cotton shipped out of Memphis.

With more than 50,000 people gathered along the bluff, the bridge was opened with great fanfare. Many doubted that a bridge could survive the strong, swirling currents of the Mississippi River and that the first time a heavy load attempted to cross it would collapse in the middle. To dispel this notion, 18 big locomotives, some festooned with flowers, lined up to make the inaugural run across to Arkansas. None of the railroads would assign engineers and firemen for the perilous trip, so all engines were manned by local volunteers. After the crews had been given bon voyage kisses by a coterie of pretty girls, a cannon boomed and the locomotives moved slowly and cautiously onto the span. Upon their safe arrival on the other side, another cannon boomed and a second train of loco-motives, with steam up, left the Arkansas side like a shot. With each bell clanging and each whistle wailing, they roared back across the bridge to Memphis. Every factory whistle in town cut loose while, down on the river, bells and whistles on excursion boats, crowded with observers, rang and tooted and the Navy's *U. S. S. Concord*, sent for the occasion, fired salutes of black powder salvos. The train's arrival inspired a cheer of such magnitude from the hordes along the bluff that it even drowned out all the attendant din. The governors of the two states then met at mid-bridge on decorated flatcars to conclude the ceremonies.

Some of the romantic aspects of the river were shifted to the lure of the rails. When that last spike was driven in at Promontory, Utah on May 10, 1869 providing the first rail connection from the Atlantic to the Pacific, 54,000 miles of tracks had been laid nationwide. In the next ten years 40,000 more miles were put down and between 1880 and 1890 an additional 69,000 miles, as a vast network was established connecting cities and towns throughout the country. The great, powerful steam locomotives pulling long trainloads of agricultural products, livestock, ore, timber, manufactured goods and passengers were visual symbols of the growing power and prosperity of the nation and the engineers, like the steamboat captains who preceded them, were highly respected for their skill and daring in handling these behemoths. Lacking safety features relating to such things as stabilization of rail, signaling and braking, that would come later, railroading was a dangerous business in that era. In 1900 alone, 6,000 railroad employees were killed in the performance of their duties.

As a boy, John Luther Jones always knew what he wanted to do when he grew up. He envisioned himself at the controls of one of the big locomotives that regularly passed near his home at the hamlet of Cayce, just across the Tennessee line in western Kentucky. Because of his birthplace, he was known throughout his life as "Casey." Allaying his mother's fears over his safety, he went to work for the Illinois Central at age sixteen; ten years later he had advanced to his cherished position of engineer.

With an apparent competitive streak and a reputation for bringing his trains in on time, the six-foot four-inch Jones was also known as somewhat of a daredevil. He lived with his wife and three children in Jackson, Tenn., 80 miles from Memphis but, because his runs originated and terminated in the latter city, he was making plans to move his family there when he made his last run, at age 36.

When at nine o'clock on the evening of April 29, 1900, Jones brought the northbound Chicago express into Memphis from Mississippi, he had been on duty for about seven hours. A little later he was informed that the engineer scheduled to take the southbound train to New Orleans at 11:15 was sick and he was asked to take the run. He would make the first leg of 190 miles to Canton where another engineer would take over for the remaining 200 miles to the Crescent City.

He and Negro fireman Sim Webb finally pulled out of the Poplar Street station at 12:50 a.m., 95 minutes behind schedule, pulling six cars of mail, baggage, coaches and sleepers. He was at the throttle of his own favorite engine, No. 382 – the "Cannonball" – on which, from another engine, he had just installed his familiar, personal signature and aural salute to all within range – a six-tone "Whipporwill" whistle.

With four scheduled stops and numerous flag stops enroute, the scheduled time between Memphis and Canton was five and one-half hours, with an average speed of 35 miles per hour. To make up the 95 minutes, Casey would have to average 49 miles per hour to Canton. With Sim busily shoveling coal, Casey kept the throttle open and his whistle rippled across the landscape as they roared through the dark Delta night at speeds exceeding 75 miles per hour (Sim Webb later said their top speed approached 100 miles per hour.) Between Memphis and Grenada, 102 miles, Casey had only one freight train to pass, on a siding, and by the time they arrived at that town he had made up 60 of the 95 minutes.

Leaving Grenada they had more than one train to be concerned with. Heading north toward him were three passenger trains and one freight. Ahead of him, moving in the same direction, were single passenger and freight trains. At Durant he was ordered to take a siding about ten miles away, at Goodman, to allow one of the northbound passenger trains to pass; arriving there almost on time, he was forced to wait five minutes before it came by, but it gave Sim a chance to catch up on his coal shoveling. As soon as he was back on the clear track, Casey opened the throttle wide and they headed for Vaughan, 13 miles down the line.

At Vaughan, only 14 miles from his Canton destination, there were sidings on each side of the main track. Jones' train had the right-of-way and the two short passenger trains had pulled onto the siding on the west side of the north-south main track. The two freight trains, going in opposite directions, had attempted to pull onto the siding on the east, which was 3,148 feet long, but it was found their combined length was ten cars too long for both trains to fit. The northbound freight, at the southern end of the siding, was to be backed up to allow the southbound freight to pull onto the siding, thereby clearing the north switch. The plan was to let Casey past the north switch and for him to then wait on the main track while the

Casey Jones, "The Brave Engineer"
(Courtesy of Casey Jones Home and Railroad Museum, Jackson, Tenn.)

two freights moved in behind him to clear the south switch, thereby enabling him to continue on to Canton. But as the freight at the southern end of the siding started to back up, an air hose burst and brought it to a standstill; this blocked the southbound freight's effort to get all its cars onto the siding. The southbound sat there with four cars still on the main track above the north switch. Meanwhile, Casey was barreling toward Vaughan expecting the north switch to be open.

The immediate approach to Vaughan traverses an S-curve and, purportedly, a flagman was sent out to the north end of this curve to lay down torpedoes and to hand signal the Cannonball to stop. But Sim Webb later said, "We saw no signals, we heard no torpedoes," although members of the other train crews at Vaughan claimed they heard the torpedoes. The night was murky and there were some indications that at least patchy fog may have been present. The last part of the curve was on the fireman's side, which interfered with Jones' vision down the track and being able to see the markers on the caboose of the stalled train.

Knowing he would have to stop at Vaughan, Casey had slowed for the curves from his previous 75 miles per hour plus speed, but by the time he spotted the train in front of him it was too late to avert a collision. He pulled the brake and yelled "Jump, Sim, and save yourself," but knowing he had passengers aboard he must strive to protect, he continued his braking effort and stayed with the engine as it plowed into the caboose. Damage was confined mainly to the engine, the mail car of the Cannonball, and the caboose and two boxcars of the freight. When they saw what was going to happen, the crew members of the freight abandoned it and the few injuries on Casey's train were minor. Sim Webb's leap to safety rendered him unconscious for a brief period, but he was not injured seriously. Casey died at his post with one hand on the whistle and the other on the brake. The accident occurred at 3:52 a. m., only two minutes behind schedule – Casey had made up 93 of the 95 minutes 14 miles short of his run.

The question was raised as to why he didn't make up half the lost time and let the engineer who would take over at Canton make up the remainder on his leg to New Orleans. In his report after the accident General Superintendent A. W. Sullivan wrote that Superintendent King had cautioned Jones

"... not to attempt to do any reckless running with the view of establishing a record of making fast time, a better time than other men on the run." Whether this order was in fact directed to Jones or whether it simply was a statement conjured in an effort to attribute all the blame to him, will never be known. But Casey did have the reputation of being a competitive engineer who liked to bring his trains in on time.

Mrs. Janie Jones never married again and wore black every day the rest of her life. She died in 1958.[*] Shortly after the wreck, a friend of Casey's, a Negro engine wiper at the Canton shops named Wallace Saunders, "wrote" a song that forever immortalized the "brave engineer." Saunders was illiterate and it is not known who wrote the words down for him, but the song became quite popular on the vaudeville circuit. There have been 93 printed versions of the song and 150 separate recordings have been made of it. Once when a troupe was appearing at the Orpheum Theater in Memphis, apparently thinking to put some spice in the performance, they added some stanzas that had Casey at the throttle of a train somewhere out west and carrying on with some floozies along his run. A substantial group of Memphis railroad men were in the audience and, taking umbrage at the implications of philandering, rushed the stage and roughed up the slanderous miscreants. The accepted version of Wallace Saunders' song is quite lengthy, but selected verses of it are as follows:

> Come all you rounders if you want to hear
> A story 'bout a brave engineer;
> Casey Jones was the rounder's name,
> Twas on the Illinois Central that he won his fame.
>
> Casey Jones, mounted to the cabin,
> Casey Jones, with his orders in his hand
> Casey Jones, he mounted to the cabin,
> Started on his farewell journey to the promised land.
>
> They pulled out of Memphis nearly two hours late,
> Soon they were speeding at a terrible rate.
> And the people knew by the whistle's moan

[*] In the early 1940's, the author frequently saw Mrs. Jones during Sunday mass at little St. Mary's Catholic Church in Jackson.

That the man at the throttle was Casey Jones.

The caboose of Number 83 was on the main line,
Casey's last words were, "Jump, Sim, while you
yet have time."
At 3:52 that morning came the fateful end,
Casey took his trip to the promised land.

Casey Jones, he died at the throttle,
Casey Jones, with the whistle in his hand.
Casey Jones, he died at the throttle,
But we'll all see Casey in the promised land.

In recent years Casey's modest home was moved from downtown Jackson to a site near Interstate Highway 40, where, next to an old steam engine and surrounded by shops depicting a small town square, it serves as a museum and memorial to "the brave engineer."

Nine years before Casey's crash another Memphis engineer, Lee Christmas of the Yazoo and Mississippi Valley line, ran his freight train into another. In investigating the cause, it was discovered he was color blind and could not recognize the signals at night. After being relieved of his duties, he went to Honduras to run a banana train during the day. The country was in a state of political foment and, being a man of action endowed with leadership qualities, Christmas got involved.

Over a 20 year period, General Christmas conquered and established puppet presidents in El Salvador, Guatemala, and Nicaragua. He is reputed to have fought 36 major battles and an uncounted number of skirmishes. He was wounded at least seven times, and his left arm was rendered limp and useless by machine gun fire. In one episode, after the government he was backing in Honduras was overthrown, he was chased through the streets by the insurgents' army and a mob of its supporters. Barricading himself alone in an armory with 1,500 rifles and an ample supply of ammunition, he ran from one aperture to another picking off his adversaries. During a siege that lasted for hours, it has been estimated that he killed approximately 100 of the attackers. Thinking they were encountering a squad of sharpshooters, the besiegers called a truce. When Christmas walked out and it was realized he had held them off by himself, he was cheered and made a general on the side of the insurgents. At one time he was given valuable mining and railroad concessions and operated a large hotel.

Desiring to support a revolt at an opportune time in Nicaragua, he called on President Cabrera of Guatemala to send 500 soldiers from his rag tag little army. When Cabrera vacillated, Christmas sent him a note of such directness and force as to do justice to Bedford Forrest:

> *Manuel Cabrera, Son of a Cur, President of Guatemala, Sir: You dirty dog, I put you in as president of this republic and you have refused to let me have money or men for the necessary campaign. You cowardly pup; if you would fight, I would beat your brains out; if you would duel, I would chop you to bits. I spit on you, to hell with you. I have quit you.*
>
> *Lee Christmas*

After the United States put the heat on him for running guns out of New Orleans to sponsor a revolt in a friendly nation, Christmas returned to Memphis in 1911. He had retained his American citizenship, and when World War I broke out he applied for an Army commission and a battlefield assignment. When he received a letter from President Wilson turning him down, he became so irate that he offered

Lee Christmas; filibuster nonpareil. (HD, M/SCPL&IC)

to "lick" the board that had made the decision, all at once or one at a time, with his one good arm. Christmas died in 1924 at age 61.

Around the turn of the century, through the efforts of Jacob Riis in New York, Jane Addams with her Hull-House in Chicago, Theodore Roosevelt's conservation measures, and various writers such as Lincoln Steffens, who deplored the over-crowded and miserable slum conditions in eastern and mid-western cities, the public became increasingly aware of the social value of park and recreational facilities. In 1900 Memphis, with a population of 102,320, had only six acres of parkland. Landscape architect John C. Olmsted, stepson of Frederick Law Olmsted, designer of New York's Central Park, was brought to the city to conduct a survey of needs. His plan and proposals were enthusiastically adopted by the Park Board led by Judge L. B. McFarland, Robert Galloway and John R. Godwin. In 1901 the city purchased a 342-acre virgin forest, east of existing development, that became Overton Park, 445 acres south of town that became Riverside Park, and began obtaining right-of-way for a vehicular parkway that would encircle the city and tie the two parks together. In 1904 construction began on the parkway. These decisions and their implementation were very progressive and had far-reaching and long-term positive effects on the character of Memphis. In 1905, with the acquisition of a bear, a zoo was started in Overton Park; the next year an elephant was added. In 1912 Montgomery Race Track Park, abutting East Parkway, was purchased for the Mid-South Fairgrounds and that same year the first public swimming pool was opened and a golf course constructed in Overton Park where, in 1916, Brooks Memorial Art Gallery was also built. The following year, Harahan Bridge, accommodating both rail and vehicular traffic, was opened across the Mississippi River.

Shortly after entering the Twentieth Century, Memphis became one of those select cities visited each year by the touring company of the New York Metropolitan Opera and, as befitted a major city of this era, enjoyed performances by

Enrico Caruso, the Irish tenor John McCormick, Buffalo Bill Cody and his wild west show, Sarah Bernhardt, Mae Murray, Eddie Foy, the soprano Mary Garden, Madame Ernestine Schumann-Heink and all the lesser-known of the cultural and entertainment worlds. When the new auditorium opened, Sousa'a band was there to provide the appropriate level of pomp and gaiety, and citizens were treated to humorous talks by Mark Twain and at least one boxing match involving John L. Sullivan.

Despite its economic prosperity and the efforts of some to enhance its cultural climate, Memphis' rivertown heritage of crime, vice and violence was still strong. A plethora of saloons, all types of gambling, prostitution and murders were rampant for decades. The rural roots of the newcomers had imbued them with a sense of a quick response to a challenge, or a real or imagined affront, and the right to settle differences on a personal basis; fights, frequently leading to death, were common. Nearing a population of 150,000 in 1916, Memphis had 134 homicides for the year, earning it the sobriquet of "Murder Capital of America." Journalists across the country tried to outdo each other in coming up with alliterative metaphors in describing the city: Sodom of the South; Babylon on the Bluff; Homicide Headquarters.

In a survey of 31 large American cities by Prudential Life Insurance Company, Memphis' homicide rate in 1916 was determined to be 89.9 per 100,000 population, almost three times as many as Atlanta, which was second on the list. The average for the 31 cities was 9.2. To put it in better perspective, in 1992 the District of Columbia's rate was 66.5 per 100,000, the nation's highest. *The Commercial Appeal* editorialized that it considered murder to be "the most thriving industry" in Memphis and that, "They kill them next door to the city hall and shoot them in the parks." A tragic example of this were the Wooten brothers, Jesse and William. They had had some minor disagreement that continued to fester over time. One day they encountered each other on Auction Street and renewed the dispute. Pulling pistols and firing over the head of Jesse's little boy, they continued to blaze away until William fell dead with five bullets in him. In 1935 *Collier's* magazine ran an article entitled "Sinners in Dixie," which claimed that "Memphis supports a population of about 7,000 professional sinners whose sole business is to provide everybody with a good time." These were classified as those who ran dance halls, gambling houses, prostitution, the numbers, and speakeasies.

One of these was Bob Berryman, well-known gambler and owner of a tourist court on South Third Street that, reputedly, catered to the "hot pillow" trade. He ran the gambling at Hotel Peabody and also operated the famed Silver Slipper nightclub on Macon Road off Highway 70, featuring a band, floor shows and good food. What really made it profitable, though, was the gambling that went on in the back room. One day in the late 1930s, Berryman was cruising down south Main when he spotted an adversary who had raised his ire standing outside Cooper's Waffle Shop across the street from the Chisca Hotel. Jumping out of his car, Berryman pulled a pistol and began firing at his foe. While he reloaded, the unarmed man ran into the little cafe where Berryman cornered him. With no available escape route, the burly individual began charging him and it took six shots to bring him down. The next day Johnny Schaffler and the author took the streetcar downtown and, with the curiosity and awe of little boys, searched for bullet holes in the front of the cafe.

He who serves the public is a poor animal;
he worries himself to death
and no one thanks him for it.

-Johann Wolfgang Von Goethe

Early one frigid January morning in 1894, a young man boarded a train in his hometown of Holly Springs, Miss. and 45 miles later alighted in Memphis with a quarter in his pocket and a bushel basket full of confidence and determination. The nineteen-year-old lad had only the rough equivalent of a

grammar school education and some limited business experience, but he was certain he had the ability to establish himself
and prosper in the rough and tumble burgeoning city on the
Fourth Chickasaw Bluff. The degree to which he was successful in business and politics was the determining factor in
gradually changing Memphis from its old boisterous and care-
less ways and setting it on a different course of order, environmental enhancement and governmental efficiency. It was
then it began to live up to its nickname – Place of Good Abode.

Of all the players who passed across the stage in
Memphis' historic panorama, none had more lasting impact or
was more colorful than Edward Hull Crump. His earliest
acquaintance with the city kindled a love affair that endured
and grew over the years. He had an insatiable hunger to
improve the city in all its aspects and he guarded its image
and well-being with an intensity that suggested "Horatius at
the Bridge."

He was born in 1874 in Holly Springs, Miss. His father
had been a distinguished Confederate officer and was one of
those selected to escort BrigGen John Hunt Morgan's body
home after he was killed at Greenville, Tenn. in September
1864. During the same yellow fever epidemic that decimated
Memphis, he had taken his family to an apparent place of
safety in another county and returned home to nurse his brother and a cousin who were stricken with the disease. All three
died. Ed was just four years old. His mother donned mourning
and wore it for the rest of her 97 years, not only as a symbol of
her personal grief but as a constant reminder of the loss the
family had suffered. Until the end, she remained in good
health and was active and clear-minded; she carried herself
with a somewhat austere, erect posture and when guests
called she insisted on standing until all had been received.
From her Ed inherited his red hair, indomitable will and large
physical frame.

Ed Crump's unusual capacity for order and efficiency,
combined with his vision and self-discipline, served him well
in the business world. He structured his life to live by axioms
that he considered to be worthy guideposts. Probably his
favorite was, "Observe, remember and compare." By his mid-
twenties he had attained a level of prominence and financial
stability such that he felt he could participate with other

young business leaders in pursuing political reform in Memphis. There was growing sentiment for civic betterment in opposition to those who preferred – for personal or financial reasons – Memphis continuing to be the way it had always been, and Crump aligned himself with the former group. At this time, he became the youngest member of an organization called the Committee of the People and helped establish the commission form of government – wherein commissioners elected by the people are each responsible for administering specific aspects of the governmental function. In 1902 and 1904 he was a delegate to the Democratic state conventions; in 1905 he became a member of the Memphis Board of Public Works; in 1907 he was Commissioner of Fire and Police; and in 1909 he was elected mayor and served in that capacity until 1916.

In his first two-year term as mayor he achieved substantial progress in improving the appearance of the city, providing more and better services, instituting fairer tax assessments and enhancing the lives of those who lived in conditions of poverty. To those who opposed his aims he had nothing but contempt and viewed them as selfish enemies of the common good. If they had some degree of influence and riled him sufficiently, he would take out large newspaper ads consisting of vitriolic attacks on these "opponents of progress." In his early days he was not averse to engaging in fisticuffs if the occasion demanded it, and it was at that time he earned the nickname "Redsnapper."

In 1909 the state enacted a prohibition law. Memphis ignored it and the saloons continued to run full tilt; Crump announced that the city would leave enforcement of the law to the state. This really hacked Crump's enemies in Nashville and Knoxville and the rural legislators who had pushed the law through. After about six years of trying, they finally got an effective ouster law through the legislature and Crump was forced from office. But the new mayor, in recognition of who was responsible for putting him there, hung Mr. Crump's picture on his office wall and told him that, in his mind, he was still mayor.

During Crump's first term the owners of the famous old steamboat *Kate Adams* offered him its use for one day during the summer for whatever purpose he deemed appropriate. Thus began the boat rides for shut-ins: orphans, cripples and the aged, that were annual events until his death. Through the years he took great pleasure in planning this event, and all the activities surrounding it, to ensure that each participant was comfortable and thoroughly enjoyed the occasion. He would even inveigle the aid of bank presidents, leading attorneys and others of prominence in the business and professional worlds who would roll up their sleeves and perform menial tasks in these endeavors. Later, similar activities took their place alongside the boat rides: theater parties for orphans, barbecues that were attended by not only the well-to-do but humbler segments of society, as well, and, in 1935, his "Crump Day at the Fair," when approximately 50,000 people enjoyed the Mid-South Fair as his guests with free admission to midway rides for the children and something for every age group.

Edward Hull Crump at the time of his election as mayor at age 34. (HD, M/SCPL&IC)

From 1919 to 1923 Crump served as Shelby County Trustee (treasurer) and from 1931 to 1935 represented Memphis in the U.S. House of Representatives. Seven times he was a delegate to the Democratic National Convention and from 1935 to 1945 served on the Democratic National Committee. During his terms in Congress he also was a Regent of the Smithsonian Institution.

The Crump Machine thrived on meticulous organization and teamwork. The key members of the machine were selected for their character and high degree of loyalty. An index card was kept on every voter in the county and appropriate notations made regarding anticipated support or opposition; what wasn't on the cards Mr. Crump heard about and remembered. Early on it was recognized that local Negroes represented a large chunk of votes. While in most areas of the South efforts were directed toward keeping them from voting, in Memphis they were rounded up and almost forced to vote – for the Machine's slate, of course. After each voter had entered the polling place with poll tax receipt in hand and had exercised his franchise, on the way out a silver dollar was slipped into his pocket and he was handed a pig sandwich and a Coke. When he had downed these he was sent on his way with a watermelon under his arm and a grin on his face. Reputedly, after registering for the draft during World War II, one of Mr. Crump's well-trained supporters stood uncertainly on one foot and the other for a moment and then blurted, "Whuh's my barbecue an' Coke?"

Because the political organization that he headed provided excellent services for the people in an efficient manner and without a taint of scandal, Crump's power increased and solidified over the years. Rather than "candidate Crump," he became "kingmaker Crump." In consultation with other leaders in the organization prior to an election, a slate of candidates deemed worthy of support would be drawn up. There were those who served in the same positions for many years but, for various reasons of attrition, there frequently were vacancies to fill. This also applied to appointive positions. Without the organization's support, the candidacy of an aspiring politician was an exercise in futility. Those so inclined would make a trip to "the Corner" – that is, visit Mr. Crump at his office located on the fourth floor of the small five-story building at the northeast corner of Main and Adams – seeking his nod of approval.

Mirroring its leader's penchant for efficiency, the machine had the capacity to deliver a very high percentage of the vote to the anointed candidate. An illustration of this was the gubernatorial campaign of 1928 when Crump backed Hill McAlister against Henry Horton, who, as speaker of the senate, had succeeded to the office when Governor Austin Peay had died before the expiration of his third term. Horton had the backing of Rogers Caldwell and Luke Lea of Nashville, who were partners in banking, municipal bonds and the production of asphalt for highway paving. Lea also controlled the *Nashville Tennessean* newspaper and was Crump's bitter political foe. When the votes were counted, Memphis and Shelby County had given Horton 3,723 votes to McAlister's 24,019. Some years later Crump supported the successful candidacy of Gordon Browning for governor and delivered with a percentage of the local vote comparable to what had been afforded McAlister, but Browning did not perform as Crump had expected and at the next election the same voting ratio applied, but in reverse, and Browning lost.

The machine had all city and county employees working in its behalf and, because Crump kept the CIO out of their hair, the large industrial establishments supported him with almost total dedication. The AF of L also was in the Crump column because he protected its efforts to organize the craft unions with its agreement to stay away from the large plants. Crump's public image as a benefactor, his intervention in behalf of many who needed a helping hand over the years and his prodigious memory, which enabled him to recall people's names and much of their personal history in affable conversations when he encountered them around town, inspired such loyalty that one would feel he was betraying his best instincts if he didn't get out and vote for Mr. Crump's candidate.

Crump's power in the state was due to two main factors. The first was the difference in political allegiance between its three grand divisions: the "Three States of Tennessee." In its looping course through the state the Tennessee River neatly divides it into East, Middle and West Tennessee. During the War for Southern Independence East Tennessee was strongly Unionist and has always been a stronghold of the Republican Party while Middle Tennessee has always been just as stoutly Democratic; this, in essence, left West Tennessee, containing populous Shelby County, effectively holding the balance of power. The second factor enhancing Crump's statewide influence was his close association with fellow Memphian Kenneth D. McKellar, who served in the U. S. Senate from 1916-1953.

Most states in the country have in-state rivalries between different sections and in some places it exists even at the county level. The Three Grand Divisions in Tennessee have always harbored certain jealousies and resentments and sniped at each other over the years. Particularly during the days of Crump's influence, newspapers in Knoxville and Nashville never tired of attacking him and Memphis. He had a long-running feud with the *Nashville Tennessean*, edited by Silliman Evans, which reached its peak in 1944 when one of the *Tennessean*'s writers, Jennings Perry, published an inadequately researched and poorly written book attacking Crump and his methods. Joe Hatcher was another writer on that paper who had been critical and piqued his ire over the years. Typically, Crump responded hammer and tongs in a letter to the *Tennessean*, that he had the Shelby delegation distribute to all members of the legislature and Senator McKellar insert in the *Congressional Record*, which said in part:

> *If the city of Nashville should ever follow the lead of the progressive city of Memphis and inaugurate a campaign for the extermination of rodents, Silliman Evans, Jennings Perry, and Joe Hatcher will undoubtedly take to the tall timbers. This trio of mangy bubonic rats are conscienceless liars who would stop at nothing in their unholy efforts to prejudice the good people of Tennessee against Memphis and Shelby County. ... It was easy for Father Adam to name the hog, snake, elephant, skunk and the hound dog, but when it came to the bubonic rat he evidently had a mental picture of Evans, Perry, and Hatcher.*

In his condemnation, Perry had contrasted the philosophy of the Crump Machine with the tenets of germinating democracy as espoused by the Greeks; Crump continued:

> *... The next time Perry delves into Greek history someone should tell him that Socrates taught Plato, Plato taught Aristotle, and Aristotle taught the world – he had perhaps the greatest capacity for obtaining and retaining knowledge than any man who has ever lived. Perry, to date, hasn't displayed enough knowledge of Greek to qualify him to open a restaurant.*

Crump also had his local detractors, primarily in the person of Edward Meeman, a Scripps-Howard employee who left the *Knoxville News-Sentinel* to become editor of the *Memphis Press-Scimitar*, the evening newspaper, in 1931. He assumed the posture of the crusading machine buster bent on promoting the city manager form of government and making the world safe for democracy. Crump also did not escape the notice of big city newspapers and national periodicals such as *Saturday Evening Post, Literary Digest, Time, PM, Economist* (London), and others, whose liberal slant ordinarily deigned to demean Memphis and portray him as a demagogue, or worse. In his book, *Mr. Crump of Memphis*, William D. Miller said:

> *The issue, many insisted, was that of bossism, for Crump was boss absolutely. Authoritarianism does indeed restrict the freedom of others. But the extent of freedom is bound by the ordering factor of its intrinsic worth. Had there been no Crump there doubtless would have been more freedom for independent political action, but would the people of Memphis have been as free in those areas that represent the basis for any humanized society – order and material well being? Considering the character of Memphis as Crump found it, it is doubtful that they would have been.*

Particularly as he aged, Crump's appearance took on more colorful and striking features and those who wrote about him painted him in hues according to the impression they wanted to convey. In 1937 Fred Hixson of the *Chattanooga Times* provided a most graphic and accurate description:

> *Crump is rather tall..., His hair is brilliantly white, thick and bushy at the sides and back and thinning at the middle. His eyebrows, as heavy as mustachios, are shaded in brown from cream to cocoa, and the deep blue of his eyes is made almost indiscernible by the covering of eyeglasses and by its setting in a face of deep, bright pink complexion. Often, as he talks, he*

raises his brows high in wide-eyed critical inspection of the topic under discussion; or, in reflection, purses his lips far outward. These mannerisms give him the appearance of a venerable pixie who is under no misapprehension as to the way the world wags and who will correct its shortcomings with no dilly-dallying on the way. His ... appearance was set off by toggery leaning to the dandified; a light gray suit with small checks, a blue shirt with a white semi-stiff collar, and a red tie.

Some, in the younger set around Memphis, in conscious recognition of the authority he wielded and in subconscious feelings of him as a sage, old member of the family circle, flippantly referred to him as "Uncle Ed."

In building the organization, Crump ensured that all groups in Memphis had representation and, in this instance, there probably was more altruism at work than political expediency. As a Protestant, although admittedly not a regular churchgoer, he found much to admire in the Catholic and Jewish religions. Will Gerber, a Jew, was one of the highest ranking and loyal members of the machine and for this Crump endured much criticism around the state. As far back as 1918 he had written a letter to the Sisters of the Good Shepherd, who maintained a home in Memphis for wayward girls, thanking them for a Sacred Heart badge (probably a scapular). He stated that he had worn one "continuously since you presented it to me some four or five years ago; in fact, it has about worn out from constant wear, hence the new one is doubly appreciated," and he carried it to the grave with him. When, during the presidential campaign of 1928, both Al Smith and his wife were denigrated by society matrons in the Northeast for lacking social graces and being Catholic, Crump took out double page ads in both local newspapers in defense of Smith. After disposing of the snob issue he said he supported Smith because of his "unrelenting and courageous stand for the preservation of water power against the power trust," his "... far-reaching and beneficial farm relief measures. Governor Smith ... has done more than any other living man to better the conditions of those of his people who are poor, needy, aged,

"Boss" Crump on the cover of Time magazine in 1946. (HD, M/SCPL&IC)

afflicted, diseased and distressed... He is a friend of the common people and a lover of mankind." In discussing the religion issue, he provided a long list of contributions made by Catholics to Memphis, saying in part:

> In 1841, ... Catholics founded Saint Peter's Orphanage. During the entire history of the institution 80 percent of its children, who now average 300 per year, have come and are now coming from Protestant parents.

> St. Joseph's Hospital, the first hospital in Memphis worthy of the name, was founded by the Catholics in 1888. Ninety-two percent of the charity patients of this hospital, who numbered 1,548, an average of 129 patients per month, in 1927, were Protestants.

As a Protestant and as an antisnob, I earnestly hope the people of Shelby County will reflect and deliberate fairly before casting their votes against Governor Smith merely because he is a plain man and a Catholic.

Crump counted among his friends the leading Catholic prelate in Memphis, Monsignor Merlin F. Kearney, who, quick with the ad lib and a quip, never let the seriousness of his vocation interfere with his breezy Irish good humor and love of a prank. Short and heavy-set, like Crump he loved Memphis, and he is a story unto himself. Because it would have meant leaving Memphis for Nashville, he turned down the Bishopric of Tennessee; he referred to Memphis as "GSU - Garden Spot of the Universe." He and Crump often prayed together and Monsignor Kearney blessed him just before Crump's death at his home at 1962 Peabody.

It took many years for Memphis' image as a wide-open, free-wheeling town, beset by vice and violence, to wane. Except for perfunctory police raids on the more notorious dives, the state prohibition law was ignored. Police payoffs by saloons and gambling parlors were routine. It was not that he necessarily approved of it or stood to gain financially from all of this, but the operators of these establishments and those with a laissez faire attitude controlled a lot of votes; Crump was not yet politically strong enough to buck them en masse – the mores of a community are not drastically changed overnight. A few years later "The Great Experiment" was tried on the national level and, about this time, W. C. Handy wrote in his "Beale Street Blues" :

I'm goin' to the river,
And there's a reason why.
Because the river's wet,
And Beale Street's done gone dry.

But Memphians were never at a loss to slake their thirst. Plenty of bootleg whiskey was made in the area, particularly on President's Island, whence it was brought into the city by small boats. The whiskey came in various sizes to suit the customer's desires and pocketbook: tall, thin 12-ounce bottles, half pints, short, medicine-style bottles called "slabs," and little bottles called "Austins."

Although he was out of the mayor's office, Crump was elected County Trustee and continued to build his political power base. Some of the civic improvements that occurred during this era were implemented during the mayoralty administrations of Rowlett Paine, who was his own man. When the St. Louis planning consulting firm of Harland Bartholomew and Associates was retained to recommend improvements in the existing infrastructure and provide the basis for future orderly growth, Memphis, under the leadership of Planning Commission chairman Wassel Randolph, became one of the first American cities to embrace comprehensive planning. In 1926 Memphis was the first city to require automobile inspection (conducted at one location every four months by city employees) as a safety measure.

Under Crump's leadership the police and fire departments were improved and, in relation to traffic deaths, Memphis was recognized as the nation's safest city. The efficiency of the fire department provided Memphis with the lowest insurance rates possible and it served for many years as host to the Fire Department Instructors Conference, where it demonstrated equipment made in its own shop and its techniques for preventing and fighting fires; in 1938 and 1939 it won the National Fire Prevention Award. With its pioneering annual "Clean-up, Fix-up, Paint-up" campaigns, a community-wide volunteer effort under the direction of the City Beautiful Commission, founded in 1929, and in considerable contrast to its earlier days, Memphis consistently won the trophy as the "Cleanest City in America." Parks became plentiful and the recreational programs carried out by the Park Commission were models for other cities to follow, as were those of the Shelby County Health Department with its unique mobile x-ray facilities to combat tuberculosis, programs for the control of venereal diseases and strict enforcement of ordinances governing sanitation, particularly in restaurants. And Mr. Crump was tough on air pollution. He once had the police arrest the Illinois Central yardmaster when he felt engines sitting in the yards were emitting too much smoke. With its noise abatement program, Memphis was recognized as the quietest city in the country and, in 1940, the American Public Health

Association gave it the First Place Award for the city with the most progressive and effective health program. All of these things were accomplished with one of the lowest tax rates in the country. But the one thing that probably gave Ed Crump his greatest satisfaction was municipal acquisition of electrical power that was the cornerstone of the Memphis Light, Gas and Water Division. When on November 6, 1934, by a vote of 32,735 to 1,868, citizens approved the issuance of bonds to buy a distribution system for TVA power, Crump was so elated that he had a downtown alley, known as Maiden Lane, renamed November 6th Street.

Like many public figures, Crump was subject to threats and extortion demands. On one occasion in the late 1940s he received a letter instructing him to put some money in a tree in West Memphis, Ark. He never took these threats very seriously. He said, "Mrs. Crump and I drove over and looked at the tree; I decided it would be more dangerous for me to climb the tree than to ignore the instructions." On another occasion he followed instructions and deposited a briefcase in a certain place, but it was not picked up. The only thing in it was a note from Crump addressed to "the coward perpetrating this dastardly thing. Anyone could take a white mouse with baby teeth and run you into the Mississippi River." There were other occasions, however, when plots came to light after the fact, indicating there had been attempts made against his life that, for one reason or another, were not carried out.

While he spent much of his time attending to the affairs of Memphis, Crump did not let his business lag. He had established a general insurance agency and also became involved in real estate and mortgage lending as a correspondent with Metropolitan Life Insurance Company. By 1925 additional offices were established in St. Louis, Pittsburgh and Little Rock and his company had ties with mortgage lenders in other southern cities. Billboards and other advertising proclaimed E. H. Crump and Company as "the South's largest insurance agency." In 1929 he purchased a Coca-Cola franchise covering an area in central New York state.

His ability to accomplish so much in politics would, in itself, constitute a demanding and satisfying career for the ordinary person. How he was able to do this and, at the same time, build a highly successful business can, in large measure, be attributed to his self-discipline and iron will that those who knew him well sometimes observed with awe. This was exemplified early in his career. After being in Memphis for three years and still only in his early twenties, he had worked himself to the point of exhaustion. He decided to make a trip to Hot Springs, Ark. for the baths and to consult a well-known physician. After the examination the doctor told him he must give up cigarettes, coffee and alcohol. He imbibed modestly in alcohol on social occasions but he drank a lot of coffee and was a heavy smoker. From that moment on he never again drank a cup of coffee or indulged in tobacco and confined alcoholic intake to an occasional bottle of beer, and that only on medical advice. In 1920 he made the first of his annual visits to the clinic of Dr. C. W. Post in Battle Creek, Mich., who developed the cereals that bear his name and was one of the pioneers of the holistic health movement.

His satisfactions in life were confined to those he acquired through his family – his wife and three sons and their children, his numerous kinsmen, and his mother – his accomplishments in politics and business and sporting events. Every Friday evening his sons and their families would have dinner at the home of he and his wife and every Sunday, with the grandchildren in tow, he would visit his mother in Holly Springs. He would write letters of counsel to his grandchildren away at school and a

Ed Crump in his later years.
(HD, M/SCPL&IC)

letter to his granddaughter, Betty, when she was a freshman at Ogontz College in Philadelphia, reveals a more personal side of him. Betty was the first grandchild and, naturally, received a lot of attention. She frequently would accompany him on early evening chauffeur-driven rides around the city as he looked for things that needed correction: tree limbs obscuring a stop sign, a burned-out streetlight, a stopped-up storm drain – all were written down in his thick, ever-present white note-book. He obviously felt constrained to impart grandfatherly wisdom to a girl so far from home. He trotted out all the old maxims that he tried to live by and had stood him in good stead:

> *Read, listen and ask. Observe, remember and compare Plan your work and work your plan Nothing worth while is easy and easy things are not worth while.*

He commented on various aspects of world affairs and mentioned a visit with President Roosevelt:

> *Courage is the first virtue as kindness is the final joy. Roosevelt had that. I saw him March 21st – he wired me to come to Washington. He looked weary and worn – twelve years is just too much for one man, with all the responsibility he had at home and throughout the world, I didn't see how he could live thirty days. [He died 22 days later.] And too, he has labored under infirmities – infantile paralysis.*

He continued to sprinkle his letter with homilies:

> *'Our civilization cannot survive material-ly unless it is redeemed spiritually,' said Woodrow Wilson, 'it is an inside job.'*

> *Life is giving – not getting.*

> *Eternal things never grow old – they are never out of date. The Ten Commandments and the Golden Rule are up to the minute. The Sermon on the Mount is ages ahead of us, waiting for our slow hearts to catch up. Sacred things never die.*

In conclusion, he switched to more personal matters:

*How are you getting along with all your boy
friends? Love never goes except where it wants
to go – no duty, sense of pressure can force it.*

This emphasizes the basic simplicity of the man.
Primarily self-educated and totally self-made, he dealt in
absolutes, and when encountering a problem he attacked it
head-on, gaining strength from the moral precepts that were
his lifelong standbys.

He had no inclination to be a "society lion" or any particular aspirations for higher government offices, such as governor or senator, and he belied Lord Acton's oft-quoted adage
regarding the corrupting influence of power. Before the
Democratic National Convention in 1940, the highly regarded
Blair T. Hunt, principal of Memphis' largest Negro high school,
wrote Senator McKellar: "... thousands of Memphis Negroes
will be happy if you'll use your influence in having Mr. E. H.
Crump's name presented for Vice President. Please do it." But
Crump discouraged all such efforts. Other pleasures were
garnered through intervening in behalf of someone or some
institution that needed help at a critical time. Each Christmas
he made donations to every charity in town and monetary or
tangible gifts to his servants, the garbage man, employees
and scores of people likely to be forgotten by others; wreaths
were also placed on the graves of his family and relatives in
Holly Springs and even on the graves of close relatives of his
friends and employees. At his death in October 1954 his office
was piled high with wrapped gifts, ready for yuletide distribution.

From his youthful days as a first baseman with the
town team in Holly Springs, Crump was always a sports
enthusiast. His primary interests were horse racing and football. He never missed a Kentucky Derby and frequently was in
attendance during the racing season at Oaklawn in Hot
Springs. Occasionally, he would organize a special train filled
with associates and friends for the trip, and the participants
had as much fun going over and coming back as they did at
the track. In 1939 two special trains left Memphis loaded with

most of the Shelby organization, about 50 members of the Tennessee legislature, and general racing enthusiasts. Future senator Estes Kefauver, then state finance commissioner, and the legislature were interested in horse racing as a possible revenue source and wanted to observe firsthand how it was handled in Arkansas. Also aboard was Lem Motlow of Lynchburg, distiller of Jack Daniels and Wild Turkey. Crump's observation was that anyone "who can beat the races or any gambling game can grow oysters in a cornfield or raise chickens on a mill pond," but that it was "good to be a little foolish occasionally."

He would always make the college football games in Memphis and big ones in other southern cities; he never missed a Sugar Bowl and attended most of the local high school contests, where he would walk around the track with a big box of candy under his arm and offer it to the cheerleaders of both teams.

In 1924, after completing some business at his St. Louis office, he took the train to Urbana, Ill. The next day he witnessed Red Grange's historic performance, against a good Michigan team, when he scored four touchdowns in the first quarter on long runs and added a fifth in the last quarter for 282 yards rushing for the day. In discussing the game twenty years later, with his uncanny memory, Crump could name almost every player by position on both teams and recall the contribution each had made in the game. His eldest son, Edward, Jr., loved football as much as his father and was All-Memphis and captain of an undefeated Memphis University School prep team. He was a good punter and in one game averaged 49 yards on six punts. He played two years at the University of Virginia.

Crump's amazing knowledge and enthusiasm for the game was highlighted one day when he impulsively called David Bloom, sports writer at *The Commercial Appeal*, to give Bloom his all-time All-American team. Coincidentally, it was the latter part of October 1943, the season that is the focus of this book. He said, "Funny thing, we were having a pretty full day up here at my office but we got around to talking about football and I thought about all of the players I'd seen and the discussion got pretty lively. Finally somebody said, 'Is that all you've got to do?' Maybe it wasn't much to do but I enjoyed it."

For his ends Crump chose Brick Mueller of California and Don Hutson of Alabama.

"That Hutson was a wonder at Alabama – fast as a streak. He was in a class by himself."

Then the tackles. Bronko Nagurski, for one. He could play about anything, but I liked him best as a tackle. And for the other, Wilbur Henry, who played for Washington and Jefferson a long time ago. But it's hard not to put Bruiser Kinard of Ole Miss in there. He was – and is – a wonderful player.

As guards we'll go a long way back. Truxton Hare of Pennsylvania and Pudge Heffelfinger of Yale and that huge Turk Edwards of Washington for a third. And at center Bettencourt – Larry Bettencourt of St. Mary's. Why, that fellow sort of shrunk up to knife blade size and shot through the line to make tackles. And he was faster than an end going down the field on punts. Simply great. Then there was Bob Peck of Penn, back in the teens. He was about as broad as he was high and very good.

Now the backfield. I'll have to name a lot of fellows and you can just shut your eyes and pick four. Jim Thorpe, of course. I saw him back in his Carlisle Indian days. Truly a marvelous fullback. Ernie Nevers, that Stanford fellow and Ken Strong of New York University – they were fine at that position, too. And Red Grange of Illinois and Tommy Harmon of Michigan. Benny Friedman of Michigan, too. He was a great passer.

Maybe Bo McMillan of Centre was an even better passer than Friedman. He was a better all-around man. Whizzer White of Colorado and George Gipp of Notre Dame were magnificent backs.

Of course, Willie Heston. I saw Willie Heston back in that year when Michigan was winning games sometimes 100 to 0. Never less than 30 to 0. I'll always remember Heston.

My son John was at Colorado College and I went out to see him. He was playing a little football, but he kept telling me. 'Wait until you see a fellow we've got.' It was Earl "Dutch" Clark. He was a marvel on that small college team – a fellow who could do everything. He proved it again later as a professional.

"You know this covers a period of 45 years of watching football. Long time, isn't it? But I love football, always have, and I've enjoyed traveling to all parts of the country to see the games. I like the prep school games, too."

Central was the first public high school in Memphis. Before becoming "Central" it simply was referred to as "the high school." Early records of the names, dates of establishment and locations of high schools are incomplete and a little confusing. "High School" was in existence at least as early as 1893 when it is suspected that it fielded its first football team, a year when both CBC and Memphis University School first had teams.

In this early era of high school education in the city, there were schools known as the Poplar Street School, later called Crockett Technical High School, and Fowkles School, subsequently known at the Jefferson Street School. It is presumed that these schools ultimately merged into the Vocational-Technical High School, which opened in 1911 as Memphis's second high school. "Vo-Tech" was housed in a building constructed on Poplar in 1899 that later became the offices of the Memphis and Shelby County Board of Education. A new facility was built on Poplar just west of Crosstown and re-named Memphis Technical High School.

To accommodate increasing enrollment, in 1905 the Memphis Board of Education purchased thirteen acres at the southeast corner of Bellevue and Linden as a site for a new "High School." The school opened in 1911 and was designated

Memphis Central High School. Because it was called "High School" in those early years, the practice of awarding an "H" for an athletic letter, rather than a "C," has continued until today.

Central High is a monolithic red brick structure of four stories with the lower floor being somewhat depressed. The entrance, of subdued Doric influence, is afforded by steps leading to the second floor. The architecture is relatively nondescript but could be classified as a modified Second Renaissance Revival style, which was popular during its era of construction. However, as a possible reflection of economic considerations, it lacks some of the embellishments of that style. To eliminate a boxy look, the central portion was recessed and an arched pavilion, with a low relief sculpture, was mounted as a roof cresting. In order to provide sufficient ventilation in an era pre-dating air-conditioning, 18 light, double hung windows (later changed to six horizontal lights) predominated throughout.

The new school provided multitudinous classrooms, five laboratories, a shop, a cafeteria, an auditorium, a library and a gymnasium. To accommodate increased enrollment, two large study halls were built over the shop in 1918. Subsequent additions and interior remodeling have occurred since then.

The first principal was Nicholas Williams, and three others followed before the arrival in 1918 of C. P. Jester, who served in that position for many years and was highly regarded for his scholarship and integrity. That same year military training was introduced into the curriculum.

Just before Professor (the terminology in that era) Jester's tenure began, the catastrophic influenza epidemic of the winter of 1917-1918 killed millions worldwide. Central High was turned into a temporary hospital to accommodate the overcrowded conditions at all the city's hospitals.*

In 1921 the enrollment had increased to an extent that the Jefferson Street School was used as an annex and a portable building with eight classrooms was erected behind

---

* The author's maternal uncle, just beginning his Boy Scout days, served as a "runner" at Central during this period, being periodically dispatched to the City Hospital to pick up medical supplies for transport back to Central on his bicycle; every time he entered the makeshift hospital, he would be required to don a mask.

Central High School
(Courtesy of Central High School Library)

Central's shop. In February 1923 the new South Side High School was opened to alleviate the burden.

In 1908 the Shelby County Board of Education opened Messick High School in the Buntyn area and then, in 1915, Treadwell High in Highland Heights. These two schools were annexed into the city in the mid-to late-twenties.

The Seven Wonders of the World I have seen
And many are the places I have been;
Take my advice, folks, and see Beale Street first,
I would rather be there than any place I know.

from *"Beale Street Blues"*
-W. C. Handy

To a large extent, Memphis' vice and violence occurred in and around the Beale Street area. All east-west streets in town are called avenues, but in common parlance "street" has always been tagged after Beale and, because of its fame, it was officially so designated some years back. This "Broadway of Negro America," runs east from the river for about one and one-half miles to East Street, but the approximate five-block strip east from Main Street served as the focus of black life in the Mid-South from the latter half of the Nineteenth Century up until the middle of the Twentieth. It was here they banked, saw the doctor and dentist, bought groceries and clothes, ate out, and did all the other mundane things of daily living. It provided some of the best tailors in town, for black and white, and originated the zoot suit; for those short on cash, bargain stores and pawn shops abounded. At a time when all the barbers in town were black, Jim's Barber Shop at Main and Beale, next to the Orpheum Theater, was staffed with 15 or more Negro barbers catering only to the white trade. But Beale attained its international fame and notoriety for other reasons.

Liberally interspersed among the offices and businesses customarily found on a commercial street were saloons, gambling dens, open air markets, "black magic" practitioners and, on the side streets, a plethora of bordellos, and these combined to attract and stimulate a raft of colorful characters, some harmless and others vicious. At night, and, of course, particularly on the weekends, Beale lit up and attracted throngs of blacks out for a good time, but the better-educated and more refined Negro elite stayed clear of it. The Savoy, Pastime, Daisy and Grand movie theaters were owned by the Zerilla and Pacini families. There was a saying about Beale: the Jews had the pawnshops and dry goods stores, the Greeks had the restaurants, the Italians had the entertainment – theaters, saloons, gambling – and the blacks were the customers; another said it was run by the Jews, policed by the Irish and enjoyed by the Negroes.

On Saturdays, excursion trains from the plantations and timber camps brought in hordes of excited Negroes eager to spend money and indulge in all the street had to offer. While their dandified pimps, called easyriders, kept an eye on them, prostitutes roamed through the boisterous, skylarking crowds that shuffled up and down both sides of the street. In Church Park a group of musicians with instruments that could include washboards, jugs, harmonicas, banjos, guitars or cornets, might get together for an impromptu public concert.

All the saloons had musical entertainment ranging from a single piano player to a full band and most stayed open 24 hours a day, with musicians coming and going. They offered liquor, dancing and shooting dice in a back room. One called Hole in the Ground had a gambling room in a basement; another, called Hole in the Wall, had a back exit for homegrown trouble and police raids, and another had a chute that sent bodies to an undertaker. Some of the other watering holes along Beale were the Monarch Club, the plushest Negro nightclub in the South, with mirrors covering the lobby walls and a brass-railed mahogany bar and featuring the barrel-house piano skills of Benny French and Sonny Butts, the Panama Club, a favorite of horse racing fans until the sport was outlawed by the state in 1905, the Red Front, Midway, Wagonyard and Gray Mule with its baked ribs, black-eyed peas, candied yams, turnip greens, cornbread and cobblers.

Sometimes a place would get a bad reputation and, to allay the fears of the general public and city hall officials, it would change its name; Sunset Hall became the Cotton Club and, after that, Blue Heaven. At the Royal Gardens, located over a drugstore at Beale and Hernando, a dice game got too intense and after someone's throat was cut he was dumped out a three-story window. At another place, after a crap shooter was killed his body was shoved under the table and the game continued unabated. Battier's Drug Store at Beale and Third patched up many who had been shot or cut and it wasn't uncommon to see trails of blood going in and, for the more serious cases, out again as the injured person headed up the street to a clinic.

There was frequent animosity among some of the saloonkeepers, mainly white, due to the competition for patrons. During the nineties Jim Kinnane and Ed Ryan and their cohorts engaged in a bitter struggle for control of prostitution and gambling, and their escapades made the decade a turbulent one. At the turn of the century and almost up until World War 1, John Persica ran a saloon on Hernando Street where an observer suggested that, "some 20 penal statutes were violated day and night in Persica's place, but still he ran it openly with each change in government of the city." He held the rights for all gambling activities south of Madison Avenue down to the Union Depot. "...anything went in Persky's place from murder on up," but he strictly forbade fighting and, if necessary, he had the ability to enforce the edict himself. He also promoted boxing matches. George Honan, "one of the most desperate men that ever lived in Memphis," controlled gambling north of Madison.

In 1903 Memphis had 504 saloons, or one for about every 200 inhabitants; many family grocery stores and soda fountains had attached saloons and on Front Street whiskey bottles were piled in bushel baskets and sold on the spot. On May 7, 1907 *The Commercial Appeal* said, "Dives have been flourishing as they have never flourished before. Hundreds of lewd women, equipped with vials of chloral and knock-out drops, have been imported. Street-walkers have been as thick as wasps in summer time." About the same time the newspaper also commented that, "few people can appreciate the extensive use of cocaine in Memphis," and estimated that 80 percent of the Negro population and "a considerable number of whites" used cocaine to the extent that about a dozen drug stores and several grocery stores relied on its sale as a chief means of support. The newspaper went on to say that drug addiction "seems to be growing" and also mentioned the use of opium, while the police department reported to the mayor that "the sale of cocaine has reached such an alarming extent that the department is unable to cope with its ravages."

Persica's two lieutenants, Mike Haggerty and Bud Deggs cut their own personal swaths of lawlessness through Memphis before World War I. To ensure that those of their ilk continued to have the freedom to operate, it was important they be active in politics. Haggerty and Deggs operated out of the well-known Turf Saloon at the corner of Gayoso and Second, and it became the Fourth Ward's headquarters and a beehive of activity prior to elections.

Another who was prominent in the Memphis underworld was Mike Shanley. He first distinguished himself by killing Ed Ryan in a shooting affray at Montgomery Park race track. On a later visit to the track to observe a balloon ascension, some unthinking dolt, in a manner that piqued the sensitive Mr. Shanley, curtly ordered him to extinguish his cigar around the balloon. In a snit, Shanley went back to his saloon and rounded up some of his Irish buddies and they returned to the park and proceeded to bring the ascending balloon abruptly back to earth with some well-placed blasts from their shotguns. Shanley's saloon was the site of a number of spectacular brawls. On one of these occasions when 28 Negroes had been arrested and hauled before a justice of the peace, Shanley followed them to court. Pulling a "small-sized cannon" from his pocket he pointed it close to the justice's head and threatened to send him to Hell if his patrons were not released. When he was subsequently brought into court for his intemperate act, the same judge, upon due consideration, felt constrained to agree with Shanley's lawyer that Mike had only innocently reached into his pocket for tobacco and had, inadvertently, pulled out the pistol which he was taking to a repair shop for a friend. Although he was never convicted of any of his outrageous deeds, Shanley was killed in 1908 by a city detective while "resisting arrest." In its obituary, *The Commercial Appeal* commented that he had been a good family man.

Most of the other underworld figures also met violent deaths. John Persica was killed in an automobile accident in 1913 while speeding down Madison Avenue. After someone took affront at George Honan fatally wounding a girl, he died in a pistol duel. When Mike Haggerty jumped a liquored-up Negro for striking one of the waiters in his saloon, both pulled pistols and fired simultaneously. Haggerty lived "barely long enough to be told that his bullet had gone through his slayer's heart."

A forerunner to McDonald's and Burger King et al, was William A. Latura, ordinarily referred to as "Wild Bill." He had a number of hamburger stands around town, but he also was an inveterate gambler and had a place on the southwest corner of Poplar and Dunlap where he ran dice games and sold liquor.

He had many friends, including policemen and Negroes, that he got along with just fine, but when someone crossed him or significantly disagreed with him in conversation, he frequently would fly into a rage. While at a baseball game he got into an argument with a young white man and beat him to death with a bat. Although he was arrested 35 times during his relatively short life, he never suffered any serious consequences as a result of them.

Hammitt Ashford, a light-skinned quadroon who wore a diamond stickpin in his cravat and carried a thousand-dollar watch in his pocket, owned a nice saloon at Fourth and Beale with a mahogany bar and marble-topped tables. Latura came in on the night of December 10, 1908 and went into the back room where some pool games were in progress. He, purportedly, had recently lost heavily gambling at Ashford's and that might explain why he was in such a foul mood; another story reported that the noise the pool players were making irritated him and his request, or demand, that they be quiet was ignored. In any event, he announced he was going to turn the place into a funeral parlor and pulled his pistol. He emptied it, reloaded it, and emptied it again. By then, five Negroes lay dead and two others were seriously wounded. He told the police, "I shot them and that's all there is to it." He was acquitted at a trial, but four years later he shot and killed another Negro.

Latura's activities fostered a lot of newsprint and he was enraged when *The Commercial Appeal* referred to him as "Wild Bill." One day he called editor C. P. J. Mooney and threatened to kill his entire editorial staff if they ever did it again. The practice ceased for some years until some unknowing cub reporter applied the appellation when he referred to Latura as one of the city's main tourist attractions. This was about the same time that everything seemed to start going downhill for him.

In 1916 Mayor Crump's enemies in the legislature were putting pressure on him and formulating a law that ultimately would drive him from office for not enforcing the state law against liquor sales. Memphis police began some symbolic efforts, at least, toward curtailing sales. They raided Latura's place and found 1,274 bottles of beer. Although they had been getting conflicting signals from headquarters regarding enforcement, the two policemen assigned to Latura's area, J. C. "Sandy" Lyons and Charlie Davis, were called in and fined ten days pay and put on probation with instructions to keep people away from Latura's.

Wild Bill, too, was confused. He had been operating without much of a problem, but he had recently been arrested and convicted on a gambling charge. He had the conviction on appeal and, now, the police were turning away his patrons. One day he called the chief of police and said he would kill him and any other policeman involved if he were required to serve the three year sentence.

On the night of August 22, 1916, a quiet Tuesday, Lyons and Davis were patrolling Latura's area when they encountered a familiar character and in no uncertain terms told him to stay away from Wild Bill's establishment. They later passed by again, just before midnight, and Latura came out a side door, almost as if he had been awaiting them. He lit into the officers verbally, berating them for interfering with his help and said that he would "get" them, "And as for that smart aleck reporter who called me 'Wild Bill,' I'm going to fix him so he'll never write up anybody else."

The more he talked the madder he got. Then, purportedly, he went for his gun, but Lyons pulled his first and hit him with the first shot. Three more shots found their mark and Latura staggered across the street and collapsed. Lyons and Davis left him there and walked back to headquarters where they said they had left the scene to avoid more shooting in the event some of Latura's employees came to his aid.

His Negro driver drove to his home and, intemperately, returned with his five-year old daughter who ran to Latura as he lay dying on the street. Two other policemen, summoned by a telephone call from a neighbor, arrived in an automobile and picked him up and drove to the nearby City Hospital. He died as they carried him in. The next day a coroner's jury ruled he had been resisting arrest and cleared the two officers.

The newspaper reports on the shooting went back to calling him "Wild Bill," but The Commercial Appeal expressed sympathy for his family and in an editorial placed some of the blame for his horrific actions and tragic end on the community at large. One wonders at the extent of mayhem he might have wreaked had he had to contend with today's drivers in big-city traffic.

In 1923 a Negro named "Two-Gun" Charlie Pierce had shot two policemen in a fight at Trigg Street and Louisiana Avenue. On other occasions he had shot two others and somebody down on Beale made up a song about him. He eluded capture for about a year but Detective Sergeant Lee Quianthy, who had killed several whites and even more Negroes, got on his trail. A tip came in from one of his informers one night that Pierce was at a South Memphis "ark," a Memphis name for a black dive. Quianthy and his partner sped to the place in a big Hudson. With his partner on his heels, he threw open the door and plunged into a large, smoke-thick room filled with reveling black men and women. A momentary hush fell on the crowd, immediately broken by the sound of shuffling feet as people tried to scramble out of the way. Then Quianthy was on "Two-Gun" and a series of shots roared as people shouted and screamed – and it was over. Pierce lay there on his back in his classy suit, blue bow tie, and yellow, pointy-toed shoes. His red and black checked hat had fallen off and a pistol lay near one outstretched hand. When his suit coat was thrown back, a holstered pistol also was revealed. Some of the shots were at such close range they had caught his coat on fire. One of the policemen who had come in as back-up stomped out the little flame and then gave the body a kick: "Two-gun; he's shot his last policeman."

Gamblers like Slop Crowder, Casino Henry and Mac Harris were the high society of Beale. Jimmy Turpin, supposedly the street's best poker player, ran the gambling at the Monarch. But Harris was called the "King of Gamblers," and he dressed the part. He favored a double-breasted, knee-length frock coat, striped trousers, Chesterfield topcoat, and a Homburg hat. When he strutted along Beale in the evening with his trim Vandyke beard and elegant curled-up mustachios, his omnipresent cane, glittering in the lights, was the crowning touch. In a four-day marathon poker game he took $2,000 from an imported sharpie from Baltimore and relieved a famous cross-eyed gambler in New Orleans by the name of Nine Tongue, of $10,000. Others would come in from Chicago, St. Louis and New York to try their skill against Harris. According to McKee and Chisenhall, in their book *Beale Black and Blue*, another well-known gambler was Red Lawrence, who looked almost white. He is reputed to have killed 13 people between 1915 and 1941 and was never convicted of any of the slayings.

The largest gambling enterprise, one that provided employment for up to 5,000 people, was the numbers game. Tickets were sold by every legitimate and illegitimate enterprise on Beale as well as at many other businesses in the city. A thriving sideline business developed in the sale of "dream books" that advised which three numbers to select based on a particular dream the bettor may have had the night before. Some others, looking for more occult advice, went a little farther east out Beale to a low-lying marshy area and received their guidance from various conjurers who congregated there. A throwback to their African roots, these witch doctors and

Memphis detectives in front of police headquarters, circa 1930. Benbow Clark is on the left, and the third man from the right in the light coat is Lee Quianthy. Their riot guns are 12-gauge, Winchester Model-97 pump shotguns. (HD, M/SCPL&IC)

medicine men types with their "voodoo" or "hoodoo" rites and incantations and "tonics," professed, among other things, to have the ability to cure any disease, bring good luck or ward off bad, punish one's enemies and predict the future. They did a flourishing business. The most prominent of these was a tall black man with strange eyes known as "Dr. Scissors," real name Will Self. An adjunct of this cottage industry was the sale of up to a dozen different types of "love potions," ranging from "Love Powder" for 25¢ to "Easy Life Powder" and "76 Black Cat Ashes" for $2.50.

Another who kept his pockets stuffed with cash was Dr. G. W. Smith, who ran a widespread dope ring. He loved to flaunt his illicit prosperity by riding along Beale in the early evening at the height of the crowds in a chauffeur-driven Cadillac limousine.

Beale Street demanded a voice for its feeling: someone to sing its songs of misery and hope; of despair and promise; of the forlorn and the high roller and, although it took him awhile, William Christopher Handy absorbed and eventually understood what he was hearing and gave the world a new kind of American music.

Handy was born in Florence, Alabama in 1873. His father wanted him to pursue the ministry, but a young man must follow the dictates of his heart and Handy's destiny lay in a different direction. Music was his consuming passion and, because of his curiosity about all its forms and his innate creativity, it was inevitable that he would end up on Beale Street. Here, in saloons and on street corners, the primitive sounds of the Delta field hand and the river roustabout were being expressed through barrelhouse pianos, crude instruments and vocalization, awaiting the sensitive talent that could combine, synthesize and hone them into something fresh and daring that would gain immediate and widespread acceptance.

Handy's first knowledge of Beale Street came in his early teens from a Memphis musician who, trying to recover from a busted love affair, showed up in Florence. While he was intrigued by what he heard about it, it would be quite some time before Handy would find his way to the Bluff City. In the meantime, he toured the country with Mahara's Minstrels for a number of years and then headed the music department at A&M Normal College in Huntsville, Ala. for two years.

In 1903, at age 29, he received simultaneous offers to direct the municipal band in a Michigan town and a Negro Knights of Pythias band in Clarksdale, Miss. While the former offered more money and, presumably, more prestige, for reasons he couldn't define, he felt constrained to head South. His nine-man orchestra, that was an outgrowth of the band, played for dances in public places and large homes and for store openings from one end of the Mississippi Delta to the other, and Handy became familiar with every square foot of that fertile, cotton-growing area. In this period of his life two things occurred that were to have a significant impact in not only broadening his musical perspective and enhancing his career but, also, helped lead American popular music in a new direction.

One night he and the band were dozing in a little railroad station at Tutwiler waiting for a train that had been delayed nine hours. Sitting next to Handy, with a guitar on his lap, was an old Negro in ragged clothes and toe-exposing shoes. With the flat side of his knife pressed down on the strings, the lean, sad-faced man began strumming the guitar and singing about, "Goin' where the Southern cross' the Dog," meaning he was going to Moorhead where the north-south Southern Railroad intersected with the east-west Yazoo Delta line, called the "Yellow Dog." The earthy rhythm and tonality produced by the raggedy man and his beat-up guitar were unlike anything Handy had ever heard and the impression was to stay with him.

Sometime later his band was playing for a white dance in Cleveland, Miss. when someone asked if he could play some of his "native music." Confused about the request, Handy played a song that was not what the petitioner had in mind, so a second note asked if he minded if a local band sat in for a few dances. Glad for the opportunity to take a break and grab a smoke, the bandstand was relinquished to three somewhat disreputable looking barefooted young black men with a battered guitar, a mandolin and a worn-out bass. The sounds they produced came straight out of the cotton fields and timber camps and off the levees and the steamboats. The music had a certain monotony, but its core contained a haunting strain. The three stomped their feet, rolled their eyes and swayed with the music, and the dancers found it irresistible. In front of the performers fell a cascade of bills and change and, when it stopped, Handy quickly noted that it represented more money than his nine-piece band of trained musicians was receiving for the engagement. He began to sense that if he took these primitive sounds and polished them up by application of his professional skills, it might be just what the public was looking for. He said, "that night a composer was born, an American composer."

Handy said:

> Southern Negroes sang about everything. Trains, steamboats, steam whistles, sledge hammers, fast women, mean bosses, stubborn mules. They accompany themselves on anything from which they can extract a musical sound or rhythmical effect, anything from a harmonica to a washboard ... they set the mood for what we now call blues.

Around Clarksdale, Handy heard the songs of the Delta field hands and, because the big river was only 18 miles away, roustabouts would come into town in the evenings and on days when they were not loading boats. With them came the many songs of life on the Mississippi.

Oh, the Kate's up the river, Stack O' Lee's in the ben',
Oh, the Kate's up the river, Stack O' Lee's in the ben',
And I ain't seen ma baby since I can't tell when.

Handy went to Memphis and operated out of Beale Street. From here, after establishing his popularity, he simultaneously ran as many as 12 bands utilizing up to 67 musicians playing the parks, excursion boats and dance halls throughout the Mid-South. He was engaged by the leading white dance spot in Memphis, the Alaskan Roof Garden on top of the Falls Building, and he opened up Dixie Park, which he called "a sort of sun-tanned Coney Island." Here, he played on Monday nights and weekends and marveled at the spectacle of color, rhythm and acrobatics of as many as 1,000 dancers on the floor at the same time.

Handy made his headquarters at Pee Wee's Saloon at 317 Beale. Because Pee Wee would let them use his telephone to receive booking calls and had a back room where they could store their instruments until their next job, his saloon was a mecca for musicians. Most lived from day-to-day and they hung around rolling dice, playing cards, shooting pool or betting on the policy game until their next gig. The saloon stayed open around the clock. Just inside the front door was a cigar stand where Handy would sometimes lean on the counter and compose or, for visiting bands, copy the lyrics of "Mr. Crump," his first blues number.

Vigelio "Pee Wee" Maffei had emigrated to the United States, ridden the rods into Memphis and found a home on Beale Street in the 1880s. He first had a saloon at the corner of Beale and Hernando; this later was torn down to make way for a public market building and he moved to 317 Beale. Still later, the market was razed and became the site of Handy Park in 1931. Through the doors of Pee Wee's passed all the colorful and legendary figures of the street. Hammit Ashford liked to come in regularly and bet Pee Wee a grand on a single roll of the dice from a Hadden's Horn. Pee Wee never hesitated to take him up on it. Whoever lost promptly paid up and looked forward to the next time. Pee Wee just as readily arm-wrestled on the bar with all comers, while a large oil painting of a scene from *Othello* looked down on them from the wall. In his later years Pee Wee turned the saloon over to his nephew, Lorenzo Pacini, and returned to Italy.

In 1909 E. H. Crump and two others were running for mayor and all three candidates hired bands to play on downtown street corners at lunch time. Crump's coterie of youthful reformers engaged Handy to represent him and Handy wanted to earn his fee and write an original song that would help his candidate. He thought back to the raggedy man in the Tutwiler railroad station, the dance at Cleveland, the field hands and roustabouts, and the sounds in the saloons and on the street along Beale. "...I was attempting to suggest the typical slurs of the Negro voice... what have since become known as 'blue notes.'" He composed a tune, initially without words, entitled "Mr. Crump." From comments by Beale Street denizens expressing their disdain for the idea of reform, Handy later wrote the following lyrics:

Mr. Crump won't 'low no easy riders here
Mr. Crump won't 'low no easy riders here
We don't care what Mr. Crump don't low
We gon' to bar'l-house anyhow –
Mr. Crump can go and catch hisself some air!

Handy and six of his well-rehearsed musicians rode to Main and Madison in a mule-drawn band wagon and set up for history's first public performance of the blues. Handy gave them the cue and the boys cut loose. In moments, patting feet in the Negro audience on the sidewalk below became dancing feet, bodies swayed to the tempo, and there were shouts of approval. In nearby office buildings whites stuck their heads out of windows and demanded more and Handy, exhilarated by the response, obliged with enthusiasm. Crump won the election.

About a year later, Handy came to Crump's office one day with the words written out on a big piece of brown wrapping paper. Handy asked permission to use his name for the

Pee Wee's Saloon
(HD, M/SCPL&IC)

title and it was granted, but it was not until two years later that he published the sheet music, without words, with the title "Memphis Blues" and "also known as Mr. Crump" in smaller letters below it. Words were later added by George Norton, who with two others had written "Come to Me My Melancholy Baby," and "Memphis Blues" became popular nationwide and provided the bases for the acceptance of a new type of music. "Beale Street Blues" was dedicated to Pee Wee and "Jogo Blues," which was a hit at local country club dances that Handy played for, was later renamed "St. Louis Blues"; remembering Tutwiler, "Yellow Dog Blues" was composed and also became extremely popular. More were to follow, but it is little known that Handy wrote many more spirituals then he did blues songs. The sounds of the Delta and Beale Street that Handy interpreted and embellished were, in effect, or led to, "boogie woogie," "jazz," "swing," "rhythm and blues," and "rock and roll."

In 1918 Handy moved to New York to enter the publishing business with fellow Memphian Harry Pace. Their first offering, "A Good Man is Hard to Find," got them up and running. But Handy's heart still was in Memphis on Beale. Regarding the lyrics of "Memphis Blues," he said one time:

Whenever I hear them new, 'smoke gets in my eyes.'
(Folks I've just been down; down to Memphis Town)
An inner voice begins to scold
(Where the people smile, smile on you all the while)
Why did you leave the town
(They've got a fiddler there that always slickens his hair)
Where everybody grinned at Handy
(It moans just like a sinner on revival day)
And every kid knew him?
(It sets me wild to hear that lovin' tune again – The Memphis Blues)

"The Father of the Blues"
William Christopher Handy and his "Silver Trumpet"
(HD, M/SCPL&IC)

On March 29, 1931, riding in a convertible at the head of a long parade, Handy arrived at Beale and Third where a park was to be dedicated in his honor. Along with other dignitaries, the speaker's platform was filled with city, county, state and federal officials present to pay homage to his musical achievements and what he had meant to Memphis. In New York Handy was losing his sight and eventually went blind, but he came back regularly to Memphis to attend the "Blues Bowl" football games between two leading Mid-South Negro high school teams. He died in 1958, one day shy of the 27th anniversary of the dedication of the park to the "Father of the Blues."

> *Way Down South Where the Blues Began*
> *Down South in Nature's own garden*
> *Where hearts never harden*
> *Like the grinding stone on old Miller's wheel*
> *You'll find the world there like a grand pageant*
> *And all a free agent, in peace alone where love is real*
>
> -W. C. Handy

Memphis' musical heritage influenced the development of an untold number of musicians who either were born there, got their start there, or spent time there absorbing its magic; it would be tedious to mention them all. Some of the old-time players and singers of the blues such as Robert Johnson, Furry Lewis, Memphis Minnie Lawler, Will Shade (Son Brimmer), Big Joe Williams, Big Bill Broonzy, Bukka White, Little Laura Dukes, Piano Red Williams and Gus Cannon, probably were more appreciated nationally and, later, internationally than they were locally. A. D. "Gatemouth" Brown, known as "Mr. Beale Street" in the late thirties, later became an eclesiastical bishop. Jimmy Lunceford was teaching music at Manassas High School when, in 1927, he formed a student jazz band he called the "Chickasaw Syncopaters," which went on to national acclaim. Its competence and style and the originality of its arrangements were so well respected that, among big jazz and swing orchestras of the 1930s, it was considered to be in the same league with those of Ellington, Basie and Goodman. During this period big bands with full horn sections proliferated on Beale.

Others of note, some of whom came along later, were Rufus and Carla Thomas, Al Hibbler, Bobby "Blue" Bland, Muddy Waters, Johnny Ace, Phineas Newborn, Jr., Memphis Slim, Ace Cannon, Aretha Franklin, Al Green, Ike Turner, Albert King and B. B. King, whose name today graces a restaurant on Beale. And then there all those of fairly recent vintage with Memphis connections who owe something of their styles to the sounds that were heard on Beale: Isaac Hayes, Otis Redding, Johnny and Dorsey Burnett, Kay Starr, Harold Dorman, Booker T and the MGs, Sam and Dave, Eddie Floyd, the Bar-Kays, the Bill Black Combo, the Blackwood Brothers and Bill Justis' band.

The sheer volume and originality of music emanating from Memphis never waned and, as it evolved and diversified into new forms, gave spontaneous birth to a plethora of studios – such as Sun, Stax and Hi – to record the seemingly unending parade of new musical artists. At one time, 28 songs made in Memphis were on the Billboard chart. Sam Phillips, whose Sun Record Co. launched the careers of, among others, Sam the Sham, Roy Orbison, Jerry Lee Lewis, Johnny Cash, Charlie Rich, Howlin' Wolf, Carl Perkins and, of course, Elvis, said in an interview in the July 1995 issue of Memphis' *Downtowner* magazine:

There is still no city so urbanized and yet so non-urbanized as Memphis. And we're built on the Father of Waters. I think there's something about being around a force you can't control. ... There will never be a place more creative than Memphis.

While it is doubtful that Beale had any particular influence on them, some others of prominence in the music field should be noted: "Snooky" Lanson left Memphis for Nashville and later spent seven years as the headliner on the televised version of "Your Hit Parade"; Elmo Tanner (the whistler on Ted Weems' "Heartaches") left Nashville for Memphis and spent several years there in the late 1920s; Kenny Sergent, vocalist ("For You") with Glen Gray's Casa Loma Orchestra and named by big band authority George Simon as the best big band male vocalist, was a disc jockey in Memphis in the 1940s and had a band that played locally; Clyde McCoy and his "Sugar Blues" trumpet settled permanently in Memphis after World War II; Marguerite Piazza has made her home in Memphis for many years and native Memphian and mezzo-soprano Mignon Dunn began singing with the New York Metropolitan Opera in 1958.

In its heyday Beale Street hosted such bands as those led by Cab Calloway, Chick Webb with vocalist Ella Fitzgerald, Duke Ellington and Count Basie. Amateurs also had their opportunity to perform. Anselmo Barrasso opened the Palace Theater and it became the biggest performance venue for blacks in the South. Broadcast over a local radio station, the weekly amateur night would begin with the emcee saying, "It's amateur night on Beale Street... where the blues began... and the stuff is here," as the house orchestra played "Beale Street Blues" in the background. Cash prizes amounted to $5, $3 and $2 and the fare provided by the contestants ran the gamut, even to such as one-legged dancers and a snake trained to wiggle to a drum beat. When the audience was displeased with a performance, the contestant could be pelted with wadded-up paper bags in the winter or tomatoes in the summer and when, despite the boos, catcalls and ammunition from the audience, he refused to leave the stage, the "Lord High Executioner" would step from the wings and shoot him with a revolver loaded with blanks. A young white boy talked himself onto the stage one night and the blacks went wild over a then unknown Elvis Presley. Saturday's "Midnight Rambles" was a weekly show for whites featuring top-flight black entertainment, such as the bands mentioned above and individual acts like Fats Domino.

In the 1950s Jim McWillie and John Murdock, Sr. went to Chicago on business. The banker they called on invited them to an evening out on the town. While playing in a dance band in his earlier days, the banker had developed a friendship with Ted (Is Everybody Happy?) Lewis, who happened to be playing at one of the city's premiere clubs. The Memphis men were a little dubious about their host's claim of friendship with the famous bandleader and entertainer, but they got a seat close to the bandstand and after the first set Lewis spotted his old musician buddy and joined them at the table. Lewis set aside his signature battered top hat and cane on an extra chair and the introductions were made. He had a routine where the band accompanied him as he sang and soft-shoed to the song "Me and My Shadow," while behind, perfectly mimicking his every move, danced a young black man. As they chatted Lewis asked McWillie and Murdock where they were from. "Ah, Memphis," he said, "I got my first 'shadow' off of Beale Street many years ago."

Recognizing a public need and pursuing it full-tilt with imagination and perseverance has been the basis for most fortunes. The validity of this precept was never better illustrated than by the amazing career of Barron Collier. Like most highly-successful people, he was eager to get a jump-start in his business pursuits. Accordingly, in 1888, at age 15, he dropped out of Market Street School, donned a derby and carried a cane to project age, and took a job soliciting passengers for the Illinois Central Railroad.

Two years later he obtained a contract to light a number of suburban streets and alleys that were outside the service area of the gas mains. Each street light was equipped with a small kerosene tank, and he hired 25 boys pushing two-wheeled kerosene carts to fill them in the morning and then light the mantles in the evening. It worked so well that he was able to obtain contracts for this service in a number of southern cities. During this period in his youth he also was briefly manager of the Appeal building and published a little newspaper, the *Bailey Hotel World*, for which he wrote and sold all the advertising. It probably didn't hurt that his father, Cowles Miles Collier, successively was a bookkeeper for the gas company and *The Appeal*. Cowles Collier had served in both the United States Navy and the Confederate Navy; he later became well-known as a painter of New England seascapes.

Ever on the alert for opportunities, while riding an elevated train on his first trip to New York Barron noticed that advertising cards on the train, being soot-encrusted and behind dirty glass, were virtually unreadable. He immediately conceived the idea of providing frequently-changed cardboards in slots without glass so they would always be clear and legible. As soon as he got back to Memphis he started calling on businesses and making sales. As is so often the case in successful ventures, his timing was opportune. Memphis was just changing from horse-drawn cars to electric trolleys and everyone began using them to get to work, go shopping, go on picnics and even have street car parties. The business flourished and expanded rapidly nationwide. At age 24 Collier moved to New York City and, from a large suite of offices in the Times Square area, directed operations that eventually had 70 offices doing business in 1,000 cities. He didn't get back to Memphis very often, but he did return in 1907 to marry a daughter of Sam Carnes, the leader of the old Chickasaw Guards and the man who brought the telephone, electric lights, and the first automobile to Memphis.

His wide-ranging interests and business pursuits led him into other areas of endeavor. At one time he was president of 15 companies, owned Luna Park at Coney Island, 13 hotels and 1,186,000 acres in Collier County, Flor., much of which later became Everglades National Park. He was instrumental in the construction of the 300-mile Tamiami Trail through swampy areas from Tampa to Miami and was enthusiastic about the development potential of the area. His estate on the coast, Useppa Island, had a private golf course with one of the tees on a wrecked ship.

Barron Gift Collier
By putting advertising on public transportation, he built a business empire that led him into various civic endeavors including formation of the International World Police (Interpol).
(HD, M/SCPL&IC)

He extended his business activities to include bus lines, banking, newspapers, a telephone company, a steamship line and various farming operations. To compliment his New York townhouse, the Memphis high school dropout also had a country estate near Tarrytown, amidst those of the eastern big-monied families and another, originally built by the Krupps, overlooked Germany's Black Forest. He was a member of country clubs and yacht clubs in New York, Chicago, San Francisco, New Orleans, Georgia, Maryland, and Memphis and numerous other business, charitable and social organizations, including being a founder and trustee of the Museum of the City of New York.

In his capacity as commissioner in charge of foreign relations of the International Association of Chiefs of Police, in July 1933 he had as his guests at a meeting in Chicago the police representatives of the largest cities of the United States and Europe, to participate in the organization of the International World Police (Interpol).

Collier also directed some of his energies to the betterment of youth. He served as acting director of the Boy Scout Foundation of Greater New York, was a director of the Boy Scouts of America and vice president of the Camp Fire Girls.

With the title of Special Deputy Police Commissioner as head of the Bureau of Public Safety, he put up $30,000 of his own money and instituted an effective public school campaign for safety. Utilizing his advertising skills and flair for the dramatic, he wrote a book entitled, *Stopping Street Accidents*, put on a daily parade for a week with 10 floats emphasizing his 10 commandments for drivers and walkers, and created "Aunty Jay Walker," a little policewoman with a bonnet and nightstick, whose image became familiar all over New York City. His safety pledge was taken by more than one million New Yorkers and within 90 days the records of the Bureau of Public Safety showed a decrease of almost 50 percent in accidents resulting from jaywalking. His business and civic activities earned him decorations from nine foreign governments.

Collier fought his way out of debt incurred by the Depression, but when he died in 1939, except for the Florida land, most of his business enterprises and his money were gone.

An early-day Jack LaLanne with a strong dash of P. T. Barnum was Christopher H. "Doc" Hottum. When the Frisco Bridge was completed, the general consensus was that a dive from it would earn a one-way ticket to eternity, but young Doc figured that a skillful diver could pull it off, and he proved his point. His instant celebrity status enabled him to open a saloon and, later, a restaurant when prohibition kicked in. It was a sort of sports bar with the walls covered with pictures of race horses, wrestlers, and sluggers from the ring and home plate.

His restaurant and a profitable beer distributorship provided him with the wherewithal to own four steamboats. He became a good friend of W. C. Handy who told in his autobiography how, during one of the periodic disastrous floods that overwhelmed the valley, Hottum took his boats to Mississippi and up the tributary rivers in Arkansas and rescued many Negro families and their livestock and possessions, bringing them to safety in Memphis where he provided them with food and shelter. They later responded gratefully by presenting him with a gold watch and other expensive gifts.

Obviously, Doc had a great zest for life, because his fertile imagination impelled him into one promotion after another. A few years after soldiering during the Spanish-American War he toured theaters around the country putting on four-round exhibition bouts between John L. Sullivan and Jake Kilrain; they had fought the last of the bare knuckle fights – 75 rounds worth – on the Mississippi Gulf Coast. For awhile, he managed Battling Nelson, a lightweight champion. And he was the driving force in making Memphis the world capital of wrestling. The sport had essentially disappeared from the local scene when, late in 1923, he brought Jimmy Londos to town for a match with Paul Schmidt. A clean-liver and a gentleman in the true sense of the word, Londos was agile and graceful and built like a Greek god. He was trained by Charles Rentrop who at one time had been a contender for the championship. Rentrop lived in the nearby community of Germantown in a home filled with fine art originals and had a son who played football at CBC.

Londos' match with Schmidt, which he won, mainly was a build-up for one the following month with Stanislaus Zbyszko, who had taken the championship from Strangler Lewis in Madison Square Garden. Hottum rented the Lyric Theater, on the south side of Madison near Fourth Street, and filled every one of its 1,400 seats. Although Zbyszko weighed 235 to Londos' 195, Zbyszko was unable to throw him. Londos was champion for 16 years.

Hottum's promotions ran the gamut. He brought Aimee Semple McPherson to town to debate an atheist, buried a man alive at Union and Second charging ten cents a look, was a leading figure in bringing Southern League Baseball to Memphis, sponsored "dance marathons" and set up a fight between a snake and a rat, but they refused to cooperate and ignored each other by taking their ease on opposite sides of a big cage.

Doc always stayed in good shape by walking briskly five miles a day, regardless of the weather. Another colorful character of well-known eccentricities also clicked off five miles on a regular basis, but Tom Collier did his outdoor running barefoot. When Hottum was 60, he and Collier competed in a five-mile run on the indoor track at the YMCA. Doc was a little older but got ahead of his opponent early and started lapping him on the short track. Each time he passed Collier he would stop and do a little jig and rub the top of the other's head.

"Doc Hottum's Annual Mississippi River Marathon," which he sponsored from 1900 to 1944, was his greatest claim to fame. It was a ten-mile race for men swimmers down the river from Island No. 40 to the foot of Mud Island at Beale. He also later added a five-mile race for women that lasted 14 years, but it was dropped in the 1930s due to a lack of participants. The best-known swimmer was a local lawyer and short story writer named George Blagdon, who won $7,500 for setting a new speed record in winning a 15-mile marathon at Toronto in 1932. Although he competed in Doc's race eight times, he never won it. In September 1943 thirteen year old Pete Dixon from suburban Whitehaven won both five- and ten-mile races for the second straight year. Over the years the income garnered from selling tickets to observers on excursion steamers and small boats possibly failed to equal expanses, but Doc thrived on the excitement of the event and the satisfaction gained from encouraging people to participate in something that promoted physical health.

Doc Hottum died in 1959 at ninety years of age. It was 14 years after he had been invalided when struck by a car in front of Hotel Peabody.

When 24 ladies of the Kings Daughters of Calvary Episcopal Church approached orthopedic surgeon Willis Campbell in the fall of 1917 with $135 to buy a wheel chair for a crippled child, he thanked them and responded, "You don't want to buy a wheel chair, you want to found a hospital." There was a huge untouched case load of orthopedic patients in the Mid-South at the time, particularly indigent children. Many would require multiple operations and continued treatment and observation, even into adulthood. In Dr. Campbell's mind, the establishment of a hospital for crippled children would be the first phase of a program that would, in turn, provide a hospital for indigent crippled adults, with both being affiliated with hospitals offering operating facilities. With Dr. Campbell's promise of a $10,000 gift from an anonymous donor to get the ball rolling, the ladies took up the challenge. With additional support from the community at large in the way of free services and plans and materials at cost, the hospital opened its doors only a year and a half later. The first year the Crippled Children's Hospital served its 36 patients at a daily cost of only $1.35 per patient!

All of the crippled children's hospitals around the country had an age cut-off of 14 or 15 years, but Dr. Campbell felt there were many physically handicapped adults who could benefit from orthopedic treatment and then take advantage of a new government program called Vocational Rehabilitation. In August 1923, with the cooperation of and donations from many close friends, the Hospital for Crippled Adults was opened near St. Joseph's Hospital, which generously agreed to supply the surgical facilities plus room for immediate postoperative care. Several years before, Dr. Campbell had moved from a downtown office to a new clinic at 869 Madison Avenue, next to Baptist Hospital and across the street from Memphis General, later John Gaston Hospital. Everything was now in place to provide the area with the level of orthopedic care that Dr. Campbell felt was needed. His new clinic was a one-story building with a waiting room, a business office, eight examining rooms, a physical therapy department and a brace shop. The foundation was designed to allow the addition of four more stories, which were later added and provided 80 beds. His credo became "Orthopedic surgery can rehabilitate cripples previously given up as hopeless."

The response was almost overwhelming; at the Hospital for Crippled Adults patients were being accepted from 19 states. In 1928 a donation of $200,000 by B. B. Jones, a close friend of Campbell who had recently moved from Memphis to Berryville, Va., made possible construction of a new 56-bed hospital for indigent adults. Rotary clubs in Memphis and the Mid-South provided wholehearted support. In a report to them by Sam Woods, a friend of both Jones and Campbell, he stated: "The purpose of this hospital is to give treatment to any adult who can be benefited by orthopedic treatment and who is unable to pay for it. The ultimate purpose is to relieve physical suffering, to restore lost hope, and to enable the patients to become self-supporting."

Willis Cahoon Campbell was the leading figure in orthopedic surgery in the United States in the period of 1920-

1940. Dr. Alfred R. Shands, the recognized historian of American orthopedics said "... no one did more for our specialty during his active years than did Willis Campbell of Memphis." Campbell was called "an orthopedic sculptor – a Rodin." Born in Jackson, Miss. in 1880 he attended Millsaps College there, Hampden-Sydney, Roanoke College, where he was "acknowledged as a champion in competitive beer drinking," and graduated Phi Beta Kappa from the University of Virginia Medical School. After a two-year internship in New York City, he set up a general practice in Memphis in 1908. He was six foot two and weighed about 230; he was robust and endowed with tremendous energy.

Within a year he switched from general practice to pediatrics, had a passing interest in anesthesia, wherein he wrote his first paper analyzing over 1,000 anesthetics, and eventually decided that orthopedics would be his life's work. He closed his office and divided months of study between London, Vienna, Boston and New York, returning to Memphis in late 1909. At this time the Memphis Medical School and the local College of Physicians and Surgeons merged and became the University of Tennessee Medical School at Memphis. When a committee was formed to select a faculty, Campbell had just returned to Memphis and he submitted his name. Dr. Hugh Smith, who has written a brief biography of Campbell, said the latter suspected that the committee deliberations went something like this:

> 'What are we going to do about Willis? I don't particularly like him, but he is a force in this town. But where are we going to put him?' 'Let him lecture to the medical students on orthopedic surgery.' 'What the hell is that?' 'He puts kids in casts and braces.' 'Well that's just fine! At least, he can't do any harm.'

After Campbell organized the department and became the school's first professor in that specialty, Dr. Smith said that "Memphis was on its way of becoming a renowned orthopedic center."

As the field became more specialized, he served as president of the Clinical Orthopedic Society in 1928. When he was elected president of the American Orthopedic Association in 1931, which was the primary professional group in the field, he took over an organization that previously had functioned somewhat like a closely-knit private club made up primarily of practitioners in the New York-Boston corridor. Campbell changed that. He was the driving force behind the founding of the American Academy of Orthopedic Surgery, which expanded the membership, and became its first president in 1933. That same year he served as president of the Southeastern Surgical Congress and pushed for the formation of the American Board of Orthopedic Surgery, which established standards of education and professionalism in the field, and then went on to serve as its president from 1937 to 1940.

Between 1923 and 1939 a tremendous number of medical papers flowed from the Campbell Clinic and were published by all the journals in the field. Campbell himself was responsible for over 100 publications, including the books, *Childhood Orthopedics*, *Textbook of Orthopedic Surgery*, for medical students and residents, and *Operative Orthopedics*, now in its tenth revised edition. Approximately 300 residents passed through and graduated from the Campbell Clinic training program, providing trained surgeons throughout the country.

Dr. Campbell's indefatigable dedication to his patients made him an exacting taskmaster of his associates, but he was generally good-humored and fair and he provided a good example by demanding more of himself than he did of others. Dr. Smith remembered a phone call one summer Sunday morning at six o'clock that illustrates this, as well as Campbell's remarkable memory:

> *'Son, do you remember those glass x-ray pictures from the old downtown office that are stored on the top shelf of the developing room?' 'Yes sir.' 'Meet me about 7 o'clock and let's go through them and see if there is anything worth keeping' 'Yes sir.' The first 40 or 50 were either of poor quality or had faded badly, when suddenly, 'Doddam, thon (Campbell had a slight lisp), that's Izzy Goldstein's boy. I remember because that is my first case of coza plana.'*

When he learned that one of his associates had made a simple adjustment of an arch support for a lady so she wouldn't have to wait hours to see him, he flew into a rage. "Doddammit, thon, these patients come to the Clinic to see me, they pay their money to see me, they expect to see me and I'm going to see them. Do you understand that?"

On another occasion, with a full waiting room, the second patient he saw mentioned to him as she was leaving that her regular doctor thought she might have diabetes. Ever solicitous of his patients, rather than sending her back to her doctor or an internist, he said, "Why that's no problem; we can find out for you in a few minutes. Irene, have Miss O' Brien get a specimen, send it to the lab, and give Mrs. Jones a report."

Willis C. Campbell, M.D.
His vision and energy brought hope to the afflicted.
(Courtesy of Campbell's Clinic)

After an exhausting afternoon, Dr. Campbell walked out into the lobby. 'Mrs. Jones, what are you doing here?' 'I'm waiting for the report on my urine.' After thirty minutes of frantic search-

ing, they found the specimen in the back of the elevator. That triggered a real tantrum. Pushing every call button on his desk, he called, 'Get Miss O'Brien, get Irene, get Mrs. Wagstaff, get Mr. Thompson, get Hugh Smith, get Harold Boyd, get John Lovejoy, get everybody!!!!' With 'everybody' lined up around his office, he shouted angrily, 'What this clinic needs it faster and more efficient service. Sixty-seven people working here this afternoon and what have we done? Not a doddam thing but ride the piss up and down on the elevator!!'

As the reputation of the clinic spread, it became a mecca for many well-known athletes who had incurred injuries, including, for example, Carl Hubbell, the great pitcher of the New York Giants. Sometime between 1909 and 1912 John Gaston, a French immigrant and former Confederate soldier who had prospered as Memphis' leading restaurateur, became Dr. Campbell's patient. Now past eighty, he had some sort of problem that was treated successfully over a five-month period. When he asked Campbell how much he owed him, the response was, "Whatever you think it is worth." Gaston wrote him a check for $10,000! Maybe that was the same $10,000 that got the ball rolling five years later for the establishment of the Crippled Children's Hospital.

Another prominent Memphis physician of this era was E.C. Ellett. He was educated at Southwestern, the University of the South at Sewanee and at the University of Pennsylvania Medical School, where he was awarded a medal for the highest average in his class.

As a lieutenant colonel in World War I he commanded a hospital in France and received a citation for "exceptionally meritorious and conspicuous service." When he came home he restricted his practice to the eye only. He was one of the organizers of the American Board of Ophthalmology, which was

E.C. Ellett, M.D.,
Pioneer Opthamalogist.
(HD, M/SCPL&IC)

started in Memphis and was the first medical specialty board of any kind in the United States. From the opening of the Memphis Eye, Ear, Nose and Throat Hospital at 1060 Madison in 1926, Dr. Ellett served as its chief of staff until his death in 1947. Through the years of his tenure, free clinics were held every afternoon.

In 1935 eye specialists from around the Mid-South assembled in Memphis to observe an "Ellett Day," and chose to honor him in an unusual and most practical way: by performing sight-saving procedures in operating rooms in every hospital in the city; Dr. Ellett performed some of them himself and described the techniques to visiting doctors.

He received numerous professional awards for his achievements and, among other offices held, served as president of both the American Ophthalmological Society and the Academy of Ophthalmology and Otolaryngology and for five years was chairman of the American Board of Ophthalmology.

He was a veritable throwback to Daniel Boone and the long hunters and a kindred spirit with Sam Fathers of Faulkner's *The Bear*. As Cap'n Richard Owen wrote of him "... he is more than just a man, he is a breed. He is a breed because he belongs more to the wild things he loves than to us..."

Such was Nash Buckingham, but he was much, much more than simply an avid outdoorsman. He was an unassuming, cultured gentleman, an all-around athlete, a peerless raconteur and a fine writer. He was born in 1880 and grew up hearing all the stories about early-day Memphis from his elders, a time when, as Cap'n said, "The cry of the panther could still be heard in the bottoms and the black bear still slept in the cane." And, because he wanted others to share his knowledge of the past and his exhilarating outdoor experiences, he wrote of them in a keenly illustrative, yet simple, style.

Nash Buckingham was broad-shouldered, ruggedly built and stout as goat breath. Although he had an ancestor who was one of the ten founders of Yale University and had a brother who was an outstanding football player at Princeton, he took his talents to Harvard. While there, however, he contracted some sort of fever that required him to leave. Later, he captained the University of Tennessee football team while attending law school. He once said he played football from 1892 to 1911. While at UT he also played baseball, participated in track and boxed. In 1910 he won the heavyweight boxing championship of the Southern division of the Amateur Athletic Union.

In his early years he was a partner in a sporting goods business on Front Street and wrote for the sports department of *The Commercial Appeal*. Joe Williams, the Memphian who became one of the nation's premier sports writers with the *New York World-Telegram*, once said that, "Had he (Buckingham) been so inclined, he could have been the greatest sports writer this country has ever known." After getting married he and his wife, Irma, spent seven glorious years hunting and fishing in Taylor's Pasture near Aspen, Colo. Then came World War I and he served as a sergeant in the Army.

After the war he became Director of Game Restoration for the old Western Cartridge Company. In 1928 he was named executive secretary of American Wildfowlers with offices in Washington, D. C.; this organization later became Ducks Unlimited. The year before, he was one of the organizers of the Outdoor Writers Association of America and later was associate editor of the magazines *Outdoorsman* and *Field and Stream*.

"Mr. Buck" received nationwide recognition as a foremost wing shot and gun authority, fly fisherman, big game hunter, judge of national field and retriever trials and as a conservationist. From 1934 to 1951 he served as a judge at the National Field Trial Championships held annually at Grand Junction, Tenn., and he co-authored the book *National Field Trial Champions*. In 1947 he received the *Field and Stream* national award for "Outstanding Service to Conservation" for stimulating the clean-up of an infamous goose slaughter pen in Illinois and pushed for stricter duck shooting regulations as chairman of the American Waterfowl Committee.

He was elected to the Field Trail Hall of Fame and the Tennessee Sports Hall of Fame. In 1962, by the votes of 4,000 outdoor writers, he was selected for the "Winchester Outdoorsman of the Year Award," winning over such competition as Dwight Eisenhower, Stuart Udall and Joe Foss.

Dr. William F. "Chubby" Andrews, Memphis surgeon, wrote and published a book in 1993 entitled *Nash Buckingham, Beaver Dam and Other Hunting Tales*. Beaver Dam was a hunting and fishing club established in 1882 by 15 Memphis men. They acquired a 99-year lease on property containing Beaver Dam Lake, a long narrow body of water on the Owen plantation three miles south of Tunica, Miss. One of the organizers was Miles Buckingham, Nash's father, and it was here that Nash killed his first duck at age ten and spent most of his early years afield and grew to love the outdoors life. In 1921, the year of Dr. Andrew's birth, his father became a member. When "Chubby" grew to manhood and got his education behind him, he became acquainted with "Mr. Buck" and hunted and fished with him for 17 years, almost up until the time of the latter's death in 1971; most of their outings were to Beaver Dam.

Dr. Andrews has hunted game on four continents, and many of the stories in his book are exciting descriptions of hunts in such places as Africa and Scotland, but the focus of his book is on Nash Buckingham, who meant so much to him. Fortunately, his sons also had the opportunity to hunt and fish with and be influenced by this fine gentleman. And they found that even into Buckingham's late eighties his mind was still razor-sharp; he could recount in detail amusing events of hunts many years before and could name, down through the years, the participants in all the heavyweight championship bouts and the dates of the fights.

One time when observing Nash Buckingham walking down the street, a man commented to a friend, "There goes a man who has done just what he wanted to do all his life." Some could construe this to mean that he had led a life of dissolution and selfishness; quite the contrary, for he neither drank nor smoked and he cherished and honored his wife up until the end of their more than 61 years together. And his six books, including the widely popular *De Shootin'est Gent'man*, and *Game Bag* and *Ole Miss*, along with his recognized efforts in behalf of conservation, are illustrative of a productive life.

For some reason, this active man never learned to drive a car. Could this have been the "throwback's" personal resistance to active participation in the "Machine Age" and industrialization that he felt were steadily destroying God's bounty of nature that he so loved? If so, it was another example of his tendencies as a true and faithful Agrarian.

In a discussion in 1955 about Mr. Buck with Hayne Barnwell, Front Street cotton broker, he told the author a little story that was indicative of the man's character and independence. A group of Memphis outdoorsmen made arrangements to meet somewhere in Arkansas for a fishing trip. Most had assembled at the meeting point, a cafe in a little town, when a Greyhound bus pulled up in front and let Nash Buckingham off carrying his gear. When his friends remonstrated with him

Nash Buckingham holding the most famous shotgun ever built in America, "Bo Whoop," so named because of the distinctive hollow roar of the big gun's report. It had the capacity to keep a small pattern at a long distance. It was bored by Bert Becker of the Ensley-Fox Corp. The dog is a Boykin Spaniel. (Courtesy of Dr. William F. Andrews)

for not calling one of them and arranging a ride over, he simply said he didn't mind riding the bus and didn't want anyone inconvenienced by picking him up.

Born well before the end of the Nineteenth Century and living into almost three-fourths of the Twentieth, probably more than for his achievements, Nash Buckingham is included in this book because his integrity, gentility, and love of the land typifies an era whose influence was still strong in the Memphis of the 1940s.

> *Nash became permeated with all that nature offered unto him. All of its secrets were made known. He sunk his teeth deep into the flesh of a raw wilderness and what he tasted and saw or felt he has written. He has captured with the rapier thrust of his pen the wood smoke of a campfire, the smell of well-oiled boots, the sting of sleet in his face, the smell of dust in the rain, the soft patter of fresh snow, or maybe just the simple beauty of a wild rose by the roadside.*

-Cap'n Richard Owen

One of the most important ingredients in the civilized development of cities and towns in the United States has been the willingness of those who have prospered to recognize their debt to the communities that provided them with the opportunity to get their start, and to return some of the fruits of their enterprise in the form of financial gifts to worthwhile causes. Some of these benefactors assume a high profile and bask in the publicity and praise that comes their way. But there are others who shun the limelight, and it is enough for them to derive their satisfaction within themselves by knowing that they have assisted in a situation that, to some degree, helped to improve mankind's lot. In Memphis the most outstanding example of the latter was a man who, although he contributed to many causes, received the nickname "Mr. Anonymous." Of course, it is not possible for someone who built an internationally-recognized business from scratch and was involved in helping the city in so many ways to not become known for his generosity, but Abe Plough studiously avoided publicity for all his good works and his business career and acts of philanthropy make Horatio Alger's creations look like pikers.

Born in Tupelo, Miss. in 1892, Plough moved with his family to Memphis when he was an infant. He graduated from St. Paul Grammar School and that's as far as his formal education went. But a teacher had taught him how to calculate figures in his head and many years later he said, "I happened to acquire thirty companies for over one billion dollars ... and at no time did I ever use a pencil." Too, he knew early in life what he wanted to do. He worked at a drug store without pay because he liked the business. The meager education and schoolboy job experience were all the tools he would ever need.

In 1908, at age sixteen, he started Plough Chemical Company in a small room over his father's furniture and clothing store. His first product was "Plough's Antiseptic Healing Oil" – "a sure cure for any ill of man or beast" – whose label featured a boy with a plow. After concocting and bottling his formula, he would set out in his father's horse and buggy and sell it to drug stores and country merchants. It was well received. Obviously, this was before the establishment of the Food and Drug Administration, which, today, would go into paroxysms of bureaucratic mania at such an extravagant claim. Two years later he acquired C-2223, a product used for rheumatism and blood disorders, and in 1915 bought the inventory of a bankrupt patent medicine company. Two years after that, following several previous moves to larger facilities, he occupied a three-story building at 132 South Second and was turning out 2,500 packages of his healing oil per day. That same year he had acquired Black and White cosmetics. Business expanded so rapidly that, only the next year, it was necessary to move into another building, at Second and Gayoso, four times as large.

His next acquisition was the Gerstle Medicine Company of Chattanooga, which had a product called St. Joseph Liver Regulator. It was at this time, 1920, that he decided to add aspirin to his product line and he utilized the St.

Joseph name for it. It was a decision that had a significant positive effect on the continued growth of the company. The next year the company began printing the St. Joseph Family Almanac Calendar, which is purchased by stores and given away to customers; it has the largest circulation of any calendar of its type in the world.

In 1924 Plough entered the foreign market with a sales operation in Mexico. In 1929, when he was nicknamed "the millionaire drug store clerk" for continuing to work on Saturday nights in his three Memphis drug stores, Plough went public and became Plough, Inc. It was listed on the New York Curb Exchange in 1936 and on the New York Stock Exchange in 1945.

When the stock market crash hit in 1929 Plough demonstrated his first significant act of philanthropy. The American Savings Bank of Memphis closed and 6,000 customers were unable to get funds out of their Christmas savings accounts. Calling on his friends for $60,000, Plough personally put up an additional $175,000 that permitted the customers to have the kind of Christmas they had been anticipating.

In 1931, Moroline, a petroleum jelly was added to the product line and Mexican Heat Powder, later renamed Mexsana, was acquired in 1939. Seeking diversification, two radio stations, one in Memphis and one in Chicago, were purchased in 1944; the company now operates six AM and six FM stations in strong markets around the country. In 1947, after several years of research, St. Joseph Aspirin for Children, with an orange flavor, was introduced and immediately received plaudits from the medical profession. During these years the company expanded its sales operations into many foreign countries and, in a 1951 opening, hosted by Jack Benny, moved out of the eight buildings it occupied into one facility of 250,000 square feet on six acres at 3022 Jackson Avenue.

Over the years Plough continued to introduce new products and acquire existing companies with names that are familiar to most Americans: Nujol Mineral Oil, Musterole Analgesic Rub, Di-Gel Antacid, Aspergum, Feen-a-Mint, PAAS, the oldest and largest manufacturer of Easter egg color kits, Coppertone, Solarcaine, QT Quick Tanning Lotion, Correctol Liquid, Sardo Bath Products, the Scholl Corporation, with its footcare products, and the Maybelline Company, now the largest manufacturer of eye cosmetics in the world. In 1971

Plough Inc. consolidated with Schering Corporation of Kenilworth, N. J., an international pharmaceutical manufacturer, and formed the Schering-Plough Corporation. Plough served as chairman until his retirement in 1976 at age 84.

His business achievements and humanitarian philanthropy were recognized by organizations, universities, the city of Memphis and the Tennessee legislature; in 1983 he became the first individual recognized by the United States Consumer Product Safety Commission for his pioneering efforts to assure safety in products for children.

In 1968, after long negotiations, a strike by the sanitation workers against the city was settled with an agreement involving a two-step pay raise. The latter two months of the first step and all of the second could be incorporated into the next fiscal year's budget, but there were no funds to pay for the two months remaining in that current fiscal year and the parties were at an impasse. Plough contacted the appropriate officials at city hall and said he would provide the necessary $558,000 on condition that his name not be made public. Plough gave money to many projects and organizations he deemed worthy of support. Among these were The Goodfellows (Christmas baskets for the needy), United Way, Memphis Area Chamber of Commerce, Memphis Boys Town, The Salvation Army, St. Jude Children's Research Hospital, Memphis Arts Council, Memphis Memorial Stadium, several colleges and universities, and $1 million to the Memphis Community Foundation.

Around 1950 he decided to give $8 million to the Memphis Zoo and he and Hal Lewis,[*] former Superintendent of Parks and Recreation, made a tour of other zoos around the country to get ideas on how best to apply the funds. Mr. Lewis says that Plough was an enjoyable traveling companion and a "character." When they would arrive at an airport Plough would say, "Let's take a walk," and they would proceed to stop by the terminal concession stands to see if they carried Plough products; if they didn't, he wanted to know, in a good-natured fashion, why not. He later decided the zoo should have an aquarium, so he donated $100,000 for it and also paid for the architect.

On another occasion, Lewis had appeared before the Park Commission requesting funds for the acquisition of a

[*] As of this writing, Mr. Lewis has just completed a history of the Memphis Park Commision.

needed small building adjacent to a senior citizens center but was turned down reluctantly due to a lack of funds. Abe Plough happened to hear about it and called Lewis on the phone and asked him how much it would cost. He didn't mention he would provide the money, but the next day Lewis received a check in the mail for the full amount. Today, a foundation Plough funded before his death continues to provide succor to charitable causes.

At a Memphis Area Chamber of Commerce function honoring him in 1975, nine years before his death, Plough said: "I hope when they throw the dirt over me, they'll say, 'Poor Abe; we thought he had a lot of money, but he's broke. He gave it all away.'"

Abe Plough
"I'd like to touch the hearts and minds of people to help them make a life." (Courtesy of Plough Foundation)

In 1910 two young women in Memphis proved that men had no monopoly when it came to exhibiting a spirit of enterprise; sisters Mary Harry Treadwell and Georgia Harry established the first insurance business in the United States owned by women. Mary, about 32 years of age, had been a widow for a year and had two young sons to raise. Georgia, two years her elder, obtained an annulment after a brief marriage and never re-married. She reverted to her maiden name but signed herself "Mrs. Georgia Harry."

Their father, Milton Harry, ran small steamboats from Memphis far up the White and Black Rivers into Arkansas. Because of his stylish clothes and manner of living, handsome features and outgoing personality, he was known as "The Aristocrat" among those who earned their livelihood along the Mississippi River, and he counted Mark Twain in his wide circle of friends. Although the family lived in Augusta, Ark., they frequently had Memphians as guests on their boats and sometimes took a suite at Hotel Gayoso for occasions of social intercourse in the city. The girls attended Miss Higbee's School in Memphis and made their debuts in the Bluff City.

In 1878 Milt Harry built the steamboat Josie Harry, named for his wife. Joe Curtis, who for many years wrote a column about famous boats and colorful characters on the river for *The Commercial Appeal*, said that it was "the most beautiful of all small steamboats that ever ran to and from Memphis." From the sweetly melodic tones of its bell, made from melting down $2,000 worth of silver coins, to its mahogany and rosewood furniture and imported carpets and chandeliers with French prisms, it was a gem. But about 1883, while a little over 10 miles below Memphis and carrying a load of cotton bales, it caught fire. The more than 40 crewmen and 13 passengers, including the Harry family, barely escaped to the Arkansas shore, and most of the boat burned as it drifted downstream. What remained settled on a sandbar near the Arkansas side and soon was covered with river silt and sand. Today the site is known as the "Josie Harry Towhead."

Mary's father-in-law, Arthur Barlow Treadwell, had functioned as a cotton factor and had a wholesale grocery business on Front Street. He suffered from catarrh and on the advice of his physician had moved to Chicago, of all places, seeking relief; he left the business in the hands of his son

Timmons Treadwell. After her husband's death, Mary, with Georgia assisting her, attempted to operate the business, which then concentrated on selling sugar and coffee to plantations. But they were in over their heads. In desperation they turned for advice to a friend, who was president of Union Planters Bank. He suggested they go into the insurance business. They looked at him quizzically, hardly knowing the meaning of the word "insurance." He explained that more and more automobiles were appearing on the streets of Memphis and, because they needed to be insured, that field offered a ground-floor opportunity.

So the women started out insuring cars, but they soon became involved in other branches of the industry. They knew many prominent Memphis families on a social basis and their beauty and charm provided an entree, but their determination and resourcefulness were equally as important to their success. In the first seven years of their operation they didn't even have a car, but they made do. One day Mary Harry Treadwell rode the streetcar to the end of the line in north Memphis and then walked the rest of the way to the office of Anderson-Tully, a large wholesale lumber company. She knew the Tully family socially, but Tully was flabbergasted by the purpose of her call and that she had ventured on foot into such a rough area of town. Before she left his office, however, she had convinced him to move his company's insurance to the Treadwell and Harry agency.

The sisters had an office on the 16th floor of the Exchange Building. One day a family friend, Frank "Streetcar" Jones, who owned all the streetcars in the city, showed up to obtain insurance on his new Packard. He had left his crisply-uniformed and shiny-putteed chauffeur with the car parked by the curb at the building's entrance. After the preliminary paperwork had been attended to, the only remaining item was to get the car's motor number to put on the form and an employee was dispatched to tell the chauffeur to get the number off the motor. After 45 minutes to an hour had elapsed with no sign of the chauffeur, just as someone was about to go check on him, in he walked. Formerly immaculate, he was a disheveled, sweaty, grease-stained mess, but he triumphantly displayed an oval-shaped piece of metal inscribed with the motor number that he had removed with a hammer and chisel. The plate, with Packard number 182709 on it, is still in the possession of the Treadwell family.

The women pursued bigger and more complex coverages with a vengeance. When it was announced that an additional bridge, accommodating both rail and vehicular traffic, would be built across the Mississippi River, they went after the primary insurance covering the contractors. J. T. Harahan, retired president of the Illinois Central Railroad, overall supervisor, and for whom the bridge would be named, knew them socially but was reluctant to consider using their company to handle such broad coverage. He did, however, supply the name of a man in New York who had the ultimate authority in the matter. "Miss Georgia" packed her bags and caught the first available train east. It's no wonder that with such resolution and refusal to take "no" for an answer that she got the man in New York to agree to let Treadwell and Harry write the big policy.

This was just one example of some of the coups they pulled off that brought in large chunks of business and solidified the future of the company. With a premium of $250,000 they insured a contractor who diverted a part of the Holston River in East Tennessee, they covered another contractor who rebuilt tracks for the Illinois Central from Paducah, Ken. to Memphis, and they insured the construction of the nation's largest Army depot.

Both ladies were very pretty. Georgia's deep religious convictions gave her somewhat of an air of self-assured sedateness while Mary had a sauciness that enhanced her attractiveness. Oddly enough, although her basic livelihood originated in writing automobile insurance, for years Mary had a running battle with downtown traffic cops who frequently stopped her car because she refused to give an arm

Founders of the first female-owned insurance agency in America. Their resourcefulness resulted in a highly-successful business.
(HD, M/SCPL&IC)

Mary Harry Teadwell   *Georgia Harry*

signal when she made a turn. Being gentlemen, they absorbed her tongue-lashings stoically and, in truth, loved her dearly.

At a dinner party in New York given by an uncle, George McGill, who was president of the New York Yacht Club, Mary was seated next to Kenesaw Mountain Landis, the federal judge who, in 1921, became baseball's first commissioner in the wake of the "Black Sox" scandal. A bachelor, Landis was totally smitten by Mary, and he pursued her with a vigor typical of his high-mindedness and tenacity of purpose. But Mary was his equal in loftiness of ideals and obduration. She finally told him, "You are a fine-looking man and a perfect gentleman worthy of the best, but I married Tim Treadwell in 1895 and I'll be married to him until I die."

Abe Plough's father, Mose, had a clothing and furniture store on North Main Street. Here, on crisp days, Mr. Plough would fire up his large, pot-bellied stove, and business people from all over downtown, in the spirit and tradition of the country store, would regularly congregate around the stove and exchange chit-chat; it became known as the "Gossip Corner." Mary and Georgia were frequent visitors and became good friends with "Mr. Mose." While, for the most part, it was a social event that evolved into somewhat of an institution, a la the "Corner Quartet," the contacts made and information acquired there undoubtedly helped their business.

As Mary's two sons, Timmons, Jr. and George, grew to manhood, they began breaking into the business and Mary and Georgia began spending less time at the office. Today, a fourth generation of Treadwells continues the legacy of resourceful enterprise established by two young women who, initially, didn't even know the meaning of the word "insurance."

Alongside the main road in Overton Park leading to the zoo is a landmark familiar to all Memphians, a rendezvous point over the years for participants in softball and touch football games on the expansive, adjacent greensward. Here, frozen in time and motion for over 70 years, a grim-visaged soldier is mounting a parapet and going "over the top" as he prepares to advance against the enemy into "no man's land" wearing his trench coat, leggings, gas mask, pack and "flat Kelly" helmet. The pose of the "Doughboy Statue" speaks volumes; it is the supreme exemplification of the American role in the "War to End All Wars."

As he climbs up out of the muddy trench ready to encounter the barbed wire, long-range German machine guns and screaming shells, the eyes and mouth of the Doughboy suggest a knowing fatalism as to what lies ahead, but the set of his jaw, the purposeful stride and the strong grip on his bayonet-tipped Springfield rifle portray his determination to fulfill his mission.

A plaque below him lists the 230 boys and men from Memphis and Shelby County who died at such battles as Chateau-Thierry, Belleau Wood, Cantigny, Saint-Mihiel and Meuse-Argonne ... Harry Baker, Samuel Cassiola, Hans Froines, Thomas Kearney, Patrick McLaughlin, Wesley Porter, Bertrum Yancey... One of the Memphians who made the trip

Forevermore "Over the Top"
(A)

"across the water" and lived, Sergeant Joseph B. Adkinson, was awarded the Medal of Honor for charging 50 yards across open ground directly into the fire of a machine-gun, kicking the gun from its parapet into the trench and capturing the three Germans manning it at the point of his bayonet.

The next time you're pushing a cart around the grocery store you might consider that the freedom to pick up and examine each item before tossing it in your cart or replacing it on the shelf, was afforded by an imaginative and flamboyant Memphian whose fortunes went up and down like a roller-coaster. Now, that doesn't sound like a big deal, but before Clarence Saunders came along shoppers would wait at a front counter while a clerk traipsed around the store filling their orders, grabbing a box of crackers here, fishing a pickle out of a barrel there or slicing a chunk of cheese off the hoop.

Saunders had spent about 15 years selling groceries wholesale and observing and analyzing store operations when he opened his own store on September 11, 1916 at 79 Jefferson Avenue. Never at a loss for dreaming up weird and catchy names, he called it Piggly Wiggly, and the opening was preceded by a billboard advertising campaign with such puzzling statements as, "Piggly Wiggly is Coming," and "Mrs. Brown Told Mr. Brown to Stop by Piggly Wiggly on His Way Home." Ultimately, the last message announced the location and the date that Piggly Wiggly would open, and when the big day arrived a brass band held forth while roses were handed out to all red-haired ladies. People would pick up a wicker basket at the front, follow one aisle through the store with the novel experience of making their own selections, and exit at a checker and a turnstile.

Most stores of the era extended credit and, naturally, suffered some losses. With Saunders it was all cash and carry and the overhead of clerks was eliminated, therefore prices were lower than competitors. The store was a huge success and in less than five months Saunders had five additional Piggly Wigglys in Memphis. The concept swept across the country and less than seven years later there were over 2,600.

When he was turned down for a patent on his "self-service stores," he called the patent chief and asked for an audience; he came back from Washington with his patent.

Clarence Saunders was born in Virginia in 1881. At age 11 he worked in both a sawmill and a stave and barrel factory. At 14 he went out on his own and crossed the mountains into Tennessee where, for three years, he clerked in a general store near Clarksville. With little education, he borrowed schoolbooks and studied them at night during those three years. After a couple of more years in other employment, at age 19 he became a salesman for a wholesale grocery company in Clarksville.

Four years later he moved to Memphis and went to work as a salesman for another wholesale grocer. Before making a sales call he would visit a store several times at rush hours and observe its operation, then he would call on the owner and make tactful suggestions about improving its operation and usually get an order. His sales increased, but he was looking for bigger things. He helped organize a lot of small stores into a group, United Stores, Inc., that enabled them to buy from him in bulk at reduced prices. Seeing that his employer was reaping almost all of the profits from his enterprise, in 1915 he got $23,000 worth of backing and started his own wholesale operation. The business sold a lot of groceries, but the profit margin was very thin. When his backers expressed concern, Saunders bought them out and started his Piggly Wiggly chain.

In order to finance his rapid expansion program he had to borrow extensively. Then he tangled with the slick-trading professional bears of Wall Street who sell stock without owning it and expect the price to fall before they have to deliver, thereby enabling them to buy at a lower price than the figure at which they sold it. Saunders presumed they were trying to drive down the price of his stock to a point where his company could be taken over at a bargain price. He borrowed millions on his stock holdings and kept buying additional stock as the price rose. When he had acquired almost all of the outstanding stock he demanded delivery from the bears; he knew they couldn't get it within the time prescribed by the New York Stock Exchange rules. But the Wall Street boys stick together. With Machiavellic cunning, the Exchange extended by five days the time for the bears to come up with the inflated stock. In the meantime, it is presumed that an "invisible hand" prevailed upon the lending bankers to call Saunders' loans forcing him to sell stock which then became available for the bears to acquire. That also forced the price down and reduced his borrowing power. He had gone to New York worth an estimated $10 million; if he had been successful in his corner, he probably would have come out of the fight worth four times that much. In a few months Piggly Wiggly was taken over by others and its founder forced out.

Saunders' first estate in Memphis, with the city's only private swimming pool, was what is now the University Club. When he lost Piggly Wiggly he was building a granite and marble mansion on 160 acres facing Central Avenue across from the Memphis Country Club. On the estate he built a lake and a golf course with one green situated on a little island. But the bottom fell out before he could finish the house and the estate ended up in the hands of St. Louis bankers. The surrounding area was developed into an exclusive residential subdivision and the house eventually was acquired by the City of Memphis; it became the city museum with space also for a planetarium and the Little Theater. Because of the salmon color of the granite, it has always been known locally

Clarence Saunders
When I go down, I go to the bottom. That's the way I do everything.(HD, M/SCPL&IC)

as the "Pink Palace." His third estate, Annswood, out in the country on Park Avenue, was later owned by Bill Terry. It, too, had a lake and a private golf course. When he died in December 1953, Saunders was living in suburban Bartlett.

Although he had been forced into bankruptcy, Clarence Saunders was resilient and never "got his dobber down." He said, "I've never walked past a Piggly Wiggly store and said to myself, 'I used to own that store,' ... and I've never driven by the Pink Palace and said, 'I built that.'" In the next 15 years he came back and failed three times. Always the innovator, two years before losing Piggly Wiggly he had started a chain of self-serve variety stores in competition with Woolworth and Kress. In 1925 he was back in the grocery business. His old enemies tried to bar him from using his famous name, but he won in court and soon had "Clarence Saunders – Sole Owner of My Name" stores in 110 cities. Then the Depression came along and in 1931 he crashed again, but in defiance of the economic times he opened another store in downtown Memphis. This time he lasted only two years. Also during this era he started a professional football team known as the "Sole Owner Tigers," or "Memphis Tigers." Being tied to his up and down fortunes, the team didn't last long, but it did defeat the National Football League champion Green Bay Packers in a challenge game when Saunders scoured the country for the best players and padded the roster for that particular game.

Going after his third fortune, he came up with another wacky name and an innovative leap into a concept that bordered on science fiction. With the usual hoopla he staged for such affairs, on February 19, 1937 he opened up the first Keedoozle at 1628 Union. Asked where he got the name, he replied, "I got it out of my noodle; it's not in the dictionary." Actually, it stood for "Key Does All." Similar to New York City's old "Automat," all the food was in little compartments behind glass. Each customer was given a coded key with a little ball on one end. When selecting a particular item, the customer would insert the key into something resembling an ordinary electrical outlet and a bulb in the ball would flash, indicating a purchase. In a storage area on the floor above untold numbers of electrical impulses went into action and one's purchases were dropped on conveyer belts and into an individual basket. When all selections had been made, the key was turned in at the cashier's stand and the groceries came down on a chute bagged, priced and totaled. A subsequent innovation moved the groceries, via conveyer belt, to a rear entrance where they could be loaded directly into one's car. Newsreel companies sent their crews to photograph the amazing store.

With 10,000 electrical connections, something was occasionally bound to go wrong. Although it happened only two percent of the time, it was enough to cause irritating problems. An electrical connection went dead and didn't record a selection, people disputed or couldn't remember what they

Clarence Saunders' Pink Palace
If I never do anything else, I'll give Memphis a landmark – a real showplace of the South. (HD, M/SCPL&IC)

had punched, or they dropped the key and broke it. Too, because of shoppers' wont to squeeze and examine, he had to relent and put the produce and meat out in their customary displays.

Saunders revised the key and came up with a pistol-shaped selector with a roll of paper and an inker which recorded the article and its price. But the two stores were still experimental and closed their doors during World War II. Right after the war he opened another one, earning a write-up in *Life* magazine, in a big Quonset hut at the corner of Union Extended and Poplar, but the futuristic concept never really got off the ground.

In 1956, less than three years after his death, the American Association of Food Chains belatedly recognized his contributions in packaging food in consumer sizes and establishing firm prices and a price tag on every item. He also was the first to run large newspaper advertisements and was cited for his original concept embodying the cost-cutting Piggly Wiggly operations which had been so instrumental in lowering prices in the industry.

Born in 1900, Richard Halliburton was a handsome young Memphian whose greatest fear was being trapped in a life of the commonplace and the ordinary. He rebelled at the strictures embodied in society's economic and social expectations of a young man whose financially comfortable family had provided with some position and a good education.

He attended the Lawrenceville prep school and, appropriately, Princeton University, where he was a member of the Cap and Gown Society and on the editorial board of the *Princetonian*. As editor-in-chief of the magazine *Princeton Pictorial*, he revamped its format and increased circulation from 400 to 2,000 while taking a heavy load of classes. He participated in a naval training program at Princeton during the summer and fall of 1918 and, frustrated by the end of the war before he could get into it, began making plans for a trip to Europe the next summer.

The following July his mother dropped him off at Union Station, ostensibly for a trip to Brownsville, Tenn. to visit a friend. Instead, he caught a train to New Orleans where he wired his parents that he had gotten a job on a freighter bound for England. Engine troubles forced the ship to put in at Norfolk, Va. for repairs and Richard got permission to visit his parents at their summer cabin at Tate Springs, in the mountains of East Tennessee.

Suffering from heatstroke, seasickness and boils when he left the ship, he had no intention of returning. He arrived at Tate Springs after a long bus ride. His mother ministered to his ailments and told him that, while they wished he could stay, he must return to the ship. He was shocked. He had expected them to want him to stay, but, wisely, his mother realized he must fulfill his obligation and carry through on his original intention. He later termed the occasion the turning point in his life, saying that if he had been permitted to remain it would have forever destroyed his self-confidence. After touring England and France on foot, he returned to Princeton for the second semester and was voted "the most original member of the class."

While in Europe his father had written congratulating him on his decision to come home for the second semester and "returning to the even tenor of your way." This phrase irked Richard and, in a response somewhat tinged with adolescent impetuosity, yet one that would become his lifelong credo, he told his father:

> *I hate that expression (even tenor) and as far as I am able I intend to avoid that condition. When impulse and spontaneity fail to make my way uneven then I shall sit up nights inventing means of making my life as conglomerate and vivid as possible. Those who live in the even tenor of their way simply exist until death ends their monotonous tranquillity.*
>
> *No, there's going to be no even tenor with me ... and I'll be happy if I am spared a stupid, common death in bed.*

Halliburton spent the summer of 1920 hunting and fishing in the Rocky Mountains with three classmates. He wrote an article about the trip entitled, "The Happy Hunting Grounds," which was accepted by *Field and Stream*. The magazine's check for $150 provided additional encouragement for him to pursue the life that was beginning to take shape in his mind – one of adventure and writing.

After graduation in 1921, Richard and a friend got jobs on the freighter *Ipswich* out of New York headed for Hamburg. The *Memphis Commercial Appeal* agreed to pay $35 for each article he sent and, with possible sales to magazines, he hoped to pay his expenses without relying on his father's assistance. Not quite two years later he returned home and estimated that he had earned $300 more than the trip cost him.

He had written about his adventures as he went and taken many photographs. When he got back he had, essentially, a book in complete form; he named it *The Royal Road to Romance*. At first turned down by a number of publishers, when it came to the attention of Bobbs-Merrill it was embraced with enthusiasm. The book was an immediate hit. Reviews were mixed, but he got good to ecstatic ones from the *Saturday Review of Literature*, *Sunset*, the *New York World*, *Detroit News*, and the *Los Angeles Times*. During his lifetime

six more books followed under the same imprint and all were
best sellers in fifteen languages.*

He became the toast of the national lecture circuit and
everywhere he appeared he drew huge crowds. For example,
the *Dallas News* panned his first book as being by one of those
"college boys from wealthy families who occupy the boring
intervals between social seasons by acting as amateur international tramps. Only one thing saves the book from being completely worthless. That is the impudence of the author." But
when he appeared at the Dallas Forum it quickly filled up and
police had to be called when 2,000 angry patrons were turned
away.

He spoke at Smith, Wellesley and Vassar and attended
the latter's graduation prom where he danced every dance,
each with a different girl. He was feted by the Chicago
Adventurers Club, Marshall Field's department store, where a
crush of society matrons showed up despite a blizzard, and in
Washington gave a talk to the National Geographic Society
with 4,000 in attendance. He crisscrossed the country, sometimes giving a lecture per day, including one at South Side High
School in Memphis. In order to portray the image that he presumed people expected of him, Halliburton began to dress for
the occasion by wearing a double-breasted Chesterfield over-
coat, pearl gray suede gloves, spats, colorful neckties, a derby
hat and carrying a black silver-tipped cane. When his second
book came out *Time* magazine described him as a "romantic,
poetic, enthusiastic, dauntless, sparkling, bubbling, impetuous,
adventurous, dramatic, enthralling, etc. playboy." He became
one of the best known and most-admired persons of the 1920s
and 1930s. But one time when a gushing lady introduced him at
one of his lectures in glowing and extravagant terms, he
ascended the dais, cocked his head and, with a wry smile, said,
"I'm none of those things; I'm just a little boy playing Indian."

---

* A first cousin, Erle Halliburton, also left Memphis for adventure and
financial independence. With no other recources other than his
ingenutiy and a dream, he toiled in the Oklahoma and Texas oil fields
until he invented a cementing process that brought him the fortune he
sought. It provided the basis for the establishment of a worldwide oil
field services company that still bears his name.

Perhaps the publicity surrounding Richard's exploits provided inspiration for the author's father and an uncle who, as teenaegers in the
1920s, worked separate summers on freighters out of Mobile that took
them to Rio de Janeiro and Buenos Aires.

Richard climbed the Matterhorn and Mount Fujiyama in the winter and ascended Mounts Vesuvius, Olympus and Popocatapetl. He swam the Hellespont (Dardanelles) and was the first person to swim through the shark- and alligator-infested locks of the Panama Canal, being charged, like ships, on the basis of his tonnage – thirty-six cents; he hid on the grounds of the Taj Mahal at closing so he could partake of the breath-taking beauty of the memorial in moonlight solitude as he swam in the pool in front of it. And, except for a few local Indians who accompanied him to the site, unsupervised and impulsively jumped fully-clothed 70 feet into the Mayan sacrificial "Well of Death" at Chichen-Itza, narrowly escaping drowning. When people in the nearby town were skeptical of his story, he repeated the act before a reporter and photographer from the local newspaper and an American archeologist who recorded the leap with a motion picture camera.

Aping Pheidippides, Halliburton ran the 25 miles from Marathon to Athens, he retraced Ulysses' journey in Homer's Odyssey – making it in five months instead of ten years – from Ithaca and back via Troy, the Isle of Jerba off North Africa, Cyclops in Sicily, Circe on the west coast of Italy, Charybdos and Scylla, Malta and Corfu, and he followed Hannibal's route across the Alps on a rented elephant. He continued his travels, always searching for new adventures with which to satisfy the insatiable demands of his captivated fans. He spent time with the French Foreign Legion at a remote outpost in North Africa, was jailed as a spy by the British on Gibraltar, lived for several weeks on Devil's Island and rode in an open cockpit biplane across the uncharted Sahara Desert and up the south face of Mount Everest, surviving a forced landing in the former instance and, when the engine temporarily conked, a near crash during the latter. While touring Russia and interviewing Lenin's widow and a man who, supposedly, was present at the murders of Czar Nicholas II and his family,

Richard Halliburton
I'm just a little boy playing Indian. (HD, M/SCPL&IC)

he was accosted by the secret police in Batum on the Black Sea. He was locked in a room in a hotel so filthy that he later wrote that, "Communism might have more appeal if the hammer and sickle were replaced by the mop and broom."

For his last glorious adventure Richard conceived the idea of building a Chinese junk in Hong Kong and sailing it across the Pacific to San Francisco, where it would be berthed and serve as an exhibit at that city's world's fair.

After eventually obtaining financing, having the junk built and then correcting some problems related to its seaworthiness that evidenced themselves during a shakedown cruise, the *Sea Dragon*, with Richard and his crew of eight, set sail on March 4, 1939. On March 23, 900 miles southeast of Yokohama and 1,500 miles west of Midway Island, the junk encountered squalls that steadily increased in intensity to near typhoon proportions. The captain of the liner *President Coolidge*, two days away, estimated the waves as more than 40 feet from trough to horizon. At midmorning the Coolidge received this message from the *Sea Dragon*:

SOUTHERLY GALES RAIN SQUALLS LEE RAIL UNDER WATER WET BUNKS HARDTACK BULLY BEEF HAVING WONDERFUL TIME WISH YOU WERE HERE INSTEAD OF ME.

Shortly after noon the *Coolidge* received another message commenting on the *Sea Dragon's* speed and estimated position and " ... may we avail ourselves of your direction finder?" The *Coolidge* acknowledged the message and periodically tried to contact the *Sea Dragon* the rest of the day and through the night, to no avail. The next morning, with some slight abatement in the weather, the *Coolidge* altered its course toward the last estimated location of the *Sea Dragon*, doubled its watches, and vainly continued trying to reestablish radio contact. Another ship, the American freighter *Jefferson Davis*, passed near the area where the junk was thought to be but saw nothing nor heard any radio signals. The junk and its crew had vanished; no trace of them was ever found.

At the Second Congregational Church of Waterbury, Conn., where Halliburton had lectured frequently, Lowell Thomas, fellow adventurer, author and lecturer presided over a memorial service. With the auditorium full, more than 1,500

Halliburton aboard "Dally," crossing the Alps
(HD, M/SCPL&IC)

people stood outside. Thousands of letters from all over the world poured into his parents' home on Court Avenue and the office of his publisher in Indianapolis, and they continued for 15 years; many were so distraught they requested a momento, some little something that had belonged to Richard or had, in any way, been a small part of his life.

In 1962 Richard's father provided the funds for the erection of a Gothic bell tower on the campus of Southwestern at Memphis, now Rhodes College, as a memorial. College offices occupy the upper floors and on the ground floor a room is filled with various momentos that he had sent to his parents from exotic corners of the world. Three of his Princeton roommates attended the dedication and one, J. Penfield Seiberling, president of the rubber company, addressed those assembled with these words:

> *For him life was something more than breathing, eating, drinking and sleeping, over and over again. Rather, it was a great, exciting, ennobling adventure of the mind and spirit, to be experienced to the full as the Creator intended.*

When Mickey Mantle was inducted into the Baseball Hall of Fame at Cooperstown in 1974, he surprised those in attendance when he concluded his acceptance speech by saying he "... hoped to live up to Bill Terry's expectations." Terry had gone into the Hall 20 years previously and, because he felt that all Hall of Fame members "owed it to the game," the night before the induction of Mantle and Whitey Ford he had privately urged them both to attend each summer's ceremonies.

The surprise of those hearing Mantle's words was due to the feeling by many that back when Terry was playing and managing, he was in baseball strictly for the money. He was taciturn and almost always kept his emotions completely under control, so his competitive spirit and love for the game were not evident to the casual observer. Fortunately, John McGraw, the crusty, legendary manager of the New York Giants was more than a casual observer; if not for McGraw's ability to recognize baseball talent, Bill Terry might never have played in the majors.

Coming out of high school, Terry pitched and played in the outfield for a season with Atlanta in the Southern League and then another year with Shreveport in the Texas League. After that he got married, quit the game to take a job with an oil company and moved to Memphis. He kept in touch with the game by playing locally on Sunday afternoons. He had been working in Memphis for four years when McGraw, who was entering his 21st year as Giants manager, heard about his Sunday afternoon exploits and came to town to look him over.

In the tall, broad-shouldered, well-muscled Terry, McGraw liked what he saw and he also admired his straightforwardness. He told Terry he would like for him to try out with the Giants. But Terry was in his mid-twenties, married, and settled into a good job and had no intention of jumping up and leaving Memphis on such a whimsical basis. He told McGraw he would come only if he were guaranteed a big-league salary. The old veteran was somewhat taken aback, but he told Terry he would let him know. On the long train ride back to New York McGraw made his decision. As soon as he arrived he wired Terry that he would accept his terms.

In 1923 McGraw sent Terry to Toledo where he pitched and pinch hit. But McGraw saw him as a hitter and after a couple of months switched him to first base. The next year at

Toledo the left-hander raised his batting average to .377 and was made manager of the club. Before the season was over he was called up by the Giants. His performance as a pinch hitter was somewhat mediocre. But when he replaced regular first baseman George Kelly, out with an infected tooth, Terry rapped out nine hits in 20 at bats, including three home runs. He had begun to live up to McGraw's highest expectations.

In 14 at bats in the 1924 World Series against the Washington Senators, Terry led both teams with a .429 average. Coming to the plate 10 times to face the great Walter Johnson, he rapped out a homer, triple, two singles and got three bases on balls. It's quite possible that even that early in Terry's career McGraw was envisioning him as his eventual successor.

From 1925-1927, Terry and George Kelly alternated at first base. Then Kelly was traded and, playing regularly, after that Terry never hit below .300. In 1930 he hit .401, and it was the last time anyone hit .400, or better, in the National League. He thrived on fast balls and was a straightaway hitter with power. It has been suggested that if he had played in the 1950s, when home runs meant bigger contracts, he probably would have concentrated on them and might have hit 70 in a season. He also was an excellent fielder. More than one baseball observer opined that "Memphis Bill," as the sportswriters liked to call him, was one of the best fielding first basemen ever to play the game.

By 1932 McGraw was in declining health and had become somewhat irascible. At this stage, he was prone to giving a plethora of signals to players in the field, and if they missed one they were subjected to one of his temper tantrums. Everyone was tense and the team was playing below its capacity and in eighth place. On June 3 McGraw retired and Terry replaced him as player/manager. By the end of the season the Giants had moved into sixth place and Terry was given a two-year contract at $30,000 a year, which wasn't too bad in the depths of the Depression.

For 1933, Terry made some trades that strengthened the club and effected some administrative changes that improved morale. Terry, "King Carl" Hubbell, the slender pitcher from Oklahoma, outfielder Mel Ott, everybody's favorite, from Gretna, Lou., who was beginning his eighth full year with the

Giants at age 24, and "Fat Freddy" Fitzsimmons, a knuckle-baller from Arcadia, Cal., were the only proven "stars" on the team. Ott had a peculiar left-handed batting style, but it always served him well. As the pitcher wound up, Ott would raise his right leg high off the ground and raise and lower his bat vertically. Just before the pitch was released he would hold his bat motionless and, as he put his right foot back on the ground, shift his weight to it, which gave him forward momentum. With his quick wrist-snap, this provided unusual power for someone of his relatively small stature. Hubbell had fantastic control, a good curve ball, and an average fast ball, but his forte was his screwball, Because he was a left-hander. the reverse curve broke away from a right-handed batter. After years of pitching it, his elbow and palm faced outward with his arm at his side.

Before the season, the Associated Press sportswriters picked the Giants to finish sixth again. Terry broke his wrist in late April but was able to return to the lineup in early June. During this period Hubbell pitched 26 scoreless innings, which earned him the nickname "Meal Ticket." By Memorial Day the Giants were in third place only three games behind the league-leading Cardinals. On June 10 they took over the lead. On June 15, confident that his wrist had healed suffi-ciently, Terry traded the backup first baseman for another needed left-handed pitcher and also Frank (Lefty) O'Doul who, although plagued by injuries, had led the league in batting only the year before. On July 2 the Giants took a doublehead-er from the Cardinals, winning both games by 1 to 0. In the first, Hubbell pitched 18 innings allowing only six hits, strik-ing out 12 and, demonstrating his remarkable control, walking none. On August 1, in a game against the Braves, Hubbell set a record of having pitched 45 consecutive scoreless innings.

The Cardinals came to the Polo Grounds on August 27 and won the first game of a doubleheader 7 to 1, as Dizzy Dean defeated "Prince Hal" Schumacher. The second was called because of darkness in the eighth with the Giants leading 4 to 1. In the top of the eighth Frankie Frisch sent a high, bouncing ball to Terry, who grabbed it and dashed for first. Frisch made a dive for the base and the two arrived almost simultaneous-ly. When Umpire Ted McGrew called Frisch safe, Terry explod-ed. He charged toward McGrew spouting appropriate invective and the umpire, with a jerk of his thumb, indicated him out of the game. Terry slammed his glove and cap to the ground and kicked them both. Fans in the upper deck came to Terry's defense and peppered the field with bottles. Terry continued to rant and Mel Ott and Coach Tom Clarke tried to calm him down. McGrew said, "Terry, you're out of here!" Memphis Bill responded, "You can't throw me out, I'm the manager and the only first baseman." McGrew then turned to Ott and Clarke and said, "OK, then you guys are out." The outburst by the usually calm Terry surprised the fans and sportswriter John Kieran wrote, "...the club won a real victory when the fans stood up and roared approval of Memphis Bill's explosion. They never knew that he cared. He lost the decision, but he won his spurs. The Old Guard among the Giant rooters had fallen in behind him."

On the season-closing road trip Hubbell beat the Braves 2 to 0 in ten innings, his tenth shutout of the season. He gave up no walks and never even got to a three and two count on a batter. When the second-place Pirates lost to the Phillies on September 19, the Giants won the pennant five games ahead of Pittsburgh. "Meal Ticket" Hubbell led the league with 23 wins, ten of which were shutouts, had an earned run average of 1.66 and was second in strikeouts to Dizzy Dean. Ott was third in home runs and runs batted in and Terry had the fourth highest batting average. The Giants beat the Senators in the Series and were the new World Champions.

In 1934, Terry managed the National League in the All Star game. His team lost 9 to 7, but the real story of the game was Hubbell. Charley Gehringer lashed a single to center on the first pitch of the game. Then Hubbell walked Heinie Manush. Coming up were Babe Ruth, Lou Gehrig and Jimmy Foxx. Catcher Gabby Hartnett called time and walked out to the mound. "Come on Hub, never mind going for the corners; just throw that 'thing' (the screwball). Hell, I can't hit it and they won't either." Hubbell's first pitch to Ruth was a ball, but then the Babe chased three straight screwballs and went down swinging. Gehrig suffered the same fate. Jimmy Foxx did succeed in fouling one off but then missed three more screwballs, retiring the side. Hubbell had struck out three of the game's all-time great hitters with 12 pitches. He started off the second inning by striking out two more great hitters, Al

Simmons and Joe Cronin. Bill Dickey got a hit, but King Carl ended the inning by fanning Lefty Gomez. It was probably the greatest pitching performance in All-Star Game history.

That year the Giants finished second, two games behind the Cardinals. Hubbell again led the league in earned run average and had 21 wins. Ott tied in home runs with 35 and led in runs-batted-in with 135. Terry was second in hits and batting average.

In 1935, the Giants fell to third place. Hubbell, Ott, Schumacher and Terry had good years, with the latter batting .341, but the team faltered in the stretch drive while the league-leading Cubs were winning 21 straight games.

Terry had planned to retire from playing after the 1935 season, but the player he acquired to replace him, Sam Leslie, came up with a severe groin pull early in the season, so Terry found himself back at first. Then he injured his knee and he and Leslie alternated, playing with their pain.

After the mid-point in the season the Giants were in fifth place but then moved up to fourth 9½ games off the pace. After a successful home stand they were just 5½ games out and then proceeded to win 17 of their next 18 games. They began a western trip only half a game behind the league-leading Cardinals. They won a series with the Reds and one with the Pirates, by Terry coming off the coaching line to belt a pinch-hit single in the fourteenth inning to win the final game. In Chicago Hubbell won his twentieth game as Ott got seven hits and won the game with a ninth inning home run; in St. Louis Hubbell beat Dizzy Dean 2 to 1 and drove in the winning run. Coming back to the Polo Grounds the Giants had won 39 out of their last 47 games and had a four-game lead over the second-place Cardinals; they ultimately won the pennant with a five-game pad. Hubbell was voted the Most Valuable Player in the league; he led with 26 wins, winning percentage and earned-run-average. Ott led the league in homers and slugging percentage.

The Yankees they met in the Series were one of the great all-time teams. They were strong in every department and had won the pennant 19 ½ games ahead of the second-place Detroit Tigers. With players like Tony Lazzeri, Lou Gehrig, Red Rolfe, Joe DiMaggio, George Selkirk and Bill Dickey, they had set a major league record of 182 team home

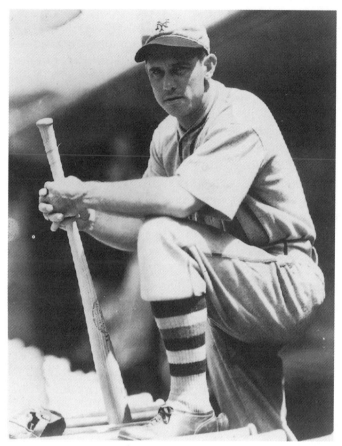

"Memphis Bill" Terry
As player/manager, he led the New York Giants to three pen-
nants and one world championship. His .401 batting average in
1930 has never since been equaled in the National League.
(Courtesy of Ray Terry)

runs and had five players who had driven in more than 100 runs. The entire National League had only six players who had accomplished that feat. With Hubbell pitching, the Giants won the first game 6 to 1. The Yanks came back in the second game to blast five Giants pitchers for an 18 to 4 slaughter. Although the Giants out-hit the Bronx Bombers 11 to four in the next game, they lost 2 to 1 on a deflected infield hit. They dropped the fourth game 5 to 2 but came back to win the next one 5 to 4 on Terry's sacrifice fly to DiMaggio. The Yankees lead in games had been cut to 3 to 2. In the sixth game the Yankees knocked out Fitzsimmons and took a 5 to 2 lead by the fifth inning. The Giants fought back with two runs in the seventh; the Yankees scored one in the eighth and the Giants matched it, but the Yankees' big bats went to work in the top of the ninth and knocked in seven runs. The game ended 13 to 5 with the Yankees winning the Series four games to two.

Terry's left knee had continued to bother him, and throughout the Series he had to sleep with pillows under his leg to reduce the swelling. Pirate manager Pie Traynor applauded Terry for his grit in playing every game on his bad leg and complimented his managerial skills. "I don't think any other man in baseball could have finagled that team into a World Series. For that matter, he did well to win a game, let alone two games, against a powerhouse like the Yanks."

Terry retired as an active player after the 1936 season but continued as manager. Late in the year he also was named general manager. He made some trades, including acquiring infielder and fellow-Memphian Lou Chiozza from the Phillies, and led the Giants to their second straight pennant. Chiozza had the distinction of having made the last putout ending Babe Ruth's career. On May 27, dating back to the previous year, Hubbell got his 24th and final victory in what would stand as the major league's longest consecutive winning streak when Mel Ott blasted a 9th-inning homer to beat the Reds, 3 to 2. The Giants again lost the series to the Yankees, four games to one. Former Memphian and renowned sportswriter of the *New York World Telegram* Joe Williams had this comment: "The turning point of the Series was when the Yanks suited up for the first game."

In 1938 the Giants started off the season by winning 18 of their first 21 games. Along the way they began to falter. Chiozza broke his collarbone, Schumached developed bone chips in his pitching arm and Hubbell sustained a serious injury to his elbow while pitching on August 18. The team did well to finish in third place. Ott had another great year. He led the league in homers with 36 and was second in runs-batted-in and walks. Terry again managed the National League in the All-Star Game, this time to a 4 to 1 victory.

In 1939, 1940 and 1941 the Giants had mediocre years, and Terry was wearying of his role as manager. After the 1941 season he recommended that Ott replace him and he was named general manager in charge of farm and scouting operations. But the war began to thin the ranks of good players, and the nine minor league franchises that the Giants owned, or with which they had working arrangements, declined to two by the end of 1942. With a reduction in his responsibilities, Terry felt it was best that he resign. He returned to Memphis and entered the cotton business.

In 1946 Bill Terry coached the CBC baseball team in the Memphis Prep League. Several years later he moved to Jacksonville, Flor. and opened up a Buick dealership.

In 1952 some young friends of the author from Houston went to Florida to play in a baseball tournament. On the way home they developed some minor car trouble and stopped in Terry's dealership for repairs. Having occasion to open their trunk in his presence, he noticed their baseball equipment and asked about it. Not knowing who he was, they needed no more encouragement to tell about the big tournament and, at least by implication, what sterling players they were and how well they had done. Then Terry said, "Come into my office for a minute; I have some things that might interest you." When they saw the plaques and all the inscribed pictures of the greats of the game, they were flabbergasted and a little embarrassed by their tales of baseball bravado.

At the same time that "Memphis Bill" Terry was beginning to make his mark with the Giants organization, another Memphian whom the Eastern press also liked to call "Memphis Bill" was making headlines on the gridiron. William Neely Mallory was fullback and captain of Yale's 1923 team that some old Elis claim was the best Big Blue eleven ever fielded. Yale forged a record that year of nine wins and no losses against such opposition as Army, Maryland, Georgia, North Carolina and, of course, Princeton and Harvard.

In addition to being a line-busting fullback, Mallory was a vicious blocker and played linebacker on defense. Walter Camp, called "the father of American football" for conceiving and implementing the first scoring system and most of the basic rules, named Mallory first-string fullback and captain of his All-America team. Because the Heisman Trophy was not instituted until 1935, this latter designation could reasonably be considered that era's equivalent of the Heisman.

Unusual for a Southerner, Mallory also excelled at hockey. As catcher on the baseball team some felt he was better at that sport than at football. At Yale he also was a member of Skull and Bones and was voted the outstanding man in his graduating class. It was said that he possessed rare qualities that made him an inspirational leader both in and out of football, characteristics also attributed to John Trent, end on Memphis Central High's 1943 team and captain of Army's undefeated 1949 team.

After leaving Yale, Mallory entered the family business, Memphis Compress and Storage Company (cotton) and, except for filling in as interim football coach at Southwestern at Memphis, left athletics behind him. He became president of the Memphis Cotton Exchange and was president and king of the Cotton Carnival. He also served Southwestern as treasurer and member of the executive committee and board of directors.

Although he would not have had to serve because of his age and having a family, his sense of duty compelled "Memphis Bill" to volunteer for the Army Air Force in 1942. He was trained as a target intelligence officer, commissioned as a captain, and served in the North African, Tunisian, Pantellerian, Sicilian and Italian campaigns. In 1943 he was promoted to major and developed a tactical bombing plan, called "Operation Mallory," which cut 22 of the 24 bridges crossing the Po

William Neely Mallory (Memphis Bill)
Captain of Yale's 1923 undefeated football team, captain of Walter Camp's All-America team, and member of the National Football Foundation Hall of Fame.
(Courtesy of W. Neely Mallory, Jr.)

River in Lombardy. This severely reduced the capability of the Germans to re-supply their troops in Italy, and for this he was awarded the Legion of Merit in late 1944. Only 44 at the time, nevertheless in 1945 the Air Force considered him "overage" and ordered him home for discharge. As the plane took off from Italy, it experienced difficulties and Mallory was killed in the ensuing crash.

Mallory was named posthumously to the National Football Foundation Hall of Fame, and Yale annually presents an award in his memory to the senior "who on the field of play and in his life at Yale best represents the highest ideals of sportsmanship and Yale tradition." In December 1954 the William Neely Mallory Memorial Gymnasium was dedicated at Southwestern (now Rhodes College) to honor him and the 41 Southwestern alumni who died in World War II. The bronze tablet at the entrance reads in part: "He was a man of honor, characterized by modesty, kindliness, a wholesome sense of humor and charm of personality."

The Memphis of the 1940s also was shaped by the city's rich heritage as a great fight town and it would be an oversight to neglect mentioning some of the good boxers that the city produced. Although he never was a champion, the best of all probably was "Pal" Moore, who fought in the bantamweight and featherweight divisions before World War I. During his career he won decisions over seven world champions. But because the fight agreement always stipulated he had to knock out his opponent to capture the crown, his lack of punching power kept him from being able to do it.

Eddie "Kid" Wolfe was an accomplished welterweight ranked as high as fourth by Ring Magazine. He fought four ten-round fights with Teddy Yarosz, winning one and losing one on decisions and fighting to a draw in the other two. Yarosz would go on to win the American middleweight championship and then move up to the light heavyweight division where he was ranked fifth. Wolfe lost two close 10-round decisions to Tony

Canzoneri who held the bantamweight, featherweight, light-weight and junior welterweight titles in his career. Canzoneri's renowned manager, Sammy Goldman of New York, was so impressed by Wolfe's guts and determination that he later became his manager. Wolfe also lost on a seven round knockout to Louis "Kid" Kaplan who, five years earlier, had won the featherweight championship before moving up to the lightweight and welterweight divisions. When Wolfe first fought these accomplished boxers he was only 17 or 18 years old and many felt he was fighting at that level of competition too early in his development.

In the latter stages of his career the Kid fought a lot of bouts in Memphis and his manager was Nathan "Nutty" Loskovitz, who ran a liquor store on Poplar at the viaduct. Nutty was a sharp dresser and always had his trademark big cigar ensconced in the side of his mouth. Jules "Pawnshop" O'Mell carried Wolfe's gear and worked his corner during these local fights. In later years the Kid operated the Green Beetle cafe on North Main with a big, green neon sign in the shape of a beetle out front. When the author walked into Jack Dempsey's restaurant on New York's Broadway in the summer of 1954 and was met with the Manassa Mauler's handshake at the door, the conversation went like this:

"Where ya from Tom?"
"Memphis."
"Eddie 'Kid' Wolfe."
"Yeah, and there was another...?"
"Pal Moore, but he died."

"Tickle" Sanders was a good bantamweight, and another sterling leather pusher was "Kid" Dugan, who was shot and killed during a holdup of a liquor store he operated on Beale Street.

Memphis Negro boxers who made names in pugilistic history were "Kid" Roux, Willie Moore, a lightweight, "Hockbones," a heavyweight, and "Gorilla" Jones, who won the middleweight title in a 10 round decision over Tiger Thomas in Milwaukee in 1931. However, he lost it a year later on a foul in the 11th round of a fight with Marcel Theil in Paris, France. One afternoon in 1932, while well-known amateur and CBC graduate Jim McWillie was working out at the old Lyceum Theater at Second and Jefferson, Gorilla stopped by in search of Billy Haack, nationally-respected referee and boxing promoter. Jim says the champ was decked out in sartorial splendor, including sporting a Derby hat and gray spats, and was driving a Pierce Arrow Coupe.

One summer night in 1941 at old Hodges Field an unknown heavyweight climbed into the ring. Although he had been promised ten dollars per round for a four round fight, he dispatched his opponent to the canvas for a ten count about midway of the first round. He had been passing through Memphis and was picked up by the police for vagrancy, probably around one of the railroad yards. After spending a few days at the Shelby County Workhouse, he was released and given twenty dollars. He noticed an article in the newspaper about a fight card the next night and he decided he would try to pick up a few extra dollars to help him along his way to wherever he was headed. Promoter Milo Solomito put him on the card as the first fight after the "Battle Royal." Six years later Arnold Cream, better known as Jersey Joe Walcott, would lose a very narrow decision to Joe Louis in a 15 round bout for the heavyweight championship. Ezzard Charles would eventually take Louis' crown and Jersey Joe won it from Charles in 1951.

Many of the big names in those days fought in Memphis: Jack Dempsey, Gene Tunney, James J. Braddock, Primo Canera, Max Schmeling, Auturo Godoy and others. One February night in 1926 in Memphis Dempsey boxed six opponents, knocking out four in the first round. There were fight cards on a regular basis at various places around town over the years. The Lyceum Theater, Phoenix Athletic Club, Winchester Stadium, Ellis Auditorium, and Hodges Field all presented plenty of pugilistic action. One of the more interesting features of fight nights was the Battle Royal. Eight or 10 black fighters would get into the ring at the same time and slug away. The usual scenario was for everyone to immediately pounce on the biggest guy to quickly put him out of the action. When two were left standing they would then fight three rounds with the winner taking the purse. The appreciative crowd would throw money into the ring.

Another popular pug around town was "Shifty" Logan Hipp known by his nickname and first name. He seemed to have the ability to show up, invited or not, ticket or not, at every major event around the Mid-South. Despite having spent a lot of time in the squared circle absorbing a multitude of punches, Shifty was quick with a quip and could ad lib with the best of them. Once when Jack Dempsey came to town, Shifty fought him in an exhibition. Using all his skills, Shifty was able to keep Dempsey from landing a solid blow in the first round and, according to Frank Liberto, local fight manager and promoter, even tagged Dempsey with a pretty stiff punch. Taking umbrage at his pal hitting him that hard in an exhibition bout, the Manassa Mauler's killer instinct came to the fore and he decided to show Shifty who was boss. In the second round he got Shifty on the ropes and flailed away, putting his lights out. Shifty's subsequent analysis of the fight was that he had scared Dempsey to death: "He thought he had killed me."

Shifty was a city fireman for awhile, but the cliched story goes that every time the alarm went off he mistook it for

Shifty "rides the rods" into the Bluff City
(He has influence – he got a lower)

Ed Barry and Mayor Walter Chandler extend the hand of welcome and the key to the city (opening all jails) to Logan Hipp, alias Shifty Logan, ambassador (still) at large of the Bum's Club. Be-tuxedoed Shifty arrives in befitting style from the Kentucky Derby where his horse, Bell Buzzer, failed to ring – coming back home to preside at the Bum's-sponsored baseball game between the St. Louis Cardinals and the Air Force's Memphis-based Fourth Ferrying Command that night and Bum's Club party the following night. He is shown emerging from his exclusive compartment. (Courtesy of Jim McWillie) a fight ring bell and wanted to tee off on the first available fireman, so he was transferred to the sanitation department. One weekday when a large group rode the train to Hot Springs for the "Memphis Derby," Shifty, of course, made the trip. Spotting Mr. Crump at the track, he went over to wish him well. Unfortunately, the Boss was accompanied by an aide, Bob Heffernan, who had obtained Shifty's job for him. He asked Shifty, "Aren't you supposed to be working?" Shifty turned to Mr. Crump, "Well, I guess I had better get on back to Memphis; the city can't run with both of us gone."

Another time, during Prohibition, Shifty walked into Foppiano's, a popular hangout at Third and Jefferson featuring a fruit stand and cafe with sandwiches behind glass containers on the counter, wire-backed chairs, sawdust on the floor and near beer; he ordered a nickel near beer. Getting his glass he raised it on high and loudly announced, "When Shifty drinks, everybody drinks." Those loitering on the premises lost no time in taking him up on his invitation and beers were passed all around. After drinking his, Shifty expelled a sigh of contentment and slapped a nickel on the counter. When Foppiano asked him about payment for those he had treated, again in a loud voice, Shifty proclaimed: "When Shifty pays, everybody pays," and walked out.

Shifty called everybody "Champ" and he was known by the great and near great. When Westbrook Pegler, former sportswriter and nationally-syndicated columnist would come to Memphis and stay at the Peabody, he always invited Shifty to come visit him at the hotel. And when Dempsey came to town he and Shifty would pal around together. In fact, according to Ed Kallaher, Dempsey would bring sports equipment to Shifty's son. Although the Kallaher boys, Ed and Wee, lived almost adjacent to South Side High School, they attended CBC and played football there; they also lived just a couple of blocks from Shifty. In honor of Dempsey, Shifty even called his son, Logan Hipp, Jr., "Champ." Ed says that Dempsey would show up at Shifty's house with baseball gear, footballs and boxing gloves for the little boy. Sporting a handlebar mustache, Shifty's father would occasionally arrive for a visit from his home in Texas; he would scandalize the neighborhood by every morning sitting on the front porch in his long underwear and cowboy hat and boots. Shifty's notoriety was such that when the famous regional artist

Carroll Cloar painted a montage of prominent Memphians, Shifty was depicted standing right next to Boss Crump.

In 1932 the CBC boxing team was featured in Robert Ripley's "Believe it or Not" for having won every fight in ten weight divisions to capture the city prep crown. Although there were only eight weight divisions in those days, to accommodate smaller boys coach Milo Solomito created "paperweight" and "tissue-paperweight" divisions. Under Solomito the Brothers won the boxing championship seven years straight. Also during this period, under the coaching of Jimmy Rudd and, later, George "Greek" Johnson, CBC won the prep wrestling title eight years running.

Solomito, owner of a liquor store at Poplar and High, was a member of the "Bum's Club," a nebulous organization of ex-fighters, pugilistic aficionados and sportswriters who periodically got together to tell tale tales, swap lies, and imbibe in good food and the oil of human conversation. There were members such as promoters Early Maxwell, Luke Kingsley, and Frank Liberto, sportswriters Walter Stewart, Emmet Maum and Ben Epstein (who went to the "Big Time" in New York),

CBC CHAMPIONSHIP BOXING SQUAD (about 1931-1932) Left to Right, standing: Charles Coburn, trainer, Marlin Johnson, Joe Sheridan, Fred Hartz, Breen Bland, Hughey Gannon, Al Brown, John Cassaretta, Ralph Gagliano, Henry Cummings, Paul Luckett, Coach Milo Solomito; sitting, Peewee Chandler, Larry Huffman, Jimmie McWillie, Ralph Turley, Garland Liles, Pete Catanzaro, Vince Tuminello.
This squad made Ripley's "Believe It Or Not" column because of championships in ten divisions. When standard names, such as Lightweight and Heavyweight, were not available, Coach Milo Solomito improvised his own designations such as Paperweight and Tissue-paperweight. (Courtesy of Jim McWillie)

attorney Ed Barry, well-known football referee Ersell "Red" Cavette and Jimmy Moore, who played for Connie Mack's Philadelphia Athletics. In addition to Shifty, another former boxer and "Bum" was "Irish" O'Mell who daily sold newspapers at the entrance to Pantaze Drug Store at Main and Madison and whose constant refrain was: "If you don't believe it, read all about it." Another newspaper vendor and general entrepreneur was Elvis Anderton, one of nine brothers, whose cry was "They got 'im" ("Any day you look through the paper, you'll see 'they' got somebody"), or, "Read all about it, the big love triangle – she shot him because she loved him."

Celebrities visiting the Bluff City, such as Dempsey and onetime leather pusher Bob "Packy East" Hope, were invited to Bum's Club wingdings and duly inducted into membership with utilization of all appropriate ancient and mysterious rites of passage.

Luke Kingsley promoted fights and had a bar on Front Street that offered the last free lunch in town. Although he wrote a popular book on how to concoct a wide variety of mixed drinks, he never imbibed alcohol in any form. But he did drink a lot of Coca-Colas. In his youth he was laid up in St. Joseph's Hospital suffering from complications from a ruptured appendix; the attending doctors, not giving him much hope for survival, told his family to let him have anything he wanted. What he wanted were Cokes, and he drank them almost constantly. Gradually, his condition began to improve and he regained his strength and made a full recovery. From then on it was reputed he drank at least two cases of Cokes a day, and Everett Pidgeon, owner of the Coca-Cola plant, offered him all the free Cokes he could down. On a train trip with a rollicking group of Memphis sportsmen traveling to Chicago for one of the Jake LaMotta and Sugar Ray Robinson fights, it was reported Kingsley had put away three cases of the refreshingly fizzy burp-producers by the time the Panama Limited entered the outskirts of the Windy City. Luke Kingsley was a nice-looking, friendly man who always was immaculately-dressed and was liked by everyone. When he died it was rumored that one of his pals slipped a six-pack of Cokes into his casket.

Frank Liberto left Memphis in his youth and went to New Orleans where he became a singing waiter. Coming back to the Bluff City he began selling cars for Hull-Dobbs and for seven straight years was the leading Ford salesman in the United States. He received all kinds of awards including numerous trips and expensive watches and jewelry. Henry Ford, himself, handed him a 16-carat sapphire ring. At one time Liberto had a stable of eight fighters, including the afore-mentioned Gorilla Jones, who later became a bodyguard for Mae West; Liberto also was a fight promoter.

Other habitues of Bum's Club gatherings were "High School Henry" and Anthony "Monk" Cassata, whose friends would pick them up and drive them to wherever the festivities were being held. Henry was a faithful Central High fan and would attend most Warrior athletic events. He was particular-ly prominent at baseball games where, standing alongside the foul line in his Central letter jacket someone had given him, he would frequently put his ever-present police whistle in his mouth and blow it furiously at the opposition.

Until he was struck and killed by a car in October 1979, Tony Cassata, better known as "Monk," was a familiar figure around Memphis for many years. There were three places where he primarily hung out: Murphy's Oyster Bar on Madison near Cleveland, Chiozza's Liquor Store at Poplar and Cleveland and Calvary Episcopal Church at Adams and Second where, cigar in mouth, he would stand in front in the morning and exchange banter with the steady stream of passersby on their way from their offices to whatever business they had to conduct at the Shelby County Courthouse across the street. Monk was very cold-natured and, regardless of the weather, would ordinarily be attired in several flannel shirts and sweaters, a couple of bandannas, and a long coat and a hat or cap – all of which he seldom shed. One of the times he did change clothes some of his buddies dressed him up in a tuxedo and, although he wasn't wearing tails, put a top hat on his head and a cane in his hand. The picture that was taken with him so garbed graced the window of the Variety Liquor Store, behind Hotel Peabody, for some years. This store was owned by Frank Liberto and run by Cappy McGrory, a former fighter.

Presumably to defend himself against some vague, potential danger, imagined only by him, Monk would carry a red, taped-up staff and have an assortment of sawed-off broom sticks and ax handles tucked in his belt. When he wanted to move his base of operations he would walk out in the street and, because he was known by so many people, would soon get a ride to where he was going. One of the places he endeavored to visit every day was his mother's grave in Calvary Cemetery.

One pleasant spring afternoon as people were getting off work and heading home, with no anticipation of the embarrassment to which he would be subjected, an unsuspecting Good Samaritan picked up Monk and drove him out Poplar Avenue. As they stopped for a red light at Poplar and Cleveland, a major transfer point for bus riders, Monk spotted a group of working girls standing on the corner. Because he presumed they were prostitutes waiting for their next trick to come along, Monk's moral indignation produced an Old Testament wrath almost fearful to behold. From the ample supply in his belt, he whipped out one of his clubs and, leaning out the window, beat on the side of the poor fellow's car and screamed, "You whores get away from here."

Anthony Cassata
Appropriately clad to forestall the frigid ravages of an early summer's day, "Monk" pauses in his busy routine around town to pose for a picture.
(Courtesy of Jim McWillie)

Monk would go to Sunday mass at St. Peter's Catholic Church downtown and afterward wait around for Sam Angier to drive him home. Sam would also take home a courtly, immaculate gentleman in his early eighties who was an usher and busied himself after mass seeing that everything was in its proper place and that the doors were locked. During Mass Monk would sometimes pull a cache of coins out of one of his plentiful pockets and absentmindedly clink them back and forth from one hand to the other. The church was equipped with hot water radiators along the walls that had metal covers, or fenders, on them. Whiling away his time until Sam was ready to leave, Monk would pull out a couple of his sticks and make like Gene Krupa on the radiator fenders. Coupled with his coin clinking, this was enough to infuriate the courtly old gentleman and he would remonstrate Tony to display more decorum in respect for his surroundings; Monk's response would turn the air blue. They detested each other but rode in the same car. To forego any possibility of Mank having an inclination to beat a tattoo on his other rider's head, Sam always insured that the former was seated in the front seat and the latter in the back.

Under the auspices of invitations acquired through a Tennessee senator's office in October 1979, Jim McWillie, Ed Barry, Monsignor Paul Clunan and Ambrose "Bud" Dudley, founder of the Liberty Bowl football game, went to Washington together to attend a reception for Pope John Paul II on the grounds of the White House. The next morning, a Sunday, they attended a mass celebrated by the Pope on the Mall and flew back to Memphis that evening.

The following Tuesday morning it was raining lightly as Jim McWillie drove downtown to work. He decided to swing by the Cassata home to see if Tony needed a ride; besides, he had a gift for him. Before he got to Monk's house he saw him walking along the street, and he stopped and picked him up. Jim was a good friend of Tony's and he told him about the trip to see the Pope; as soon as he mentioned the Pope's name, Monk made the sign of the cross. Then, from his coat pocket, Jim pulled out a gold-plated medallion on a chain, commemorating the Pope's visit, that he had bought for Monk in Washington. The little man was overjoyed. He put the chain around his neck and kissed the medallion and blessed himself over and over as they drove downtown. After Jim had dropped Monk off at his customary morning stand in front of Cavalry Episcopal Church, he sat in the car for a few minutes watching him as he walked down the street; oblivious to all around him, every few steps Monk would stop, admire the medallion at arms length and then kiss it hard and bless himself.

That night it was raining harder. About 9:30 Monk was struck by a car in front of Murphy's Oyster Bar. Monsignor Clunan received a call from the hospital and sped to Monk's bedside. He stayed there praying until the lovable little man died about 1:30 the next morning.

Two days later McWillie and Clunan met at a wake for their friend. Monk lay there with the chain around his neck and the medallion lying on his chest. The next day when Monsignor Clunan conducted the funeral mass at St. Louis Church, where he was pastor, he was assisted by six other priests who had known Monk; it was the most heavily-attended funeral ever at that church.

From initially being dubbed "the hip pocket bootlegger" by the Memphis police to later being characterized "Public Enemy Number One" by the FBI constituted a substantial leap in notoriety for George "Machine Gun Kelly" Barnes. Yet, like others of his ilk, he was a relatively brief flicker in the pantheon of Depression-era gangsterism.

Born the same year, 1900, as Richard Halliburton, George F. Barnes, Jr. was imbued with similar cravings for adventure and excitement, but he pursued a very different path to satisfy those yearnings. George came from a respectable family; he grew up in a nice home at 2098 Cowden and his father had a fairly prosperous insurance business with an office downtown in the Porter Building. But, while George was close to his mother, he never got along with his father. When his mother died during his last year at Central High School, the gap between father and son widened irrevocably.

When he was only 16 and in the tenth grade, a time when lawlessness was rampant in Memphis, George began to take advantage of Tennessee's prohibition law. He would hang around in front of the original Hotel Peabody at Main and Monroe, or at Madison and Crosstown, with half-pints in his back pockets and have no difficulty in finding a ready clientele. Some became regular customers. After accidentally catching his father in a dalliance, he blackmailed him into letting him use the family car to secretly make runs into neighboring states where he would buy whiskey by the case and then peddle it around town. He even rented a garage to store it in. He was picked up by the Memphis police a few times, but his guile and youth and the influence of his father would get him off. He never took these episodes very seriously and they didn't deter him.

The summer after graduating from high school he drove a cab, which fit right in with his bootlegging. That fall, primarily out of respect for his deceased mother, who had always wanted him to attend college, he enrolled at Mississippi A&M (State). He stayed a year and thoroughly enjoyed the experience, particularly the social aspects of college life that enabled him to make new friends and meet more girls. But at the end of the academic year when he came back to Memphis, he decided to give up college and go back to making money bootlegging. He moved out of the family home on Cowden for good and, rather than a hotel, took a room in a boarding house to make the money he had saved up go further.

He continued to cultivate the new friends he had made at college and, because he was well-dressed, clean-cut and mannerly, was invited to many local parties. It was during one of these that he met Geneva, the oldest daughter of George and Della Ramsey. Ramsey, a graduate of the University of Texas, was a wealthy contractor who constructed railroads and levees. He had built a nice, large home for his family on Clark Place, just off Poplar.

Geneva was a little younger than George, but when he was at Central High he had noticed the petite and attractive girl as she drove to and from school in a Cadillac. He immediately set his cap for her and, while initially resisting his suit, she eventually succumbed to his charms and persistence.

Being aware of George's illicit activities, Mr. Ramsey did just about everything he could to break up the relationship. including sending Geneva off to a girl's school in Columbia, Tenn. She was to enroll at a finishing school in New York the next fall, but two days before her scheduled departure George talked her into eloping to Clarksdale, Miss. where they were married by a justice of the peace. George was just barely 19 and Geneva was not yet 18.

They spent several days in Clarksdale at the home of one of Geneva's classmates from the Columbia school, whose father was the governor of Mississippi. After a round of parties they fearfully returned to Memphis to face Geneva's parents. It went better than they could have hoped. Mrs. Ramsey was hurt but determined to make the best of it and was civil toward George. And, in order to collect his thoughts and bring his emotions under control, Mr. Ramsey had left the day before to sequester himself at a camp where his workmen were building a levee. George and Geneva would have a little while longer to steel themselves for the coming confrontation. When he returned a few days later and the three got together, Ramsey was restrained, but he did congratulate the newlyweds and offered George a job running the commissary at the camp. The young couple was shocked and overjoyed.

When school was not in session during the summer, the entire Ramsey family had lived at the levee camps and Geneva had enjoyed it, so it was old hat for her to accompany George to the camp and live with him in a tent. The better acquainted he became with Mr. Ramsey, the more George liked and respected the man. With his beloved mother dead, estranged from his father, and seeing little of his older sister, young George essentially had no family for emotional support. It was only natural for him to begin to view Mr. Ramsey as a substitute father figure and he wanted to prove himself in the older man's eyes. He worked hard and was effective and Ramsey began to feel that he may have been wrong in his initial assessment of him.

An almost idyllic period of over a year went by broken only by a joyous two weeks Christmas vacation at the Ramsey home, shared by Mr. and Mrs. Ramsey, George and Geneva and the six younger Ramsey children. A couple of months later Geneva became pregnant with their first child and by mid-

October the baby was due in only two weeks. George took Geneva back to Memphis for one of her periodic medical checkups while Ramsey remained at camp near Hickman, Ken.

On October 22 a telegram arrived at the house on Clark Place; George Ramsey had been injured in a dynamite explosion and was being sent back to Memphis on a Frisco train. His injuries were severe, but, inexplicably, the train poked along stopping at every hamlet along the way, while medical personnel waited impatiently at the Memphis station. The accident occurred at 11:30 a.m. and by 5:30 p.m. the train had gotten only as far as Blytheville, Ark., about halfway. It was here that George Ramsey died.

After Mr. Ramsey's death the business was sold and, with other assets, Mrs. Ramsey was left in a comfortable financial situation, but with its leader gone the large family was emotionally devastated. George had lost his father figure and his moral compass and now, only 20 years old, he struggled to find ways to support his wife, and son, George F. Barnes, III (Sonny). He was, successively, in the used car business, raised goats and sold insurance (he had turned back to his father for advice and assistance). A second child was stillborn and then a second boy, Bruce, was born. Bruce, who attended Sacred Heart Grammar School and Central High, has lived in southern California most of his life. He recently wrote and published a biography of his father, entitled, *Machine Gun Kelly: To Right a Wrong*.

Unable to support his family, George reverted to his old ways by contacting some of his cronies in Kansas City and again hauling hooch. Before long he had enough money to buy three trucks and hire drivers for them. They operated in Oklahoma, Texas, Tennessee and Mississippi. Fed up with his illegal activities and his meanness when he drank, Geneva divorced him. Expanding his operations into New Mexico, he was caught and spent several months in the state prison. He moved his base to Oklahoma City, but within six months he was arrested again. This time he was sentenced to the federal penitentiary at Leavenworth where he served 11 months of a three-year sentence. The whole time he was gone his trucks kept running and his drivers set aside his money for him, so he had a nice stake when he was released.

While in Leavenworth he made friends with some of the era's better known gangsters, such as Frank "Jelly" Nash, Wilbur Underhill ("The Tri-State Terror"), and Verne Miller. In discussions with them he made the decision that when he was released he would phase out his bootlegging operation and enter the more lucrative field of bank robbery. He returned to Kansas City and honed his pistol marksmanship and handling of a shotgun while carefully selecting his compatriots who would assist in his new endeavor. One story says the first hit was a small bank in Oklahoma, another says it was at Tupelo, Miss.; in any event, the initial holdup didn't yield much money. But a long series of bank robberies, even as far away as Washington state, provided an income sufficient to keep him dressed in the finest clothes and the ability to purchase several custom-built Cadillac automobiles. It was at this time that he began using the name George R. Kelly. Kelly had been his mother's maiden name.

George had a second marriage that didn't last long and then was smitten by the girlfriend of a bootlegger pal in Oklahoma City. Her attraction for him was reciprocated and, as soon as his friend went out of town on a brief business trip, he moved fast. He invited Kathryn (Kit) Thorne out for dinner and proposed marriage. They were wed the next day.

The pretty, once-married Kit had been involved with those in the lower echelons of gangsterism for years, and she saw in George the chance to move up in the crime world. She bought him a Thompson sub-machine gun from a pawn broker in Fort Worth and George practiced with it on the farm of Kit's mother and father-in-law, Ora and "Boss" Shannon, near the hamlet of Paradise, Tex. After becoming proficient enough to write his name with it on the wall of a barn, he took it with him on his bank jobs and it became his stock in trade.

Robbing ten to fifteen banks a year and filling the intervening times with extravagant vacations in New Orleans, Miami or Chicago became monotonous for George and Kit. Her affinity for reading the society pages made Kit think of it first: they would kidnap a rich businessman and collect a large ransom, enough to support them for a long time. George was reluctant at first, but she kept harping on the idea and the boldness, implied excitement and monetary potential inherent in such a caper began to appeal to him. They selected as their target a millionaire oil man named Charles Urschel who lived in Oklahoma City. The ransom amount would be $200,000.

In July 1933 George, carrying a machine gun, and Al Bates, a bank robbery buddy brandishing a pistol, snatched Urschel from a bridge game he and his wife were enjoying with another couple on the screened-in porch of their mansion. They took him to Kit's folks' farm near Paradise.

After a series of notes providing instructions for Mrs. Urschel, nine days after the kidnapping George rendezvoused with one of Urschel's friends on a Kansas City street and politely relieved him of a suitcase containing $200,000. He and Bates drove back to Paradise, picked up the bound and blindfolded Charles Urschel and let him out in Norman, just south of Oklahoma City.

The nation had just gone through the agony of the Lindbergh baby kidnapping. This had prompted legislation making the act a federal crime, and George and his gang got the FBI on its trail. Except for a couple of times when George directed him to write notes, Urschel had been blindfolded during his captivity. But he had noticed that every day, except one when the weather was bad, that a plane had flown over twice each day. He would wait about five minutes and then ask his captors what time it was. This, coupled with his remembrance of riding over a long wooden bridge, overheard comments from a gas station attendant about a rain that had broken a drought and saved some of the "broom corn," and the crowing of a rooster and livestock sounds enabled the FBI to identify the location of the farm as being in Wise County, Tex. This was established when it was learned that a Fort Worth to Amarillo mail plane passed over the county at 9:45 each morning, returned at 5:45 each afternoon and, on one particular day, had been diverted due to winds and heavy rain. When two Dallas detectives volunteered that they knew he location of "Boss" and Ora Shannon's farm and that it had, from time to time, been used as a hideout by various petty criminals, the site of Urschel's incarceration was firmly established.

George buried the bulk of his share of the ransom on the farm of Cass Coleman, an uncle of Kit's. Then he and Kit got into their 16-cylinder 1932 Cadillac coupe and drove to Chihuahua, Mexico, 230 miles south of El Paso, arriving on

August 3. George had made other trips to Mexico and become fluent in Spanish, and they spent an enjoyable and relaxing nine days exploring the colorful shops and touring the countryside until George happened to hear a news broadcast on the radio. The FBI and local police had raided Shannon's farm and arrested everybody; they even picked up Al Bates in Denver. George had been positively identified in connection with the Urschel case and the FBI had a description of his car.

Kit was very upset about the arrest of her mother and Boss and they left Chihuahua immediately to return and devise some plan that would exonerate them. They stored the Cadillac in El Paso and flew to Denver and then to Des Moines where a Fort Worth friend of Kit's met them and bought another car for them. They then flitted to Coleman, Tex., Biloxi, San Antonio and Chicago. George then decided they might be safer in Memphis.

As soon as they arrived in the Bluff City, George called Langford Ramsey, one of Geneva's younger brothers, and asked him if he could put them up at his home on Mignon. Everyone had heard of Machine Gun Kelly, but they never had seen a newspaper picture of Barnes identifying him by that name, so everyone in Memphis still knew of him as George Barnes, smalltime bootlegger. Langford said he had a house full of out-of-town visitors, but he had a friend whose family was away and who probably would be glad to put them up for a few bucks. So George and Kit moved into 1408 Rayner on September 21.

Anxious to be brought up-to-date on his two sons, George called Geneva and asked if she would have lunch with him at Hotel Peabody. Geneva was re-married to a well-to-do businessman, but he sympathized with George's interest in the children and gave his approval. George drove over to Della's house on Clark Place and they got into Geneva's car and rode downtown. Geneva had a huge, cream-colored Franklin touring car. It was a four-door convertible with a spare tire on each front fender and a windshield separating the front and back seats – a one-of-a-kind in Memphis. When they got back to Della's George saw the boys. He was introduced as a family friend, but the older boy undoubtedly knew who he was. They noticed his pistol in a shoulder holster and he told them he was on a secret mission for the FBI. Before he left he peeled two twenties off a big wad of bills and told each of them to go buy new bicycles.

A few days later George was apprehended and his identity as Machine Gun Kelly became public knowledge. Geneva and her husband were panic-stricken that someone would remember seeing her and George together in the Franklin and notify the authorities. Their terror was well-founded, for with unprecedented fervor and zeal the FBI was rounding up everyone it presumed had any connection with the kidnapping or any other of George's illicit activities. A good friend of Geneva's was Camille Doyle and she called on her for help. Camille was the mother of Jimmy, who 10 years later would be a starting end on CBC's 1943 football team. For over a month, until the "heat" was off, she hid Geneva's big Franklin in the Doyle family garage.

The FBI finally tracked George and Kit down at the Rayner address and two agents flew into Memphis on September 25. At daybreak the next morning, two months to the day after the kidnapping, police surrounded the house. Sensing that the net was tightening, George stayed up all night with a .45 automatic in his hand. When the paper boy threw *The Commercial Appeal* on the front porch it was still

George F.(Machine Gun Kelly) Barnes, Jr. , after his arrest in Memphis.
(HD,M/SCPL&IC)

dark. George went out and picked it up but forgot to re-lock the door on the way back in.

When Detective Sergeant Bill Raney, CBC graduate, and detectives A. 0. Clark and P. M. Wiebenga, of the Memphis police, entered the house shotguns in hand, George was standing in the bathroom relieving himself. His automatic lay nearby but he had no opportunity to grab it. He surrendered peacefully. Some writers have attributed to George the coining of the term "G-man" during his arrest, saying something like, "Don't shoot G-men." However, he told his son Bruce, who visited him at Alcatraz, that he never said it. But he got a laugh out of it and said that if they wanted to claim that he had, it was okay with him, besides it was the Memphis police who actually effected the arrest.

Twenty-one people were convicted in the Urschel kidnapping and received sentences of varying lengths. The indictments came quick and the trials were speedy. As this was the first case prosecuted under the new "Lindbergh Law," making kidnapping a federal offense, the Justice Department was eager to make an example of them and pursued the case with vigor. Kit received a life sentence but was released in 1959. She lived a reclusive life in Oklahoma City and died only a few years ago. Still living at 94, Geneva resides with her son Bruce in southern California. George was given three 99 year sentences to run consecutively. He spent a year at Leavenworth and then was transferred to Alcatraz when it opened in 1934; in 1951 he was sent back to Leavenworth.

Despite his notorious nickname, George never killed anyone. Although he was a "model" prisoner, his requests for parole were never taken seriously and the 17 years he spent at a place like "The Rock" seem unwarranted and excessive punishment. George had had a heart problem all his life and on July 17, 1954, his fifty-fourth birthday, he had a heart attack. He died a few hours later in the prison hospital of coronary thrombosis. From her federal prison cell in West Virginia, Kit directed that he be buried at Paradise, Tex.

Like E. H. Crump, Barron Collier, Clarence Saunders, Abe Plough, and other successful men of his era in the South, James K. "Jimmy" Dobbs was essentially self-educated and imbued with a strong desire to succeed. But, also like his notable compatriots, this desire did not make him a humorless, all-business drone, for he faced the world with a sunny disposition and thoroughly enjoyed the intellectual challenges generated by his many enterprises.

Born the son of a blacksmith in Fort Payne, Ala. in 1894, Jimmy Dobbs was eager to make his way in the world and, to the consternation of his school-teacher mother, dropped out of school after the fifth grade. After various sales jobs that took him to Birmingham, Memphis and St. Louis, he returned to Memphis and got a job selling trucks for John T. Fisher Motor Company.

In the course of this job he became acquainted with city engineer Horace Hull, nine years his senior. Hull had worked his way through Vanderbilt and Dobbs admired his practical business sense and logical approach to problem solving. When the opportunity to buy a Ford agency arose, Dobbs talked Hull into quitting his job to take over as manager. John T. Fisher put up the bulk of the purchase price and Hull-Dobbs was poised to make history in the automobile business. Jimmy Dobbs was the energetic idea man with Hull serving as the perfect foil to temper his enthusiasm with just the right dose of practicality.

From their headquarters at Second and Gayoso they branched out to eventually control 14 dealerships from San Juan, Puerto Rico to Honolulu. With two in Chicago, they also were located in, among other cities, Louisville, San Francisco, Minneapolis and Cleveland. By 1939 Hull-Dobbs was known as "The World's Largest Ford Dealer." During the Depression they stayed open 24 hours a day, six days a week. If necessary for customer convenience, they did repair work at night and established a shop in the suburbs for those who found it difficult to get to the downtown location. Along the way, they set up their own financing company and automobile insurance agency. An employee profit-sharing system established in 1938 helped business to zoom.

With the entry of the United States into World War II and plants shifting from making cars to war materials and the rationing of tires and gas, many dealers around the country threw in the towel and closed their doors for the duration, or sold out. Hull-Dobbs saw the situation from a different perspective. They borrowed $6.5 million and dispersed their agents all across the country to buy as many cars and parts as they could lay their hands on; then they put them in storage and waited. As old cars began to wear out, Hull-Dobbs had the needed parts, the Navy bought $60,000 worth of cars and then the federal government authorized the purchase of some new cars. When the dust settled, Jimmy Dobbs' idea had generated a huge profit. It was in this era that Memphis became known as "The World's Largest Used Car Market."

Hull-Dobbs' ventures into other areas were just as successful as their automobile business. Starting with a $1,000 investment in 1936, the Jack Sprat Co. grew into a chain of highly-profitable snack bars. Out of this enterprise was developed the Dobbs Houses chain of restaurants grossing $20 million a year in the 1950s. Dobbs then acquired, for $22 million in stock, the 162-unit Toddle House chain of 10-stool fast food restaurants, operating on the honor system (payment was dropped in a box by the door as one left), that also had originated in Memphis.

In the mid-thirties Dobbs Houses entered the airline catering business. In 1935 Dobbs was on a flight from Dallas to Amarillo. The stewardess was on her initial trip, scared and airsick, and when it came time to serve the food Dobbs helped her. As he helped pass the food around and then tried it himself, it was obvious to him that all of it was unappetizing in

Jimmy Dobbs
His ability to recognize opportunities led he and Horace Hull to become the "World's Largest Ford Dealers" and caterers to the nation's airlines passengers..
(HD, M/SCPL&IC)

appearance and unpalatable; it was then he saw the opportunity and made the decision to enter that business. In 1966 Dobbs Houses' stock had a value of more than $81 million; that year it was purchased by Squibb Beechnut, Inc., which later sold it for about $100 million. In personal ventures Dobbs had an interest in 25 producing oil wells in Texas and ranches near Fort Worth and Memphis.

Jimmy Dobbs died in 1960. In 1965 his estate established the James K. Dobbs Medical Research Institute in Memphis.

In 1928 Thomas W. Briggs founded Welcome Wagon in Memphis, the organization that welcomes newcomers to town with gifts from local businesses, and it spread to cities all across the country.

In the 1930s local insurance man Lester Rosen, in a meeting at Hotel Peabody, conceived the idea of that industry's Million Dollar Roundtable.

In discussing those who shaped Memphis' character, there are two others worthy of mention who typified the Mid-South, one for the aspects of his occupation and the other for the genteel flair he put into his. With the area economy reliant on the productivity of its soil and the exploitation of its timber resources, the power needed for breaking the ground and snaking logs out of the woods came from the strength of the long-eared mule. Memphis became "The World's Largest Mule Market," as millions of the stubborn beasts were sold through half a dozen commission houses from around 1900 until mid-century. The paragon of this activity was auctioneer M. R. Meals who, at 368 pounds, certainly had the capacity to make an imprint on Memphis one way or another. During his 31-year career, the colorful and personable Colonel Meals sold about 1.5 million mules and once auctioned 1,274 in one day.

The antithesis of Colonel Meals in size, color and occupation was Alonzo Locke, a dapper Negro man who was head-waiter of Hotel Peabody. The original Peabody was situated at the corner of Main and Monroe; it was torn down to permit construction of another building and the second Peabody was built facing Union Avenue between Second and Third Streets. It opened in 1925. Billed as "The South's Finest, One of America's Best," except from 1970 to 1981 when economics closed its doors, it has lived up to that slogan. With its commodious and comfortable old-fashioned lobby and dining rooms, and the Skyway supper club and Plantation Roof Garden on the top floor, it has been a focal point of the Mid-South for 70 years, and no one was more instrumental in spreading its reputation than Alonzo Locke.

He had worked as headwaiter at Hotel Gayoso and the old Peabody and assumed that position when the new one opened. In his career he served numerous world figures such as Theodore Roosevelt, William Jennings Bryan and Sarah Bernhardt. One of his few trying moments came when the great, yet temperamental, actor Richard Mansfield, who liked to eat at Luerhmann's, became dissatisfied with his unopened eggs and hurled them at Alonzo. Locke said, "I just ducked and ordered Mr. Mansfield two more eggs."

In his heyday, Locke's domain consisted of nine dining rooms with a hundred waiters under his direction. Meticulous in dress and with an erect bearing, "'Lonzo" strove for perfection in all aspects of the dining regimen. At the every-afternoon training sessions he conducted for his charges, he made sure they could pronounce and describe properly all the items on the menu. And, so they would reflect favorably on their race, as well as the hotel, he insured they conducted themselves with dignity. In his early days at the Peabody, Locke would spend at least part of the summer seasons at hotels in large cities and resorts to learn whatever he could that would help improve his own service and that of the Peabody.

Despite his executive position, Locke was not someone who retreated to the background and pulled the strings; he was highly visible and more akin to a platoon leader in the forefront of his men. Moving quickly among the tables with no suggestion of haste as he supervised the flawless serving operation, he seemed to have a built-in antenna that sensed the arrival of the next diner, for he would arrive back at the door at the opportune moment to provide a warm and dignified greeting. It was at these times that he was at his uncanny best, for he had perfected a simple system for recalling names and associating them with faces. After meeting someone a time or two, invariably, he would remember them and, to their surprise, greet them by name with a slight bow; they, of course, remembered his, as well. Once, when an Englishman, who had visited Memphis years before, encountered a Memphian in Europe, the first thing he asked him was, "Is Alonzo still at the Peabody?"

The respect and affection he commanded locally was illustrated by a particular occasion in which he took pride and satisfaction. When the word got around town that he and his wife were attempting to set up a day care center for the children of working Negro mothers, he promptly received a number of unsolicited checks from his white Memphis friends.

"The South's Finest, One of America's Best."
The new Hotel Peabody, shorlty after opening in 1925.
(HD,M/SCPL&IC)

The morning after the failure of the Fraternal and Solvent Savings Bank on Beale Street, that had wiped out the savings of many depositors, a stranger summoned Alonzo to his breakfast table. "He said he had read in the newspapers that I was one of the big losers and handed me $100. 'Take this and do something with it. From what I've read and know of you, you'll know what I mean.' I put that $100 in the bank that same day and it is still there."

Taught by a private tutor when he was growing up, Locke was well-educated and well-read; he regularly devoured such magazines as *Harper's, Atlantic Monthly, Life, Saturday Evening Post, Collier's* and others and could discuss just about any topic with authority. He was active in many organizations in the Negro community, particularly the Boy Scouts.

Alonzo was known throughout the country and when he was confined with a kidney ailment and heart trouble in December 1946 hundreds of letters and cards, wishing him a speedy recovery, arrived at his private room at John Gaston Hospital and, later, at his home. Some of his wealthy white friends who visited invited him to their winter homes in Florida or California to convalesce, but he felt he could get better quicker in familiar surroundings. He kept talking about returning to work when the weather got cooler, but he died of a heart attack at his home August 3, 1947. The news of his

Alonzo Locke and the graduates of one of his waiter's schools. (HD,M/SCPL&IC)

death went out over the wire services and by early the next morning calls had come in to the Peabody from people in New Orleans and Nashville who expressed their sorrow and made reservations so they could attend the funeral. Clark Porteous of the *Press-Scimitar* led off his article on Locke the next day like this:

> *Alonzo of the Peabody, a tradition in his own time, has gone to his heavenly hotel.*
>
> *Alonzo Locke, the courtly Negro headwaiter of Hotel Peabody, who probably knew more people from outside Memphis than any other Memphian, and who was well known to most of Memphis, died quietly at his home, 699 Edith, at 10:25 a.m. yesterday.*
>
> *Alonzo of the flashing smile, the Chesterfieldian courtesy, the humble yet proud demeanor – Alonzo who was a Memphis institution and one of the leading ambassadors of good will not only for the Negro race but for mankind, was dead.*

Another well-known personage at the Peabody during that era was a white woman, known at "Big Mama," who was a waitress in the basement grill. She had been a school teacher in Mississippi, but lacked a degree, and came to what is now the University of Memphis to obtain one. In working her way through school, she soon found she could make more money waitressing than getting that degree and going back to the schoolroom, so she was at the Peabody for many years. With most businesses still located downtown at that time, the grill had a big lunch crowd and, like Alonzo, she had a remarkable memory for names. She also had a constant, cheery disposition, but, at the same time, a touch of the schoolmarm about her demeanor. If her patrons didn't order what she thought they should – what she deemed to be good that day – she would tell them "no" they weren't going to have that, she was going to serve them such-and-so. Also like Alonzo, she became a beloved Memphis institution.

After some years of neglect and becoming a little tattered around the edges, in 1976 the Peabody was acquired and refurbished in a joint effort by the City of Memphis and the local Belz Enterprises. Lovingly restored to her former grandeur and elegance, the old lady was reopened in 1981 with a new sense of purpose. Once again, the famous ducks dunk and paddle and quack in the lobby fountain from 11 a.m. to 5 P.M.

The ducks first made their appearance in 1934 when the Peabody's general manager was Frank Schutt. There are at least two versions of how the ducks were first introduced. One has it that two of Schutt's buddies, Chip Barwick and Howard Brinkley, decided to play a prank on him. Although Schutt was dependent on his eye glasses for seeing at a distance, he was an avid duck hunter. So he couldn't see what devilment they were up to, Barwick and Brinkley first temporarily pilfered his glasses and then, with consummate stealth, deposited three quackers into the lobby fountain. Schutt's immediate reaction can only be speculated on, but his small daughter was enamored with them and begged that they be allowed to remain. Always on the lookout for a promotion that would help publicize the hotel, Schutt apparently thought it was a good idea, for, except for the period when the hotel was closed, ducks have graced the lobby fountain ever since.

Another version of the story has it that Glenn Miller, the great band leader, and Smith Ballew, another musician, were in town on a lengthy gig and went duck hunting with Schutt. Coming back to town with no kills, reputedly they took their live decoys and put them in the lobby fountain. That story was recently told by 95 year old Ray Johnson, who played with Miller.

In 1940 chance and destiny coalesced and Edward D. Pembrooke entered the picture. In town as an animal trainer with Ringling Brothers, Barnum and Bailey Circus, he was tired of the constant traveling. Somehow he and Schutt met and Pembrooke was offered, and accepted, the job of Duckmaster of the Peabody, a position he held until his retirement in 1991, three years before his death. Just before giving up the position Pembrooke and his feathered charges appeared on Johnny Carson's "Tonight Show."*

Each morning at eleven o'clock, seven days a week, the ducks leave their cages on the hotel's roof and ride the elevator down to the lobby. To the inspiring strains of a medley of Sousa marches, beginning with "King Cotton March" and ending with "Stars and Stripes Forever," the ducks waddle across a red carpet, especially rolled out for them, mount the three steps of the fountain and hop into the pool. When they have completed their daily frolic at five o'clock in the afternoon, the process is reversed before an ever-present and appreciative audience lining the red carpet.

The ducks live in their caged "Penthouse Palace" on the Plantation Roof Garden, which is equipped with a fountain and an Arabian style tent where they do their snoozing. Incidentally, one would look in vain for "duck" in any form on the Peabody's menu.

In 1931, 59 years after the establishment of Mardi Gras, and 49 years after its demise, Memphis held its first Cotton Carnival. It was instituted to promote the crop that was the basis of the economy, but like the celebration that preceded it, it also was designed to help pull the community out of a psychological malaise – caused this time by the Depression. Under the leadership of Everett R. Cook and A. Arthur Halle, it was a resounding success from the start with daytime and nighttime parades, a carnival midway along the bluff, an air show, private parties by every club in town and many other activities.

A king (usually married and middle-aged) and queen (a debutante type) with family connections in the cotton business were crowned and reigned over the week-long festivities. They were tended by uniformed "Royal Guards" (young men) and "Pages" (young boys). There also was a large group, called the "Royal Court," consisting of college-age girls, each

---

* Tony Lanier, bellman, and 18 year employee, and James Means, current Duckmaster, told the story of the ducks. Lanier has two mottoes that typify the tradition of excellence at the Peabody: "It's not the White House, but it's the right house," and "The best for our guests, and then we rest."

representing a business or social club, wearing a uniform
color of evening dress, while their escorts all wore summer
tuxedos. To put the celebration into high gear, the whole
assemblage boarded a brilliantly-lighted and decorated
barge at the U. S. Corps of Engineers landing, just south of the

*Ducks in lobby fountain of Hotel Peabody. (Courtesy of Richard
Langford.)*

*Across their red carpet to the elevator.
(Courtesy of Richard Langford)*

bridges on the Arkansas side of the Mississippi River, which
was pushed upstream. When the barge landed at the foot of
Monroe just after dark, its arrival prompted a fireworks extrav-
aganza behind it on Mud Island. The mayor dutifully tendered

to the king the keys to the city and for the next five nights the royalty and court, with police motorcycle escort, zipped around town in convertibles and buses to put in an appearance at every club's social function, usually making four or five parties a night. Half a dozen "secret societies," some reactivated from Mardi Gras days, with names bespeaking Memphis' Egyptian connection, such as Memphi, Osiris, and Ra-Met, selected their own king and queen and maintained club rooms at downtown hotels during the week. Girls from throughout the cotton producing states of the South and Southwest vied for the title of Maid of Cotton, to reign for a year and tour throughout the country as a "goodwill ambassador" staging fashion shows and appearing before various trade groups to promote the usage of cotton. Down on Beale Street the "Cotton Makers Jubilee" was celebrated.

The barge bearing the King and Queen of Cotton Carnival and the Royal Court, arrives at the foot of Monroe Avenue to inaugurate the 1946 Carnival. (HD,M/SCPL&IC)

Book Two

One Autumn
from a distant window

0, Skylark
I don't know if you can find these things
But my heart is riding on your wings
So, if you see them anywhere
Won't you lead me there?

Skylark
-Johnny Mercer and
Hoagy Carmichael

Memphis skyline in 1940. Wolf River flows between Mud
Island and the waterfront on its way to the Mississippi.
(HD,M/SCPL&IC)

On the Plantation Roof Garden in 1944. (A)

Memphis, Tennessee was exciting,
We went to the hotel there.

I had always known about Memphis, Tennessee
It looked as it should, Memphis, Tennessee
All except the hotel; the hotel was a good hotel
We did eat very well.

And there seemed to be so much social life there,
very many girls and very many men
And they all seemed to be there as if there were
no other anywhere
All the life they lived there.

Everybody's Autobiography
-Gertrude Stein

A Sunev party in the Skyway in 1944. (Courtesy of Julius Smith)

The period of the late thirties and early forties was a turning point for Memphis. The city administration began a clean-up of vice and the nation was girding for a war that would be the impetus for a tremendous social and economic upheaval, the momentum of which would carry into future decades.

In May 1939 as he and two others were touring North Mississippi promoting the upcoming Cotton Carnival, Mr. Crump's youngest son, John, was killed in the crash of a small plane at Grenada. A year later, almost to the day, Mr. Crump's mother died. Whether these personal tragedies prompted him to institute the clean-up or whether, as previously noted, he only now had achieved sufficient political power to effect it, is arguable. In any event, Police Commissioner "Holy Joe" Boyle led the crackdown that eliminated the gambling and booze on Beale, closed the nearby brothels and ran the gamblers with their floating crap and poker games out of the cheaper hotels on South Main. The blatant gambling that was the norm at the Peabody, Gayoso, Devoy and Claridge hotels, and at several restaurants downtown, also was shut down. Prior to this, while one munched his lunch, he could bet on the horses, play blackjack, shoot craps or wrestle with the one-armed bandits. As noted in the section describing life on Beale Street, the numbers game was big and quite a few respectable small businesses were engaged in this activity.

In a scenario somewhat reminiscent of Little Vigor and the expulsion of the prostitutes a hundred years before, the ladies of the evening were summarily rousted out and sent on their way. After years of paying protection, the prostitutes were shocked and dismayed. Some of them temporarily set up shop in Oxford, Miss., 80 miles southeast of Memphis and site of the University of Mississippi, and then probably drifted on to New Orleans. According to a lady who was an Ole Miss coed at the time, during the whore's brief sojourn there a date was hard to come by.

In 1940 Congress passed the Selective Service Act and, in the initial registration, 49,000 Shelby County men, 21 to 35 years of age, were put on the rolls of potential draftees. In the fall the National Guard was federalized and the reserves called to active duty (for one year, it was said), and soldiers coming home on leave provided the first opportunity for many to see men in uniform. Convoys carrying baby-faced soldiers in canvas-covered trucks occasionally rumbled through town. Some Memphians went to Canada to join the Royal Canadian Air Force and ended up in England in an "Eagle Squadron" like those who had flown in the Lafayette Escadrille in World War I.

Early in the year President Roosevelt had signed a bill expanding the Navy Air Corps by 10,000 planes and then another, called the "Two-Ocean Navy Act," which projected building 35 battleships, 20 aircraft carriers and 88 cruisers. He then asked Congress for an additional $4.8 billion in "defense" funds, promising when he made this request: "We will not send our men to take part in European wars." But not many people were fooled by such statements; a Gallup Poll showed that 67 percent favored universal military training. Roosevelt ran for an unprecedented third term and in a speech in Boston, presumably to ensure the "mother vote," he said, "I have said this before, but I shall say it again and again and again: Your boys are not going to be sent into any foreign wars." He defeated Wendell Willke with 55 percent of the vote.

It was somewhat of a sad joke that the size of our standing army approximated that of Ecuador's or Liechtenstein's or some other small, peaceful country. But before the end of 1940 several hundred thousand Americans had volunteered for a year's military service, essentially negating the need for the first draft quota. Because of a paucity of equipment early on, during training whatever was handy was used to simulate the real thing; trucks were sometimes used for tanks, stovepipes for mortars and sacks of flour for bombs.

In order that the collective mind of the general populace be cajoled into a fighting mood, Hollywood and Tin Pan Alley spewed out a plethora of crass and stupid movies and songs. While they did produce some good material, it was overshadowed by such inanities as *Confessions of a Nazi Spy*, starring Edward G. Robinson, and pabulum-like combat films typified by *Bataan* and *Guadalcanal Diary*, usually featuring some naive, clean-cut young hayseed from the Midwest and his wise-cracking, smart-aleck sidekick-buddy from Brooklyn who were fighting so they could take up their lives again at the "malt shop." When they "got it," it always was a nice, neat clean wound with a minimum of blood that permitted sufficient time for the utterance of a few last words for posterity.

Some of the songs which, fortunately, received little air time equally were as bad: "The Japs Don't Stand a Chinaman's Chance" and "We're Gonna Find a Feller Who is Yeller and Beat Him Red, White and Blue," were prime examples, although Spike Jones' silly, but cute, "Der Feuhrer's Face" was a hit. Rex Stout wrote a magazine article entitled "We Shall Hate or We Shall Fail," and an advertisement in the *New York Times* depicted a sinister Japanese face with the heading "Rat Poison Wanted": below, a caption said "There's only one way to exterminate the slant eyes – with gunpowder."

In Memphis the Kuni Wada Bakery, run by Hanichi Nakajima and located on the north side of Madison just west of Cleveland, was a particular favorite of the after-show crowd to get a sack full of big, fluffy powdered-sugared doughnuts. Not too long after the attack on Pearl Harbor it quietly closed; this action roughly corresponded in time with the bulldozing, by official decree and universal agreement, of the Japanese gardens in Overton Park.

To its credit, during this period Hollywood did turn out *Casablanca* and *For Whom the Bell Tolls* and, rather than monotonous, tuneless inanities and bawling despair and degradation and unintelligible claptrap appealing to the glands that has assaulted the ears in recent decades, the music and lyrics of that era conveyed a message of hope and elegance and have never been equaled in their capacity to endure and to touch the hearts and minds of a people: "Laura," "Stella by Starlight," "That Old Black Magic," "Dream," and those that related specifically to the tenor of the times, "Shoo Shoo Baby," (your Papa's off to the Seven Seas), "Till Then," "We'll Meet Again," "For All We Know," (we may never meet again), "You Are Always in My Heart," "I'll Be Seeing You," "I'll Walk Alone," "Don't Sit Under the Apple Tree," (with anyone else but me), "Don't Get Around Much Anymore," "Love Letters," "I Miss You," (since you went away dear), "I'll Be Home for Christmas," and the Academy Award Winner of 1943, "You'll Never Know" (just how much I miss you). Then there were the wacky songs such as: "Mairzy Doats," which sounded something like, "Mairzy Doats and Dozee Doats and Little Lamsydivy, akiddleedivytoo, wouldn't you?" "Cement Mixer" (Cement Mixer, puttee-puttee), "Too Fat Polka" (I don't want her, you can have her, she's too fat for me) and something along the line of: "Hut Sut Ralston on the Riddlerah and the Brawla-Brawla Suet..." And with most of the young studs off somewhere in uniform, a maiden's lament might be:

> They're either too young or too old
> They're either too gray or too grassy green
> The pickings are poor and the crop is lean
> What's good is in the Army
> What's left will never harm me

> -Frank Loesser and
> Arthur Schwartz

Terse and emphatic newscaster Walter Winchell would come on the airways for 15 minutes five nights a week with, "Good evening, Mr. and Mrs. North America and all the ships at sea, let's go to press! Flash!" And then, in rapid-fire staccato, he would launch into a series of gripping bulletins, each heralded by the impatient sounds of a telegraph key, regarding ominous threats to the domestic tranquillity. Another newscaster, but one who discoursed on the latest in such dark and somber tones as to almost impel one to frantically seek out a single-edged razor blade and go into a frenzy of wrist-slashing, was Gabriel Heatter. He would start off intoning, "Oh, there's bad news tonight." Even when the news was good he could make one despondent just listening to the tenor of his voice.

In 1940 Memphis had a population of 292,942. There were an additional 64,678 people in the county, with most of them on the city's fringe. Memphis had dropped to sixth place in size among the cities of the South and Southwest. Annexation of some of the adjoining areas would have pushed Memphis past Atlanta and Dallas, each of which had only a few thousand more inhabitants, and probably past Louisville, but livability was more important than size. The effects of the Depression lingered and a little over 14 percent of the labor force was unemployed or working for the WPA.

The Chickasaw Ordnance Works, operated by DuPont and located between Millington and Shelby Forest, began making explosives for the British, and other local industries started re-tooling for the war effort. The Ford plant discontinued automobile assembly to produce airplane engines, Firestone began making rubber life rafts and tires for Army trucks, Fisher Body built wings and fuselages for bombers, Continental Can manufactured shell casings and Pidgeon-Thomas built LCTs, small amphibious landing craft. The speed with which American industry shifted from making consumer goods to production of armaments and the resultant flow of war materiel was phenomenal. In Roosevelt's State of the Union address in early 1943 he reported that the year before American industry had produced 48,000 military planes, 56,000 combat vehicles and 670,000 machine guns.

From Pearl Harbor to mid-1943 close to 40,000 people flocked to Memphis to find employment in war-related work. Because of material shortages the War Production Board prohibited all new home construction and an acute housing shortage developed. Some owners turned their homes into rooming houses or remodeled them to provide small apartments. Even abandoned gas stations were converted to housing. A new arrival in Memphis was usually put on a waiting list for a telephone and some who had them might share their line with one to three other users.

Other real or presumed shortages brought on rationing.

Just after Christmas of 1941 rationing was instituted for tires. Shortly thereafter sugar (eight to 12 ounces a week, per person), coffee (one pound, per person, every five weeks), gasoline and shoes were rationed. Windshield stickers (letters A to E) indicated gas allowances. Those with "A" stickers (pleasure driving) were issued stamps good for, depending on the region of the country, three to five gallons a week. A thriving black market developed, particularly for the acquisition of meat and gas. Coupon books were issued for sugar, meat and a variety of food products. Butter was in short supply and oleomargarine became popular; it came in a white cake that looked like lard and had to be mixed with an orange colorant. The dairy lobby had effected this and Congress finally passed legislation to permit pre-coloring. Meatless Tuesdays and Fridays were the norm and to stretch the meat people started eating creamed, chipped beef on toast; in the military that took the form of ground beef and servicemen referred to it as S. O. S. Spam, a canned meat developed for shipment to England, was served to the troops and eaten on the homefront. Johnny Mercer wrote a song about it:

> *They've got Spam and Wham and deviled ham*
> *And something new called Zoom*
> *You take it home and heat it*
> *To the temperature of the room*

To save on tin cans, dehydrated soup in packets was developed; powdered milk and eggs became common. Due to a shortage of sugar and chocolate, candy bars were hard to find. To take up the slack in the shortage of canned vegetables, the government pushed the idea of "Victory Gardens" and 20.5 million were planted in 1943. Because of paper shortages there were very few Christmas cards available in 1943 and, during the holiday season, people were asked to limit long distance calls to five minutes so circuits would be available to servicemen calling home. Regardless, they usually had to wait hours to get through.

To save cloth, men's suits no longer came with vests or two pairs of pants, cuffs were eliminated and coat lapels narrowed. By decree of the Office of Price Administration, women's skirts ended an inch above the knee. When the war cut off the supply of silk, and then nylon, "bottled stockings" enjoyed some currency. Women would smear on this tannish leg make-up and then, sometimes, take an eyebrow pencil and create the semblance of a seam up the backs of their legs. It was said that with luck and no baths (yuk) it would last three days. It caused a problem for men because, as the song said, "... it decants on your pants." When former Heisman Trophy winner and Air Corps pilot Tom Harmon and actress Elyse Knox were married her dress was made from a silk parachute he had used during one of the two times he had been forced to bail out of his plane. There was a shortage of doctors and dentists and that's when the former stopped making house calls.

The Navy started construction of the big base at Millington, just north of Memphis, that would accommodate the Naval Air Technical Training Center and an air base and a hospital. Tens of thousands of men were trained there and sent out on the flattops in the Pacific. On pleasant-weather weekends sailors on liberty would unload buses at Ellis Auditorium and turn Main Street into a bobbing sea of white. Particularly at Norfolk and the Hampton Roads area of Virginia, headquarters of the Atlantic Fleet and home to naval installations for many years, professional gamblers, and all the unsavory characters of their ilk, had moved in and prospered on the naiveté of young sailors. Mr. Crump undoubtedly was aware of this and it's likely that, as much as for any other reason, if not the paramount one, the aforementioned clean-up can be attributed to his determination that the sailors from Millington would be exposed to a wholesome environment when they came "ashore" in Memphis.

Other military facilities that came to town were the Army Quartermaster Supply Depot on Airways, the Air Force Depot on Jackson and Kennedy General Hospital (Army) at Park and Shotwell – with the latter street name later, more appropriately, changed to "Getwell." The Fourth Ferrying Command, which ferried military aircraft around the globe, was located on the north side of the Memphis Airport.

The headquarters of the Second Army, under initial command of old cavalryman LtGen Ben Lear, was at the Mid-South Fairgrounds from 1940 to 1946. Gen Lear had entered the Army as an enlisted man in the Spanish-American War and also had fought in World War I. He had come up through the ranks, went by the book and was as tough as a nickel steak.

On a broiling Sunday afternoon in July 1941 Lear was playing golf at the Memphis Country Club when a convoy of 45 Army trucks came rolling by on Central Avenue carrying 350 soldiers from grueling field maneuvers in Middle Tennessee to Camp Robinson, Ark. Spotting some attractive young ladies in shorts on the course, some of the soldiers began howling and yoo-hooing at them. Witnessing the whole thing, Lear was embarrassed and incensed. Attired in casual, civilian clothes he took off at a trot, hurdled the low hedge along Central, stopped the convoy and spoke to the commanding officer. When the trucks arrived at Camp Robinson, near Little Rock, they were ordered to turn around and come back to Memphis to Second Army Headquarters. After all 350 men were thoroughly chewed out, they were sent back to Camp Robinson, but Lear ordered them to put on their packs and make the first 15 miles on foot. Becoming one of those quirky things the media loves to elevate to the status of a cause celebre, the "yoo-hoo incident" received national publicity. Naturally, some congressmen did some posturing about it and the crusty old soldier was pilloried and depicted as an insensitive tyrant. Gen. Lear was named commander of Army Ground Forces in 1944 and wound up as deputy commander of the European Theater of Operations under Eisenhower. He retired to Memphis and was a contributor to causes working on behalf of civic betterment.

When the Japanese attacked Pearl Harbor on December 7, 1941, as Admiral Isoroku Yamamoto said, they "awoke a sleeping giant." However, not yet fully comprehending the fighting capability and dedication of the Japanese, people were outraged that what they considered a pip-squeak island country of copy cats and toy makers would have the audacity to pick a fight with "the greatest nation on Earth" – and in such a cowardly fashion. Immediately, recruiting stations were swamped and had to go on a 24-hour basis to accommodate the long lines of volunteers. For example, after a particularly gratifying blast in the Skyway the night before, a local attorney and two of his fellow celebrants joined the Marine Corps the next afternoon, December 7. Getting bombed twice in the same 24 hour period was more than they could tolerate.

In the early days of the war, some people in coastal

cities, like Los Angeles and New York, expected to be bombed at any time. A couple of false alarms in the former city and San Francisco sent people into panic and the front of the New York Stock Exchange was piled high with sandbags. The 1942 Rose Bowl game between Duke, quarterbacked by Memphian Tommy Prothro, and Oregon State was moved to Durham, N. C. for fear the Japanese would bomb the Pasadena arena during the game.

Air raid drills were conducted all across the country. During these drills all vehicular traffic was prohibited, and if lights were used in a home, blackout curtains had to cover the windows. Parttime national civil defense director Fiorello La Guardia, mayor of New York City, was succeeded in the post by James M. Landis, dean of the Harvard Law School. His austere, legal mind envisioned a formula for achieving a blackout that was imparted with seriosness but, in fact, elicited a guffaw from those who read it: "Such obscuration may be obtained by the termination of the illumination." Even a place as remote and militarily inconsequential as Jackson, Tenn. had drills. Here, state guardsmen were instructed about how many plane lengths to fire in front of low-flying enemy aircraft. In Memphis the Office of Civilian Defense trained 25,000 people in first aid, to serve as air raid wardens and in other related capacities. A pamphlet entitled "What to do in an Air Raid" was distributed to 57 million people, and the best selling book of 1942 (eight million copies) was "Red Cross First Aid Manual."

There were four instances of enemy military activity in the United States. One was when a Japanese submarine surfaced at night off the coast of California and used its deck gun to lob a few shells that hit near an oil refinery and knocked out a well close to Santa Barbara. The second was actually a series of events wherein the Japanese launched thousands of 30 pound balloon-borne bombs to send to the United States via high-altitude wind currents blowing across the Pacific. About 300 actually made it and a few drifted as far as Iowa and Kansas, but most were duds. There was only one instance that ended in casualties. In 1945, on a mountain in Oregon, a woman and five children on an outing came upon a bomb on the ground; it exploded and killed all six. On September 9, 1942, Flying Officer Nobuo Fujita, in a Zero airplane, was catapulted off of a submarine lying off the coast of Oregon. His mission was to drop incendiary bombs to start a forest fire that, hopefully, would sweep down the coast. The flames from the bombs sputtered out and he flew back to try again on September 29 with the same result.

On June 13, 1942, four specially-trained Germans were launched from the U-boat *Innsbruck* and came ashore in a rubber boat on Long Island. They carried a large supply of explosives and their mission was to sabotage specific military installations and war production facilities. Four days later, another four-man team landed in Florida. All had lived in the United States before the war and spoke fluent English, but within two weeks – before they could do any damage – they were all rounded up by the FBI. They were tried before a military tribunal and sentenced to death. Because two of them had, in essence, defected, President Roosevelt commuted their sentences; the others were electrocuted.

Burning freighters that could be observed at night along the Atlantic Coast and the Gulf of Mexico and the debris and oil that washed ashore were frequent reminders of the presence of German U-boats near our shores. The Civil Air Patrol, with 40,000 part-time volunteers too young or too old for combat, flew their own light aircraft on missions such as ferrying military passengers and mail. However, in July 1942 they were armed with real bombs and began submarine patrol duty off the coasts. They bombed 57 subs and were credited with several kills.

Many people, particularly children, saved all sorts of things and carried them to collection centers for use in the war effort: newspapers and magazines, old tires, all types and sizes of scrap metal, including lead toothpaste tubes and tin foil from the lining of gum wrappers and cigarette packages, silk stockings for recycling into powder bags for naval guns and bacon grease for use in making explosives. Kids, particularly, were adept at the "tin can stomp." After a can had been emptied of its contents it was washed out and the top and bottom removed with a can opener and placed inside; a well-placed "stomp" then flattened it out for ease in transporting to a collection center.

Unless one could scuffle up the gas ration tickets to go by car, traveling any distance from one city to another could be a problem. Airline tickets were ordinarily issued only to those having a priority based on their activities in the war effort and riding a train or bus frequently meant standing up all or most of the way. In 1944 railroads logged three times as many passenger miles as in 1941 and buses more than twice as many.

With almost total employment and many working long hours in defense industries, in stark contrast to Depression days, most people had more money to spend than ever before. It was a thoroughly tragic time, yet, because of the commonality of effort and sense of mission, it was an exciting time that touched everything in a frenetic sort of way. People worked hard, but they also played hard. Even with those away in the service and overseas, wartime nightclub business increased 40 percent. Central High athlete Gayden Drew worked three evenings a week, for three dollars a shift, at Hotel Peabody's Skyway his last semester in school in the spring of 1943, and the club was packed every night.

Particularly in bars, signs decorated the walls urging maximum effort to defeat the Axis. With the implication that the country was overrun with spies with unusual hearing capabilities, one sign depicted an attractive girl with a cautionary index finger raised to pursed lips to discourage talking about such things as troop movements and ship departures. Another, with a drawing of a burning freighter sliding beneath the waves in the background, said "A slip of the lip can sink a ship." All mail arriving from overseas had been scanned by a censor to insure that the writer had not mentioned something not deemed suitable for civilian eyes. After the censor's scissors had done their work, many letters were delivered that resembled paper dolls' clothes. The envelope would be taped back up and stamped "Opened by Censor."

Before his big hit in *Shane*, Alan Ladd had broken into the movies in the early 1940s playing a semi-tough-guy in gangster-type flicks. One time William Bendix would be his pal and the next time out he would be a bad guy and bounce Ladd around a little bit. Veronica Lake, also a newcomer, customarily provided the female interest. Needing a gimmick to enhance her attractiveness and overcome her apparent lack of acting skills, she affected a sort of husky voice and what the studio publicity people referred to as a "peek-a-boo" hairstyle:

her long, honey-blonde hair was waved at just the right spot so that it partially covered one eye. In some limited female quarters this style became all the rage, but for those working around machinery in defense plants the long tresses provided the potential for a scalping, or worse. Accordingly, the War Production Board issued its edict and, thereafter, "Rosie the Riveter" and her compatriots, making another sacrifice in behalf of the war effort, wore their hair "up" and covered with a snood.

With so many cigarettes being distributed to the troops, well-known brands frequently were unavailable and hand-rolled "tailor-made" cigarettes made a comeback. Occasionally, some strange brands, that possibly had been put together from sweepings at the tobacco warehouses, would make their appearance. The author remembers Richard Langford showing up at a party one evening with a package of "Home Runs." Something in the green dye of Lucky Strike's package was needed, so with the advertising announcement that "Lucky Strike Green Has Gone to War," the package was forevermore changed to white.

All of these concerns and preparations to forestall enemy attacks seem rather silly now, but one wonders what might have happened if the war had lasted long enough for the Germans to complete development of an atomic bomb and increase the range of their rockets. And there is some evidence the Japanese had just developed "the bomb" contemporaneous with our dropping the first one.

Walter Stewart, sports editor of *The Commercial Appeal*, was in the Army Reserve and was called to active duty. He served as a major at Guadalcanal and other locations in the Solomon Islands. After contracting malaria he got to come home to Memphis on leave. He then was reassigned to the China-Burma-India Theater where he served with General Bob Neyland, head football coach at the University of Tennessee.

Stewart had cut his sports writing teeth on the rings at New York's St. Nicholas Arena and Madison Square Garden. Maybe the eastern media establishment was miffed at his leaving the Big Apple and returning to the hinterlands of the Mid-South, because it always referred, in somewhat reverent language, to Red Smith (after all, doesn't he write for the *Times*?) as being the top scribe in the field with some now-forgotten fellow with the *Los Angeles Times* running in the place position. Stewart received national recognition when some of his columns were judged to be among the best in a particular year, but he still didn't get the respect to which he was entitled. In the author's opinion, Smith just told the facts in a drab, unimaginative manner, whereas Stewart's writing, while not sacrificing the elements of the story, was colorful and interesting.

World War Two's call to arms and industrial mobilization decimated the ranks of the normal civilian work-force, and the vacant jobs were filled by retirees, teenagers and women who never before had worked. The coaching field was hit just as hard as any. Ruffner Murray, the Central High football coach in 1940, was in the naval reserve and was called to active duty in early 1941. His replacement, Bob Porter, who had played college ball at Southwestern at Memphis, assumed the position for that fall but entered the Navy in the spring of 1942. Like Walter Stewart, Porter also made it to the Solomon Islands, where he had occassion to see Stewart briefly. Emil Beopple was the head coach that fall with Kenny Holland and Fleet Edwards, former Central and Southwestern stars, as assistants. Beopple went into the Navy before the final game with Tech and Holland and Edwards took over for that game. By the next fall they, too, were gone and C. P. Jester, Central principal, and Ernest Ball, superintendent of education, selected Cecil Glass as the replacement.

Cecil Glass was a graduate of Hillsdale College. Hillsdale is a fine, independent liberal arts school in Michigan that, today, 150 years after its establishment, has never received any aid nor accepted any control from the federal government. The year before Glass had coached at Fairview Junior High in Memphis and the year before that at Bolles Military Academy in Jacksonville, Flor. He chose as his assistant Churchill Roberts, a native of Gastonia, N. C., who had played freshman football at Duke and later coached at Christ School, his alma mater, in Asheville. Several years before, his family had moved to Memphis.

Ensign Bob Porter, former Central High football coach, and Major Walter Stewart, sports editor on leave from The Commercial Appeal, get together on a naval vessel between Guadalcanal and Savo Islands in 1943.
(Courtesy of Bill Buckles)

In 1943 Ralph Hatley had been head coach at CBC for two years. The native of Jackson had played tackle and guard in Major Bob Neyland's single wing system at Tennessee and in 1934 was captain of the team and an All-Southeastern Conference guard. While on "The Hill" he had played with such Volunteer greats as Beattie Feathers for two years and Gene McEver for one. Like most coaches, Neyland would occasionally pad his schedule with a team that assured an easy victory, but he also sought out the best and Tennessee played some of the finer eastern teams of that era, such as NYU and George Washington.

Although the nickname "Seven Blocks of Granite" for the line of the Fordham Rams did not come into currency until two years later, in 1934 Hatley had the opportunity to go head-to-head with one of its future members – a then unknown sophomore named Vince Lombardi. Behind 13 to 12 in the fourth quarter the Vols put on a long drive that reached the Fordham 12 yard line. On fourth down and short yardage Tennessee ran a play that apparently picked up the first down, but the official ruled it short. In frustration, the Tennessee tailback slammed the ball to the ground and it bounced up and hit an official. By now, home cooking at the Polo Grounds had reached a boiling point for, rather than exacting a penalty for unsportsman-like conduct, the official ejected the tailback from the game. In those days when a player was substituted for he could not return in the same quarter. As the second-string tailback had been in when the fourth quarter started and been replaced by the first-stringer, who now was sitting on the bench, Tennessee had to go with its third-string tail-back the remainder of the game. When Fordham got the ball the Vols held and forced them to punt, but the lack of punch at tailback kept Tennessee out of the end zone and the score stayed the same.

Tennessee won eight and lost two that year. The other loss was to Alabama 13 to 6. In this game Hatley blocked on another who then was relatively unknown but would later become a legend in the game; Paul "Bear" Bryant was at end for the Tide. An incident occurred in this game that ended up being somewhat amusing. The man playing alongside Bryant was Alabama's 245 pound tackle Bill Lee who, in the heat of competition, slugged Tennessee tailback Phil Dickens. But the referee thought Bryant was the culprit and tossed him out of the game. That Alabama team, with the legendary Don Hutson at end and Dixie Howell at tailback, went on to clobber a favored Stanford team, 29 to 13, in the Rose Bowl.

After graduation Hatley's coaching career took him to every corner of the state. He spent one season as line coach at University of Tennessee Junior College at Martin and then, successively, was head coach at Carter High in Knox County, Polk County High, and then Dyersburg High in 1939 and 1940. In 1939 the Jackson Golden Bears, a perennial powerhouse in that era, had beaten Dyersburg 55 to 0, but in 1940 Hatley pulled a big upset and beat Jackson 13 to 7, with all the points being scored within two minutes.

Central coaches Churchill Roberts and Cecil Glass.

CBC had gone through several losing season and needed a competitive team to go along with its new school and expansive campus on Parkway. Things had gotten so bad that at mid-season in 1939 Brother Luke Joseph, then principal, called a meeting of the team and invited them to cancel the remainder of the season – he was afraid someone out of the only 28 or so players would get killed. In 1940 CBC lost to Tech High 64 to 0 and Central 38 to 0. At the end of that season Brother Matthew contacted Bob Neyland for a coaching recommendation and he suggested Hatley. After talking to several other prospects, the search committee decided that Hatley was the best qualified and it invited him to Memphis for a serious discussion of the job.

The meeting was held in the law office of Ed Barry in the Commerce Title Building. Also in attendance were Brothers Mathias and Luke Joseph, J. E. McCadden, Herbert Moriarty and "Monk" Godman. Hatley, a Methodist, felt somewhat out of place amongst all these Catholics. He had never before met a Christian Brother and didn't really know the difference between one and a priest. After the discussion had gone on for awhile and reached a point where it was apparent that an offer was on the table, Hatley felt it necessary to mention something that, to him, apparently had been overlooked. He got a serious expression on his face and the room fell silent. "Gentlemen, I'm flattered by your confidence in me and I would like to accept the job, but I think you should be aware of something – I'm not a Catholic and I don't know how well I

Freshman Coach Harold Hatley and Head Coach Ralph Hatley of CBC.

might fit in at CBC." After a burst of hearty laughter by all but Hatley, he was assured that they wanted him to only take charge of the athletic program with the primary duty of turning out a good football team and that he would not be responsible for any religious duties. Somewhat appropriately, Hatley reported for work on St. Patrick's Day, March 17, 1941.

In those days coaches did not have the luxury of the large staffs that are common today. In fact, the football coach ordinarily was responsible for coaching all the other major sports, such as basketball, track and baseball. He frequently would be conducting two at the same time. The assistants would be hired only for the duration of the season of a particular sport. Hatley's first football assistant was Andrew "Pop" Calhoun, who had played at Memphis State College. He entered the Army Air Corps early in the war and was killed when his P47 Thunderbolt fighter plane was shot down over France. Others who helped out at one time or another were Lloyd McDougall, Bill Speros and John Michael, another former Memphis State player. Hatley's brother, Harold, also coached the ninth-grade team that fed players to the varsity.

Hatley's top assistant in 1943 and 1944 was an all-around athlete whom he had admired for many years. Leo Davis, a native of Drummond, Okla., had been offered a football and baseball scholarship to Vanderbilt when he came out of high school. Showing up in Nashville to enroll, he was told that his high school transcript had been evaluated and that he lacked the requisite two years of a foreign language for admission. Discouraged, and not having any specific plans at that point, Davis started hitchhiking back to Oklahoma. While between rides in McKenzie, Tenn. he began chatting with a local resident and told him what had happened. The man suggested that he go out and talk to the officials at the local Bethel College, which had a well-rounded athletic program. Davis followed through on the recommendation and was accepted at Bethel where, for four years, he starred in football, baseball, basketball and wrestling, later serving as head coach in the first three sports. Today, the field house at Bethel is named in his honor and in February 1993, two years after his death, he was inducted posthumously into the Tennessee Sports Hall of Fame. Just before joining Hatley at CBC he had been an assistant coach at Memphis State, which discontin-

ued football during the war. His primary responsibility at the Brothers was to
get the team into good physical condition and coach the backs. He regularly
stayed in shape and could do anything
in the way of calisthenics or running
that he directed the boys to do.

When Hatley arrived at CBC in
the spring of 1941, he had already conducted spring practice at Dyersburg
High and now had to do it all over
again. In those days spring practice
normally began the first Monday of
February and lasted for six weeks. The
first day approximately 100 boys came
out for the team. One week later, after
Hatley's strenuous drills emphasizing
conditioning and fundamentals, all
but 13 had turned in their uniforms.
Those who remained loved football
and had a strong desire to acquire the
necessary skills to excel; they stayed
with the program and constituted the

CBC assistant Leo Davis.
He tutored the backs and
got the boys in shape.
(Courtesy of Rebecca (Mrs.
Leo) Davis)

core of the teams that over the next several years would have
winning seasons and turn out some outstanding players.

In addition to fundamentals and conditioning, Hatley
stressed quickness and morale. To enhance school spirit and
develop competitiveness, with the help of the Brothers, he
organized an intramural program from which he ultimately
obtained some players for the varsity. Overriding all was getting the boys in shape whereby they could perform effectively
on both offense and defense for as long as they might be
required to stay in a game. This was an area in which Leo
Davis was particularly proficient during 1943. In the early part
of the season practice would begin with about 40 minutes of
calisthenics frequently followed by 10 laps around the quarter
mile track with an occasional player momentarily pausing
along the way to throw up. One year, after a poor performance
one Friday night wherein they beat a team over which they
were heavily favored by only 6 to 0, those who were deemed
not to have played to their capabilities ran 50 laps the next

morning in the rain. In a similar circumstance on another occasion an extra practice was held on a Sunday and another time, after being cautioned not to eat prior to practice, on a Thanksgiving afternoon.

Theories about conditioning have changed over the years. In that era there was no such thing as a water break during practice, although one or two players would sometimes bring a lemon onto the field and suck on it to slake their thirst. It would end up being passed around and, after the juice was gone, the rind would be chewed up and totally consumed. The duck waddle exercise was a favorite until it was realized years later that it stretched and weakened the muscles and made one more susceptible to knee injuries. There was no organized weight training program – it made one "muscle bound" – although some players lifted on their own. By restriction of water and the emphasis on calisthenics and running, the goal was to develop speed, quickness and endurance – resulting in a "greyhound" type of player – that was necessary at a time when almost everyone played both offense and defense. It also encouraged a physical and mental toughness.

At the end of each CBC practice it was customary for the squad to split up in pairs for full speed, head-on tackling, for eight or ten times, with each participant alternately tackling or running with the ball; good technique was stressed. Sometimes this was done with helmets on and sometimes without. (The mark of a good blocker and tackler in those days was scrapes and scabs along the cheekbone, providing evidence that one had consistently used good form in getting the head alongside the opponent's hip pads or the blocking dummy.) While this drill was being carried out a couple of days prior to an out-of-town game, Al Huebner, sans helmet and using proper technique, almost tore an ear off. It was taped up against his head and he made the trip and helped beat CBC of St. Louis. The following year he was a first-string all-state guard.

In this era, football was played with leather helmets and, regardless of position, every player's shoulder pads were pretty much the same, except that a few linemen were starting to wear ribs pads. Face masks, called nose guards or "bird cages," ordinarily would be worn only by someone with a broken nose. There were no mouthpieces, neck rolls, sweat bands, gloves for receivers or "flak jackets" for quarterbacks and all shoes were high tops. Trainers were students and there was a lot less taping of joints; sideline medical care left much to be desired.

Like every Marine is a basic infantryman, every football player in the forties had first to be a blocker and tackler. An end might throw a block on a safety that enabled his runner to score and then on the ensuing kickoff go down and make the tackle.

With such formations as the single wing, double wing, and short punt in vogue, blocks were resounding things designed to put people on the ground rather than the brush blocks of the T-formation and option offenses that only momentarily interfere with the defensive player until the ball carrier can zip through the gaps. Many of the "blocks" John Madden gushes about enthusiastically on Sunday afternoons would have been laughed at in the forties. In a conversation with University of Texas two-time All-American linebacker Don Manasco in 1951, he told the author that when Tennessee tailback Hank Lauricella cut back over tackle and ran something like 70 yards for a touchdown in that year's Cotton Bowl, that he, Manasco, was blocked to the ground twice on that one play. And a tackling performance was deemed admirable only when the tackler's shoulder made vicious contact with the runner and the latter was "wrapped up" by clamping his legs together and driving him back.

Coach Hatley had been thoroughly indoctrinated in the single wing system playing under Neyland at Tennessee and had coached it for eight years since leaving college, so he knew what it took to succeed with the formation. Basic to its effectiveness were two fast and agile "running" guards who not only could block on the line but, equally as important, could pull and lead power plays on sweeps and cutbacks off tackle. These two positions were amply filled by Al Huebner and Percy Roberts. At 150 or so pounds Huebner was the prototype guard – low-slung and muscular with good balance and speed. One player said that in dummy scrimmage Huebner's blocks hurt even through the blocking dummy. Percy was about 10 or 15 pounds heavier, but his almost six feet in height made him leaner and he was fast enough to run track. They had run plays together for so long that each knew instinctively where the other would be at any split-second point on blocking assignments, and they were a devastating pair when the ball was snapped.

While there was more emphasis on the running game in the forties, the passing aspect was certainly a necessary component and Hatley needed a fast receiver who had the moves to get open and the agility to catch almost anything thrown in his direction. Bill Burke, a graceful, all-around athlete stepped forward at end to fulfill that need.

But the heart and soul of the offense focused on the tailback who had to be able to run and pass and, if necessary, punt. CBC was well-stocked at this position with versatile George "Bubba" Whitehead, hard-running John "Sleepy" Ross, and sophomore comer Jack "Hoot" Gibson.

On defense, Hatley told his linemen to watch the center's hands and as soon as they moved to drive into the opposing lineman to blunt his initial charge, to fight pressure and then try to control the line of scrimmage, which is the basic key to winning any football game. The ends would box by crossing quickly over the line and setting up facing the offensive backfield and then hand-fight the blockers to keep all the play inside of them, thereby limiting the scope of the action and making it easier to contain.

For two weeks prior to the beginning of classes, CBC began preparations for the 1943 season with morning and afternoon workouts. These were grueling affairs in full uniforms with no water breaks under an unrelenting August sun and consisted of long sessions of calisthenics, running laps and 100-yard wind sprints, technique drills and daily scrimmages.

After the morning practice and a quick shower, the team would eat a hot lunch in the school cafeteria and then have a couple of hours off before the afternoon session. Most would leave the campus, just to get away, with no particular destination or purpose in mind. Sometimes a boy would have the family car for the day and a group would pile into it or, if not, they would hitchhike somewhere. An unsuspecting girl might receive an impromptu visit at her home by half a dozen young bucks or they might drop by the Pig 'n Whistle, the primary CBC-Central hangout at 1579 Union Avenue.

The "Pig" was a gabled, brick, stucco and batten Tudor

style building more resembling a big, comfortable home, chimney and all, than a commercial establishment. A tall sign in front depicted a pig on its hind legs tooting on a piccolo emitting neon musical notes. The building was on a big lot with parking front and back and had "curb" service, but most people parked in the large area in back and entered through the rear door. Across the back of the lot was a four-foot concrete retaining wall topped by a six-foot wooden fence.

Fortune's, at the southwest corner of Union and Belvedere, was another favorite hangout with its "Cellar" being the focal point. Access was down steep, concrete steps on the east side of the building that led to a low-ceilinged, cozy room that resembled a large wine cellar. As was the case anywhere else in town, no one was "carded" and getting a beer was no problem.

Another place that got some play from the younger set was Fortune's Jungle Garden, which mainly was a Tech High hangout. It also was on Union, closer in toward downtown, and was razed to make way for the expressway that crosses at that point. Billed as "The World's First Drive-in" restaurant, it was leveled during a time when little consideration was given to historic landmarks. A scribe who occasionally essays historical trivia for the *Dallas Morning News* recently claimed that title for a nondescript little barbecue stand that once was located somewhere in "Big D." This boast can be dismissed as

The former Pig 'n Whistle at 1579 Union Avenue. (Courtesy of Mike Mosteller)

failure to do adequate research and the knee-jerk proclivity of some Texans to make extravagant claims for their state. When Fortune's got started Dallas probably had not yet shed its swaddling clothes.

Because the Jungle Garden's main building, fronting immediately on Union, contained limited seating and, essentially, was a soda fountain, it was more of a drive-in facility. It was aptly named. Between the many mature oak trees on the large lot, owner Harold Fortune directed that a type of heavy chicken wire be connected, parallel to and about 15 to 20 feet above the ground. Over time, as vines snaked their way through the wire, driving under these canopies between the trees at night was akin to entering the depths of a rain forest. A carhop at Pig 'n Whistle called it the "Honey Hole." One signaled for service by turning on the car lights.

Starting as the Fortune-Ward drugstore in Hotel Gayoso in 1883, Fortune's occupied several sites downtown. At one time it was at 9 North Main across from Court Square. After evening concerts in the Square people would drive their buggies over to Fortune's for refreshments. The store would become so crowded that there were requests for drinks and ice cream to be brought out to the buggies. By 1906 there were enough cars in town for Harold Fortune, son of the owner, to advertise: "Honk, honk; drive up and blow twice for Fortune's auto soda service." When traffic increased to the extent that curb service in the downtown area became impractical, Harold moved out and opened up the Jungle Garden in 1920. To complement the restaurant/soda fountain, in 1929 Fortune erected a cypress-slabbed "Jungle Lodge" on the back of the lot serving sandwiches and drinks. There was seating both indoors and on a patio outside. There was also a greenhouse and stuffed animals consisting of a tiger, a couple of foxes, a monkey, a bobcat and parrots. Live birds flitted about and fish swam in a stream.

Fortune made his own ice cream that he distributed throughout the Mid-South. Being 16 percent butterfat, it was probably the richest ice cream in the country. His soda fountains turned out such things as lime cokes, cherry cokes, cherry phosphates and undoubtedly the most tantalizing ice cream soda ever made. The soda jerks made their own chocolate syrup, cooking up to 20 gallons at a time, and one of the by-products of this was a popular drink known as a chocolate coke. The secret of the ice cream soda was having the carbonated water very, very cold. To achieve this they ran it through 40 feet of copper tubing packed in ice. After combining the rich ice cream, home-made chocolate syrup and carbonated water, they topped it off with real cream, whipped by hand, and a bright-red cherry.

Other drive-ins, frequented to a lesser extent, were "The Pit," located on the north side of Poplar a couple of blocks east of Parkway, whose lot, like that of the Jungle Garden, contained massive oak trees that made it almost as dark without the overhead vines, "Alta Vista," for eating watermelon outside on picnic tables under strings of lights, and the "Cotton Boll." These latter two were situated on East Parkway North across from Overton Park and were both felled by the expressway program. The Cotton Boll also was owned by Fortune and, at one time, had a beer garden and bandstand where four or five young black men played guitars and banjos for tips. Another drive-in, at Bellevue and McLemore in South Memphis, was "Leonard's," a famous barbecue restaurant frequented by South Side High students.

The Pig 'n Whistle, designed by Memphis architect Daniel McGown, was opened in 1929 by a company operating out of Atlanta. It was acquired by Herbert Hood, Jr. in 1933 and in 1945 he sold it to Dr. Will Cramer who gave it to his wife, Louise, as a birthday present. Mrs. Cramer operated it until 1966 when a decline in business, as development moved farther east, forced its closing. From the late 1960s on it housed a variety of businesses, the last a leaded glass-making facility. The name derived from an old English pub sign, "Piggen Wassail." A "piggen" was a drinking stein and "wassail" was the Anglo-Saxon "was heal" – be in health. The day the Pig closed Herbert Hood and his wife dropped by along with a lot of old customers who stopped in to say good-bye. Head carhop James B. "Preacher" Gordon, who had worked there all but two years of the restaurant's existence, said, "To me it brings a lump, a feeling hard to explain. Probably sometime I'll be sitting across the street just looking at the place."

All of these old favorite haunts are gone. The Pig was the last to survive, being torn down in early 1994, for no apparent good reason. Two restaurants perpetuating the Pig 'n

Whistle name are located in Bartlett and on Winchester Road. Two new Leonard's are on Elvis Presley Boulevard and in East Memphis.

The Pig was the headquarters for many high-schoolers. Almost any afternoon after school a group of girls would show up to sip cokes and share a plate of french fries. They could be from Central or Tech or one of the girls' schools such as St. Mary's, St. Agnes', Lausanne or Miss Hutchinson's. Naturally, they attracted the boys. It was said that if one sat there long enough he eventually would see everyone he knew.

The main dining area with padded booths along the walls and tables and chairs in the center, was large enough to seat a good crowd but not so large as to lose its intimacy, which was enhanced by the low ceiling and a fireplace on the back wall. Near the front door sat a large Wurlitzer jukebox and, in those days, it seemed that whenever one walked in the door either "Rum and Coca Cola," by the Andrews Sisters or "Till Then," by the Mills Brothers was on the turntable.

Up against one wall was a phone booth framed with heavy polished wood containing thick glass panels, wherein one actually could sit comfortably on a padded seat and carry on a conversation in relative solitude. The ladies restroom was entered at one corner of the dining room and the men's was situated behind it on the outside of the building. So, when the call came, one went out the back door, inclement weather notwithstanding, and entered it off the parking lot. Typical of its time, it was a narrow, unheated little thing with minimum facilities and graffiti-decorated walls. Of course, Kilroy had been there – probably more than once – but the best-remembered was the admonition: "Please do not throw cigarette butts in the urinal; it makes them soggy and hard to light. "

All of these drive-ins had Negro men in white coats as inside waiters – a circumstance that added an element of decorum to the scene – and some had attended Alonzo Locke's training classes. The Pig also had as many as 18 carhops at one time. Particularly after a Friday night high school or Saturday college football game, cars would be lined up for several blocks on Union awaiting access to the parking lot. Before each shift Preacher Gordon would casually inspect all the carhops to ensure that their clothes were clean and freshly-pressed, their ties properly knotted and straight, and their shoes shined and hair cut appropriately short. During the winter they wore black jackets and pants, black caps and a white shirt with black tie. In warm weather they changed to white coats. Cuties in short skirts or tight pants on roller skates, a la California or Texas, would be totally out of place in Memphis.

It was the character and quality of the carhops and waiters that put the finishing touch on the Pig to make it the intimate, friendly and comfortable place it was. It wasn't that they were just efficient and courteous. To those who frequented the place on a regular basis, some became friends and confidantes. They are remembered fondly by many and, of those of their thinned ranks who survive, they too, after all these years, remember some of their customers by name. While Preacher, who began his 35 year tenure in 1929, kept the outside service running smoothly, the inside was the domain of Wright Redwood, known by his last name. Tom Neal, known by his first name, usually worked the dining room with Redwood in the evening. They were both somewhat portly gentlemen, probably in their late fifties, with kind and intelligent countenances, and they moved their ponderous bodies around the room with an easy grace and dignity. If not too busy, they always were ready to engage in sincere and friendly chitchat on any subject of the day and were genial with no hint of obsequiousness.

Some of those there during the war years whose personality made them unforgettable were Brown Sikes, Melvin Trojan, Turley Becton, Samuel Peace, George Scott, and the Jackson brothers, Warren, William and Vernon. Then there were those given nicknames by their colleagues: "Deacon," "Hoppy Red" (had a bad leg), "Rail" (tall and thin), "Shine" (very black), "Gypsy," Winston "Whitone" Adair (for the ointment of that name he sold on the side), Tillman "Jet" Hinds, Carl "Cadillac" Herndon ("they call me that cause I'm long and black"), and Criven "Dizzy" Dean.

Dizzy was a thin, good-humored, lovable little fellow in his mid-twenties who had an unfortunate romance with the bottle. It didn't affect his work but did impinge on his health and general well-being. He loved to talk and was alternately serious or silly. Although one couldn't be sure, one eye sometimes seemed to be looking in a direction different than the other. Dizzy seemed to chronically be short on money and his

Pig 'n Whistle carhops scan Union Avenue for their next customer. The sign next to them shows the mileage to various cities. (Courtesy of the estate of Herbert Hood)

white high school friends usually helped him along out of their meager personal supply. Sometimes with him and the other carhops or waiters it worked the other way around. If a boy drove in with his date and put in an order he couldn't pay for, he might excuse himself and go inside to surreptitiously borrow a few bucks from Redwood, Dizzy, or whomever, so he would have the money when the order was delivered. There were a few daddys who had an arrangement with the management to let their kids have whatever they needed and then be sent a bill. And Redwood ran a lot of tabs for the boys themselves.

Another who was there many years, made a lot of friends and has a storehouse of memories is T. J. "Junior" Murray, better known as "Flopsy." Originally from Blackfish Lake, Ark., his family was displaced by the great flood of 1937. His father had a weakness for gambling that nettled T. J.'s mother, and when he lost a bale of cotton in a dice game, she decided to leave him. A Memphis veterinarian was in the area tending to some livestock hurt in the flood and met Mrs. Murray, who told him of her plight. When he asked her if she would like to move to Memphis and cook for his family, she readily assented. T. J. and his mother shared a backyard servant's house in the 1400 block of Peabody that he says was "real nice." It was only a few blocks from the Pig and he began hanging around there hoping to get on as a carhop. At age 14 and five feet three inches in height, he was told he was too young and too little. Eventually, however, the carhops started letting him pick up trays from cars when the customers were finished with their repast and then would give him part of the tip. An older man, Andrew Young, whom the other carhops called "Big Flopsy," took him under his wing and helped him get started. Naturally, he became "Little Flopsy" and, later, the "little" was dropped. The nickname was a natural, because being eager to do a good job and make as much money as he could, he hopped and scooted as quick as a bunny.

Over time he became regularly employed and moved up the chain of command to dishwasher, kitchen helper, cashier and carhop, spending 15 years at the Pig. But, being small, for awhile he had trouble putting the trays on the cars. Once he dumped a whole trayfull in the lap of a prominent local businessman. But the man was not all that perturbed by the minor catastrophe and graciously told Flopsy that he realized he was small and was doing the best he could. Some idea of the extent of the mess and breakage can be appreciated when it is remembered that the Pig was still using real glasses and china for curb service at that time.

Flopsy and others on the evening shift would come to work at four p.m. on weekdays and five or six p.m. on weekends. On weeknights they closed at one a.m. and on Friday and Saturday nights at three a.m. Both Mr. Hood and Mrs. Cramer were sticklers for cleanliness and the carhops would be there for at least another hour washing trays and cleaning up the parking lot.

The early morning hours held potential peril for those who walked home from work with their hard-earned dollars. The police knew them all by sight and would cruise by, shine a spotlight and then keep going after recognizing them. Leutenant Littlejohn was the best-remembered and highest-ranking policeman in that area of town. He told the Pig employees to walk in the gutter facing whatever traffic might be about that time of night and away from any shrubs along the sidewalk that could hide a possible assailant. He frequently had a partner that drove him whose eyes seemed to stay at half mast and when he looked at someone would tilt his head back slightly. The carhops called him "Mr. Sleepy."

Next to the Pig on the corner of Willett and Union was a

two-story house that must have been inhabited by a recluse. It was always dark and was surrounded by big trees and wild hedges at least ten feet high bordering the sidewalk. Flopsy was in love at the time and he remembers walking home and looking up at the night sky through the trees and hedges and Big Jimmy Rushing's refrain from Count Basie's Drum Boogie" would come to mind: "Don't the moon look lonesome shining through the trees." The object of his affection then has now been his wife for 56 years.

In the parking lot or in the dining room the atmosphere at the Pig was informal and friendly. Flopsy recalls Mr. Crump standing next to his car and eating off the tray so he could chat with whoever happened by. He remembers the mother of Fred Smith, founder of Federal Express, driving into the back lot with her children in a 1941 black Cadillac with a white top; when the toddlers needed to go to the bathroom Flopsy would lead them by the hand and knock on the back door and one of the inside waiters would take them to the women's restroom.

And he remembers another, a well-known rich lady who shall go nameless, who would order white speckled trout to her car and insist that Flopsy be the one to carefully remove the bones before it was brought out to her. She was quite fussy about this and every aspect of the service, but her tips never exceeded 10 or 15 cents.

The old-timers at the Pig probably had the capacity to at least qualify as guest lecturers at a college-level course on public relations or psychology. Up front in the carhops' den , where they congregated when things were slow, was a thick book containing all the automobile registrations for Shelby County. If they served a customer they didn't know and who happened to be in a cranky mood, they would look him up in the book. The surprise of being called by name and the attentive courteousness he received in response to his ill temper usually improved the customer's humor and resulted in a good tip then and on subsequent visits.

Naturally, the Pig could not have survived all those 37 years unless it served good food. From a choice Kansas City sirloin steak for $1.25, to an oyster and shrimp cocktail for 35 cents to a jumbo banana split for 20 cents, it was all fresh and tasty. A wide variety of sandwiches were available, but a barbecue, of course, was the favorite. It had a distinctive flavor

like no other pork barbecue ever served anywhere. It was prepared from Boston butts, which are cuts off the shoulder and
front legs. These were cooked in gas ovens and when done the
meat could easily be pulled from the bone. The fat and gristle
were trimmed off and the meat was put in pans and a special
barbecue sauce applied. After sitting in the refrigerator for 24
hours it was taken out, chopped up, and put on the steam
table. Unfortunately, the key ingredient, the sauce recipe,
seems to have been lost to posterity. Instead of slaw, which is
customary today, the meat was topped with a couple of slices
of dill pickle. In the 1940s this aromatic gourmet's delight was
available for 40 cents. The Pig also was widely-known for its
crisp fried onion rings. As late as 1960 a whole platter of these
crunchy morsels could be had for 40 cents.

Memphis has always been known for its barbecued
pork. Dwyer's, way out east, was another favorite spot and
when Mae West, Bing Crosby and other celebrities came to
town they invariably made a pilgrimage to Johnny Mills' place
across from Hotel Peabody at Hernando and Gayoso. Johnny's
son says that Mae told his father to save his nickels and dimes
and when he got a dollar to come up and see her sometime. On
weekends when the Pig stayed open until three a.m. and the
big bands had ended their evening performances at the
Peabody and the Claridge, the musicians frequently would
drop in for a late night snack. Flopsy says he remembers one
night when Harry James showed up with a growling stomach.

One of the favorite drinks at the Pig was a "Goo." This
was a malt type drink that came out of a machine. The Pig
used milk in its mix and didn't cut it with water as is done in
today's fast-food restaurants, therefore while the Goo was
thick, it also was smooth and not icy. They came "White"
(vanilla) or "Muddy" (chocolate).

The kids showed up at the Pig attired in such as cash-
mere and angora sweaters, suede pants, sharkskin pants,
pedal pushers, wool skirts, cordovan wing tips, white bucks,
saddle oxfords with argyle or lacy little white socks, and but-
ton-down oxford cloth shirts with a knit tie knotted in a double
Windsor the size of Jack Dempsey's fist.

The carhops and waiters did so well with their tips
(George Scott built and paid for his house while there) that
they all dressed like fashion plates on their time off. Flopsy

says after getting up in the morning and taking a bath he would put on a suit and ride a cab for 35 cents from Dixie Homes, a public housing project, to Beale Street. He would mess around until 11 a.m. and then go back home to eat a bite and take a nap. He would then put on a different suit and head back down to Beale until time to go to work when he would dress in yet a third suit for the day.

There were 13 tailor shops on Beale or around the corner on Main that catered to a black and white clientele. Suits went from 25 to 45 dollars and all the tailors knew the waiters and carhops around town by name. Dino Paccasassi the "King of Drapes," Eggelston the Tailor, Lansky Brothers, Harry Kabakoff, King the Tailor, Louis Lettes and H. Moskovitz all had Flopsy's sizes on record. They would have employees, dressed to the nines out in front of the stores, strutting around modeling their latest offerings

One might see Flopsy across the street and holler, "Hey T. J. (or "Junior"), I've got some new material in."

"What kind is it?"

"It's a hickory stripe!"

"Make me up one; I'll be in Monday and pick it up."

Allen Gary had been a manager of the Pig in its infant days, and then a partner. In 1941 he and George Early, another former partner, converted the old John Harris horse stable near Bellevue and Union into a restaurant called "The Stable." When they had a special event there requiring extra help that coincided with a slow night at the Pig, with Preacher's blessing, Flopsy would help serve the dinner and make good money. At one of these special parties one night a man was there from Arkansas with a hat Flopsy greatly admired. When he commented on it, the man told him to try it on and then asked, "How does it fit?" "Fine, fine, it fits perfect," replied Flopsy. The man told him, "Good, you can have it." When Flopsy looked inside at the band, he was astonished. It was a Cavanaugh 50, a brand whose prices started at $50. From then on Flopsy bought nothing but Dobbs and Cavanaugh 50 hats from Julius Lewis, an upscale men's and ladies' store on Main next to Hotel Gayoso.

As previously mentioned, the zoot suit originated on Beale and that was the style that Flopsy and the other younger fellows preferred, with a coat "as long as a Baptist preacher's."

To round out his ensemble, he bought Florsheim "knob" shoes that were so long "I would almost need a chauffeur to turn a corner."

When the CBC football boys stopped by the Pig after their morning practice in the hopes of encountering some girls, they usually were disappointed. School had not yet started and the girls were off doing whatever it was they did during the summer. So the boys would sit in the booths and shoot the breeze, spend about a dollar between them, and then head back to school as their respite expired. If there wasn't a car amongst the lot of them, they would be forced to hitchhike. A favorite ploy was to operate from a corner with ample vegetation, and while two would stand on the curb with their thumbs out, four or five more would hide behind trees and bushes and come with a rush when an unsuspecting motorist stopped with a four-door car.

Through the years the Pig became steeped in warm romanticism as couples remembered it as the site of a first date with a particular person, marriage proposals and recognition of wedding anniversaries. Like old walls layered with multiple coats of paint or rolls of wallpaper, it was saturated and sheathed with the overlapping memories of gaiety and good cheer by patrons from several generations. But the yin of soft and dreamy moments and easy-going conviviality was balanced by the yang of other events providing tension and excitement, for young men fueled by overheated libidos and ego and the innate urge to express what they deemed to be an exercise of manhood invariably would produce conflict. Single fights and an occasional brawl of sizable proportions were not unknown at the Pig.

One February night in 1943 six Central football lettermen went to the Memphis Prep League boxing matches at the YMCA on Madison. They were Clarence Cotton, Gayden Drew, Jack Hall, Robert Koen, Bernie Lewis and Louis "Hot" Napier. In order to make the train for boot camp on time, the previous December Russell Swink and Maurice Chism had to leave the Central High football banquet before its conclusion and Drew had driven them to the station. So with Swink off in the Marine Corps, these six were probably the toughest guys at Central. Lewis had been a four-sport letterman and named best all-around athlete in 1941-42; he also had been an honor student and at the moment was home on leave from the Merchant Marine. That spring Drew would win the West Tennessee championships in the high hurdles, high jump, shot put and discus. Muscular Jack Hall had been the starting fullback that previous fall and had a wonderful singing voice that he occasionally would unlimber at parties; he was particularly good on "Night and Day." He also thought he was a boxer, an idea he should have dispelled. The others were good football players and pretty tough dudes. Hall was in the ring that night and Gayden Drew served as his second. Jack had the misfortune to draw Rabbit Cook, of South Side High, one of the better amateur boxers around town. The beating was so bad that Gayden tried to talk Jack into letting him throw in the towel after each of the first two rounds, but Jack refused and stuck it out for all three.

Another Central boy, Warren Leffler, was fighting Freddie Hamlett from Humes, who had won the lightweight championship the year before. Wanting to make things more interesting, Gayden scuffled up ten or fifteen dollars from among his buddies to bet on Leffler and got a like bet on Hamlett from a nearby group from Humes with Central halfback A. G. "Aggie" Wellons holding the money. The first round was fairly even, but Leffler's first punch in the second round knocked Hamlett out.

After the fights the Central boys went out to the Cellar at Fortune's and got a large table near the door. It was fairly warm for a winter night, but there was a little bite in the air. Not long after they took their seats the door opened and a few boys from Humes stepped tentatively into the room; behind them were others, maybe 12 to 15 in all, their mass holding open the door. Feeling a cold breeze on the back of his neck, Lewis turned around and ordered them to close the door and wondered aloud if they might possibly have been raised in a barn. The Humes boys stiffened as if hit across their faces with wet dish rags and with somewhat surprised looks went back out the door. It was apparent they were not happy about the loss of the bet on the fight and also didn't like the idea of the Central boys using their money with which to refresh themselves. But it ran a little deeper than that. There was a latent antagonism toward Central on the part of many students at several of the other high schools in town. It was a class thing wherein, probably with little or no justification, they felt that Central people were "stuck up" and considered themselves better than they were.

A little later the Central boys moved a couple of blocks down Union Avenue to the Pig. They were standing around in the back parking lot when they noticed people peering at them from around the corner of the building. The Humes bunch had called down to Leonard's Drive-in and talked to some South Side High football players and were awaiting these reinforcements before unleashing their anger and moving into action. In the meantime some of them had gripped rolls of dimes in their palms and taped up their hands.

When the South Side boys arrived the antagonists' ranks now numbered about 30. A big tackle, his body language pregnant with menace but also exuding confidence and nonchalance, ambled up to the outnumbered six. Although everyone present except Gayden Drew had on a Central letter jacket, with challenge in his voice he inanely demanded to know: "Are you guys from Central?" Feeling it was obvious no verbal response was necessary, Gayden knocked him sprawling. He immediately was beset by several guys who knocked him down, and as they kicked him he could see sparks flying as the steel taps on their shoes scraped the rough pavement.

When the Humes and South Side boys began assembling in front of the building, it was apparent to the carhops that all these unfamiliar and glowering faces hadn't been drawn to the Pig to partake of a barbecue and a goo. The bricks making up the chimney on the back of the building were staggered in such fashion that it was almost like walking up steps for the carhops to climb up on the roof and, resembling a row of gargoyles, they hunkered down and perched there to observe the action. As the crowd gathered the manager was alerted and he called the police, but before the three squad cars arrived there were at least five minutes of frenzied fisticuffs.

Lewis ended up under a car and someone else was knocked into and scattered the garbage cans. Hot Napier said he just kept swinging at whoever was available and had a lot of fun that night. As evidence of this, Slick Williams said Napier's hands were as big as hamhocks at school the next day. The arrival of the police brought an immediate end to the festivities and people scattered in whatever direction they thought offered the best avenue of escape. Some scaled the retaining wall and fence in the back, some sprinted through the adjacent lot behind the filling station next door and others ran toward the front around the side of the building. As far as is known, they all got away. The cops probably viewed it all as a big joke, anyway.

Oddly enough, it was just before this time that Gayden and Jack Hall had become good friends with Bevo Covington, who had been an outstanding athlete at Humes, highly respected at the school for his football and fighting ability. He arrived on the scene at the Pig about the same time as the police and helped to smooth things over. For some reason Bevo had dropped out of Humes after the previous semester and was attending a small private school located a few blocks from Central High. He knew a few people at Central and after the school day would stop by on his way home. He met Gayden and Jack and they started running around together.

Dateless one evening, they made plans to spend the night at Bevo's house and stopped by Rex Billiards for a few

Gayden Drew clears the high hurdle in 1943. (Courtesy of Gayden Drew)

games of snooker. Rex's was located in the basement below the Warner Theater, was entered from an alley just off Main Street and was a favorite Humes hangout. As soon as they opened the door and started down the steps the cacophonous sounds of balls clicking together, whoops and hollers and cries for "rack" assaulted their ears. But as Bevo and his new friends (they attired in their Central letter jackets) stood prominently on the wide shelf-like bottom step surveying the room, the decibels diminished gradually as their presence was noted: talk ceased, pool cues were laid upon tables with studied precision and cigarettes were stubbed out with dispassionate deliberateness until an ominous and stifling stillness pervaded the room; a mute and motionless tableau with narrowing eyes, almost comical in its incongruence, stared blankly at the trio with menace and, because of Bevo's presence, a touch of bewilderment; the only discernible movement was a slight drift of the clouds of tobacco smoke hanging lazily over the tables. Bevo knew most of the pool players and, as the atmosphere became more threatening, he was the first to break the silence in an effort to ameliorate the situation. Taking each of his two pals by an arm, he stepped into the room and announced loudly, "I want everybody to meet my good friends Gayden Drew and Jack Hall," and proceeded to introduce them all around. Only someone like Bevo, with a reputation for being a tough guy yet commanding respect for being a nice guy, could have pulled it off.

The Pig 'n Whistle, Fortune's and the other aforementioned hangouts fell within the primary geographic confines of what was known as "The Frog Pond." Generally, it took in the picture shows and hotels with their dance bands downtown, went east out Union Avenue to Parkway to include the Jungle Garden, the Pig and Fortune's, and then looped north encapsulating The Pit, Alta Vista and The Cotton Boll. An evening on the town was called "froggin'" – hopping from one place to another. However, the Frog Pond's boundaries were elastic on demand and could be extended, for example, to include the Casino ballroom at the Fairgrounds and, for outings, the popular picnic area at Ellendale, east of town, Horseshoe Lake across the river in Arkansas or the lodge at Shelby Forest State Park north of town. Froggin' was mainly a nighttime activity, but daytime fun in the summer was offered by swimming pools at Maywood, just south of the Mississippi line, Clearpool and Rainbow out Lamar Avenue and East End on Madison Avenue; the latter two also had skating rinks.

Basically, froggin' was a somewhat unplanned and aimless venture, like a pinball bouncing from light to light, and the types of places visited related to the number and diversity of pictures of famous Americans reposing in one's wallet. As an example, one Saturday night in the fall of 1943 three high school couples embarked on an evening of merriment with the boys, at least, having the foreknowledge that, due to a paucity of funds, an exercise of imagination would be a strong factor in determining the evening's success.

The first frog jump landed at Friedel's, formerly an old, high-ceilinged house, just east of town, that had been converted to a restaurant. If one did not desire to eat, as was the case in this instance, then there was a large room with settings of deep couches and coffee tables for chit-chatting and drinking. Although in those days a teenager could sometimes be served a mixed drink, after one round of cheap cokes they took off with no particular destination in mind. One of the boys carried a saxophone around with him all night and, as he had upon their arrival, signaled their departure and startled the other patrons by playing the first bar of "Memphis Blues."

The next adventure was a cruise down Beale Street where, as they were stopped for a red light at Second Street, the saxophonist spontaneously jumped from the car amidst the skylarking throng on the sidewalk and cut loose with several bars of "Beale Street Blues" and threw in a couple from "Memphis Blues." As he returned to the car several voices shouted "Hey man, come back and play some more." But the silly six were off to the Skyway supper club on the top floor of Hotel Peabody, where a name band was playing.

With the saxophone still in tow, and not having proper attire, much less the cover charge for admittance, they stood a little self-consciously outside the Skyway's entrance and lis-

216

1943 Central High School Football Squad

Bottom Row (left to right)- Joe Highfill, Louis Daltroff, Ray Brown, Maurice Keathley, Capt. Elwyn Rowan, Co-Capt. Billy Williams, Billy Buckles, Jim Laney, Malcolm Baker.

Second Row (Left to right)- Louie Hansberger, Bill Roberds, Jack Callicott, Bobby Ladd, Vance Cartwright, Bobo Meriweather, Billy Bolton, Billy Trickett, Joe Powell, Frank Halford, John MacIntosh.

Third Row (left to right)- Mgr. Ira Whitley, Robert Jeffrey, Paul Barton, Buddy Malmo, Henry Bateman, Emil Golden, Harley Jeffery, Louis Jones, Ralph Baker, Vince Skillman, Herbey Abraham, John Trent, Mgr. Jerry Hanover.

Fourth Row (left - right)- Don Hollowell, Ted Hay, Babe Welch, Ralph Beard, Bobby Newton, Buddy Halle, Joe Crim, Minor Tate, George Sneed, Billy Finney, Eugene Jones.

(Courtesy of Don Hollowell)

tened to two songs before leaving. The last stop was at a packed and noisy Pig 'n Whistle, for a homeward-bound snack, where they burst through the back door with sax wailing, engaged in raucous repartee with familiar faces in the affable assemblage as they munched, and then departed with the "Memphis Blues" echoing stridently throughout the neighborhood.

Each year, just prior to fall practice, it was customary for the Central football team to attend an out-of-town camp for a week to ten days. In 1942 the team had gone to Shiloh National Military Park, a little over 100 miles from Memphis. In 1943 the camp was in the Ozark Mountains at the village of Hardy, Ark., a summer retreat that had been a favorite of Memphians for many years.

The emphasis of these camps was conditioning. Probably of more importance, however, was the influence of the isolated environment which encouraged camaraderie and cohesion and provided the atmosphere for the emergence of additional leaders necessary for a successful team. The seniors were experiencing their third coach in as many years and they had to become familiar with a little different system and what the new coach expected of them.

Practices were held in a pasture, but it first was necessary to clear it of rocks and boulders, so part of the conditioning process involved picking these up and running with them until they all were off on the side of the field. After a couple of days the field had been cleared and practice began with full pads, morning and afternoon. A swim in the adjoining Spring River completed the day.

Bob Porter, who had been head coach in 1941 when the current seniors were in the tenth grade, had been a big influence on them. He had provided the basis for their development into good football players by stressing fundamentals and instilling those attributes of character, such as perseverance and unselfishness, essential for effective teamwork. He had known that these tenth-graders had excellent potential and, with affection, began calling them "my little nubbins," a term coined by assistant coach Don Owens. To a large extent, the 1943 Central team played in the shadow of Bob Porter. The boys had agreed among themselves that no one would smoke or drink during the season. When a certain boy, in particular, was lackadaisical about this stricture, the others, recognizing his presence could cause disunity, made his life so miserable during practice that he eventually turned in his uniform, but for awhile longer he carried his bruises with him.

Under Porter Central players learned the single wing. Under Beopple in 1942 they ran the short punt formation and scrimmaged four days each week. In 1943 Glass brought in some T-formation plays. The end result was they ran plays from all three of these systems as well as some double wing and a spread thrown in for good measure. However, the emphasis was on the single wing and the "T."

Co-captains Elwyn "Rip" Rowan, at fullback, and William "Slick" Williams, at right halfback, led the Warriors into their first game with Treadwell at Crump Stadium on Friday night, September 17. Treadwell was in a rebuilding mode with an entirely new line. On the other hand, Central fielded a seasoned, talented team. Except for Slick, out with a knee injury sustained in practice, they were at full strength. Jack Callicott started in Slick's place.

The game was no contest. Central scored six touchdowns and was threatening to score another at the end of the game when their fumble was covered by the Eagles at the goal line. All attempts at extra points were failures: two were blocked, two kicks were missed, and both a run and a pass had failed. The final score was 36 to 0 as Treadwell never threatened to score.

Central's first tally was set up when Bill Wright tossed a flat pass to Rip Rowan at the Eagle 28, which he carried down to the eight. Three plays later Rowan crashed over from the three. The next touchdown came when Rowan scored from the one after a 35-yard drive was set up by a punt return of 24 yards by Wright. Another short drive set up a three-yard run for a score by quarterback Louis "Butch" Daltroff, which made the score 18 to 0 at the half.

Taking the second-half kickoff, the Warriors drove to the Treadwell 35-yard line. From the single wing, tailback Bill

1943 Christian Brothers High School Football Squad

Top Row (left to right)- John Nash, Jimmy Foley, David Steffan, Jack Gibson, Bob Burke, John Schaffler, Sam Angier, Joe Gold, Basil Crone, George Bland, Ralph Giles, Ed Glasgens, Coach Hatley.

Middle Row (left to right)- John Ross, John Walt, Louis Sampson, Bill Dulweber, Gene Berretta, Julius Smith, Bertie Huebner, Arvin James, Leon Shahun, Al Guthrie, Merrick Coles.

Bottom Row (left to right)- George Whitehead, Joe Smith, Jim Doyle, John Fox, Al Huebner, Tommy Mulroy, Percy Roberts, Mark Follis, Bill Burke, Harry Costello, Phil Turner.

(Not Shown)- Managers: Tony Evangelisti, Don Crone.

Wright then hit end Ray Brown on a post pattern for the game's fourth touchdown. The next score also came in the third quarter when Rowan went around right end for 45 yards and into the end zone standing up. Central scored the final tally early in the fourth quarter when Wright ran the ball in from the 10-yard line.

Although it was apparent Treadwell was one of the weaker teams in the league, the decisiveness of Central's victory suggested that it had to be the favorite to win the Prep League championship. The game marked the first appearance in a green and gold uniform of sophomore reserve tailback Vance Cartwright – all 122 pounds of him. When he tucked a football under his arm he was as quick as a water bug. He also was quick and tough in the boxing ring when he won the novice and, the next year, the open Mid-South bantamweight title in the Golden Gloves. It was almost impossible to find a pair of hip pads small enough to stay on his slight frame; besides, they were heavy and cumbersome, so he never wore them. The thick plastic thigh pads that other players slipped into sleeves in their pants slowed him down, so, in lieu of them, he would insert a couple of Kotex into each pants leg.

Christian Brothers opened its season against the Whitehaven Tigers at Fairgrounds Stadium Wednesday, September 22. The Tigers already had a game under their belt, having tied Catholic High 7 to 7 the week before. A county school, that had been Whitehaven's first game as a new member of the Memphis Prep League. Fearing Whitehaven's passing attack, featuring halfback Red England, the Brothers had worked hard on pass defense in their practices.

The game was scoreless in the first quarter. To get his team out of holes, England quick-kicked on two occasions sending the ball over the CBC safety man's head and pinning the Brothers back in their end of the field. Early in the second quarter the Tigers scored the first touchdown of the game. With the ball on Whitehaven's 37-yard line England hit halfback Dike Sandridge with a pass at midfield. Dike juked a defender off his feet and then turned on the speed to sprint the rest of the way for the score. Eschewing a place kick for the extra point, fullback Clarence White's plunge was stopped short leaving the Tigers ahead 6 to 0.

After the ensuing kickoff Whitehaven held CBC for three downs. Harry Costello punted to England at the Tiger 25 and he returned it to the 32. Then a bad snap from center went past England and Phil Turner recovered for CBC on the 16. Three plays later Turner carried it in for a touchdown. Costello's kick for the point after was wide and at the half both teams had six points.

CBC, while scoring twice, kept the Whitehaven offense in check throughout the second half. England's passing was Whitehaven's primary offense as he completed eight of 16 passes during the game. "Sleepy" John Ross, substitute tailback for the Brothers, came off the bench in the second half and, as sportswriter Henry Reynolds described him, "ran like Beattie Feathers," the great Tennessee back of the early 1930s. Carrying only nine times the junior racked up 95 yards and scored CBC's second touchdown from eight yards out. Again, reeling off gain after gain, Ross carried the ball to the Tigers' seven-yard line, at which point he left the game with a leg injury. Phil Turner hit over tackle to the three and then carried the ball in for the final touchdown. Costello made one of two extra point tries in the second half and the Brothers came away with a hard-fought 19 to 6 win.

Central took to the rails for its next game and rode the train to Louisville, Ken. for a meeting with du Pont Manual High on September 25. Arriving on Friday they had time for a practice session and then settled in at the venerable old Seelbach Hotel. During a taxi ride from the train station the cab driver asked Slick and some others why they were in town. When he was told the purpose of their visit he said, "You might as well get back on the train and go on back to Memphis, those guys are tough, there's no way you can beat them." When Central worked out that afternoon several hundred Manual students lined the field and heckled the Warriors, telling them how bad they would get beat the next day. Manual, long a power in the upper South and Midwest, was coming off an impressive win over Bowling Green the week before.

Manual had a big line. John Pope Wilson, who played tackle, says it averaged 235 pounds per man and that when he suited up for Central he pushed the scales up to 270. While there might be some hyperbole involved in his statements, Manual's line was bigger than Central's. One end, Bill Guthermuth, was six four and weighed 210; the other end was six two and one-half and correspondingly filled out. It was common for high school teams in that era, but more particularly in the 1920s and 1930s, to play teams in other parts of the country. Manual played Miami Central of Miami, Flor., as did the Jackson, Tenn. Golden Bears, and beat perennial power Erie, Penn. 13 to 12. When Harry Gilmer, the great University of Alabama and Washington Redskins back, went to Louisville with his Birmingham high school team in 1943, he beat Manual with a 60 yard touchdown pass for a 7 to 6 win.

Game day was cloudy and blustery and the wind had an effect on the outcome of the game, which was largely a defensive struggle. Central had only eight first downs and 102 yards of total offense, while Manual managed only three first downs and 52 net yards. Manual did not penetrate the Warriors' 35-yard line until a short pass on the last play of the game put the ball on the 29.

In the second quarter a 33-yard pass from Daltroff to

Bill Wright bangs into the endzone against Louisville Manual for the only score of the game. (Courtesy of Bill Buckles)

Trent, followed by a 15-yard completion from Butch to Rowan, put the ball on Manual's four-yard line, but the hosts' big line stiffened and held and took over on downs. But they could not move the ball and Pat McNeil, punting into a brisk wind, booted it out on his 13. Daltroff then hit Rowan with a ten-yard pass and on the next play Bill Wright cut over right tackle for the score. Rowan kicked the extra point for a 7 to 0 lead, which ended all scoring for the day.

Central threatened two other times but couldn't produce any points. Just before the half they intercepted a pass and then moved downfield to a first down on the Manual 23, but four consecutive passes were unsuccessful. In the third quarter the Warriors recovered a fumbled punt on the Manual 29 and then drove to the 10 where they lost the ball on downs. In the same quarter Manual's gritty little 145-pound fullback, Don Marmillot, went out to block on Central's big, rangy end John Trent. As he tried to throw a cross body block on him, Trent, reacting instinctively, brought his knee up and flattened Marmillot's nose. Don says he has had trouble with it ever since.

One peculiar thing about the game was the ball that was furnished by Manual. Several players commented that it seemed to be slightly oversized and soft which, ordinarily, would make it more difficult to throw. Could this have been a ploy for Manual to stack the defense to contain the run and force Central to pass on a windy day? Reputedly, however, the officials were competent and fair.

The riverboat *Island Queen* arrived on September 30 and tied up at the foot of Monroe for a 12-day stay. It offered "Moonlight Dance Excursions" with music by Clyde Trask and his orchestra, with advance tickets for 75 cents or $1.00 "at the gate."

Autumn meant not only football games but plenty of social activity on the weekends, as well. Girls always liked autumn; it was their favorite season. When they were little kids they would drape themselves with their mother's or big sister's clothes and preen and primp in front of the mirror. The cooler weather in the autumn provided the opportunity for the selection of a greater variety of types of clothes and more colors corresponding with nature's bounteous seasonal hues. Girls could then put together an ensemble that really made them feel good about themselves.

Parties were diverse and plentiful: afternoon outings and wiener roasts at Ellendale that lasted into the evening; backward dances (where the girls asked the boys to the dance and then did the "cutting in") at Peabody Community Center or the Casino Ballroom; progressive dinner parties (each course at a different house), scavenger hunts, hay rides, costume parties, etc.

Memphis probably was one of the few cities (possibly the only one) with extensive high school sororities, fraternities and related social clubs. They all did a modicum of charitable work but, of course, their main focus was fellowship and fun. The girls had such as Beta Delta, Chi Sigma, Delta Alpha Delta, Delta Beta Sigma, Delta Sigma Delta, Phi Sigma, Sigma, Sigma Kappa Sigma, Tau Delta Sigma, Zeta Beta Theta, We Moderns, Decem, Sunev (Venus spelled backwards), and La Jeunesse (Webster: gilded youth). Many belonged to a Greek letter sorority and also one of the clubs. The boys had Delta Phi Kappa, Delta Phi Omega, Phi Kappa, Sigma Phi Omega, Tau Delta Phi, Tau Delta Tau and Theta Kappa Omega. Most had their big Christmas and spring formal dances and lesser galas throughout the year.

For its next opponent, CBC took on Catholic High for the city parochial championship. CBC had probably the smallest team in the Prep League and before the season started it was not considered to be a serious contender for the title, but on this night against Catholic it demonstrated what Ralph

Hatley and Leo Davis had wrought: a quick, savvy, hard-hitting bunch of guys with a lot of spirit and grit who could stay on the field with any team, regardless of size. The Brothers had emerged as a serious contender for the loop championship. Years later Hatley would say that this team gave more effort than any he ever coached and that, in actuality, it played over its head the entire season.

CBC kicked off to start the game and after three plays Catholic had been stopped cold and found itself in a punting situation. Phil Turner broke through from linebacker and blocked Bill Garibaldi's punt and the Brothers recovered on the 26-yard line. On the first play tailback George "Bubba" Whitehead, behind precision blocking, carried the ball in for a touchdown. Costello missed the extra point kick leaving the score 6 to 0.

After the kickoff CBC's Purple Wave again held and Catholic went into punt formation on their 27. Disaster again struck the Terriers. The center fired the ball over Garibaldi's head all the way into the end zone. Bill ran back and retrieved the ball and tried to run it out, but guard Al Huebner tackled him for a safety making the score 8 to 0. Before the first quarter ended CBC scored again. After moving the ball to the Terriers' 38-yard line, quarterback and captain Tommy Mulroy slipped through the line on a sneak and sped through Catholic's confused secondary all the way for a score. This time Costello tried to pass for the extra point but, it too, failed.

Catholic made its only serious threat of the night in the second quarter. With the ball on his own 40-yard line, quarterback Tony Federico hurled a long aerial that was caught by Terrier captain Bill Jeter on the Brothers' seven yard line. Then misfortune again plagued Catholic. After a five-yard penalty for offsides, wingback Cooper was thrown for consecutive five yard losses by the alert Purple Wave line. A pass failed and then one from tailback Milton Lockridge to Cooper was complete, but only to the 14-yard line on fourth down.

Harry Costello was the leading ground gainer in the game, but early in the third quarter backup tailback John Ross, who had run so well against Whitehaven the week before, showed he could also pass. He hit wingback Costello with a 34-yard strike at the Catholic five-yard line, and Harry pranced on into the end zone. This time Costello's kick was good and the score was 21-0. Later in the third quarter, with the ball on the Wave 37-yard line, Costello took a reverse and started around his left side. Bill Jeter, Catholic's fine end, hit him in the backfield but couldn't wrap him up. Off balance, Costello spun completely around and stumbled for five yards before regaining his footing and straightening up; he then faked out two would-be tacklers and had clear sailing for a brilliant 63-yard touchdown run. His kick for the point after again was good for a 28 to 0 lead.

In the fourth quarter neither team scored and Coach Hatley cleared the bench, but even against the reserves the Terriers could get no closer to scoring than the CBC 20-yard line.

Ralph Hatley tells a story about Harry Costello on an occasion when CBC played another Catholic High team. The year before, when Harry was only a sophomore, the Brothers had traveled to Arkansas to play Little Rock Catholic High. Every player was responsible for ensuring that he arrived at a game with his equipment. In the stadium dressing room shortly before game time Harry approached Hatley and told him he somehow had neglected to pack his football shoes. Beside himself, Hatley went outside and spotted a group of dented up old garbage cans near the dressing room. After a few minutes of rummaging through them, miraculously, he dug out a pair of football shoes. Naturally, they didn't look like then had just come out of the box from the Wilson factory nice and shiny black and leathery smelling: the cleats were almost all worn down, the arches were as flexible as day old carrot sticks, the

John "Sleepy" Ross, Harry Costello, and Terry Tracy. Note the keychains on Costello (gold football attached) and Tracy, which were popular items at the time. (Courtesy of John Fox)

strings had been broken and re-tied in several places and they were one big scuff. When they swallowed little Harry's size six feet it was apparent some adjustment would be necessary. Fortunately, Coach Hatley had access to plenty of tape and Harry's feet soon resembled those of Billy "White Shoes" Johnson. Possibly attempting to atone for his oversight, on these uncertain clodhoppers Harry then went out that evening and proceeded to make four long runs for touchdowns and having a fifth called back on a penalty. This had been an extreme example of adherence to the government's wartime recommendation for everything: "Use It Up/Wear It Out/ Make It Do/Or Do Without." It's a pity those beat-up bluchers weren't saved for eventual deposit in a CBC trophy case.

Six days after playing in Louisville, Central tangled with the tough Whitehaven Tigers. The Tigers gave a good account of themselves and at the end of the first half Central led only 7 to 0.

The Warriors threatened early by driving down to the Whitehaven 12-yard line, but Rip Rowan fumbled and the Tigers recovered. After being held on downs in their end of the field, Whitehaven got off a nice punt upfield, but in two plays the Warriors were back on the Whitehaven 20. Rowan again fumbled and Central lost the ball when Charles White recovered at the 23.

Early in the second quarter Central took over at its 46 after a Whitehaven punt. Wright completed a pass to Rowan at the Tiger 39 and on the next play Bill ran 27 yards to the 12. Bill picked up another nine yards and then Rowan took it in for the score. Rip's kick was good for a 7 to 0 lead.

Due to the sterling play of linebacker Jerry Lunceford, end Charles White, guard Neal DeLong and tackle Lawrence Rice, Rowan, obviously being keyed on, was thrown for losses on a number of occasions. But Ripper could be bottled up for only so long, In the third quarter Central recovered a Whitehaven fumble on the Warrior 43 and, after Trent had lost nine yards on an end around, Rowan scampered 66 yards for

Versatile Central tailback Bill Wright.
(Courtesy of Bill Buckles)

Central's second touchdown. He then kicked the point for a 14 to 0 lead.

As the fourth quarter began the Warriors had the ball on their 37. They then proceeded to drive 63 yards with Judd Williford carrying the ball in for the final six yards. Rowan's attempt for the extra point was low. That ended the scoring with Central ahead 20 to 0.

Late in the game Whitehaven recovered a Central fumble on the latter's 32-yard line. Tiger captain Red England carried to the 27 but, on the next play, Whitehaven fumbled the ball back to Central ending their best scoring opportunity of the evening.

Singled out for excellent defensive play in behalf of Central were Billy Buckles, John Trent and Malcolm Baker. The Warriors suffered a big loss when John "Sonny" Glasgow went out with a broken leg on the fourth play of the game. Glasgow, with the potential to be an all-state player, was lost for the season. Harley Jeffery, only a tenth grader, moved into his slot and did an excellent job.

With two wins to their credit and seemingly gathering strength as the season progressed, Christian Brothers' next opponent was Messick High. CBC again was facing a team that outweighed it. The Messick Panthers had lost their first game to defending Prep League champion South Side by 12 to 6 and had rallied and scored twice in the final four minutes of their game with Catholic to beat the Terriers 13 to 7. This game was considered a tossup, but the Brothers' domination of the Panthers illustrated the fallacy of that prediction.

Messick had several outstanding players in quarterback Billy Goodwin, tackle Allen Hover, end Jeff Adams, guard Red Watkins and team captain Douglas Krell, fullback and linebacker.

With only three minutes having elapsed in the first quarter, Sleepy John Ross carried the ball into the end zone from the four-yard line. Costello kicked the point after and the Purple Wave led 7 to 0. In the second quarter Leon Shahun, subbing for Bill Burke at left end, took a handoff on a reverse from Costello and went around right end untouched 22 yards for the second touchdown. Costello's extra point try hit the crossbar and bounced back and CBC led 13 to 0. Later, the Brothers drove from the Panthers' 49 yard line to the one, but Ross' plunge for the touchdown was stopped short.

Messick came out in the second half full of fight and did its best to make it a close game, holding CBC scoreless in the third quarter. The Brothers put on a drive that again carried to the one but, as before, the Panthers' big line reared up and kept CBC out of the end zone. When Messick couldn't advance the ball, long punts by Krell got them out of holes on both occasions.

Another punt by Krell was fielded by Costello on his own 38-yard line. He shook off two potential tacklers, sidestepped two others and returned the ball 62 yards for an apparent touchdown, however the play was called back for a clipping penalty. In the third quarter Messick put on a drive of its own. After moving the ball to CBC's 20-yard line Billy Goodwin tried to hit end Jeff Adams with a pass near the goal line, but Tommy Mulroy diagnosed the play and intercepted the ball at the five and returned it to the 19.

Early in the fourth quarter CBC tailback George "Bubba" Whitehead cut back over the right side of his line,

All-State Al Huebner and Percy Roberts, CBC's devastating guard duo.

broke a couple of tackles and raced 45 yards to cross the goal line standing up. However, it was called back due to a penalty. Then Whitehead and Costello alternated in carrying the ball and moved it to Messick's three-yard line. The Panther defense again stiffened, but on fourth down fullback Phil Turner plunged into the end zone. Costello's point-after was good and the 20 to 0 lead stood up for the remainder of the game.

CBC guard and co-captain Al Huebner came out of the game in the third quarter after re-injuring an eye originally hurt against Whitehaven. He had played a sterling game on defense and the crushing blocks he and fellow guard Percy Roberts had laid on Messick's fine fullback and linebacker, 6'2," 195 pound Doug Krell throughout the game, forced the latter to the sideline in the third; he did, however, return for a few plays in the fourth quarter.

While the boys of CBC and Central were engaged in their gridiron wars, the girls at Central, as well as girls from the other public and private schools in town, were busy with their own extra-curricular activities. Many of the boys would soon be entering military service, but the girls also were doing their part in behalf of the war effort. They visited and entertained patients at the Army's Kennedy General Hospital and the Navy's hospital at Millington; they performed duties as Pink Ladies at other hospitals in town; and some were in an organization called the Motor Corps wherein they drove pilots, passing through town, back and forth between downtown hotels and the Fourth Ferrying Command and sometimes even drove prisoners of war to Kennedy Hospital for medical treatment. One of the training requirements for the Motor Corps was learning how to change a tire on an ambulance. At Central, Jane Bratton had the imposing title of Commissioner of War Activities. Presumably under her direction, with a goal of $10,000, $11,080.35 was raised the first semester for the purchase of War Bonds. The girls made hundreds of small stuffed animals to send to children in bomb-ravaged England; stressing originality and quality of work, it was put on a competitive basis. Arlene Coleman came in first with her six-animal collection. Others doing "best" work were awarded 25-cent War Bond stamps. But the girls did other things, too, not related to the war effort, like sneaking down to forbidden Beale Street to the "Home of the Blues" record shop searching for bluesy platters not available in other record shops.

On Friday night, October 8 Central played Humes in a league game at Crump Stadium that drew 7,500 fans. In their first game Humes had defeated the Jackson, Tenn. Golden Bears 7 to 6, but in their next outing they pulled a big upset in running over defending Prep League champion South Side by a score of 31 to 14.

Due to a sprained ankle, Rip Rowan was slated to play little, if at all, and the team physician had benched halfback Bill Wright due to "water on the knee." But when the ball was kicked off both were on the field, although Rip limped noticeably. Slick Williams had recovered sufficiently from his preseason knee injury to step back into his starting right halfback slot, but he would wear a brace on the knee the rest of the year. On the line, Joe Highfill was moved from his guard position to tackle to fill in for the injured Sonny Glasgow and smallish Joe

Powell was promoted to the first string and put in Highfill's old slot.

Central wasted no time getting on the board by scoring their first touchdown within the first five minutes of the game and adding another three minutes later. After taking over on their 30, Slick and Rip lost four yards on respective carries. Then Daltroff tossed a short pass to end Ray Brown who lateraled to Rowan at the 40; the defensive halfback was sucked in to commit on Brown and Rip had an alley down the sideline 60 yards all the way to the goal. Rowan's extra point kick was good for a 7 to 0 lead. Then Tilford Flowers fumbled Buckles' kickoff and Bill Wright recovered at the Humes 25. Seven plays later Wright scored from the one and Rowan kicked the point.

Humes held the Warriors scoreless for the remainder of the half and in the second quarter made their only scoring threat of the game. After downing Wright's punt at the Central 46 Nick Speros made a first down at the 36. Jerry Crook picked up two yards and then Speros fired a pass to Cliff Milton who lateraled to Mike Strauss who was downed on the 22 with another first down. The Warriors stopped the Tigers as that point and a field goal attempt by Don Kaurez was unsuccessful.

Early in the third quarter Central recovered a Humes fumble on the Tigers' 27 and scored in three plays. Butch Daltroff tossed a short pass to Brown who lateraled to Wright who carried to the 16. Then Butch hit John Trent with a quickie pass to the nine. From there Louie Hansberger, who had replaced Rowan, ran wide around right end for the score. Wright's kick was good and Central led 21 to 0.

In the fourth quarter Buckles, playing at linebacker, intercepted Speros' pass on the Humes 30 and returned it to the 21. After two incomplete passes and a run by Hansberger were ineffective, Louie hit end Bill Roberds with a pass on the Tigers' five. Rowan carried to the two and Judd Williford scored standing up on the next play. Rowan's point after was good.

A few minutes later Warrior Bill Bolton, who backed up Rip Rowan at fullback, intercepted a pass thrown by Bob Bilger on the Humes 40 and raced to paydirt for the final touchdown. Williford's try for the extra point was low leaving the final score 34 to 0. Assistant Coach Churchill Roberts' younger sister, Joyce, was dating Bolton, later to become her husband, and she would occasionally send notes down to the bench urging her brother to put Billy into the game.

Buckles and Highfill were outstanding in stopping Humes' offensive efforts. On offense Trent and Brown shone, as well as Rowan and Wright, despite their injuries. Humes put up a gallant fight but simply was outclassed. Back Nick Speros and linemen Cliff Melton, Don Kaurez and All-Memphis performer Red Williams turned in fine games, but their efforts were not enough to contain the talented Warriors.

The birth of high school football in Memphis probably occurred in 1893 when it is believed that CBC met High School (Central). But Memphis University School, a private preparatory school, was also in existence and fielded a team that year. In the early years there were a few occasions when the Brothers didn't even sponsor a team and others when they had two different teams, presumably based on grade levels. Sometimes small colleges were played. Games were played at CBC on Adams, at Red Elm Park, later known as Russwood Park, which was across from Baptist Hospital on Madison, and at old Hodges Field.

CBC had outscored their three opponents 61-6, while Central, against four foes, had tallied 97 points to the opposition's none; the upcoming battle between the two was on the minds of every football fan in Memphis. Interest in the game was heightened by the fact that many colleges did not field teams in 1943. Except for Sonny Glasgow's season-ending injury, both teams were in good physical condition.

Now in his third season at the Brothers, Ralph Hatley had developed a group of boys that were well-grounded in fundamentals and ran their plays with precision. And assistant Leo Davis' relentless conditioning program had honed them into a lithe toughness, akin to a buggy whip, that inspired unswerving determination. From a team that a few years before had been a doormat in the Prep League, it now was poised to contend for the state championship.

The CBC team of 1913. Inset, upper right: CBC and Central tangle.
(HD,M/SCPL&IC)

A comparison of the physical sizes of the two starting teams illustrates their contrast. CBC's line averaged only 157 pounds per man compared to Central's 171, a difference of 14 pounds per man. If Glasgow had still been in the lineup, Central's average would have been 181. There was even a greater differential in the backfield weights with CBC averaging 150 pounds per man to Central's 171.

CBC				CENTRAL		
6'	155	Bill Burke	LE	John Trent	6'2"	185
5'11"	170	John Fox	LT	Malcolm Baker	6'5"	185
5'11"	165	Percy Roberts	LG	Jim Laney	5'9"	165
5' 8"	135	Joe Smith	C	Bill Buckles	6'2"	185
5' 8"	155	Al Huebner	RG	Joe Powell	5'7"	135
5'10"	165	Mark Follis	RT	Joe Highfill	5'10"	165
6'	155	Jim Doyle	RE	Ray Brown	5'11"	175
5'8"	145	Tommy Mulroy	QB	Louis Daltroff	5'6"	150
5'9"	155	George Whitehead	LH	Bill Wright	6'	180
5'9"	140	Harry Costello	RH	William Williams	6'	175
5'11"	160	Phil Turner	FB	Elwyn Rowan	5'10"	180

There also was a contrast in the formations employed by the two teams. As previously discussed, CBC adhered strictly to the single wing while Central utilized several formations including the "T," which was something no one locally had ever seen before.

The superiority of CBC and Central in comparison to the other league teams is illustrated by the number of players each placed on the All-Memphis teams selected by the two newspapers. *The Commercial Appeal* picked five from Central and three from CBC while the *Press-Scimitar* tapped three from Central and four from the Brothers. CBC guard Al Huebner and Central fullback Elwyn Rowan were both selected on the first string all-state team while Rowan was named first-string All-Southern, meaning he was chosen as the best player in Tennessee.

Had it not lost three starters that had been scheduled to return from the 1942 team, Central would have fielded an even more powerful eleven. End Leslie Morgan at 6'1" and 180 pounds and guard Russell Swink at 5'7", 150 pounds, went into the service and Dick Shannon, 6'2", 215 pound tackle left when his father was transferred out of town. Reserve guard Maurice Chism left with Swink for the Marine Corps.

CBC also had lost an outstanding player to the war. At 5'11" and 165 pounds, Lamon Kelley had made All-Memphis as a junior playing center and linebacker for the Brothers in 1942, but he joined the Marine Corps in May.

Huebner was quick and fast and generated an amazing amount of power out of his relatively small stature. He also was very tough as was illustrated by the time he almost tore off an ear in practice and played a game a couple of days later. In track, Rowan was the city's 100-yard dash champion and it was said he could run almost as fast sideways as he could head-on. It he hit the line and encountered only a narrow gap, he had the agility and balance to "crab" through it sideways and then, once past the line, square up his shoulders and head downfield. He was well-muscled and had good leg strength, which made him a hard runner, and he was capable of a vicious stiffarm. Central wingback Slick Williams and CBC guard Percy Roberts were the city's fastest men in the 220-yard dash and Huebner could hang right with them. Central tackle Malcolm Baker ran the half-mile.

Each team had a player who was an anomaly. Joe Smith at 135 pounds was the starting center for CBC; Joe Powell, at about the same weight, played guard for Central. But both were tough enough to get the job done. It was said of Joe Smith that every time he centered the ball it was a perfect pass. His father had died when Joe was a small boy and a few months after the 1943 season his mother passed away; his older brother was killed in military service during the summer and Joe was left without any family in Memphis. Tommy Mulroy and some of his other teammates frequently would go over to his house and keep him company by spending the night with him. After selling the house Joe lived with Mulroy and Sandy Kincannon until he went into the Merchant Marine.

Central quarterback Louis "Butch" Daltroff lost his mother at an early age and his father farmed near McGehee, Ark. about 180 miles south of Memphis, so most of the time Butch lived with his "Auntie" Bloom in an apartment on Madison near Cooper; he also lived for a time with Bill Buckles' family.

At CBC the boys who kept the equipment clean and in good order and shuttled the footballs and blocking dummies to the practice field and back were Tony Evangelisti and Don Crone. Over at Central the head manager was Ed Larkin. He was assisted by Ira Whitley, whose playing career had been terminated by an injury, Jerry Hanover, who had a lot of heart but not enough size to keep playing, and Billy Lacy.

Generally "running around" in the same social circles, boys from both teams dated some of the same girls, were members of the same fraternities and hung out at Pig 'n Whistle and Fortune's. A few years later a CBC boy would help rescue a Central boy on the battlefield and boys from each school would be in the weddings of boys from the other. But when they met on the football field they got after it.

Out at Christian Brothers High School for Boys on Parkway, Brother Lawrence David, principal, ran the school of about 400 boys with efficiency and benevolence. He was a big, easy-going man devoted to his calling. Anyone who ever attended school there during his tenure remembers him every morning standing outside the south end of the building, which was the main entrance, loudly exhorting the stream of late-arriving students hurrying from the bus stop up the long driveway. He regularly reminded them of the requirements for punctuality and haste they would encounter when entering military service or the business world.

Coach Ralph Hatley remembers with fondness and gratitude the lengths Brother Lawrence David went to in order to ensure that he and his family were comfortable in their new environment in Memphis and at Christian Brothers. The first thing he told Hatley was, "Just do your job, you don't have to answer to anyone but me." Hatley says he was "a great man" and "like a daddy to me."

Except for Mr. Miller who ran the business office and taught typing, all the courses were conducted by Christian Brothers, a time when more young men were attracted to a religious vocation. In the main, the Brothers were from Chicago and the Midwest, however, Lawrence David, originally from Kentucky, was an exception; naturally, his compatriots referred to him as "the Colonel." Most of the brothers were of Irish descent, although some were of Polish or German extraction. Most had a good sense of humor, but they brooked no nonsense. Those students who tried to get away with something that they shouldn't or who smarted-off usually got the back of a fist or an open palm up the side of their head. Although there was a substantial number of non-Catholics in the school, prayers were conducted in each home room every morning.

Brother Lawrence David, president (principal), of Christian Brothers High School for Boys

The Brothers had, of course, been boys once, too, and they knew pretty well how the adolescent mind worked. They had more anticipatory equipment than just eyes and ears and could be quite adept at sensing mischief in the making. One day Richard Langford, Jimmy Foley and Bert Rathheim decided they would cut the last class of the day, so right after the bell rang and the classroom doors closed on an empty hallway they scooted out the door on the north end of the building and made a dash across the lawn to a big storm drain that went under the railroad tracks that bordered that side of the campus. When they emerged from the drain on the other side of the tracks one of the Brothers was calmly standing there with his arms folded and a look of displeasure on his face. He pointed toward the school: "Go right on back the way you came."

As Langford says, "They won most of the time." But on another occasion one of the older Brothers, who was getting a little absent-minded, left his keys on his desk one day as class ended and he headed for lunch. On his way out of the room Richard scooped them up and dropped them in his pocket. He soon found that one would open any classroom door, so when he had a free period he would locate an empty room and go back in the corner and take his ease and have a smoke. He learned that another key opened the door leading from the lower level of the school into the long underground tunnel that ran to the boiler room and the Brothers' residence, so this provided an even better hideaway for enjoying his nicotine and satisfying his rebellious urges. Along one wall of the tunnel ran a multitude of big steam pipes extending several feet out from the wall and close to the floor. Whenever Langford heard someone coming he would lay prone under the pipes and escape detection in the dimly-lit tunnel. Richard says he never got caught and "I won that time."

Over at Central High C. P. Jester was justifiably proud of his school with its almost 1,300 students. One time when a new student, transferring in from out of town, and her mother met with Mr. Jester, he told them Central was the best high school in the country. Jester was about six feet five inches tall and carried himself in a dignified manner that made his integrity apparent. In his youth he had been an amateur boxer. He was a good judge of character, but there were instances when his probity permitted him to be had. Once when Elwyn Rowan, a distant relative, had some piddling matter he felt demanded his attention away from school, he took an eraser and spread a light coating of chalk dust on his face to effect a pallor and told Mr. Jester he didn't feel well and sought permission to go home. It worked.

Rowan's father drove a truck for Stewart's Mayonnaise Co., calling on local grocers. He died of a heart attack on the job one day when Elwyn was 16. His mother, Molly, was some-what physically impaired from a youthful bout with infantile paralysis, but she didn't let it slow her down. His sister, Bitsy, was married to a Memphis attorney. His older brother, Walter, Jr., had played football with Bob Porter at Southwestern and had acquired the nickname of "Ripper." Elwyn was referred to as "Little Rip" and the "Little" was later dropped as he came into his own.

With few exceptions the faculty at Central had many years of teaching experience. Most were spinsters. A very few were not particularly good teachers, but most of them had the ability to impart knowledge in such a manner that their charges were not even aware it was being absorbed.

The faculty had a strong allegiance to the school and its sports teams. One elderly lady had a long row of potted ferns on the window ledge in her classroom with each named after a Central football captain from previous years. On game days another teacher would tell the football play-ers to lay their heads down on their desks so they could rest up for the game that night. With smirks and winks they would do her bidding so as not to hurt her feelings. One of those desks that Slick Williams occupied had a name carved into it that ten years earlier had become well-known to Memphis police and the FBI: George Barnes, Jr.

C.P. Jester, principal, Central High School. (Photo taken in 1924) (Courtesy of Central High Library)

From Tuesday of one week, when they played Messick, until Thursday of the next week, CBC had six regular practice days to get ready for Central. Central played Humes on Friday and now had only three days to prepare for CBC. With some concern for Central's T-formation plays, the Brothers had sufficient time to install some defensive variations or an offensive wrinkle or two of their own.

Cecil Glass began to worry. He knew he had the best talent in town, but he also knew that well-coached and spirited CBC had the capability to upset his Central team. A loss would be personally embarrassing and the Brothers' extra practice days might provide them with enough time to make some adjustments that could make the difference in the outcome of the game. Rather than simply fine-tuning his own team, he began to fret too much and to ponder how he might be able to eliminate the advantage that he was sure was enjoyed by CBC. He needed to find out what the Brothers were up to out there on Parkway! As he saw it, there was only one thing to do.

Glass sat down with his assistant Churchill Roberts and told him what he had in mind. CBC was on the northeast corner of Parkway and Central and Fairview Junior High was on the southeast corner of the intersection. From Fairview, across four-laned Central Avenue and then open fields to the CBC practice field, it was a distance of a little over 300 yards. Someone could sit at an open window in a second-floor classroom and, with a pair of binoculars, observe everything transpiring as the Brothers went through their drills. Having coached at Fairview the year before, Glass was familiar with the layout of the school and at what time of the day the students and faculty vacated the building.

As he began to detail his plan, Roberts was somewhat taken aback. While such action would not establish a precedent in the game of football, there were certain ethical standards to consider, and if Central was caught spying on CBC's practice there could be Hell to pay. Glass was able to rationalize his proposal in Roberts' mind and assure him that, if he proceeded as Glass told him, there was no danger of detection.

Glass decided to test the practicality of attempting to observe the practice from as far away as Fairview. Before leaving his office to go to his afternoon study hall on Monday, he quickly slipped his binoculars and, as a cover, a few irrelevant papers in his empty brief case. When he got to his desk in the study hall he transferred the binoculars to a drawer. After the bell had rung and the class settled down into a homogenous lethargy, Glass removed the binoculars, slapped the drawer shut, and walked to the back of the room. Passing by football player George Sneed as he walked down the aisle, he quietly directed him to accompany him to an open window.

He handed the binoculars to George. "At the far end of the stadium and across the street from it is a drugstore; look through these and tell me if you can see it clearly."

They were above and about ninety yards behind the west goalpost, so there was an unobstructed view down the field and to the drugstore. As he looked through the glasses, George wondered what was going on. He focused on the store, a tree off to the side along the street, one end of the stadium stands and back to the store. "Maybe he's trying to tell me something," he thought, as he peered intently trying to discern some writing on the plate glass windows, a sign — something! Seeing nothing of significance, he handed the glasses back to Glass.

"Yes, sir, I can see it fine, very clearly," he said.

A slight smile of satisfaction creased Glass' pudgy face. "Thank you, George," he said, and lumbered back to his desk, leaving a bewildered George Sneed.

That night Ralph Hatley got a phone call at home.

"Ralph?"

"Yes."

"This is _____" (a local high school coach). "Did you know that some of the wrong people have been watching your team work out?"

Hatley thanked the coach for his courtesy in calling, but he presumed he had been ill-informed and refused to believe that something that outlandish could occur.

The next night the same coach called back. "You must not care about your practice being spied on," he kidded, referring to Hatley's inaction in the matter. Hatley now began to believe there might be some truth in what he said, after all. His concern was reinforced the next morning, Wednesday, when several of his players told him that some of their Central friends razzed them about knowing everything the CBC boys were doing in their practices.

That afternoon Central assistant coach Churchill

Roberts and student assistant manager Billy Lacy again drove out to Fairview Junior High School and climbed the stairs in the tomb-like hallways to assume their regular positions at a window on the second floor of the school's north side. They scooted their chairs up to the window, got their clipboard, pencils and binoculars out of Cecil Glass' briefcase and were ready for business.

Ralph Hatley now had heard enough to warrant an investigation. From the practice field he surveyed the area and determined that if, in fact, someone was observing his team's drills that it was likely they were at Fairview, across Central Avenue, to the south. Looking cautiously in that direction, it appeared there might be someone in a second floor window. He noticed Brother Vincent, biology teacher, nearby doing some bird-watching in the fields and woods on the campus with a strong pair of binoculars. Hatley sent student manager Tony Evangelisti over to borrow the glasses and then gathered the team around to cover him. As he peered toward Fairview he saw two figures in white shirts looking back at him; apparently thinking they had been spotted, they suddenly dropped below the window level. Some students were standing along the sideline observing the practice and Hatley inquired if any of them had a car. When he found one that did, he asked him if he would drive over to Fairview and see if he could detect anyone looking out a window.

Burke Cranford, Hall Crawford, an All-Memphis end the previous year who was only a few days away from entering the Army, and Don Lutenbacher got in Burke's Model T and headed to Fairview. The route they had to take would not make it apparent to anyone at Fairview that someone would be leaving the CBC campus for that purpose. The parking lot at CBC was a good hundred yards off Parkway and, because the driveway sloped downward, when they got to that street the terrain and the Brothers' residence and the steam plant put them out of the line of sight from the junior high. Because of the approximate 75-foot wide wooded median separating opposing lanes of traffic, they actually had to turn away from the direction of Fairview and go north until they came to a break where they could make a U-turn and head south toward Central Avenue. Turning left off Parkway onto Central they had to drive past the side of the large school building, facing the CBC campus, in order to pull into the parking lot in the rear. To the unsuspecting snoopers they were just another car traveling along Central.

Burke, Hall and Don walked around the corner of the building and then backed up toward the street to get a better visual angle on the window. They recognized Roberts and Lacy who, for a few moments, were too intent in their clandestine activities to notice they, too, were being watched; then they jumped back from the window. The boys tried to gain access to the locked building but couldn't find a janitor to let them in. They returned to the CBC practice field and reported to Hatley, specifically identifying by name the two covert culprits.

Now, that what initially he had deemed to be preposterous had definitely been confirmed, Hatley became enraged. It was beyond his comprehension that someone would so blatantly cast aside the concept of good sportsmanship and engage in such skulduggery. He told Leo Davis to take over the practice and, with manager Tony Evangelisti trailing behind him, he left at a trot headed toward Fairview. As he ran through the big field and then across Central Avenue to the junior high turning over in his mind the rash and audacious actions of the rascals perched in the window, his anger rose with every step.

Fairview Junior High School. CBC's practice was observed from the middle second floor windows on the north (left) side of the building. (A)

When he got to Fairview's locked doors, Hatley's anger had almost rendered him out of control. Roberts and Lacy had seen him coming and told the janitor to not let him in under any circumstances. When he pounded on the door the janitor, aware of the situation, came quickly and shook his head and told him he could not allow him to enter the building. Hatley then asked him to go tell them to come outside, that he wanted to talk to them. When the man came back he told Hatley, "They have no intention of coming out; they haven't the guts." By now, Hatley's ire had cooled somewhat and he realized it was fortunate that he had not been able to gain admittance; in the frame of mind he had been in a few minutes before he likely would have wreaked considerable havoc had he gotten inside. He went on back to the practice field and continued preparations for the game the next night.

News of the incident quickly became known across the city. Henry Reynolds, a sportswriter at *The Commercial Appeal*, dubbed Coach Cecil Glass "Spy Glass," and in Friday's newspapers every high school coach in the league deplored the incident in strong terms. Murel Nemecek of Tech High said, "There are certain ethics in regard to coaching and business and that was the most unethical thing I've ever seen in sports."

At the CBC pep rally at noon Thursday, the energetic spirit that normally infused the students at these events had been accelerated by news of the spying incident. Brother Josias Bernard, an irrepressible cut-up, made an appearance attired in what he deemed to be an exemplification of the guiding force at Central High. Attaching a fake mustache to his lip and parting his black hair in the appropriate manner, he became a ringer for Adolph Hitler. When he donned a long, leather coat with swastikas on the collars and hung a pair of binoculars around his neck, his authentic ensemble was complete. He later posed for a picture peering out a window with binoculars while behind him a blackboard, with the chalked heading: "Unfairview Junior High School," was covered with notations of football plays and kindred comments.

Illustrative of the emotions surrounding the game was the situation involving two sisters who attended a local private girls school. Because one was dating a boy who played for CBC and the other dating a boy who played for Central,

Brother Josias Bernard's interpretation of Central's scouting efforts: "Unfair Junior High School" "We Stoop to Conquer," etc. (Courtesy of Richard Langford)

weeks passed without the two girls speaking to each other. Their exasperated father finally sat them down and told them they were going to have to call a truce and start acting normally again before they drove their parents to vexatious desperation.

In full realization that the outcome of their game would likely determine the ultimate champion of the Memphis Prep League, neither CBC nor Central needed any additional incentive to mentally get them ready. But the spying incident obviously served to heighten the intensity of emotion that had been building as game time drew nearer. When the teams trotted onto the field at Crump Stadium, Thursday, October 14, 13,000 fans were awaiting eagerly what they knew would be a thrilling and hard-fought contest.

Predictably, all the players were somewhat tight in the beginning. After CBC fullback Phil Turner took Billy Buckles' kickoff, he was making a nice return when he was hit and fumbled with Central recovering on the Brothers' 27-yard line. From his fullback position on a quick snap, Rip Rowan broke through the line on the first play and sprinted for an apparent touchdown, but the Warriors were offside and the play was called back. After a couple of running plays for virtually no gain, quarterback Daltroff faked to Rowan up the middle and handed off to wingback Slick Williams; Slick handed off to left end John Trent who, in turn, gave the ball to right end Ray Brown who ran an end around down to the eight. Rowan took it to the five and then Daltroff lobbed a little pass to Brown just over the goal line for the score. Rowan missed the point after but Central was ahead 6 to 0.

Near the end of the first period CBC took possession on its own 40 and started a drive that ended early in the second quarter. Merrick "Dippy" Coles faded back and heaved a long pass in the direction of Billy Burke, who was streaking toward the goal line. Judd Williford, playing defensive halfback, jumped and gave the ball a mighty swat, convinced he was sending it into oblivion. The ball caromed crazily to the side and behind Judd and he turned to see Burke come back and make a sensational diving catch and fall to the ground at the Central 20-yard line.

Dippy picked up three yards and then Tommy Mulroy ran six more out of bounds at the 11. Dippy plunged for a first down and then he and Sleepy John Ross alternately banged away to move the ball to the two. At this point Ross went wide right, cut back over tackle and crossed the goal with three Warriors hanging on. Costello's extra point try was blocked by John Trent. Neither team threatened the remainder of the second quarter and at the half the score stood 6 to 6.

The second half started with Costello kicking off to Bill Wright. It turned out to be a repeat of the first half kickoff, only in reverse. Wright took the ball on the ten and returned it to the 28 where he was hit and fumbled. A gang of CBC players fell on the ball. Phil Turner picked up one yard and then George "Bubba" Whitehead broke away for 12 yards to the Warrior 15. On the next play Central was offside and the penalty made it first and five at the ten. Ross and Turner moved it to the one and then Phil hit the middle for the score. Costello's extra point try again was blocked, but Central was offside. Turner again tried the middle and his forward motion carried him over the goal line, but Central tacklers drove him back and the officials ruled that he had been stopped short. This left the score at CBC 12 Central 6.

On two occasions in the third quarter Central drove deep into Purple Wave territory only to lose the ball on downs and a fumble. It was not until the middle of the fourth quarter that Central was able to catch up. A bad snap from center deep in its own territory shoved CBC back to its three-yard line and Costello punted out of bounds at the 47. At the end of the play Mark Follis, who had been clipped, stayed on the ground hoping the official had seen it and would call a penalty on Central. Coach Hatley thought he had been hurt and dashed out on the field. But Mark got up before Hatley reached him and the Brothers were slapped with a 15-yard penalty for the coach coming onto the field without permission.

With a 30-yard difference in field position, this gave the Warriors a big boost. Two plays failed to gain and then Daltroff passed to Ray Brown at the 15. A running play was stopped cold but Daltroff again hit Brown on the three. Plunges by Rowan and Daltroff moved the ball to the half-yard line and Rowan took it in from there; his kick was good and it put Central ahead 13 to 12.

With only a couple of minutes left in the game, Bubba Whitehead's pass intended for Burke was intercepted by Bill Wright at the CBC 42. Rowan and Wright took turns in carrying the ball to the Brothers' 24. Then Rowan slanted through left tackle, was slowed by but shook off several would-be tacklers, and broke loose to finally be brought down on the one-yard line. With 15 seconds remaining on the clock Wright plunged over for the touchdown. Rowan missed the point after but Central had extended its lead to 19 to 12.

CBC returned the kickoff to their 42. Time was called with five seconds left and the Wave drew a five-yard penalty for too many times out. On the final play fleet Bill Burke got behind everyone, but a slightly-too-long, desperation pass slipped through his fingers. If the pass had been successful, CBC would have had the opportunity to tie the score.

Regardless of the outcome and the disappointment of the CBC coaches, players and fans, those on hand had been privileged to witness a contest containing all the elements that the true lover of football could hope for: a meeting of a good, big team and a good, small team, teams utilizing different formations, several lead changes, spectacular individual performances, gritty, leather-popping action from start to finish and the ultimate result in doubt right up until the last play. The Brothers had ended up on the short end of the scoreboard, but it had taken all the skill and determination of their opponent — probably the best team in the state and one of the best in the country — to accomplish the job, and the CBC players and coaches knew that maybe at another time... a different bounce of the ball...?

Disgruntlement, taunting, hot words and flashes of anger served to produce a couple of fights at the game and several more at the Pig 'n Whistle for the next week or so.

Right after the game a reporter caught up with Coach Glass on the field at Crump Stadium.

"Coach, I see your new scouting system paid off some big dividends tonight."

"What scouting system?"

"The Fairview incident."

"You mean you're going to print that?"

"I sure am, it's a good news story. Coach Hatley said he saw Coach Roberts and the student manager in the window and Professor Wadley (Fairview principal) said they were there. I'd like to get a statement from you."

"I don't have any statement."

"What about Coach Roberts?"

"You'll have to see Coach Roberts."

The reporter approached Churchill Roberts. "Coach, do you have any statement to make regarding the Fairview incident yesterday?"

"I don't have a thing to say. Any statement will have to come from Coach Glass."

The reporter walked off. When he reached the middle of the field he heard a whistle and turned around; the two coaches were walking toward him.

"Coach Roberts has a statement for you," Glass said.

"I was at Fairview School on Monday delivering some tickets to Professor Wadley for tonight's game," said Roberts.

"Did you deliver them to him on the second floor?"

"Yes, we were up there."

"What were you doing there Tuesday afternoon?"

Roberts didn't respond.

"What were you doing there Wednesday afternoon?"

"I wasn't there."

"That was when Coach Hatley and some boys said they saw you," rejoined the reporter.

"I was at the football game at the Fairgrounds field," (to watch a junior high game).

"But Ed Molinski (former great Tennessee guard) said you left the game at four o'clock along with the student manager."

"We went to see Fairview practice," Roberts responded.

Friday's newspapers quoted Central's principal, C. P. Jester, as saying that he promised to look into the matter. "I personally would not endorse anything unethical in prep school football and especially with CBC, with whom we have had such pleasant relationships through the years."

Saturday's newspapers reported that all the other coaches in town had asked Harry Sharp, Treadwell coach and president of the coaches association, to call a meeting for Monday night at the Chisca Hotel to discuss the situation. It was mentioned that while there was nothing in the by-laws prohibiting scouting another team's practice, there was a tacit "gentlemen's agreement" barring such an activity. Now that it had occurred, consideration probably would be given to making it officially illegal.

Given Mr. Jester's high sense of honor and integrity and his pride in Central High, it undoubtedly was an extremely trying time for him. What was said when he called Coach

A 'SPY' GLASS VIEW OF A CBC PRACTICE

"A Spy Glass View of a CBC Practice." A Press-Scimitar photo taken through binoculars with a telescopic lens from the window at Fairview.

Glass on the carpet is not known, but it can reasonably be assumed that after Jester had his say Glass was sufficiently humbled.

On Sunday night Glass apologized to Hatley and, as a result, the meeting of the coaches' association was called off. Hatley accepted the apology and said, "the matter is closed." The other coaches agreed with Hatley that the continued pursuit of the matter would only make things worse and, presumably, no coach would ever again be so reckless as to do something like that in the future.

In a statement Glass said he took full responsibility for the incident. "I want to express my apologies to Coach Hatley of CBC and all other people concerned in the unfortunate scouting episode which preceded the Central-CBC football game. I trust that the relations of Central and CBC will continue in the future in the same fine manner they have been carried out in the past. As far as I am concerned, I have learned my lesson and in the future no such practices will be connected with any coaching endeavors with which I am associated. I hope that this apology to Coach Hatley, to CBC, and to the football public of Memphis will bring to an end an unhappy incident."

The CBC players put the spying incident and the loss to Central behind them and buckled down to concentrate on the four remaining games on their schedule. They had only a few days to get ready for Treadwell on Tuesday night at Fairgrounds Stadium. After having lost their first three games, Treadwell had pulled an upset in defeating defending league champion South Side by 7 to 0 and then beat Bartlett, a suburban team in Shelby County.

The Purple Wave got things going midway of the first quarter when they began a drive at their 39-yard line. Dippy Coles, Harry Costello and George Whitehead alternated running the ball down to the Eagle two-yard line where John Ross carried it in for the touchdown. Harry's kick for the extra point was good and CBC led 7 to 0.

In the second quarter Treadwell tried to make a first down in its own territory with fourth down and short yardage, but the Eagles' backfield ace Wayne Franklin was stopped cold on his 43-yard line. Six plays later Phil Turner burst over his right tackle from the Treadwell 10-yard line and scored standing up. Costello's kick again was good and the score was 14 to 0.

With just two minutes remaining in the first half, CBC substitute tailback Jack "Hoot" Gibson, standing on his 25-yard line, wound up and fired a long pass to end Bill Burke. Bill cradled the ball in and sped untouched across the goal line. Hoot's plunge for the extra point was short and the score remained 20 to 0.

With the third quarter drawing to a close, CBC guard Percy Roberts broke through the Eagles' line and blocked Billy McCalla's punt. The ball rolled into the end zone and Percy fell on it, but a swarm of Eagles piled into Percy and when referee Red Cavette had untangled everyone McCalla was on the ball; instead of a touchdown the Brothers were awarded a safety. CBC now led 22 to 0. Percy was injured on the play and had to leave the game.

The Eagles never gave up but couldn't get any closer to scoring than the CBC 25-yard line. Once Wayne Franklin broke loose for a nifty 44-yard run to the Brothers' 21, but the Eagle backfield had been in motion and the play was called back. With only a few minutes remaining in the game Treadwell was desperate to score, and Franklin hurled a long pass to the CBC 15 yard line. Bubba Whitehead had it gauged all the way and stepped in front of the potential receiver and picked it off on the run. Breaking four tackles and keeping his balance, he raced down the sideline 85 yards for the final score of the game. Once he broke clear five CBC players set up a wall behind him that eliminated any possibility of his being caught from behind. Costello's kick made it 29 to 0.

Center John Walt, tackle Arvin James, end Billy Burke and guards Huebner and Roberts played outstanding games for CBC.

Arvin James backed up Mark Follis and started two games for CBC. He always played solid football. (Courtesy of Arvin James)

After the emotionally draining game with CBC, Central's next game was Friday night of the following week with Little Rock Central at the latter's homecoming. But during the week as they prepared for the game, some of the Warrior stars received some unusual mail. In the eyes of some CBC students, the "H" awarded for an athletic letter at Central was too suggestive of the shape of a pair of binoculars to ignore and they felt, given what had happened the previous week, that the letter was an appropriate symbol for Central. Accordingly, imaginative and anonymous drawings expounding on this theme and making reference to "Spyglass High" ended up being delivered to the homes of several Warriors.

Memphis Central was heavily favored in their game with Little Rock. The Warriors moved the ball well, but almost every time they got within striking distance of a score they would commit a mistake. Four of their passes were intercepted and they lost seven fumbles to Little Rock. They also incurred four penalties for a total of 60 yards. In helping their cause, Little Rock punted four times for a 49-yard average.

Neither team could score until late in the third quarter

when Memphis drove, almost entirely on the ground, from its 17 to the Little Rock 27 where Wright hit Trent with a pass in the end zone. The extra point was missed. Little Rock responded immediately by scoring in three plays. Big John Hoffman, who later starred at Arkansas and with the Chicago Bears, returned the kickoff to his 44-yard line, but a penalty on the play, downfield, put the ball on the Memphis 31. Halfback Hal Pevia scampered to the two on the next play and Hoffman, at about 6'2" and 220 pounds, hammered it in from there. The extra point was good and that ended the scoring with a 7 to 6 Little Rock win.

The Warriors had 16 first downs to Little Rock's six and gained 217 yards rushing to their host's 142, with only 30 of those coming in the first half. In the air Memphis picked up 46 yards while Little Rock could manage only 12.

Had they held on to the ball and taken advantage of their scoring opportunities, Memphis likely would have put the game out of reach in the first half, but the innumerable fumbles and interceptions were its downfall. As the line was effective in opening up holes most of the night, Rowan and Wright consistently reeled off nice gains; Buckles and Trent stood out on defense.

When some of the Warriors encountered some CBC players at the Pig 'n Whistle the next night, they were razzed unmercifully about the loss.

After its game with Treadwell CBC had ten days to get ready for the Tech High Yellowjackets on Friday night, October 29 at Crump Stadium. Tech almost always fielded a strong team and this year seemed to be no exception. So far, the Jackets had stung Treadwell 36 to 0, Catholic 14 to 0 and South Side 20 to 0, so they definitely were in contention for the prep championship. Tech was led by All-Memphis tailback Clyde Hooker and Dutch Bauer in the backfield and Leo Wood and Gene Caudle at ends. Wood, along with trackman Joe Johnson at wingback, constituted deep threats on passes from Bill Crumby at quarterback. Tech was in good physical condition for the game, but injuries and illness slowed or eliminated from action CBC backs Coles, Whitehead and Ross.

As 13,000 looked on, CBC played probably its best game of the season. Neither team scored in the first quarter, but about midway of the second CBC's defense had bottled up Tech's offense in the latter's end of the field. Trying to kick away from Harry Costello at safety, Hooker punted from his eight-yard line but netted only 15 yards as the ball went off the side of his foot and was downed on the 23. Costello picked up a yard and on second down Ross was sent in for Whitehead at tailback. The Tech defense assumed that Sleepy John had come in for a specific purpose and keyed on him. Instead, left end Bill Burke came on an end around, took a handoff from Costello at wingback and went the distance for a touchdown. Costello kicked the extra point and the Brothers were out in front 7 to 0.

With less than a minute to go in the half, CBC took over deep in its own end of the field. Two successive penalties against Tech put the ball on the Purple Wave 30. Then the "Burke Special" was called. Bill pulled from his left end posi-

Tommy Mulroy, CBC co-captain and All-Memphis blocking back.

tion and swung around through the backfield. Mulroy had taken the snap from center and handed off to Costello who had started to his left from his wingback position. As Burke passed by Costello he took a handoff from Harry and continued heading for the right sideline. It appeared to be the end-around that he had scored on only a few minutes before and the Tech defense scrambled to cut him off. Meanwhile, right end Jim "Red" Doyle, not known for his speed, had gone down and faked a block on the safetyman and then kept going. Suddenly, Burke stopped, and the all-around athlete reared back and heaved a looping pass toward Doyle; just as it left his fingertips he was clobbered by two or three Tech defenders and knocked sprawling out of bounds. Hooker, the Tech safetyman, had been sucked in by the fake end-around and when Burke's pass settled into Red's arms he was at least 15 yards behind Clyde. Hooker wheeled around and started pursuit. The little speedster caught Red at about the Tech 25, but Doyle shook him off and continued to lumber goalward. Hooker got up and caught him again at the ten and finally dragged him down on the four. Thinking Red had scored, the CBC players on the bench were jumping up and down and celebrating prematurely. It all worked out, however, for Hatley sent Julius Smith into the game with a play and Costello flipped a pass to Burke in the end zone with 12 seconds remaining on the second-quarter clock. However, Red Doyle was not too happy about not having scored the touchdown. Harry's kick was good and the Brothers went into the dressing room with a 14 to 0 lead.

In the third quarter an exchange of punts put Tech in a hole and CBC kept them from making a first down. Again, trying to punt away from Costello, Hooker kicked off the side of his foot and out of bounds at the Tech 31. Bubba Whitehead picked up nine yards and Costello added five more to the 17. Bubba then hit Harry with a pass to the two and carried it over on the next play. Costello missed the extra point and it was 20 to 0 at the end of the quarter. At this juncture Tech had not even been able to make a first down.

In the fourth quarter Coach Hatley substituted liberally. Jack Gibson opened up with a passing attack that connected with Costello, Leon Shahun and Al Guthrie. Costello caught a 23-yard touchdown pass and the fleet "Gaddy Goose"

Guthrie scored on a 36-yard aerial.

In between those two scores Tech made its only significant offensive outburst of the game. After driving to the CBC 16-yard line on passes, Hooker darted in for the score. He kicked the point after and that made it CBC 27 Tech 7. Late in the fourth quarter Hooker made a sensational 57-yard run from his 23 to CBC's 20, but the Brothers held and kept the Jackets out of the end zone making the final score 33 to 7.

At 3 a.m. the day of the game Leo Davis' wife, Rebecca, gave birth to a girl at Methodist Hospital, just a couple of blocks from Crump Stadium. As she lay in her hospital bed Rebecca heard the CBC band play the fight song time after time and knew the Brothers were winning big.

Never let it be said that center Julius Smith was ever lacking for an opinion on anything, and he never hesitated to be certain that everyone was aware of what it might be. In those days of limited substitution the coach couldn't send a player in with a particular play he wanted called on every offensive down, so it was incumbent upon the quarterback on

Ralph and Ruth Hatley and Rebecca and Leo Davis enjoy a traditional post-game repast at the CBC cafeteria with "Mr. Jack" Bondurant, whose son had played for the Brothers some years before. (Courtesy of Rebecca (Mrs. Leo) Davis)

the field to make the decision about what play to run. One of Coach Hatley's axioms that he relayed to his quarterbacks was "When in doubt call number 21 (the old single wing off-tackle power play), or punt."

The next year during the course of the 1944 season occasions arose when Smith would disagree with the quarter-back's call and would interject his opinion about it in the hud-dle. Tailback Jack Gibson would usually side with Julius and also add his thoughts on the matter. Either Hatley observed from the sideline that it was taking too long to get plays off or the quarterback complained to him about what was going on. In any event, he told Smith and Gibson to keep their mouths shut in the huddle and let the quarterback call his own play.

In their 1944 game with Tech at Crump Stadium CBC had driven to the Yellowjackets' 20-yard line but faced fourth down and short yardage. The situation obviously called for a run or a pass, but the quarterback, with a big question mark over his head, was definitely in doubt. He remembered Coach Hatley's adage, but instead of Number 21 he called for a punt. Bent over in the huddle, Smith started to say some-thing and then remembered Hatley's admonition. He looked up and across the huddle at Gibson. Hoot, a fine punter, gave Julius a big wink. The Brothers lined up and Julius centered the ball deep to Gibson. Rather than trying to kick out of bounds near the goal line, Hoot stepped into the ball and sent it sailing over the goal post, over the cinder track, and into the west endzone stands. It was, of course, a touchback and the ball came back to the 20-yard line where the play had originated.

After the play Julius ran off the field to the CBC bench and, with a smug grin on his face, glanced at Coach Hatley who quickly turned his head to avoid his gaze.

Some girls could go out on dates on weeknights, but unless it was a special occasion like a particular football game, most stayed home and studied and went out on Friday and Saturday nights with a midnight curfew. It there wasn't a party or dance, the usual routine was a downtown movie and a stop at the Pig 'n Whistle or Fortune's. Or, for a special date, maybe the dark recesses of the Jungle Garden or The Pit.

Although gas was rationed, there always seemed to be enough to get to wherever the occasion demanded. Of course, there were no tape players and, as the evening wore on in driving here and there, the radio dial came alive as the 50,000-watt stations across the country turned up their power: WSM and WLAC in Nashville with disc jockey Gene Nobles advertising Randy's Record Shop in Gallatin, WCKY and WLW "the Crosley station" in Cincinnati, KVOO in Tulsa with the call letters spoken as in an echo chamber, WSB in Atlanta, which signed off at midnight with "Dixie," KMOX "the voice of St. Louis with studios in the Marx Building," WWL in New Orleans "with studios in the Roosevelt Hotel," evermore playing Dixieland with intelligent commentary about the historical roots of particular songs and the performers thereof, WOAI in San Antonio, WFAA in Dallas, WBAP in Fort Worth and KDKA in Pittsburgh, with a cowbell sound. And then WMC and WREC in Memphis. On the latter, they tied in with the nation-wide network at nine to present whatever band happened to be playing in the Skyway or on the Peabody roof: "Good evening ladies and gentlemen, from the Plantation Roof Garden high atop Hotel Peabody overlooking Old Man River in downtown Memphis, Tenn., CBS brings you the scintillating rhythms of Chuck Foster and his orchestra." Then, the band would strike up with Foster's theme song, "Oh, You Beautiful Doll," while the announcer continued with his patter and introduced the first song. Between songs, as the announcer advertised something or other or the next song, could be heard the background murmurings and laughter of the crowd and the tinkling of glasses.

Getting on toward midnight a couple of stations operated by Americans just across the Mexican border, whose call letters always started with an "X," would turn up their power and advertise all sorts of outlandish things. Also, about that time of night, when things were closing down in Memphis, an oily-voiced individual who identified himself as "your friend Morris," would come on touting his nightspot across the river in little, gravel-roaded, rough and tumble West Memphis, Ark. where, if so inclined, one could go to romp and stomp until the sun came up.

A few youthful gadabouts around town drove Buicks that had radios with five push buttons that spelled out the name of the car. It was a rather cornball, gauche thing to do, but some rearranged the letters to stand for something they considered cute, e.g., "BICKU — Bet I Can Kiss You," or "ICKUB — I Can Kiss You Babe." A girl in a little North Mississippi town shattered syntax but got her point across with "UCKIB — You Can't Kiss I, Bailey." While driving around and listening to romantic music with a date, a valuable steering wheel appendage was a knob, a little smaller than a tennis ball, called a "necking ring." This gizmo allowed reasonably good control of the automobile with the left hand while freeing up the right arm for other important matters.

A favorite program at one o'clock on Saturday afternoons, always featuring a well-known "Big Band," was "Matinee at Meadowbrook," located "on the Pompton Turnpike near Cedar Grove, New Jersey." On Saturday night from nine until midnight a local station broadcast the "Rhythm Express." This was largely a request program with songs being introduced by the disc jockey saying such as, "this one is going out from Jack to Beverly," or "this one is from Mary Ann to you know who; why don't you call me?"

Central occasionally would have informal weekend dances in the gymnasium at the school. Everybody would doff their shoes and, as they dipped and slid around, dirty up their socks and put a nice luster on the hardwood. A couple of regional jitterbugging styles in those days were known as "The Memphis Shuffle" and "The Memphis Stomp." The terpsichorean talents of Bill Wright made him the acknowledged master of these mini-galas. Towering over the crowd and ever vigilant for breaches of decorum and moral rectitude, Professor Jester circulated with a poised right index finger ready to tap the shoulder of a boy whom he deemed was dancing too close. He reminded everyone that in his day a boy would take his handkerchief out and place it on the girl's shoulder where his hand would lie as they danced.

Prior to a game, it was the custom of Henry Reynolds, *Commercial Appeal* sportswriter who covered local high school football, to arrive early at the stadium and stroll around the cinder track. As people began arriving and taking their seats and then the teams came out on the field for their pre-game warm-ups, Henry would slowly walk the quarter mile circuit allowing his sensory perceptions to acquire the necessary "feel" for the game before he mounted the steps to the pressbox to observe the action and record his impressions.

As Henry approached the Central bench prior to its game with Catholic, he noticed Mr. Jester turn his way and look at him. Jester still was agonizing over the spying incident that had sullied the good name of his beloved school and he resented Reynolds' front-page story that had played up the unfortunate matter and his dubbing Coach Glass as "Spy Glass"; he felt that Henry had been too zealous in his handling of the story. As Henry approached, Jester stepped toward him and said, "Mr. Reynolds, I'm going to slap you," and, with that, he hauled off and gave Henry a good swat up side his head. Reynolds recognized that Mr. Jester's touchiness could, at least to some degree, probably be attributed to his advancing age. He had had many conversations with Jester about football and Central's past athletic glories, and he liked and admired the man. After taking his lick, Henry acknowledged to himself the older man's need to respond to his personal code of honor — a hundred years earlier it might have been the first act in a drama that played itself out in a duel across the river at Hopefield; Henry stepped back, smiled, almost nodded in obeisance, and mounted the steps to the pressbox.

Central moved another step closer to the Prep League championship with their fifth win in the circuit, a 19 to 0 victory over Catholic High. The Terriers took Buckles' opening kick-off and when they couldn't move the ball punted only to Central's 45. Judd Williford, starting in place of Bill Wright due to the latter's recurring "water on the knee," reeled off 15 yards on the first play. Rowan then swept wide and picked up 10 more. Catholic stiffened and two runs gained nothing, followed by an incomplete pass. Despite his inability to cut on his injured knee, on fourth down Slick Williams took a reverse handoff and went around left end 30 yards for the first touchdown. Rowan's extra point try was wide.

In the second quarter Williford intercepted a Bill Garibaldi pass, intended for Bill Jeter at midfield, and fought his way down to the Catholic 28. Rip picked up 17 yards through the middle and then Slick and Judd moved it down to the six; Rowan carried it in from there and his extra point kick was perfect for a 13 to 0 lead.

As the outcome of the game never was in doubt, Coach Glass substituted freely in the second half, and it was in the fourth quarter before Central scored again. After a Garibaldi punt went out of bounds on the Central 20, Rowan took charge. First, quarterback Daltroff tossed him a lateral and he bulled his way up to the 40, taking several Terriers to bring him down. Two more running plays netted him 26 yards. Butch then faked a handoff and raised up and threw a pass to Ray Brown on the Catholic 16. Rowan pounded down to the ten but Central was penalized five yards for an illegal formation. Daltroff then froze the defense with a fake handoff and looped a little pass to Trent who lateraled to Rowan coming around the left side; Rip carried it in standing up. Bill Rainer's dropkick for the extra point was blocked.

Catholic had trouble moving the ball all night. Their deepest penetration came on a pass interception at the Central 30, but they were stopped cold at that point. The Terriers were able to manage only four first downs to Central's 19, but Bill Riley at tackle and Bill Jeter at end turned in good games on defense.

A week after the Tech game CBC played Humes at Fairgrounds Stadium. The Humes Tigers had wins over South Side, Whitehaven and Messick but had been clobbered by

Central 34 to 0 a month earlier. They had talent and were determined to improve their league record of three wins and one loss; they gave the Brothers a tough fight. Much of the first quarter was played in Humes' end of the field, but neither team could score. On one occasion CBC drove to the Tigers' 11 yard line, but third and fourth down passes failed to connect.

Early in the second period CBC drove to the Humes 24. Seeming to vent his frustration at his team's previous inability to score, on the next play Phil Turner picked up 15 hard-running yards to the nine. Bubba Whitehead then circled right end for the score. Costello kicked the extra point and it was 7 to 0.

A little later in the same quarter the Brothers drove to the Tigers' 36 at which point John Ross, following his blockers and breaking arm tackles, bulled his way to the 16. Turner and Ross then moved the ball to the four where Sleepy John spun through right tackle for the touchdown. John Walt kicked the point after for a 14 to 0 lead.

The Brothers displayed their depth of talent at tailback when they took over the ball at the Humes 45 in the third quarter. Hoot Gibson circled right end, cut back to the middle of the field and darted to the Humes 25-yard line. Two plays later Gibson looped a pass to Whitehead inside the five and he overpowered two Tiger defenders to cross the goal line. Walt missed the extra point and all scoring had ended with a 20 to 0 CBC lead.

Humes' only serious offensive threats, led by tailback Nick Speros, occurred in the fourth quarter. The Tigers drove to the 16 on one occasion and, later, to the CBC three but were stopped both times. After taking over at the three, the Brothers drove all the way to the Humes 24 before being halted just before the end of the game.

Situated on the low hills just across Wolf River northeast of Memphis, the village of Raleigh, with its many springs, had for decades been a favorite place for outings and picnics.

In fact, a trolley line had once run out to it. The family of George Sneed, a Central football player, owned property there out in the nearby woods on which was situated a large lodge. It was called "Sneed's Cabin," which was a misnomer, because it was a larger structure than that. It was a rustic, rectangular building containing one big room with lofts at each end of it. On one end wall was a huge fireplace; above it, the mounted head of a bighorn sheep surveyed all with mute indifference.

The night after the CBC-Humes game George's fraternity, Theta Kappa Omega, held a wiener roast and hayride at the "Cabin." On a somewhat frosty evening about 20 boys (most from Central but some from CBC) and their dates clambered up into a stake-bodied, horse-drawn wagon and gratefully snuggled into the luxurious, crackling agglomeration that provided some slight protection from the country chill. After about an hour of riding around the property and abutting rural lanes, laughing at silly witticisms, poking good-natured fun at each other, and singing a song or so, they unloaded back at the Cabin.

For overnight stays by a group of boys, the Sneeds kept a big bunch of cot-size mattresses on hand to lay on the floor. When not needed they were tossed helter-skelter in one of the lofts. After they had warmed up around the fire, consumed the hot dogs and had tired of dancing to a record player, half a dozen couples, "going steady" and "pinned," climbed into the loft and sat in amongst the bumpy and tiered mass of mattresses where they talked in low tones.

A week after their game with Catholic High, the Warriors again took to the road to play another "Central" team, this time Knoxville Central. The Knoxville school consistently turned out good football teams and, as there was no statewide playoff system, the victor would have a good shot at ultimately being designated the state champion. The rivalry between Tennessee's "Three Grand Divisions" was never more apparent. When the Warriors got off the train after a 400 mile ride, they were greeted by headlines in the *Knoxville News-Sentinel* that trumpeted: "Team From Crumptown Arriving to Vie For State Title."

On a cold East Tennessee Thursday night Memphis took the opening kickoff and promptly fumbled the ball away on their own 35-yard line. The Bobcats tried a pass over the middle, but Butch Daltroff, who had dropped back in coverage from his linebacker position, slapped it away into Rowan's arms at the 20. The Warriors then drove 80 yards for a touchdown and a 7 to 0 lead.

Highlights of the drive were two short passes by Butch to Ray Brown that resulted in 14- and 25-yard gains when Ray did some nifty running after the receptions. The second one put the ball on Knoxville's 25. Several runs moved the ball to the 11 for another first down. On the next play, from the T-formation, Butch faked to Williford and Williams as they crossed in the backfield and then handed off to Rowan who blasted up the middle for the touchdown. Judd and Slick's blocking responsibilities on the play were the two linebackers against a 6-2-2-1 defensive scheme. Judd got a good angle on his man and put him on the ground. As they both lay there they looked up in time to see Rip hurtling through the hole and the Bobcat linebacker was heard to remark, probably more to himself than to Judd, "Look at that son-of-a-gun go!"

On kickoff returns Knoxville used a wedge formation to convoy the kick returner upfield. The Warriors' feisty little guard Joe Powell, who had entered the starting lineup after Joe Highfill had moved to tackle to replace the injured Sonny Glasgow, was determined to stop it. When the ball was kicked off he went flying downfield and threw all his 135 pounds of grit headfirst and low into the point of the wedge. Joe succeeded in breaking it up, but after everyone else had gotten up he still lay on the ground. Slick went over to check on him and found him totally cold-cocked. With arms outstretched and legs crossed at the ankles he lay flat on his back with eyes closed and snoring loudly.

Although the mistakes were not as extreme, the game was somewhat reminiscent of the one with Little Rock Central. The Warriors would churn out large chunks of yardage then shoot themselves in the foot after having driven into scoring position. Once they drove to the Bobcats' 19 and lost the ball on a fourth-down play mix-up. On another play that almost always worked in practice, Slick went in motion to the left from his wingback position, took off on a fly pattern down the sideline and got behind everybody as Butch laid a perfect pass right in his hands. Slick took it over his right shoulder and brought the ball to his chest, but it slipped through to the ground. Too, it seemed there might have been a slight tilt in Knoxville's direction in the officiating. The referee was rumored to be an uncle of one of the Bobcats' starting linemen, and it seemed that he made a habit of calling questionable penalties against Memphis. Once, when a supposed offender, who protested his innocence, was called for clipping, Billy Buckles told the official "If you'll put on a jersey, we'll block you too." Needless to say, the referee's blood pressure rose to an alarming degree and he uttered a few choice words of his own.

Late in the third period Rowan ran 52 yards down the sideline to the Knoxville five. Three plunges into the line moved the ball to the one, but on fourth down Bill Wright fumbled and Knoxville recovered on their three. The Bobcats then began their best drive of the night. Mixing runs and passes in a desperate effort to possibly salvage a tie, they moved to a first down at the Warrior 24-yard line. However, their hopes faded as four straight passes fell incomplete.

Late in the fourth quarter Rowan broke loose and dashed 28 yards to the Knoxville 48 but, inexplicably, was caught from behind. He, of course, and Wright and Williams stood out for Central while Brown and Trent also played good games. For Knoxville, end Gaylon Wilson was outstanding as he made a number of tackles on plays trying to turn his end and was an effective passing target, particularly on the long drive in the fourth quarter.

The T-formation, a big part of Central's offensive scheme, had just recently been used effectively by Stanford's Rose Bowl team led by Frankie Albert and the Chicago Bears with Sid Luckman at quarterback, but it still was somewhat of an unknown quantity in the football world. After the game, area high school coaches and local media prevailed on the Warriors to put on a demonstration of the intricacies of the system in a gymnasium adjoining the dressing room. So, in

Elwyn "Rip" Rowan, Central's All-Southern fullback.

shorts and socks the boys lined up and walked through their "T" plays. Coach Cecil Glass had purportedly gotten the plays through a personal contact with someone affiliated with the Chicago Bears and he was quite gratified at the attention he received for his ingenuity.

Christian Brothers wrapped up its regular season with a game against the South Side Scrappers on Friday, November 12. CBC was heavily favored. This was quite a contrast to the previous year when the South Side juggernaut had rolled over the Brothers 45 to 7 and run roughshod over every other team in the league on their way to winning the championship. But in the intervening period the Scrappers had lost a slew of outstanding players. Some had graduated, but there also were some boys who were a little older than normal high school age who now were in military service, as was their coach. Age eligibility for participation in high school athletics was more liberal in that era. In 1937, for example, the age breakdown for the All-Memphis team was as follows: one player was 16, three were 17, two were 18, two were 19 and three were 20 years of age. That same year Mississippi raised the maximum eligible age from 20 to 21!

Two years before, in 1941, CBC and South Side had engaged in a literal slugfest. That first year under Hatley the Brothers were already showing improvement and beginning to display the fortitude that would so characterize the 1943 team. By the end of the first half in that game neither team had scored and the favored Scrappers were getting increasingly frustrated. This was compounded by the fact that two of the CBC starters lived in the South Side neighborhood. Ed Kallaher, 190-pound center and linebacker, and his brother William "Wee" Kallaher, a 180-pound tackle, lived very close to South Side High and knew all the boys on the Scrappers' team, but because they were Irish Catholics it was a given for them to attend CBC. Naturally, there was some resentment.

South Side took the second half kickoff and, starting from its 20 yard line, drove down the field. The Scrappers got to about the CBC 15 with a first down, but two successive running plays were stopped cold by Ed Kallaher at linebacker. On the next play a Scrapper tackle charged out and hit Ed on the side of his face with his fist. At the same time, big Frank Davis, South Side tailback, cleared around end 12 yards for a touchdown. The blow that Ed took was the first of many passed that night. The playing field soon was a roiling melange of players on the field and from the benches, spectators out of the stands and police. Although he had the physical capacity to participate in a meaningful way, it is not known whether a certain Christian Brother was on the field to join the affray or to try to break it up, but it was reported that he got knocked down.

The police waded into the mob with billy clubs and Ed Kallaher says "they were really laying it on us." After maybe up to 30 minutes of fisticuffs and attendant activity the teams were reseated on their respective benches. The Kallaher boys at center and tackle and the CBC guards, Westy Harsh and Jack Gillespie, were ejected from the game and received a police escort to the dressing room where they were locked in.

Only two South Side players were expelled. One report has it that third-string players from South Side were sent in to instigate a fight in order to get the first-string CBC boys thrown out; however, Ed says it was a first-stringer who hit him and it is generally agreed that the South Side coach would not condone such an action.

After things simmered down, the game continued. In the fourth quarter South Side recovered a CBC fumble on the Brothers' 23 yard line and punched across its second touchdown for a 14 to 0 win. Fullback Kenny Sigman blasted in from the two yard line, but he was met with a ferocious head-on tackle by CBC's little tailback Gene Doyle. Sigman at about 190 and Doyle at 135 were both knocked out and Gene left the game with a concussion. The seriousness of his condition was not realized until he was taking a shower after the game and someone noticed that he was looking up at the water spray with his eyes open. When his pulse was checked it registered only 19 beats per minute.

After the fight there was no serenity in the CBC dressing room where the four banished boys were angry as ever. The remainder of the CBC team had been corralled on its bench by the police and, after the game, the South Side team walked to its bus, which was parked at the end of the stadium behind Central High School. When they arrived at the bus, the police concluded it then was safe to allow the Brothers to go to their dressing room under the stands. Little did they know.

There also was a back door to the dressing room. It was locked, but the four incarcerants battered it down and made a beeline for the South Side bus, being joined by their teammates arriving from the field. When the Scrappers' coach saw what looked like a herd of stampeding cattle headed for him and those of his team who had not yet boarded the bus, he put up his hands like a defensive end preparing to ward off blockers, but he was flattened as the wave rolled over him and fists again began to fly. In something resembling a Three Stooges comedy, one CBC player, who had a reputation as an amateur boxer, would peep out from under the bus and wait for a Scrapper to stick his head out a window; then he would jump up and bop him. In all the confusion that same boy swiped a pistol from one of the cops. The next morning at school Brother Lawrence David made an announcement over the public address system that carried to all the classrooms: "If, during lunch, whoever took Officer _____'s pistol at the game last night will lay it on my desk, there will be no questions asked."

William "Wee" Kallaher got his nickname when, as an infant, his grandmother would rock him and call him a "wee, tiny baby." However, he grew up to be a big boy. Wee's natural ebullience would sometimes get him in trouble and he was dropped from the CBC team; later he was expelled from school. He transferred to Catholic High. One morning Ed was reading the sports section of *The Commercial Appeal* at the breakfast table and saw where a "Harper Simmons," playing football for Catholic, had blocked a punt and scored a touchdown in a game at Corinth, Miss. the night before. Wee walked in and Ed asked him who this "Harper Simmons" was. Wee replied, "That's me; I'm ineligible to play at Catholic, so I play under that name for away games." Wee went into the army and was in the 42nd Rainbow Division, Sergeant York's old outfit. He fought in southern France and into Germany earning a battlefield commission, a Silver Star and two Bronze Stars. He and a Col Michael Fellons were the first Americans to enter the Dachau Concentration Camp. They were so upset and enraged by what they saw that they pursued the fleeing SS guards and killed them to a man. Col Fellons always sent Wee a Christmas card addressed to "Wild Bill" Kallaher. What he had experienced during the war, but more particularly the soul-shattering events at Dachau, had a lasting effect on Wee and he never was able to put those things behind him.

The 1943 CBC Purple Wave football team shot the works against South Side in their last game of the season and came out a big winner. The Brothers kicked off and held the Scrappers who then were forced to punt. Harry Costello took the kick at midfield and returned it all the way to the South Side 23-yard line. On the play, while trying to throw a cross-body block, Red Doyle, Gene's little brother, caught a knee in the side which broke three of his ribs. After finally getting his breath back, Red stayed in the game for awhile. He was taped up in the dressing room and played some in the second half. Phil Turner and George Whitehead carried the ball to the 11 and then Turner smashed down to the one. On the next play Phil dove in for the touchdown and Costello added the extra point. A little later in the quarter CBC got the ball on its 40 and drove for a touchdown in six plays with Whitehead scoring from 18 yards out. Costello's kick again was good for a 14 to 0 lead.

Early in the second quarter the Purple Wave took over on its 43-yard line and made another impressive drive to pay-dirt. Costello, Turner and Ross alternated in carrying the ball with the latter ripping off gains of 25 and nine yards. With the ball on the two-yard line, Turner carried it in for the score. Harry added the extra point and the Brothers were ahead 21 to 0. Near the end of the quarter CBC again was on the move when Jack Gibson fumbled the ball up in the air on his 40-yard line. With an alert move, South Side end Kirby Brubaker grabbed the ball and raced untouched to the end zone. Clifford Stewart kicked the point after and the Brothers' lead had been cut to 21 to 7.

Just before the end of the first half the Scrappers brought the crowd to its feet with a little razzle-dazzle. Clyde Holley passed to end Gilbert Mills who lateraled to Stewart who passed off to back Billy Sears who, in turn, lateraled to Hackney. The play was good for 30 yards and moved the ball to CBC's 21 where Hackney was knocked out of bounds. But CBC held at this point and South Side was unable to add any points.

Early in the third quarter CBC drove to the South Side 13-yard line at which point Whitehead passed to Bill Burke for a touchdown. Tackle Mark Follis attempted a drop kick for the extra point but it was blocked. A little later in the quarter Burke blocked a South Side punt and recovered the ball on the Scrappers' nine-yard line. Turner ran it in for a touchdown on the next play. Costello's kick for the extra point was true and the Brothers were now out in front 34 to 7.

A CBC drive in the fourth quarter reached the South Side eight from where Dippy Coles carried the ball in for the last touchdown of the night. Harry kicked his fifth point-after of the game and the Brothers came away with an utterly decisive 41 to 7 victory.

The following Sunday, with "Submarine Ball" Moss pitching and "Rocking Chair" Bassett catching, the Negro American League All-Stars met the Kansas City Monarchs, with Satchel Paige on the mound, at Russwood Park on Madison across from Baptist Hospital. Paige, who customarily pitched three times a week, was in his seventeenth year in the game.

BOOK THREE

Showdown
in memphis

Let there be one man who has a city obedient
to his will, and he might bring into existence
the ideal polity about which the world is so
incredulous.

-The Republic
Plato

On Monday, November 15, three days after CBC's game with South Side, E. H. Crump proposed publicly that CBC and Central play again on December 4 in a game to benefit the blind of Memphis and Shelby County. Purportedly the suggestion for the game had been made to Mr. Crump by Lake Hays, a local attorney who was past president of Lions Clubs International. Having completed their season, the boys out at the Brothers' campus were, that day, turning in their uniforms and some were ready to start playing basketball. Tackle John Fox was being processed for entry into the Marine Corps and expected to be leaving soon. Central still had three Prep League games to play and was looking forward to the possibility of a game with Boy's High of Atlanta, or maybe some fun in the sun with a week-long trip to south Florida involving a game with Miami Central and a possible cruise to Havana. Miami Central was led by "Pistol Pete" Williams, who later would star at the Naval Academy.

Approval of a postseason game was dependent upon a ruling from the Tennessee Secondary School Athletic Association, but if Mr. Crump wanted a favorable decision from that body, it was a foregone conclusion. In addition, post-season games had been held for years. Of particular note in this regard was the record of the fine Tech team of 1940, coached by Charley Jamerson. The Yellowjackets won the city championship and, along the way, beat some outstanding out-of-state teams. The latter part of October they traveled to Indiana and defeated previously unbeaten Culver Military Academy 12 to 7, outgaining the Flying Squadron 299 yards to 71. On November 30 they downed Atlanta Tech 12 to 6 on a rainy day at Crump Stadium, with the game sponsored by the Shrine as a benefit for the Crippled Children's Hospital. The score was no indication of the Jackets' dominance. Led by backs Jack Bishop and Marvin Curland and ends Harry Sayle and Billy Hildebrand, Memphis gained 362 yards without even attempting a pass while Atlanta picked up 125 yards; Tech had 18 first downs to the visitors' one. Atlanta scored when their All-Georgia tailback, Jack Pounds, broke loose for an 89 yard run from scrimmage against Memphis Tech's second and third stringers.

A week later Tech again played the host at Crump Stadium when it met Soldan High, which had romped through an unbeaten season and won the St. Louis championship. Soldan was led by Tom Lombardo, who later would captain the great 1944 team at West Point. The game was no contest. The Yellowjackets led 36 to 0 — six touchdowns and no extra points — before Soldan was able to put 13 points on the board against Tech substitutes in the fourth quarter.

In 1936 through the efforts of Frank Ahlgren, editor of *The Commercial Appeal* and a Chicago native, a game was played in Memphis between the Austin High Maroons, Chicago city champions, and the Robert E. Lee Generals of Columbus, Miss. Lee had won eleven straight games beating Clarksdale for the Mississippi championship and Blytheville, the Arkansas champion, both by 7 to 0 scores. Lee won the game with Austin 7 to 6, outgaining the Maroons on the ground 241 yards to 106 but was on the short end of the passing yardage, 36 to 98. Austin's coach, W. C. Heiland, was anxious for a return engagement in Memphis so his boys could redeem themselves.

In 1937 Austin again swept through their Chicago opponents. As was the custom in the Windy City, after winning the public school championship they played the Catholic league champs for the city title. Austin had a halfback who probably was the most publicized high school player in history. Bill de Correvont had scored at least one touchdown in every game of his three year high school career, and largely through his gridiron exploits Austin had gained a national reputation. In a 93 to 0 rout of Chicago's McKinley High, "Wild Bill," playing not much more than a quarter of the game, touched the ball 10 times and scored nine touchdowns. In nine games in 1937 the Maroons had scored 351 points to their opponents' 19 and de Correvont with 204 points — 34 touchdowns — led the nation; his picture was even on the cover of *Look* magazine. When Austin met St. Leo for the city championship, it was the kind of high school game that would draw a big crowd in that era, but it was de Correvont's fame that brought out the largest crowd ever to attend a football game — anywhere, or anytime. According to newspaper reports:

> *Soldier Field has 76,000 seats, but every aisle was packed with fans. Others crammed themselves in between the rows of wooden bleachers. Thousands of standees ringed the field. Overflows stood six deep around the top of the stands. The north end zone was packed with standees going back almost to the Chicago Park District administration building.*

A private usher service was hired to attempt to control the crowd, and their special police had their hands full trying to keep them out of the north end zone. The usher service estimated the frenzied throng at 125,000. Chicago police estimated 115,000. A figure of 120,000 was accepted as a compromise. The next day, only 4,188 showed up to watch the Chicago Bears beat the Cleveland Rams at Wrigley Field. Exhibiting his unparalleled blend of instinct, quickness and speed, Wild Bill did not disappoint the huge, expectant crowd. He ran for three touchdowns and passed for another as Austin defeated Leo 26 to 0.

When it was learned that Austin was willing to play one more game, offers poured in from various places in the eastern half of the country: Arkansas, East Tennessee, Georgia

Before a crowd of 120,000 people at Soldier Field in 1937, the great Bill de Correvont breaks past the line of scrimmage on one of his runs in Austin High's game with St Leo for the Chicago city championship. In the 26 to 0 victory, "Wild Bill" scored three touchdowns and passed for a fourth. (Courtesy of Howard "Bud" de Correvont)

(Riverside Military Academy, where Memphian Tommy Prothro was the star), Mississippi, Missouri, Illinois, Florida and Massachusetts. But Coach Heiland wanted to return to Memphis.

It was decided that Austin would play the West Tennessee champion, who would be decided by playoff games between Covington and Union City and Jackson and Memphis Tech. During the regular season Jackson had beaten Covington 13 to 6, Union City 25 to 6 and played a scoreless tie with Tech. In ten games the Golden Bears had scored 295 points to their opponents' 19. In rankings, for some strange reason Covington was rated number one in West Tennessee, Jackson second, Union City third and Tech fourth. In the first game Union City upset Covington and in the Jackson-Tech game, pitting two teams that obviously were on a par with each other, the Yellowjackets lost on a missed extra point, 14 to

13. Jackson then took the crown with a 20 to 0 win over Union City. The Golden Bears had played a very tough game with Tech on a Friday, beat Union City the next Wednesday and now had to face Austin on the following Saturday afternoon, December 11. Joe Fly, who played for Jackson in the mid-forties, says his brother Hugh, a starting guard for the Golden Bears' 1937 team, told him he was so sore before the Austin game he could hardly move.

Austin High had a distinct advantage. Because it had completed its season two weeks prior to the game with Jackson, it had ample time to lick its wounds and had scouted all the West Tennessee playoff games. Then canny Coach Heiland came to town and, in a controversy that raged almost up until game time, insisted that the game be played under intercollegiate rules rather than high school rules. In a colloquy at *The Commercial Appeal* that involved Jackson coach Tury Oman and lasted late into the evening the night before the game, it finally was agreed to use high school rules. If there was any particular reason for Heiland's strange request, it is not known, but it could have been a ploy to interfere with Jackson's preparations for the game. After the two tough games in six days, one only two nights before, the haggard Oman should have been attending to other matters. Heiland also insisted that there be at least one game official from the Midwest. To meet this demand, editor Ahlgren was able to obtain the services of a high school friend, the great Ernie Nevers, as head linesman. The former Stanford player, a member of the National Football Foundation Hall of Fame and one of the finest backs in the history of the game, added a lot of interest to the upcoming battle.

After being informed on the evening of December 1 that the eventual West Tennessee champion would be the Maroons' foe, Coach Heiland and his peerless all-around back, de Correvont, flew to Memphis on a Chicago and Southern airliner the following day. The next morning they visited the Ole Miss campus and that afternoon attended the Tech-Jackson game in Crump Stadium.

When the Austin team and their fans arrived on the Illinois Central's City of New Orleans at Union Station the night before the game, they were greeted with rousing football fight songs played by a part of the 80-piece All-City Band that would perform at the game. Meanwhile, Ernie Nevers, who then was backfield coach at the University of Iowa, had come to town the day before and on Friday, accompanied by a Chicago sports reporter and one from *The Commercial Appeal*, made a tour of West Tennessee high schools giving brief talks at Bartlett, Covington, Ripley, Dyersburg and Union City.

There was not much difference in the sizes of the teams. Austin's line, end to end, averaged 184 pounds per man while Jackson's averaged 180. The average backfield weights were the same for both teams, 168 pounds. Jackson's most effective back, Billy McKinney, formerly of Memphis South Side, had hurt a shoulder in the Union City game and wasn't able to start and played very little. The 5'11" 185-pound de Correvont was the difference between the two teams.

On a brisk, partly-cloudy day with temperatures in the thirties, as Acme Telephoto and the Associated Press wired pictures of the game to various part of the country, Jackson drove into Austin territory the first two times it had the ball but just barely missed on a first down try on the first series and lost the ball on a fumble the second time. De Correvont responded both times with quick kicks that were effective. Jackson couldn't make a first down on its third possession, and when Ross Long punted the ball went off the side of his foot and traveled only four yards to his 43-yard line. Austin moved the ball to the 38 and then de Correvont cut over left tackle, picked up good interference, faked out a tackler and outran the Golden Bear secondary for a touchdown on his first rushing attempt. This kept intact his record of having scored a touchdown in every game he ever played in.

Wild Bill set up the Maroons' second touchdown late in the second quarter with a 15-yard run but was hurt on that play and went out of the game with a broken collarbone. It was a hard-fought contest with several penalties for unnecessary roughness and one player being ejected for that violation. Austin gained 195 yards to Jackson's 145; almost unstoppable, de Correvont had 79 yards on five carries as the Maroons won 13 to 0. Jackson substituted only five players while, indicative of its depth, Austin use 15 replacements. Coach Heiland immediately declared his team the best in the country. Obviously, his claim was not an empty boast.

Bill's older brother, Howard "Bud" de Correvont, had been an all-city tackle at Austin, but their father died in 1935 and he had to quit school and go to work to help support the family. He worked for a few years and eventually attended Northwestern for a semester, but his budding football career was a casualty of the Depression. There were many good high school football players in the 1930s who never attended college. They either had to work or had no particular interest in furthering their education, nor were they encouraged to do so by their parents. Too, today's sophisticated scouting systems used by colleges to identify outstanding players did not exist then. Bud came down for the big game with the Chicago entourage and said the trip to Memphis was an interesting and enjoyable experience for everyone. He said they were a little taken aback by the Jackson players "wanting to fight the Civil War all over again," but, in mature reflection, "I understand why." The game was rough, but engendered by the mutual respect that good athletes have for one another, at least one friendship evolved from it as Bill de Correvont and a Jackson player kept in touch for a number of years.

Two years later de Correvont was in college, but the Maroons again swept aside all their Chicago opponents and looked south for a post-season game. Heiland was dickering with Greenwood, Miss. – and Memphis Central was undefeated – but he preferred to play Jackson again, which had won all eleven of its games. The game was played in Jackson and the Golden Bears won 7 to 6. However, in first downs and yards gained Jackson had a larger corresponding edge than that indicated by the score. Jackson started three sophomores in the line, including Charlie Hoover at center and linebacker. In his senior year, at six foot six and 225 pounds, Hoover made All-Southern. With his jersey sleeves rolled up to his shoulder pads and in a crouch with his muscular arms bowed in readiness at linebacker, Hoover was a formidable figure on a high school football field. He was headed for all-American stardom at Vanderbilt after the war, but broken legs in both his sophomore and junior seasons brought his career to an end. After the Jackson players had raised a little money with a public performance of a "womanless wedding," as a reward for their 1939 season a Jackson booster club made up the difference in cost and sent about 25 of the boys to New Orleans for the Sugar

Bowl game featuring Tennessee and Boston College.

Memphis was treated to a lot of good football at Crump Stadium in the several weeks before Christmas in 1937. On December 3 Jackson defeated Tech 14 to 13 in the first playoff game, the next day Tennessee, with George "Bad News" Cafego starring, beat Ole Miss 32 to 0, Jackson and Austin played on the 11th, and the following Saturday the Chicago Bears, champions of the NFL West, met a team of professional All-Stars. The All-Stars fielded such players as Don Hutson and Jim "Buster" Poole at ends, Bill Lee at tackle and Arnie Herber at fullback. The Bears had gridiron greats Joe Stydahar at tackle, Danny Fortmann at guard and Ray Nolting, Jack Manders and Beattie Feathers in the backfield. A cousin of the author, Henry Hammond, who had starred at Southwestern at Memphis the year before, started at end for the Bears and was designated game captain by Coach George "Papa Bear" Halas. The Bears won 28 to 13.

De Correvont went on to play at Northwestern, however he didn't quite live up to his promise. But he led the Wildcats in total offense in 1939 and 1940 and in rushing in 1941, and he made some long runs when Northwestern beat Notre Dame 20 to 0 in 1940. Batting over .400 on Northwestern's Big Ten championship team, he was about as good a baseball player as he was a terror on the football field. In his senior year he shared tailback duties with sophomore Otto Graham, a future college and pro Hall of Famer, who later quarterbacked the Cleveland Browns. Austin High teammate Alf Bauman, who probably was the best lineman on the field against Jackson, also went to Northwestern where he was an All-American tackle.

Bob Voits, an All-American tackle at Northwestern when de Correvont was a freshman and who later coached the Wildcats' only Rose Bowl team until the Cinderella squad of 1995, said of Bill, "Oh, boy, was he terrific. He was the thing in football." After college de Correvont went into the Navy for three years and, after the war , played five years of pro football for four different teams. George Connor, College Hall of Fame tackle at Notre Dame and NFL Hall of Fame linebacker, was a teammate of Wild Bill's for two years on the Chicago Bears. He said of him:

I was in the stands that day when they played Leo, and you've never seen anything like it. He was unbelievable. He had the speed, maneuvers, cuts ... it seemed like he scored a touchdown every time he touched the ball. He was the greatest prep athlete I've ever seen in my life. He was a phenomenon. But he was just the nicest, unassuming guy. He got more press than Red Grange, but it never affected him.

In 1990 de Correvont suffered a severely debilitating stroke. After that, he resided in a nursing home in Florida until he passed away, at age 76, on September 6, 1995. Later that month in Chicago about 150 people, including many of his old high school and college teammates, gathered for a memorial mass to remember a modest, blonde-haired boy who had been the talk of the football world and whose gridiron greatness had attracted that record-setting crowd to Soldier Field 58 years before.

The Central Warriors were tired when they arrived back in the Bluff City from their game with Knoxville Central. They had played a tough game sandwiched between two 400-mile train rides, and now they had the Tech game coming up in only four days.

Central and Tech were in the 25th year of their bitter rivalry. On the eves of these games Professor Highsaw over at Tech always had a dream about the outcome, and the newspapers would regularly contact him about his prediction. The year before he had accurately divined an upset and Central came out on the short end of a 7 to 6 final score. The Yellowjackets had four league victories and only the sound drubbing by CBC marred their record; they definitely were looking forward to a repeat of the previous year. Because of scheduling confusion when the season began, both teams were playing the game between other regularly scheduled games.

Ray Brown had suffered a hip injury at Knoxville and Joe Powell a concussion. Given the overall condition of the team with such an important game coming up, Coach Glass felt the emotional buildup and distractions of the city over the weekend should be avoided, so on Saturday morning the boys loaded up in cars and drove out Lamar Avenue 45 miles to Holly Springs, Miss. They checked into an old hotel near the railroad depot and stayed there for two days working out and even scrimmaging the local high school team. Being the big team from the nearby metropolis, they were quite a curiosity in the little town and small boys followed them around and showed up at their practices. During one of their workouts they ran the play that Slick Williams had dropped the pass on at Knoxville. Chugging at full speed 40 yards down the sideline Slick didn't have to break stride as Butch laid it in his hands. The involuntary gasps of awe from the assembled railbirds were audible across the field. On Monday morning they drove back to Memphis and got in their final workout that afternoon.

Tech was in top shape for the game and Coach Murel Nemecek, taking a cue from Professor Highsaw, expressed publicly his expectation for another upset. Bill Roberds started at end for Ray Brown but Joe Powell, seemingly recovered from his wedge-busting concussion, moved back into his regular guard slot.

Before approximately 17,000 fans, Tech kicked off short to Central's 26 and Trent returned it to the 36. The Warriors could pick up only four yards in three plays and, trying to keep the ball away from safetyman Clyde Hooker, booted it out of bounds on the Yellowjackets' 33-yard line. Tech likewise could not move the ball and punted to Central's 22. Rowan fumbled on the first play and Tech's Leo Wood recovered. Bill Crumby hit Joe Johnson with a pass on the 15, but on the next play he was intercepted by Bill Wright on the eight. Central made a first down and then, after being held on the next series, Wright got off a nice punt that Hooker fielded on his 30 and returned to the 35.

Staying on the ground with Wood, Hooker, Crumby, Johnson and Dutch Bauer running the ball, the Jackets moved to the Warriors' 40. On the next play Joe Johnson, running the same pattern from his wingback slot that Slick had wowed them with at Holly Springs, got open at the 20. Crumby's pass was perfect and Johnson scooted in for the touchdown. Hooker's try for the extra point was blocked by Trent, leaving the Jackets ahead 6 to 0.

In the second quarter a punt off the side of Hooker's foot went out of bounds on his 39-yard line. In three tries Wright and Rowan picked up a first down at the 28. Bill then slipped off tackle and picked up 16 yards before being brought down by Bauer. Wright gained four more and then Rowan blasted through the middle and scored from eight yards out. His kick put Central ahead 7 to 6.

Rip Rowan blasts eight yards up the middle for the first touchdown against Tech. Number 41 is Tech's Charles Turner; number 75 is John Trent. (Courtesy of Bill Buckles)

Later in the second quarter Hooker made a stunning 41-yard broken field run to the Central ten yard line. But the scoring threat ended when Wright jumped up and batted a Tech pass that landed in Rowan's arms on the eight. Central couldn't make a first down and kicked back into Tech territory. The Yellowjackets responded with a flurry of mainly incomplete passes that failed to put them back into scoring range before the half ended.

Buckles kicked off to Hooker to start the second half and Clyde returned it from the Tech five to the 32. The Jackets rolled for three successive first downs to the Central 17.

Caudle slipped and lost six yards on an end-around and a pass by Crumby was batted down. But then he hit Caudle on the 16 and, on fourth down, tossed to Hooker in the end zone. Hooker missed the extra point, but Tech had re-taken the lead 12 to 7.

There was no more scoring until the opening minutes of the fourth quarter. Despite his hip injury, Ray Brown came into the game. With the ball on the Warrior 20 Daltroff threw to Ray on the 40 and he raced 60 yards, outrunning three Tech defenders for a touchdown. Rowan kicked the point after and Central was back in the lead 14 to 12.

Three minutes later Bill Roberds blocked Hooker's punt on the Tech 31. As the ball bounded backwards, Trent picked it up on the 19 and was brought down on the 15. Three running plays put the ball on the seven and then Rowan got the first down at the three. Rip plunged to the one and then Daltroff slipped through center for the score. Rowan's kick for the extra point was wide and all scoring had ended for the night with Central winning 20 to 12.

In a game pitting two long-time rivals, previous results frequently can be discounted. Tech entered the game with only the one loss, administered by CBC, and they had a lot to gain by beating Central. They basically outplayed them for

Ray Brown, Billy Buckles, and Jim Laney on Central's hard-packed dirt and rock practice field; Crump Stadium is in the background. (Courtesy of Bill Buckles)

three quarters but, like the champions they were, the Warriors knew what they had to do to win and did just that in the fourth quarter. Maybe Central wasn't up to par because of the tiring trip to Knoxville less than a week before, but they had enough stamina left to run all over Messick only two nights after the Tech game for their third win in eight days. Tech, on the other hand, undoubtedly had a big letdown; three nights later they lost a battle with Humes for third place in the league by a surprising score of 25 to 7. Central's 13 to 0 shutout of Tech in the fourth quarter was, in large measure, due to the blocking and defensive play of John Trent at end, Joe Highfill at tackle, Jim Laney at guard and Bill Buckles at center.

Going into the Messick game Ray Brown still was bothered by his severely bruised hip, but he was able to start. Bill Wright again was plagued by "water on the knee" but he, too, started. In the line Lewis Jones and Maurice Keathley started at guard and tackle, respectively, for Powell and Highfill. Messick was handicapped by having three of their better players out with injuries, particularly Doug Krell who played fullback and linebacker.

Central was initially somewhat sluggish but seemed to gain momentum as the game progressed. Midway of the first quarter, on the running of Rowan, Williams, Wright and Daltroff, they drove 45 yards to the Messick 12. Behind good blocking, Daltroff then circled left end and crossed the goal line standing up. Rowan kicked the extra point.

Early in the second period they repeated the play that had broken open the Tech game. With the ball on their 30 Daltroff hit Ray Brown with a pass at midfield and, picking up blocks by Rowan and Wright, he went all the way. Rip's try for the extra point was blocked leaving the score at 13 to 0.

In the third quarter, from the Messick seven-yard line, Daltroff scored on the same play that he had in the first quarter. A little later Rowan broke past the line, bulled his way over the Messick safetyman and ran 53 yards for a score. Judd Williford's attempt for the extra point was wide and Central now was ahead 25 to 0.

After a long drive the final Warrior tally came with only 30 seconds to play. On a double reverse Brown tossed to Trent on the Messick five and he trotted across the goalline. Having missed on three out of four extra point tries, the Warriors decided to try something different. Tall, rangy Malcolm Baker was called into the backfield from his tackle position and, just for fun, smashed up the middle and into the end zone for the final point of the evening, making the score 32 to 0.

Messick crossed the Central 40-yard line in the first half but never penetrated deep enough to present a serious scoring threat. The Panthers' only other foray into Central territory came on the last play of the game with a pass completion to the Warrior 40.

Ed Crump's proposal for a second game was not a popular idea among the players on the two teams. If Central couldn't make the trip to Miami, or even Atlanta, then the preference was to play a team of Memphis high school all-stars. The Central seniors had been playing the CBC seniors since junior high school and didn't feel like they had anything to prove. Some of the Brothers' players would like another crack at the Warriors, but their season was over and, like the latter, they were a little tired of football.

On Thursday, November 18 Ralph Hatley passed the word that there would be a team meeting on an important matter in the chemistry lab on the second floor during lunchtime. The players strolled in and leaned against the walls or hunched over the experiment stations with their sinks and gas jets. Everyone was aware of Mr. Crump's proposal for the Blind Game, so Coach Hatley's expected message was brief. He told them that Brother Lawrence David had been contacted about CBC playing in the game and was awaiting the team's feeling in the matter before giving his reply.

Hatley said he recognized that the season was over, that most of them were tired of football and some were already practicing basketball, but the school was obligated to the City of Memphis to participate in a game like this. If CBC refused to play it would never live down the stigma of being unwilling to help a worthwhile cause. Hatley, himself, didn't want to play Central again, but he told the boys: "It's up to each of you, individually, whether or not you play. If you want to play, draw your equipment next Tuesday after classes and we'll start practice Wednesday afternoon. Those who decide not to play will not receive a letter for this year. In the meantime, I've got to try to whip a basketball team into shape."

As the boys filed out of the lab everybody seemed to want to talk at once. Some felt they should have won the first game and were tickled to be presented with the opportunity for another go at the Warriors; they were voluble in their glee. Others kept their thoughts to themselves until they had left the room and were out of the hearing of Hatley and athletic coordinator Brother Luke Constantius and his assistant Brother John Michael. For those who had no expectation of getting into the game and would watch it from the bench, it meant donning clammy shoulder and hip pads for about ten more afternoons and going through the unrewarding grind of practice. Particularly because the desire to play was not enthusiastically embraced by the entire team, one had to be inordinately

In his box at a Saturday afternoon college game, Mr. Crump discusses plans for the Blind Game with Henry Reynolds. (Courtesy of Henry Reynolds)

imbued with team spirit to the level of zealotry to want to go back on the field and knock heads in order to get the boys who would play ready for the game.

Late that afternoon, before the Central-Messick game that night, and again early the next morning before school, the phone lines were busy as leaders from both teams cussed and discussed Crump's proposed game. It was finally decided that a majority on both squads was opposed to playing again and that if anything was going to be done about it they needed to move quickly. In light of the exigency of the situation, the only recourse was to beard the lion in his den by going directly to the Boss. Because Central had won the game the previous

"The Corner." Mr. Crump's office was on the fourth floor. (A)

month and ultimately would play three more games than CBC, it was felt that it had a more valid case against the game and should take the lead in the discussion.

On that Friday afternoon, players from both teams rendezvoused on the sidewalk outside "The Corner." Representing Central were Rip Rowan, Slick Williams, Ray Brown and Bill Wright; from CBC were Tommy Mulroy, John

Walt, Harry Costello and Bill Burke. Although they didn't have an appointment, they took the elevator up to the fourth floor and told Evelyn Humphreys, the Boss' secretary, they would like to see Mr. Crump. After letting them wait for a respectable period of time he appeared in the doorway to his office. He raised a long arm toward the ceiling in greeting and in a loud, friendly voice said "Boys! Good to see you, come on in."

He knew most of them by sight and knew something about those he didn't know personally; in fact, Slick and John Walt were dating two of his granddaughters at the time.

After enough chairs had been rounded up to seat everyone, introductions had been made and things had settled down, Uncle Ed picked up an ornate letter opener off his desk and reared back in his chair. He was confident the boys were there to tell him what a good idea the proposed Blind Game was and how much they were looking forward to playing in it. As he toyed with the letter opener, balancing it on this finger and the next, he launched into a lengthy discussion of his vision of the game and what a great thing it would be for the City of Memphis.

As the boys were anxious to tell him the reason for their visit, most of what he said probably went over their heads. Finally, Rowan saw an opening. "Mr. Crump, it's been a long season and we've still got the South Side game on Thanksgiving next week. We've been talking among ourselves and the general feeling on both teams is that we would rather not play each other again." There was a general nodding all around the room, then Ray Brown drove in the final nail: "Besides, our parents are behind us on this."

As Rip spoke the old Red Snapper's countenance began changing from a friendly demeanor to one resembling a thundercloud; his eyes flashed anger and he started shaking his massive head of white hair. When Ray piped up with his statement that essentially constituted a challenge, the Boss lurched forward in his chair and slammed the letter opener down on his desk with terrific force; it bounced off and clanged across the floor. The boys sat erect, immobile. The oppressive silence was momentary, but seemed interminable. Mr. Crump had gotten their attention.

The Boss gradually composed himself and relaxed; he ignored the letter opener and what he had done with it. He spoke quietly with a touch of weariness in his voice that perhaps reflected a recognition of the undeveloped sensitivity of youth. "You boys have the opportunity to provide a significant service to your community by helping a large number of unfortunate people. Already the wheels are in motion involving many people who are donating their time to make this a successful enterprise. The printing of the tickets and programs is being done at no cost, there will be no charge for the use of the stadium and its lighting and after-game cleanup, the officials are donating their services, as well as those selling and taking up the tickets, and all concession profits and program advertising will be going into a fund for the blind."

As he elaborated on the plans for the game and what it could accomplish, his voice became stronger and more enthusiastic. "There will not be one penny of overhead expense! We are in the process of identifying those – without regard to race or sex, or whatever – who are blind and in need of financial assistance and they will be given checks directly without any bureaucratic red tape, probably about 600 in all. The efforts of all those involved will bear no fruit without your services; you fine boys are the star attractions; you have the ability to attract a large crowd that wants to see you perform. God gave you your talents and you have the rich opportunity to utilize them to help those who are not as fortunate as you. With the Christmas season upcoming it is particularly timely that we help our blind citizens; it will mean a lot to them to receive a financial gift that time of the year."

The room was silent for several moments as if all he had said was gradually being absorbed and analyzed. Then a couple of the boys moved in their chairs and shifted their feet; it was like a signal had been given to Rip and he spoke again. "We've had our noses to the grindstone with school, practices and games for so long that I guess we haven't been able to come up for air and look at the bigger picture. Now that I have a better understanding of what the game means, I'm ready to play." He glanced around at the others and they nodded acquiescence. "There again, though, we are a little tired of playing each other. Maybe Central could play a team of all-stars from all the other teams in town."

Crump spoke calmly, "I see your point Elwyn, and it's an idea that has merit. But I really doubt that we could attract a capacity crowd without CBC. Interest would be too dispersed. There wouldn't be as much spirit involved as there would be with two evenly-matched teams. The two of you played a heck of a game last month and everyone will come out expecting more of the same this time." He avoided any reference to the spying incident.

"I suppose you're right again, Mr. Crump." Rip made eye contact with Slick to see if he agreed and then looked at the three CBC boys and grinned. "I guess we'll be seeing you guys again."

"It'll be a different story this time," Billy Burke said with a laugh. Then the meeting broke up with the joshing and good-natured comments that the occasion and Mr. Crump's presence seemed to warrant.

Except for Joe Highfill, who had incurred a head injury against Tech, Central entered its last regular season game against South Side on Thanksgiving Day with its starting line-up intact, although Ray Brown, Bill Wright and Joe Powell were still dogged by nagging injuries. Before several games Coach Glass had said that Bill Wright would not play, yet he invariably ended up starting and making substantial contributions on offense and defense. South Side's squad was in good shape for the game.

Three minutes after Billy Buckles' kickoff, South Side was on its 43 preparing to punt when the center fired the ball over the kicker's head; Central took over on the 29. Wright, Rowan and Daltroff moved the ball to the 11 in five plays and then Slick Williams carried it to the five. Wright scored off tackle on the next play and Rowan kicked the point for a 7 to 0 lead.

A few plays later Ray Brown blocked a Scrapper punt on their 27-yard line. Rowan, Daltroff and Williams moved the ball to the South Side one and Daltroff went over on a quarter-back sneak. Rowan's kick was good for a 14 to 0 count.

The Warriors threatened again at the end of the first quarter but the drive was stopped when South Side intercepted a pass on its seven-yard line. Then on the first play Scrapper quarterback Clyde Holley was hit hard and fumbled with Central recovering on the six. Rowan was stopped at the line, but on the next play Hansberger went around left end to score. Rowan kicked his third extra point for a 21 to 0 lead early in the second quarter.

The Scrappers took Buckles' kickoff, got a nice return and finally started moving the ball. They produced some momentary excitement on this drive when Holley tossed a short pass to Crisp at end who lateraled to Mole Stewart who, likewise, lateraled to Billy Sears. For a moment it looked like he would get away, but Central closed quickly on the play and stopped it after a 14-yard advance. From the Central 46 Holley fired a pass out in the left flat to Mills, but Rowan, timing it perfectly, stepped in front of him and picked it off and went 60 unchallenged yards for the touchdown. This time Rowan's kick was wide, but the score had mounted to 27 to 0.

Immediately after this score about 15 to 20 men came down out of the stands and congregated on the track behind the Central bench; some even approached the coaches. From their railing at Glass and Roberts it soon became apparent they had all placed bets on South Side but had not gotten enough points to feel comfortable with the rapidly mounting score. Their antagonism was heightened by having probably imbibed a little Wild Turkey to go along with their Thanksgiving turkey. Mr. Jester arrived on the scene and then policemen came from several directions. After some minutes of pushing and shoving and angry words the thugs were gradually dispersed and escorted away from the bench.

In the closing minutes of the first half Judd Williford intercepted another Holley pass on the Scrapper 40 and returned it to the 13. He and Rowan smashed it to the five and Rip carried it in from there. Bill Rainer, a tackle, who had in a couple of previous games tried drop kicks for extra points, threw a pass for this attempt, but it was batted down leaving the score 33 to 0.

In the second half Coach Glass cleared the bench to provide an opportunity for all the boys to play in this last game of the season. South Side took the second half kickoff

and marched 80 yards for a score with Billy Sears doing most
of the running. Central pretty well contained the Scrappers for
the rest of the game but could not score in the second half. The
final score was 33 to 6.

The day of the Central-South Side game the two daily
newspapers published their All-Memphis football teams. As
previously mentioned, the afternoon paper, the *Press-Scimitar*,
had four from CBC and three from Central. Representatives
from the Brothers were Al Huebner at guard, Billy Burke at
end, Tommy Mulroy at blocking back and Harry Costello at
wingback; Warriors were Ray Brown at end, Billy Buckles at
center, and Elwyn "Ripper" Rowan at fullback. On *The
Commercial Appeal* team CBC boys were Huebner and
Costello and Mark Follis at tackle. For Central it was Buckles
and Rowan and Malcolm Baker at tackle, John Trent at end
and Louis "Butch" Daltroff at blocking back. Boys who made
both teams were Huebner and Costello, Rowan and Buckles,
as well as Clyde Hooker, tailback from Tech, and Louis "Red"
Williams, guard from Humes.

The *Press-Scimitar* also picked second and third teams.
On its second team were CBC's Follis and tailback George
"Bubba" Whitehead and Central's Trent, Baker and Daltroff.
The third team contained CBC guard Percy Roberts and full-
back Phil Turner and from Central tackle Joe Highfill and tail-
back Bill Wright. *The Commercial Appeal* selected only a sec-
ond team with Burke, Roberts and Mulroy from CBC and
Brown and Wright from Central.

Had it not been for Central's John "Sonny" Glasgow's
season-ending broken leg, incurred in the Whitehaven game,
and Billy "Slick" Williams' pre-season knee injury that
plagued him throughout the campaign, their names would
likely have appeared on these teams. As it was, in competition
with seven other teams in the Prep League CBC and Central
captured 15 of the 22 first team positions selected by the two
newspapers.

(Courtesy of Bill Buckles)

The Commercial Appeal
Thursday, November 25, 1943

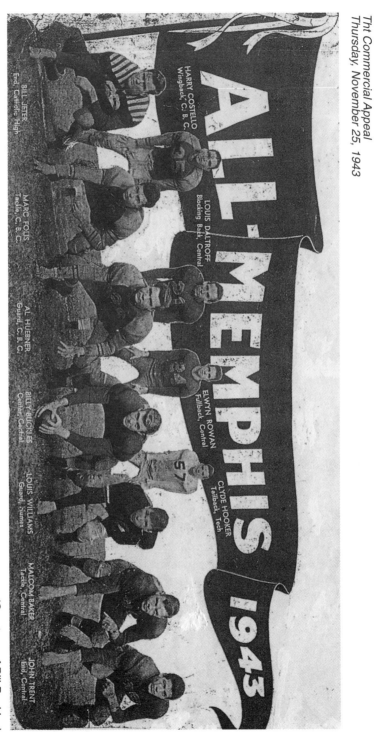

ALL-MEMPHIS 1943

HARRY COSTELLO
Wingback, C. B. C.

LOUIS DALTROFF
Blocking Back, Central

ELWYN ROWAN
Fullback, Central

CLYDE HOOKER
Tailback, Tech

BILL JETER
End, Catholic High

MARC FOLIS
Tackle, C. B. C.

AL HUEBNER
Guard, C. B. C.

BILLY BUCKLES
Center, Central

LOUIS WILLIAMS
Guard, Humes

MALCOM BAKER
Tackle, Central

JOHN TRENT
End, Central

(Courtesy of Bill Buckles)

As the Blind Game was only a week away, it naturally was uppermost in everyone's mind. Over the weekend players from both teams ran into each other at Fortune's and Pig 'n Whistle, but there was a tendency to withdraw and less of one to engage in light banter than there ordinarily would be. There were some remarks passed that were seemingly in jest and not caustic enough to raise hackles sufficient to precipitate any physical aggression, but the competitive fires smoldered just below the cloak of civility.

As the countdown to kickoff began, each new day brought a heightened anticipation and eagerness to don a game jersey and run out on the field under the lights at Crump Stadium. Particularly at CBC the practices daily became more spirited and harder-hitting with lots of hollering. Even those who initially had been opposed to playing another game became swept up in the building excitement. Percy Roberts, Al Huebner and others couldn't wait to get at the Warriors again. They felt that the difference in the first game had been when the clip on Follis, after Costello's punt, had not been noticed by the official – although everyone else had seen it – and, instead, a penalty was called for Hatley coming onto the field to check on him that made a difference of 30-yards in field position. Maybe the Central seniors had won every game over the years since junior high playing against those who were now CBC seniors, but the Brothers felt they had outplayed the Warriors in the 7 to 2 loss in 1942 and, under Hatley's tutelage, had progressed to the point that they were on a par, or better. They wanted desperately to prove it to themselves, to Central High, and to the rest of the City. It was time for a Showdown in Memphis.

Through the organizational genius of the Crump Machine, arrangements for the game proceeded full tilt. Large signs advertising the game were hung in prominent places on Main Street, theaters interspersed slides about it on their screens and 40 of the Boss' minions hit the trail with their fists full of tickets to sell to businesses all around town. The date of the game was changed from December 4 to Friday night, December 3. An appeal for support of the game was mailed to several hundred businessmen on November 27 over the signatures of Mayor Walter Chandler, E. W. Hale, chairman of the Shelby County Commission, and Mr. Crump. The day before the game *The Commercial Appeal* quoted Crump:

The tickets are going like hot cakes. And there's a reason. A worthy cause for the blind and a great football game between two magnificent teams, probably the best Memphis has ever had. It looks now as if we will have to put sideboards on the stadium to hold the crowd. Extra seats are being put around the cinder track. The game will be played rain or shine.

John Fox, CBC starting tackle, was scheduled to leave for the Marine Corps on November 26. However, the day before, Brother Lawrence David called him into his office and told him that he had received notification of a one-week deferment, which would allow him to play in the game. Brother had put in the request for the deferment, but one wonders if the hand of Mr. Crump was not somehow involved.

In the mid-thirties CBC and Central played four games that had particular significance. The beloved Notre Dame Coach Knute Rockne had been killed in an airplane crash in 1931 at age 42. Prior to his death this creative genius of the gridiron had guided the Fighting Irish to 105 wins and only 12 losses and 5 ties, including five undefeated seasons. In 1933 the Notre Dame Club of Memphis established a plaque in his honor to be awarded to the winner of a Prep League game whose team coaches had played for the Irish and used the "Notre Dame shift." Prior to each game one of the club members would present a memorial address to the memory of Rockne and the combined CBC and Central bands played "Notre Dame, Our Mother."

These games were played 1933 through 1936. Part of the proceeds went to the Crippled Children's Hospital. Whichever team would be the first to win three games would receive permanent possession of the plaque. Hugh Magevney was the Central coach for all four games. For the first game Emmett Murphy was at the Brothers' helm, in 1934 it was Norb Christman and the last two years Sturla Canale was the coach.

Central won the first two years 20 to 6 and 18 to 0. On a muddy field in 1935 they played a scoreless tie with both teams just missing field goals. The game was highlighted by the punting of Central's Billy Barnes, later a Tennessee standout.

In 1937 the favored undefeated and untied Purple Wave led 7 to 6 in the fourth quarter, but the Warriors came back to score with about six minutes remaining in the game to win 13 to 7 and gain permanent possession of the plaque. CBC halfback Lew Chandler, climaxing an 87-yard drive, ran the ball into the end zone from Central's 10-yard line for the first tally. But Central's Tommy "Red" Harrison connected on a number of long passes to his backs and ends to set up Central's two touchdowns. A favorite target was Irwin "Buddy" Elrod who later would be an All-American performer at Mississippi State. In addition to Chandler at halfback and Esgro at fullback, another star for the Brothers was big Gene Laurenzi, 282-pound tackle, "who figured in nearly every play through the line."

As game time neared influenza touched a few players on both teams, including Rip Rowan and Harry Costello. Joe Highfill had suffered a concussion in the Tech game, had not played against South Side, and his status was doubtful. Bill Wright continued to be plagued with "water on the knee" and Red Doyle was still bothered by the ribs broken in the last game of the season against South Side. On Thursday night Rowan and Tommy Mulroy were interviewed about the game on the radio and the next morning a parade was held downtown. Accompanied by the bands from both schools and the one from Whitehaven High School, players rode in open convertibles down Main Street from Ellis Auditorium to Beale Street and then back up Second Street.

As an early December darkness settled on Memphis, an air of expectancy permeated the city. Kickoff was scheduled for 8:00, but people started arriving at the stadium much earlier than that. With no nearby parking lots, the only off-street spaces available were at a few scattered businesses that had closed for the day. With traffic backed up in all directions and people parking along the streets as much as half a mile away, it obviously was going to be the largest football crowd ever seen in Memphis. Mr. Crump got there early and visited every ticket window to insure that everything was going as planned. City policemen tried to keep the traffic moving and there were firemen, state guardsmen, military police and shore patrolmen spaced every few feet around the stadium to fend off gate crashers and keep the crowd orderly. A steady stream of excited fans began filling up the stadium. A large block of them were female sponsors – two for each player – who arrived at their 50-yard line seats bedecked with corsages. These were the players' girl friends, mothers and, at Central, female faculty members.

When the teams came out on the field for their pregame calisthenics and warm-up drills Central's first exercise was side-straddle hops, what some call "jumping jacks." In time with their movements, the Warriors began a derogatory chant aimed at the Brothers. CBC quickly responded with a chant of their own casting aspersions at Central. When Coach Cecil Glass was spotted walking across the field in relative isolation, in recognition of his portliness the CBC band struck up "The Beer Barrel Polka."

After undergoing a doctor's examination Joe Highfill was cleared to play, so he was back at his tackle position. Rowan and Wright and Costello and Doyle also started. Possibly because they were seniors, Coach Glass started Louis Jones and Buddy Malmo at guards, instead of Jim Laney and Joe Powell, but the latter two played a lot.

Accompanied by three bands, the CBC and Central team members paraded through downtown the morning of the game.

302

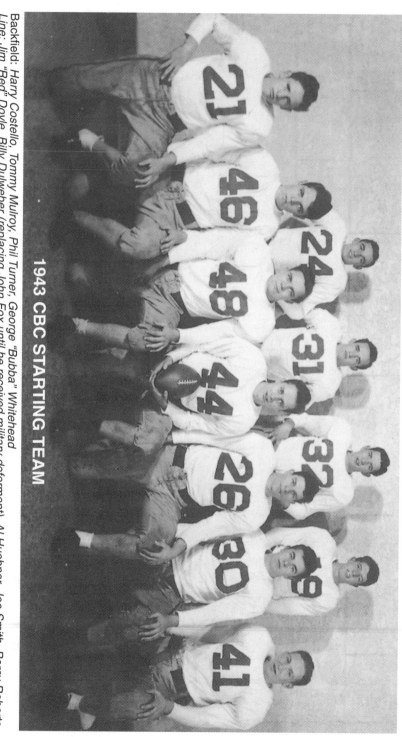

1943 CBC STARTING TEAM

Backfield: Harry Costello, Tommy Mulroy, Phil Turner, George "Bubba" Whitehead
Line: Jim "Red" Doyle, Billy Dulweber (replacing John Fox until he received military deferment), Al Huebner, Joe Smith, Percy Roberts, Mark Follis, Billy Burke
(Courtesy of Patsy (Mrs. Bill) Burke)

1943 CENTRAL HIGH STARTING TEAM

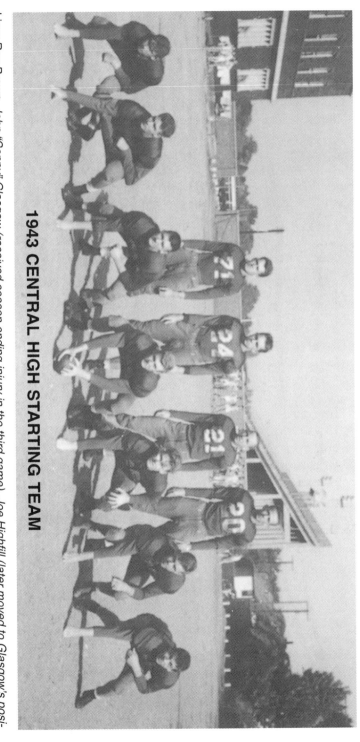

Line: Ray Brown, John "Sonny" Glasgow (received season ending injury in the third game), Joe Highfill (later moved to Glasgow's position and Joe Powell moved into his guard slot), Billy Buckles, Jim Laney, Malcolm Baker, John Trent

Backfield: Jack Callicott (subbing for starter Billy "Slick" Williams out with a knee injury), Elwyn "Rip" Rowan, Louis "Butch" Daltroff, Bill Wright

(Courtesy of Bill Buckles)

As the teams lined up for the kickoff it was a damp, chilly night with a temperature of about 45 degrees, almost the exact temperature when the first game was played seven weeks previously. There still were throngs of people waiting to get into the stadium, so the word was passed to Billy Buckles to delay kicking off until they could be admitted. Rather than continuing to take up individual tickets, Mr. Crump said "Open the gates" and the remaining crowd hurried in with many taking seats on the steps of the aisles; standees filled the track around the field.

After the 10- to 15-minute delay Buckles kicked off to Whitehead at the CBC 10 and he returned it to the 19 where he was tackled by Ray Brown. On the first play Whitehead tossed a pass to Doyle for a first down at the 30, but Mulroy fumbled on the next play and it was recovered by Trent. Rowan, Wright and Daltroff moved the ball to the nine and a first down. Daltroff tried a quarterback sneak into the left side of the line but was stopped by Huebner and Fox after a two-yard gain. Bill Wright could pick up only a yard, but then Rowan powered his way to the two-yard line. With fourth and goal the little CBC line dug in. Rip again blasted into the line but was stood up after only a yard gain and the Brothers took over on downs.

CBC couldn't move the ball and Harry Costello got off a fine punt to put Central back in its end of the field. The rest of the first quarter was played around midfield, as neither team could mount a sustained drive. Late in the quarter Ray Brown was hurt and carried from the field. Right after this Central punted. As Red Doyle rushed the punter from his end position he was blocked. With the punt away he now became a blocker; he took two steps back and got set. When short Butch Daltroff came at him Red dipped and came up with a forearm. Rather than receiving the blow up under his shoulder pads, Butch caught it up side his head and he dropped to the ground cold as a wedge. When he couldn't initially be revived Doyle got scared. A doctor examined him and an ambulance drove on the field and carted him off to Methodist Hospital. The doctor said he would be all right but he wanted him kept overnight as a precaution. Butch ended up spending several days there.

In the second quarter CBC drove to Central's 11-yard line. On first down Phil Turner picked up seven yards, but the play was called back and the Brothers penalized five yards for offsides. Phil received a hip injury on the play and left the game for good. Replacing Phil, Dippy Coles went back to pass but was trapped by John Trent and dropped for an eight-yard loss. Costello came around his left side on a reverse and gained four yards. On third down Dippy dropped back and hit Whitehead with a pass. When Wright tackled him, Bubba fumbled and Trent fell on it at the 10. Later in the quarter Huebner put a block on Rowan that caused an injury – probably to the ankle that had continued to bother him – and Rip was forced to leave the game. The first half ended with neither team having scored.

Mr. Crump spent the first half in his box on the CBC side of the field accompanied by Mayor Chandler, Ernest Ball, superintendent of education, C. P. Jester, Brother Lawrence David, Brother Luke Constantius, athletic coordinator at CBC, Will Hale, chairman of the County Commission, and Will Prescott, president of the Board of Education. During halftime

Rip Rowan, Ed Crump, and Tommy Mulroy pose for a quick picture at halftime of the Blind Game.

they journeyed to the Central side of the field to occupy a box there for the second half. The Whitehaven High School band performed on the field and then all the stadium lights were turned off. On a pre-arranged signal each of the 27,000 spectators lit a candle. The beauty of the moment and the amount of light produced was startling. The stunt was used to symbolically illustrate what is possible to accomplish when each one does his part when working in concert with others in an endeavor, in this instance, providing a light for the blind.

When the second half started Brown and Rowan were back in the lineup. The early part of the third quarter was much like the first half with neither team being able to mount much offense. Then from the Central 41 Rowan shot a pass out to Bill Wright that Costello' intercepted at the CBC 45 and returned to the Central 39. Helped by two offside penalties called on the over-eager Warriors the Brothers moved to the 25 with a first down. Coles and Sleepy John Ross moved the ball down to the 16 where it was third and one. Central braced for a plunge for the first-down, but the Brothers crossed them up with a pass. Dippy tossed it high to Billy Burke in the back, right corner of the end zone and Billy leaped and grabbed the ball. When he came down his feet were barely inbounds and he knocked the marker over as he staggered out of bounds clutching the ball. Although CBC got a penalty for delay of game after celebrating the touchdown, Costello kicked the ball true for the extra point and the Brothers led 7 to 0.

Central took the kickoff and came fighting back. At the end of the third period they had moved the ball to the CBC 37. Rowan picked up a few yards and then Slick Williams came around left end on a reverse with a lot of running room in front of him. He picked up 20 or so yards before Whitehead made a low, touchdown saving tackle. Slick's right heel hit his other foot and as he fell it caused his injured knee, with the brace on it, to lock up. It didn't hurt, but he couldn't get up. He started to call time out but he kept messing with it and pounding on it. It finally unlocked and he bounded back up and trotted to the huddle. The Warriors now had a first down on the Purple Wave 12-yard line, but, reminiscent of their stand in the first quarter, the Brothers bowed their backs and after four downs Central was back on the 17.

As the fourth quarter wore on neither team was very

effective moving the ball and most of the action occurred around mid-field. Costello got off another of his fine punts and Central took over on their 27-yard line with five minutes left; they knew this might be their last opportunity to get back in the game. With little respite both teams had been hustling and hitting hard throughout, and they were nearing the point of exhaustion. Each team had used only eight substitutions and, as previously mentioned, some had just gotten over the flu; Red Doyle had played every down with his broken ribs. Billy Buckles, at center, had been given a pretty good working over by CBC guards Al Huebner and Percy Roberts and he complained to Rowan that they were holding and pounding on him. He wanted Rowan to say something about it to Charley Jamerson the head linesman or Harry Sharp the referee, but Rip didn't want to take the time; he was more interested in putting points on the board. Ray Brown tells the story:

> Billy had a slight lisp and had trouble pronouncing a few letters such as "L" and "R." You have to visualize the picture. We're leaning over in the huddle, grabbing for air, getting the hell beat out of us, all grimy and tired, and Billy says 'Wipper, those guys are swugging me.' When Billy voiced his complaint, Rip, who was about to call a play, stood up straight, looked Billy right in the eye and said 'Well, Biwie Boy, you just tell them to twit it.' That sort of relaxed all of us.

On the first play Bill Wright fired a pass to Rowan in the flat and he scampered 24 yards to the CBC 49. Then Wright threw to Brown, but the Brothers' secondary knocked it down. Rowan dropped back as if to pass. It was not clear if the play was diagrammed that way or whether he saw an opening; in any event, Rip took off and picked up 14 more yards to the Purple Wave 35 with the secondary again having to bring him down.

Wright again dropped back to pass. The CBC defensive backs moved to cover the deep receivers and those on the line reached deep into their waning reservoirs of energy to summon up enough strength to again rush the passer. Rowan floated out to the left and seeing some room in front of him took off and crossed the line of scrimmage. Wright dropped the ball into his hands at the 30 and the CBC backs shifted over toward him, but Rip cut sharply back to his right and then swung downfield as he neared the sideline. He went all the way without being touched, as Bubba Whitehead's strenuous efforts to catch him were futile. Louie Hansberger held for the extra point and, as Rowan kicked it through the goalposts and tied the game 7 to 7 the largely Central crowd let out a huge cheer.

Bubba Whitehead is just a few steps too late as Rip Rowan scores the tying touchdown with less than five minutes remaining in the Blind Game.

After the kickoff the Brothers took over in their end of the field and moved to a first down. They were then stopped and Costello punted deep into Central territory. On the return Buckles was near Huebner and saw him angling toward the ball at about the 20 yard line. All the frustration from the pounding he had been getting from the CBC guards suddenly welled up, and he caught Al star-gazing and rolled into him low and cut him down with a vicious leg whip with the heels and cleats of his shoes across Huebner's shins. Huebner lay there and said, "Well, you finally got me." Billy replied, "I sure hope so." Huebner got up and said, "Nice block." It wasn't in Buckles' nature to purposely hurt someone and when he saw Huebner begin to limp from the field remorse overcame him and he hollered at Huebner's back, "Al, I'm sorry."

Central couldn't make a first down and after receiving

the Warriors' kick the Brothers came roaring back downfield. Rowan again injured his ankle and was helped from the field. CBC moved all the way to the Central nine-yard line but had a pass intercepted to end the threat. Shortly thereafter the clock ran out of time and one of the most exciting and hardest-fought games ever played in Crump Stadium was over.

Having recovered from his concussion received in the Blind Game, Butch Daltroff smiles from his bed and says he's ready to leave the hospital. (Courtesy of Bill Buckles)

The 7 to 7 deadlock probably was an appropriate way for the game to turn out. If CBC had won it would only have led to additional speculation and, in the extreme, the impracticality of a call for a "playoff" game. In a relatively few short months, many would be in a different kind of uniform playing in games with higher stakes in Europe and the Pacific; one would be killed and half a dozen wounded. If Central had won CBC would have been forever silenced. As it was, both teams could claim some bragging rights for having thrilled a crowd of 27,000 people with their skill and guts and having participated in one of the most unusual and significant episodes in Memphis sports history.

The next morning John Fox boarded a train and headed for Marine Corps boot camp at San Diego.

A week after the Blind Game Mr. Crump wrote a letter to his old nemesis Edward Meeman, editor of the *Press-Scimitar*. He accused Meeman of having tried to sabotage the game and, while he was at it, went on to excoriate him for other past sins. To emphasize his indignation, some of the letter, reprinted in part below, was in all capital letters.

> *You are running true to form in your hate – tried to break up the Central High and Christian Brothers College CHARITY FOOTBALL GAME FOR THE BENEFIT OF THE TERRIBLY AFFLICTED – THE BLIND – A DASTARDLY TRICK ON YOUR PART. YOU HAD YOUR REPRESENTATIVE TO CONTACT THE HIGH SCHOOL ATHLETIC ASSOCIATION OVER THE STATE, WHICH PASSES ON POST-SEASON GAMES – THROWING COLD WATER – HOPING TO PREVENT THEIR APPROVAL. FURTHER, YOU REWROTE YOUR EDITORIAL PAGE – SOMETHING YOU RARELY EVER DO – PROTESTING AGAINST THE GAME FOR THE BLIND.*
>
> *YOUR WHOLE CONDUCT ADMITS OF NO DOUBT YOU WERE TRYING TO BREAK UP THE GAME FOR THE BLIND, SIMPLY BECAUSE I HAD A HAND IN IT AND YOU WERE NOT CONSULTED.*

Changing topics, Crump went on to accuse Meeman of unfairly trying to discredit the governor, the mayor and two judges because they had not sought the support of the *Press-Scimitar* in their election campaigns.

> *Your nature is so steeped in suspicion, disappointment, vanity, hate, envy and lust for power, you are a deadly enemy to fair play, charity and truth.*
>
> *You haven't been a happy man since you came to Memphis thirteen years ago, because you have not been able to elect anybody to office in Memphis, Shelby County or the State of Tennessee.*

The scandalmonger, the tale-bearer, one who bears false witness against his neighbor, is not only a a despicable creature in any community, but sooner or later gets his just desserts.

You should have a first-class funeral inside yourself for your hates, jealousies, grudges, griefs and selfishness.

STRIP YOU OF YOUR PAPER AND NOBODY COULD FIND YOU AROUND HERE.

After signing the letter Mr. Crump added a postscript:

I have written you before in answer to some of your unfair articles, but you have declined to publish my letters. In this case I am sending a copy of this letter to a great many over the City. I want them to know what your purpose is – what is running through your mind – what is in your heart.

In recent years it had been the practice at Memphis' Central High School for the students to send Christmas gifts to schools attended by poor children in the Appalachian Mountains. This year the various home rooms provided Yuletide presents for the injured and maimed of the war who were being treated at Kennedy General Hospital. After each room was asked to contribute at least a dollar, $61.87 was collected. Gifts purchased were ties (khaki, of course), handkerchiefs, utility bags, picture frames, cigarette cases, shaving lotion and wallets; 300 ornaments also were donated for the Christmas trees at Kennedy. In the four sewing classes several hundred sewing kits were made for distribution to camps around the country. Dorcas Thomas was recognized as having done the most outstanding work and the leader in each class received a 25-cent War Bond stamp. Central High's Red Cross chapter gathered used clothing and 60 pounds was sent to the British War Relief Society.

The various clubs had their parties at school just before the holidays. A quote from the student newspaper, *The Warrior*, is indicative of wartime shortages: "The Spanish Club met in the recreation room (everyone spoke only in Spanish) and part of the refreshments were *Chocolate Bars*! Yes, each and every person had a chocolate bar, but how they obtained them is a secret."

The Warrior described the football banquet at Hotel Peabody thusly: "All in all, the dinner was unexpectedly good for wartime. The boys, sighing with relief that the training season was over, brought out great cigars and seemed to enjoy them immensely. Coach Glass would have awarded the sweaters, letters and footballs to the members of the team who had earned them, but because of the war situation the awards had not yet arrived." Billy Buckles was named "the boy with the best spirit" and Joe Highfill the "best tackler." Jim Laney and Joe Powell were elected captains for the 1944 season.

Although he was only 17$^1/_2$ years old and had just finished his junior year, Lamon Kelley, CBC's 1942 All-Memphis center and linebacker and his backup at that position, Roy Key, together had joined the Marine Corps in May. After boot camp at San Diego they were assigned to the Fourth Raider Battalion, which had a lot of Memphis boys in it and was commanded by James Roosevelt, the president's son. While in advanced combat training in California they became friends with a boy from Vicksburg, Miss. named Shelby Flowers, whose familiarity with gambling joints in Mississippi and Louisiana had made him quite proficient with the galloping dominoes. When the three got liberty to visit "Dago" or "L.A." and were short on funds, Flowers would get into an omnipresent crap game and soon acquire enough cash for the three to enjoy a riotous weekend ashore.

Christmas of 1943 found them in the hills above Noumea, New Caledonia, a non-combat area and headquarters for the South Pacific fleet under Admiral William "Bull" Halsey. While "the troops" were bivouacked up in the hills with little or nothing to remind them of the Christmas season, Navy and Marine officers, with an adequate supply of music, spirits and Navy nurses, were having a gay old time at a late afternoon wingding down near the beach. The party went splendidly until it was rudely broken up by incoming 60mm mortar shells lobbed its way by the boys up in the hills who had taken umbrage at the inequity of the situation. The next morning Marine tanks were sent up into the hills to forestall any similar future activity.

A little later Kelley and Key were sent to hot, humid, stinking, pestilence-ridden Guadalcanal in the Solomon Islands. This island had been invaded by elements of the First and Second Marine Divisions on August 7, 1942, in what was the first offensive action of the war by Allied forces against enemy-held territory. "The Canal" had been the place where the Japanese juggernaut, which had swept all before it in its drive through Southeast Asia heading toward Australia and New Zealand, had been brought to a grinding halt; a place where, despite food, equipment and ammunition shortages, miserable weather and environmental conditions and against seemingly overwhelming odds, Marines had triumphed. Although the battle had lasted into early 1943, the island was now secure when Lamon and Roy arrived, but they still had to contend with such things as a 180-inch annual rainfall and mosquitoes bearing a dozen different types of diseases, particularly malaria and dengue ("bonebreak") fever. Almost everyone contracted the former, some more than twenty times and, in the early days of the battle when there never seemed to be enough manpower to contend with the swarms of Japanese reinforcements, some risked dehydration by continuing to fight with a high fever in the oppressive climate. Key would later come down with filariasis, another mosquito-borne disease that causes swelling of the lymph nodes. There have been cases of such severity among Pacific Islanders that some have had to carry their gonads around in a wheelbarrow.

In the stifling dank and grubby environment of The Canal, Marine dungarees, collapsing in limp futility and sticking to the body, were destined for an early rotting death in the survey pile, so when Roy's Marine-pilot uncle showed up for a visit in pristine, starched khakis, he turned heads like a sudden materialization of a Varga girl at Main and Madison at high noon. Sensitive to his nephew's most pressing need of the moment, he brought two cases of beer for him.

Despite having attended CBC, Lamon Kelley was not a Catholic. But he became friendly with the Catholic chaplain, who thought he was making headway in converting Lamon to the faith. Their friendship reached a point where Kelley felt he could take certain liberties. Because of the scorn, jealously, and concomitant political manuevering by the larger branches of the military resulting in disproportionate smaller budgets for them, Marines have usually been under-equipped and, to some extent, their effectiveness has been due to their ability to patch up outmoded gear and to effect daring and imaginative midnight requisitions to acquire needed equipment. Somewhat in accord with this spirit, Lamon would help himself to what he deemed to be excess communion wine, appropriate the chaplain's jeep and make a 40-mile trip to a "Seabee" base on Guadalcanal where he would trade the wine for ice cream, film and other items unavailable to the Marines.

On his trip back to South Bend from attending the Sugar Bowl, Notre Dame coach Frank Leahy stopped off in Memphis for a visit with Rip Rowan. All Rowan would say later was "I enjoyed my talk with Coach Leahy." Former Boston College coach Denny Myers, in the service and stationed at Millington, had seen some of Central's games and, in a newspaper interview, said "Rowan and center Bill Buckles could have made my Boston College team."

John Trent:

He always had a smile and a nice word for everybody. He would look at you and his eyes would dance and sparkle.

-Bill Lacy

He was a man's man. He had integrity; he was straightforward. He loved life; he liked to have fun.

-Bill Wright

CBC and Central were now into basketball season. The Warriors were tops in the city and were picked to win the state championship. Judd Williford was captain and first string All-Memphis. At the end of the season they clinched the Prep League title in a game at Tech. Somewhat reminiscent of the cause of the brawl at the Pig 'n Whistle between Central boys and those from Humes and South Side, this was another time that the long-standing resentment against Central by other public schools surfaced.

Most of the Central players had showered, dressed and left when a Tech football player, accompanied by a handful of his compatriots, showed up at the door of the dressing room and asked for John Trent, who had just come out of the shower and was drying off. When Judd Williford told Trent that _____ wanted to see him, John said, "What does that so-and-so want?" Trent was well-acquainted with the Tech player due to the latter's considerable mouthing-off during the Central-Tech football game. Judd cautioned him, "Watch it, there's a bunch of them out there." Trent was nonchalant and matter-of-fact,

"Don't worry about it." He quickly donned the minimum and walked to the door.

"You want to see me?"

"Yeah, Trent, you know Central people act like they are hot stuff, but I don't think they are."

"Are you looking for me?"

"You've been getting a lot of publicity, All-Memphis and so forth, and I'm getting tired of hearing about you."

"That's not what I asked you. I asked if you were looking for me?"

"Yeah, I guess so."

"Well I'm tired of your crap, too; let's get it on."

They were almost exactly the same height and weight and it was a pretty good fight for awhile. Then Trent started landing with a jab whose telling effect enabled him to get in some hooks and crosses that really began making a difference. At this point a couple of Tech lineman jumped in and attempted to pull Trent back. Someone said to Trent, "You're going to kill him," and he retorted, "That's exactly what I'm trying to do." At this point the Tech coach, who had been leaning against the wall in the background, stepped in to break it up.

The next morning, a Saturday, Trent and Williford were walking down Main Street when they encountered John's much-bruised adversary of the previous evening wearing dark glasses and accompanied by some of his buddies. After an initial moment of tenseness, reasonably cordial greetings were exchanged and both parties continued on about their business.

In a single-elimination district tournament leading to the playoffs for the state championship, Central was upset by South Side, a team they had beaten twice during the regular season by approximately 20-point margins.

Harley Jeffery says he thinks Trent ran into the same problem that season after a game at Treadwell. It usually was the guys that had a reputation of being able to take care of themselves that the other guys who thought they were tough wanted to test. Harley, then in the tenth grade, said by the time he was a senior he decided to stop going to basketball games at other schools. "Every time you went there somebody would challenge you and you would end up having to fight your way out."

There was another boy at Tech who, in addition to being tough, was generally considered to be a pretty nice fellow, but it seemed that his preferred form of recreation was fisticuffs. He carried a pair of black kid gloves with him that he would put on just before going into action. One night at a football game at Crump Stadium he tried to get Harley to fight him under the stands. Harley maintains the guy was polite about it, saying something like, "Come on, let's just you and me go to it, just for fun." On another occasion, for no particular reason, he selected Slick Williams as an opponent. He had been pestering Slick during some athletic function in the gymnasium at Memphis State. Later, as Slick walked down the gym steps the war-lover stood waiting at the foot deliberately donning his gloves as he described the mayhem he was preparing to wreak upon Williams' physiognomy. The instant Slick got on level ground he hauled off with everything he had and knocked the loquacious lad, gloves and all, over a low brick wall surrounding a tree. Known for his ability to take a punch, the boy said, "That was a good lick," and quickly scrambled back over the wall; just as quickly, Slick sent him back whence he had come. On the third trip out, just as the campus cops arrived on the scene, the boy raised his gloved hands and said, "That's enough."

BOOK FOUR

Fields of Strife:
friendly and otherwise

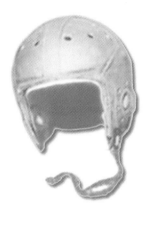

*War was our condition and our history,
the place we had to live in.*

-Martha Gellhorn

*On the fields of friendly strife
Are sown the seeds
That, upon other fields, on
other days
Will bear the fruits of victory.*

-Gen Douglas MacArthur

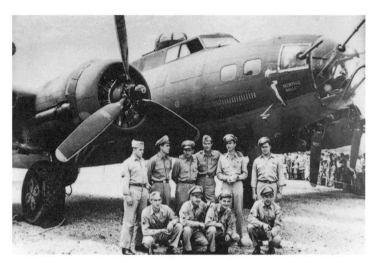

The "Memphis Belle" and her crew. This was the first B-17 to complete all its required bombing missions over Europe. (HD, M/SCPL&IC)

As the calendar was turned to a new year, most boys who were high school seniors in 1944 realized they had only a short time left to experience life as they had known it. Before them lay an uncertain future stretching out for an indefinite time. Eighteen-year-olds had been drafted since the fall of 1942; some waited for the call while others went ahead and enlisted. In his personal memoir of his wartime experiences in the Pacific, *With the Old Breed: At Peleliu and Okinawa*, E. B. Sledge said:

> *But the awesome reality that we were training to be cannon fodder in a global war that had already snuffed out millions of lives never seemed to occur to us. The fact that out lives might end violently or that we might be crippled while we were still boys didn't seem to register.*

Allied troops were still fighting their way up the Italian boot, the skies of Europe were daily blackened by hordes of bombers flying out from England, warships and carrier planes were engaged in vicious Pacific battles and the Merchant

Marine, carrying suppplies to the Russians, was dodging U-Boats on the perilous Murmansk run. Only six weeks before, the Marines had captured Tarawa Atoll, an idyllic, lonely dot of coral, sand and palm trees in the central Pacific, in a battle of such bloody ferocity and primitive savagery that the nation was shocked when some of the details were made public and pictures in *Life* magazine showed the bloated bodies of dead Marines. Prior to this, civilian photographers were not permitted to release pictures showing war dead. But President Roosevelt and his advisers were concerned that people on the home front, particularly war industry workers, were becoming complacent, viewed the war effort as consisting of rationing and scrap drives and had no conception of what was going on in the combat zones. Too, Hollywood, essentially under government directive, was turning out films that showed the good guys always winning and making it all look too easy. It was decided that the civilian populace needed to be jarred into realizing that it was a tough war with a long way yet to go to achieve victory, hence the still pictures in *Life* and newsreels showing American dead in the water off Tarawa rising and falling with the waves. War Bond sales jumped, but during the same period Marine recruitment dropped 35 percent.

*The Marines have a way of making you afraid –
not of dying, but of not doing your job.*

　　　　lstLt Bonnie Little (killed on first day),
　　　　last letter to his wife.

Tarawa Atoll, a part of the Gilbert Islands, is a nine by 17 mile looping chain of 47 very small islands, surrounding a lagoon, only 90 miles from the Equator. Pronounced TAR-a-wa, most of those who fought there call it Ta-RA-wa. Betio (BAY-she-oh), the flat island where the battle occurred, was just two and one-half miles long by a half-mile at its widest point and consisted of only 291 acres, less than half the size of Manhattan's Central Park. Its configuration resembled a bird with a long tail. The northwest corner was referred to as the "Bird's Beak," while the eastern end was called its tail. The island was so heavily fortified that its Japanese commander had boasted that a million men couldn't take it in a hundred years, but the Marines did it in 76 hours.

As the Second Marine Division sailed from New Zealand bound for Betio, Tokyo Rose came over the radio and announced, "There are 90 ships underway from Wellington, and we have a submarine waiting for each one of them." Lieutenant junior grade Edward Albert Heimberger, known as Eddie Albert when he was nominated for Academy Awards for his roles in *Roman Holiday* and *The Heart-Break Kid* and for his portrayal of Oliver Douglas, the city lawyer drawn to the country in the TV comedy *Green Acres*, was salvage boat officer on the attack transport *USS Sheridan*.

> *One of her messages was directed to us on Sheridan. She identified one of our sailors by name, stated that his wife worked in an airplane factory in Rochester – which was correct – then claimed she was shacked up with the factory foreman. This was false, but it devastated the man and spooked all of us.*

The Japanese had occupied Tarawa Atoll for two years and for the previous eleven months had worked feverishly to fortify it. By the time of the battle they had emplaced 104 machine guns, 42 artillery pieces, including four eight-inch coastal defense guns, purchased from the British well before the war, plus the cannons of 14 tanks, which were buried in the sand, and scores of mortars. These were all set up with interlocking fields of fire focused on the lagoon and reef area which the Marines would traverse to get to the beach. There also were more than 500 blockhouses and bunkers, steel pillboxes and other fortifications connected by trenches and underground tunnels; some of these were built of reinforced concrete five feet thick and overlaid with angle iron, sand, coral rock and coconut logs. The reef itself was dotted with concrete tetrahedrons, sprinkled with mines and laced with coils of barbed wire. Betio was garrisoned with almost 5,000 troops of the Japanese Special Naval Landing Forces – their equivalent of Marines – who were veterans of Asiatic conquests. Their warlords had indoctrinated them in the Bushido Code which, in homage to the Emperor, obligated them to fight viciously to the death while taking as many of the enemy with them as possible.

During the Japanesse occupation of the Gilberts, five Europeans and 17 New Zealand coast watchers had been rounded up and sent to Betio to help construct fortifications. When one of the prisoners cheered during an American air raid in October 1942, the garrison commander at that time, Cmdr Matsuo, became enraged. He had the prisoners rousted out for execution while some of the native leaders from adjoining islets were assembled and forced to witness the atrocity in order to impress upon them the reality that the Japanese were firmly in control. When Cmdr Matsuo drew his sword Rev Alfred Sadd, a retired missionary, stepped forward to offer himself as a sacrifice for the others. He simply became the first to die. As the natives watched, all the prisoners were brutally bayonneted and beheaded.

The Joints Chief of Staff had been convinced by advisors that a naval campaign through the Central Pacific would be feasible, in part, if spearheaded by "battle-tested shock troops with amphibious training," further identified as either the First or Second Marine Divisions. During months of rigorous training in New Zealand the men of the Second Division had been fed good and worked hard. Their high level of physical conditioning and their inherent aggressiveness, ingrained in them in boot camp and enhanced in the field by their combat leaders, would serve them well during the ordeal they would endure at Tarawa. Some of the battalions developed a sort of competition for bragging rights regarding their ability to hike long distances, but none would surpass Major Henry P. "Jim" Crowe's 2ndBtn, 8th Marines, which hiked over the hills and dales of New Zealand for 70 miles and then promptly turned around and covered the same distance back to camp.

A large number of the men had been through combat at Guadalcanal, some had fought in the Central American "Banana Wars," or Haiti, in the twenties and thirties, and a few had even done battle with the Germans in World War I. Living through the Depression, many had known only sacrifice in their lives; now they had been called upon to continue in that mode, to respond to "duty" – the word that Gen Robert E. Lee called "the most sublime word in the English language" – even to the lofty extent of possibly surrendering their brief lives to win a war for their country. Some had served in the Civilian

Conservation Corps in an effort to eke out a living and learn a trade to improve their lot in life. They were all volunteers in what they considered to be the world's elite fighting force and their character and manhood, forged in the crucible of hard times and Marine training, were about to be put to their ultimate test.

Using old charts drawn up in 1841, the Navy assured the Marines that when the landing occurred there would be five feet of water covering the shelf of coral extending as much as 1,000 yards out from the beach, thereby permitting access by all boats utilized by the landing force. The Navy brass ignored warnings by the former British administrator of the Gilbert Islands and a New Zealand Army major, who had lived on Tarawa for 15 years, that the autumn tides might not be high enough for the boats to get over the reef.

In his book on Tarawa, *Utmost Savagery*, published in 1995, Col Joseph H. Alexander, USMC (Ret), brought to light new information about the battle. Regarding Japanese preparations and the formidability of the defenses, he said:

> *Good intelligence saved lives at Tarawa, no doubt, but the disturbing fact remained that Betio Island appeared about as accessible as a porcupine. Just about every hydrographic and topographic feature on Betio favored the defender, from the unpredictable tides and fringing coral reef to the flat nature of the terrain, which would permit near universal machine-gun coverage by simple traverse. The senior [Marine] officers could see some of the mines ... sown in the waters; each fresh batch of aerial photographs reflected even more of the weapons. They could also see the abundance of horned scullies, steel-tipped tetrahedrons, and coral rock cairns dotting the offshore approaches, along with double-apron barbed wire and steel cables. Moreover, what seemed to be hundreds of machine guns and antiboat gun positions covered each cluster of obstacles.*

Two types of troop-carrying craft were available for the

assault. The Landing Vehicle Tracked (LVT-1 or LVT-2) was equipped with treads and had the capacity to ride through the water, cross the reef and traverse land at up to 20 miles per hour. It was referred to as an amphibian tractor, shortened to amphtrack. The LVT-1 was colloquially called an alligator and the later, modified version, LVT-2, a water buffalo. The other craft was designated Landing Craft Vehicle/Personnel (LCVP). This was just a little open boat with a motor in the back and a ramp that let down in front to disgorge the troops; it could not cross any kind of impediment. The amphtrack was exited by jumping over its sides. Both craft ordinarily carried mounted .30 and .50 caliber machine guns and could transport up to about 30 men.

The amphtracks had been brought to Tarawa by Landing Ship Tanks (LSTs) and the plan was to unload the troops on the transports down cargo nets into the amphtracks. Others would load into LCVPs, stowed on the transports, and later transfer into amphtracks, while both were in the water, after the latter had returned from the initial landings. The big problem was that there were not enough amphtracks. Of the 125 brought to Tarawa 90 were destroyed by mines, mortars and artillery fire – most early in the landing operation – and of the 500 men who operated them, 323 became casualties.

Time/Life correspondent Robert Sherrod went in with the fifth wave and wrote about his experiences in *Tarawa: The Story of a Battle*:

> *We jumped out of bed at midnight, swimming in sweat. Nobody took more than fifteen minutes to eat his steak, eggs, and fried potatoes and drink his two cups of coffee, but everybody was soaking before he had finished. This was the hottest night of all.*

> > *... we had received a little mail in the New Hebrides (where two practice landings were held), and among that mail was a letter from my mother. She had included a scripture that had to do with a psalm: 'A thousand shall die at thy right and ten thousand at thy left, but nothing shall come near you.' I also had my*

New Testament that I carried with me all the time, and the night prior to the Tarawa opera-tion — I had seen it many times, but this time it appeared and I used it for my prayer: 'Greater love hath no man than this: That he lay down his life for his friend.' And that's how I was going in, because I had no way of know-ing I was going to come out.

-PFC Carroll Strider[*]
Hendersonville, N. C.

The admiral commanding the fleet that would attempt to neutralize the Japanese firepower before the landing assured Marine officers: "Gentlemen, we will not neutralize Betio. We will not destroy it. We will obliterate it."

We had been led to believe we could go in and stake off our souvenir area and it would be a pretty easy deal.

-PFC Eugene Erikson
Rapid City, S. D.

Nineteen-year-old PFC Eddie Moore of Dallas, Tex. would be the driver of LVT-1 #49, but while cleaning one of the amphtrack's .50 caliber machine guns several days before the landing, a roll of the ship knocked the gun's 54 pound receiver off of an ammunition box onto his left foot, severely bruising it and relegating him to sick bay. However, when he heard the order come over the transport *LaSalle*'s public address system for Marines to start boarding their landing craft and noticing that no doctors or corpsmen were around to object and inter-fere, he dressed in his dungarees, informally released himself

---

[*] On November 20, 1988, the forty-fifth anniversary of the Battle of Tarawa, veterans of the Second Marine Division returned to Betio to erect a monument in memory of their fallen comrades. They replaced one erected by the British in 1963, when the Gilbert Islands were a pro-tectorate. It was removed in the mid-1980s to accommodate a cold stor-age warehouse for Japanese fishing interests. At the Second Division's annual reunion in Dallas in August 1988 some of these veterans were interviewed by Bill Burrud-Milas Henshaw Productions for their video *Return to Tarawa*.

from sick bay, climbed the two ladders to his amphtrack on the top deck and reported to his crew chief that he had been discharged and was ready for duty.

The amphtracks began loading about 0300 and at 0505, when it was still dark, the first 16-inch shell was fired from a battleship, searching for a target on the island.

> *The show had begun. The show for which thousands of men had spent months of training, scores of ships had sailed thousands of miles, for which Chaplains Kelly and McQueen had offered their prayers. The curtain was up in the theatre of death.*

Soon, two more battleships joined in the shelling, then five heavy and light cruisers and nine destroyers "... with many five-inch guns on each, firing almost as fast as machine guns. The sky at times was brighter than noontime on the equator." Then a hundred planes from the aircraft carriers — torpedo bombers, dive bombers and fighters — swept over and dove on the burning and smoking conflagration on Betio dropping bombs and spitting hundreds of .50 caliber bullets per minute. The sense was nothing could be left alive on that little piece of coral and sand. But the air strike was 30 minutes late. It was supposed to last 35 minutes but was over in seven. A scheduled massive bombing with 2,000 pound bombs by Army Air Force B-24s from a base in the Ellice Islands never showed up, but waiting for it delayed the landing another 45 minutes as the tide began receding from over the reef. All the while the amphtracks, awaiting word to move to the line of departure, were moving slowly in a score of circles, half a dozen in each, and the troops were being tossed around in the little boats getting seasick and soaked with spray.

At 0620, led by the minesweepers *Pursuit* and *Requisite* and supported by the destroyers *Ringgold* and *Dashiell*, the amphtracks churned through a channel in the atoll and entered Tarawa's lagoon. When the bombardment ceased the Japanese opened up with their big guns and the *Ringgold* took three hits. The transports, followed by the defenseless amphtracks, moved quickly out of range. The warships opened up again.

*If there had been an unearthly flash of lightning
before daylight, now, at close range, there was a
nether world of pandemonium. Hundreds of
shells crashed with hundreds of ear-rocking
thuds as they poured toward the Jap big-gun
positions.*

But much of the shelling was ineffective. As the shells
hit those Japanese strongpoints which were conically-shaped
or landed on the island in a relatively flat trajectory, they
glanced off or skipped away and exploded in the ocean on the
other side of Betio. Errors were made in range, deflection, trajectory, ammunition selection, and fuse settings. Many salvos
missed the island entirely.

At 0855 a Scout and Sniper platoon led by 1stLt William
Deane Hawkins, along with some engineers under 1stLt Allen
Leslie carrying flamethrowers and demolitions, landed at the
end of a long pier extending out from the island past the edge
of the coral reef. Their task was to clear the pier of enemy
troops who could pour enfilading fire into the amphtracks as
they approached the beach.

Then came the order from *Pursuit*, which was coordi-
nating the attack: "Land the landing force." The tractors peeled
off out of their circles and formed three parallel waves 300
yards apart at the line of departure 6,000 yards from the island.
Three battalions were to land abreast with each hitting one of
the invasion beaches: Red One, Red Two, and Red Three.
Moving east to west, one behind the other, the amphtracks
chugged along, parallel to Betio, getting lined up with their
respective beach. LVT -1 #49, which had been nicknamed "My
Doloris" by crew chief Plt/Sgt Lester Hairston of Cordele, Ga.,
was driven by Eddie Moore and was on the extreme western
end of the first wave, nearest to *Pursuit*. The crew chief in each
amphtrack held aloft a flag, and when Hairston received the
word he dropped his flag and the signal was relayed down the
line. The tractors executed a left flank movement and faced
the beach; the drivers pulled their throttles wide open and the
scores of little amphibians, cutting swaths of wake through
the deep blue water, headed full-tilt for Betio.

Fires burned fiercely on the island and much of the
beach was shrouded in smoke, naval shells rocketing toward

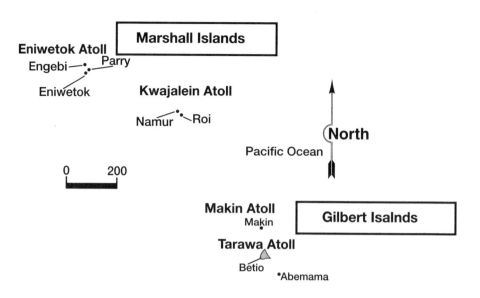

Marshall Islands

Eniwetok Atoll
Engebi — Parry
Eniwetok

Kwajalein Atoll
Namur • Roi

North

Pacific Ocean

0   200

Makin Atoll
Makin

Gilbert Isalnds

Tarawa Atoll
Betio
•Abemama

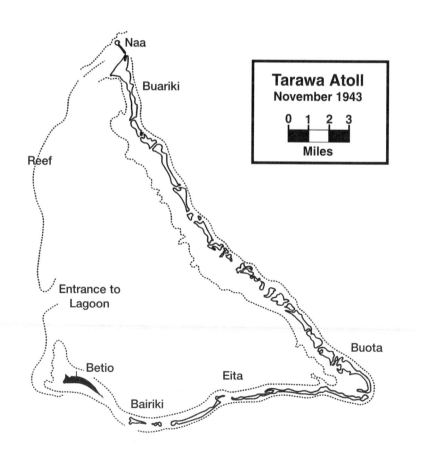

Naa

Buariki

Reef

Tarawa Atoll
November 1943

0 1 2 3

Miles

Entrance to
Lagoon

Buota

Betio

Eita

Bairiki

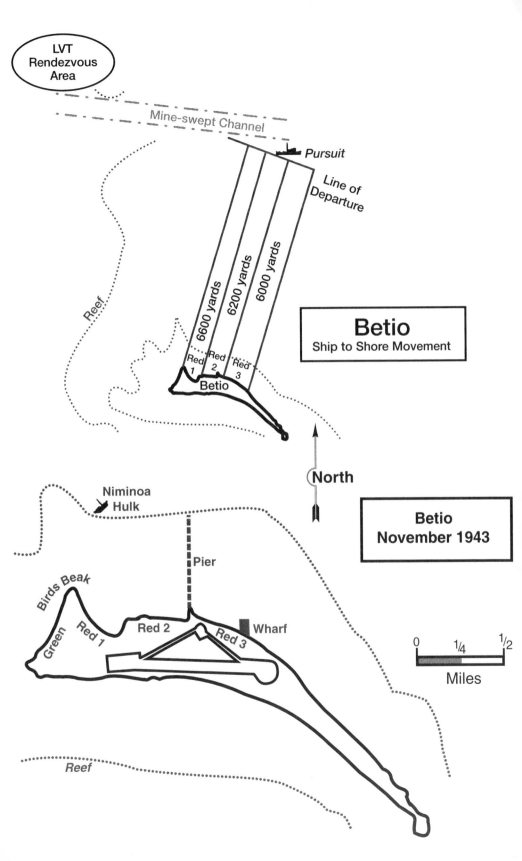

LVT
Rendezvous
Area

Mine-swept Channel

Pursuit

Line of
Departure

Reef

6600 yards

6200 yards

6000 yards

Betio
Ship to Shore Movement

Red 1

Red 2

Red 3

Betio

North

**Betio
November 1943**

Niminoa
Hulk

Pier

Birds Beak

Green

Red 1

Red 2

Red 3

Wharf

0   1/4   1/2

Miles

Reef

Betio rent the atmosphere with a sound like ripping cloth and the .50 caliber bullets of strafing fighter planes resembled the angry popping of grease in a red hot skillet. The tropical sun blazed down and the air was filled with wisps of burnt powder bags from the naval guns, bringing a burning odor to the nostrils with each breath; fish killed by the bombardments floated on the water's surface. When the amphtracks were 3,000 yards from shore the Japanese renewed firing of their artillery.

Over the crash of the shore batteries and naval guns and the roar of the amphtracks' engines, Eddie Moore could hear Marines singing in the other tractors. With a takeoff on an old song they bellowed, "Ta-Ra-Wa-Boom-Di-A, Ta-Ra-Wa-Boom-Di-A." Undoubtedly, all were fearful to some degree and each individual, in his own way, tried to keep the fear submerged and not permit it to envelop him. As he steered his tractor into the terrible crescendo of noise, the roiling clouds of black smoke and the angry flashes of enemy gunfire, Eddie prayed out loud and sang, "I'm Headin' for the Last Roundup."

Three religious medals, including a St. Christopher, were in Eddie's pockets. With these, he also carried throughout the war a picture of a nun, dressed in her habit, who had been his teacher four of the years he had attended Sacred Heart Grammar School in Dallas. Signed "Your Mother in Christ," in those unoccupied, stand-by interludes common in the military that provided a setting for bull sessions, whenever anyone asked if he had a picture of his girl friend, Eddie would show them the snapshot of Sister Teresa Joseph Ingram.

When the amphtracks were 2,000 yards from the beach the Japanese began firing their 70-mm howitzers and 50-mm grenade throwers. The long barrels of the 75-mm anti-aircraft guns were lowered to a horizontal position; at that angle they could fire 15,200 yards and, as close as the amphtracks were now, they could hardly miss. They fired high explosive shells with a muzzle velocity of 2,450 feet per second and the crews of each gun sought to maintain a firing rate of one shot every four seconds. The tractors hit the reef and bounced and lurched, tossing their occupants around as they traversed the coral shelf. The concrete obstructions, with iron rails projecting outward toward the landing craft, were designed to divert them into lanes where the Japanese artillery and mortars were zeroed in on and where the mines were positioned. The steel and lead shower of fire rippled the water surface like rain. Some of the tractors took direct hits, and if a shell was from one of the larger guns the amphtrack and its occupants disappeared in a ball of fire and a towering plume of water. The admiral had been grossly inaccurate in his assessment of the capability of the warships and planes to "obliterate" the Japanese and their firepower. The enemy simply had retreated to his tunnels and bombproof redoubts and came out ready to fight when the bombardment was over.

The amphtracks, firing their .50 caliber and .30 caliber machine guns, plunged ahead into the acrid smoke and toward the discordant and unremitting ear-splitting booms and clamor emanating from Betio; they clanged and scraped through two aprons of barbed wire entanglements, dragging wire and posts with them. Bullets hitting armor plate, hastily installed around the amphtracks' cabs and gun mounts before leaving New Zealand, "sounded like bells ringing." A four-foot high coconut log and coral rock seawall ran along most of Betio's shore and, now, at low tide, there was 20 to 30 feet of sandy beach between it and the water. A Japanese officer stood atop the seawall brandishing a sword, another waved his pistol, daring the Marines to come ashore and fight. Some of the Japanese Marines, eager to live up to their Bushido Code, left their fortifications and waded out to meet the amphtracks, firing their rifles and throwing grenades; they were quickly dispatched.

"My Doloris" was coming in on the extreme right flank of the first wave and was the first tractor to arrive at the beach, landing on the western end of Red Beach One at the Bird's Beak at 0910. Armorplate, with a slot cut out for driver visibility, had been installed over the amphtrack's windshield and the sides of the cab, but it was riddled with armor-piercing machine gun bullets on the way in. Eddie tried to drive over the seawall, but as the front end of the tractor raised up, exposing its underbelly, more machine gun fire knocked out its dashboard wiring, rendering it inoperable. An infantry sergeant stood up and yelled, "Everybody out," and was hit immediately, causing non-fatal wounds to his neck and shoulder that spattered everyone nearby with blood.

After the troops had rolled over the sides of the tractor to the sand, the Japs opened up with small arms fire and the bullets ripping the air all around the Marines sounded like the sharp cracking of strings of tiny firecrackers going off next to their ears. Less than 200 yards down the beach, Moore's best friend, Claire E. "Goldy" Goldtrap of Hobart, Okla., also 19, was killed as he drove his tractor onto shore. Before the battle would be over, Moore would lose his platoon sergeant, platoon commander and company commander to wounds, his battalion commander would be killed and the officer replacing him would be wounded.

In *Utmost Savagery*, Alexander noted:

Inland from the beach the battlefield took the form of a deadly barroom brawl. Japanese sallied forth from their gun positions and magazines to meet the Marines hand to hand. Bayonets inflicted several casualties among the Americans, but the Marines were adept close-combat fighters themselves. The sands became littered with the fallen from both sides: stabbed, hacked, choked to death.

Far off to the left, at Red Beach Three, the seawall was lower and it was into this area that 1stLt Aubrey Edmonds of Livingston, Ala. was leading his company of men from the 2nd Battalion, 8th Marines. When the driver of Edmonds' amphtrack got to the beach, the terrified man said "This is as far as I go." Edmonds, an old China Marine and Guadalcanal veteran who had come up through the enlisted ranks, cocked his .45 automatic and stuck it in the man's face. "Keep this thing going as far as it will go. You can die right here or you can take your chances with the Japs." The amphtrack plunged inland and reached the edge of the airfield where everybody jumped out. Sans his helmet, which he had given to one of his men who couldn't find his on the transport, Edmonds positioned his people behind some 55 gallon oil drums. They set up their automatic weapons and started mowing down Japs on the other side of the airfield who, lined up like a bucket brigade, were feeding shells to a large artillery piece. Two counterattacks by the Japs were repulsed.

Edmonds twice sent runners back to the beach to report his position to the battalion commander, but neither one returned. It's likely they were picked off by snipers, who were everywhere – lashed into palm trees, in covered holes called "spider traps," which frequently were steel drums buried in the ground with camouflaged lids, and in pillboxes. Edmonds finally went to the beach himself and found the battalion commander and legendary Marine, Major Henry P. "Jim" Crowe, a native of Kentucky. Like Edmonds, he also was a "Mustang," having come up through the ranks to achieve commissioned officer status. When Edmonds encountered him he was erect and walking around with his waxed and pointy, red mustache, cigar in mouth and carrying a shotgun. An internationally-renowned marksman and coach of the Marine Corps rifle team, Crowe was exhorting everyone else, who were laying prone: "Come on, get up and let's get after 'em. Those sons-of-bitches can't shoot; see, they can't even hit me." In retrospect, the small breakthrough achieved by Edmonds probably should have been exploited, but Crowe was concerned about the mass confusion and the flanks of Edmonds' company being exposed and ordered him to bring his men back to the beach.

The flagship *Maryland* carrying the fleet admiral and MajGen Julian Smith, commander of the Second Marine Division, had been repaired and refitted after being damaged in the attack on Pearl Harbor, but the first time it fired its 16-inch guns the communications system was knocked out and there was only intermittent contact with the troops on the beach. In addition, many of the radios carried in by the landing force had been destroyed or become water-logged and contact between landed units was severely reduced. Some units had landed on the wrong beaches and become intermixed with others. One of the battalion commanders was killed wading in, just off the beach, and many company and platoon officers were killed or seriously wounded in the early going leaving it up to non-commissioned officers and others of lower rank to assume command positions. Displaying initiative, in some cases privates paired up with other privates and began attacking the Japanese fortifications. Col David Shoup took command of the landed forces and set up his command post just three feet from a Japanese bunker with walls so thick neither could get at the other.

Shortly after Aubrey Edmonds had returned to the beach a shell hit nearby and a fragment tore a large hole in his back, rendering him unconscious. With other wounded Marines he was laid crosswise on a rubber raft, which was pushed by hand through the water to the end of the reef where they could be transferred to an amphtrack or LCVP that could take them to a ship affording medical care. A corpsman on the raft examined Edmonds and couldn't detect a pulse. He announced to those nearby that he was dead and asked for help in pushing his body overboard to make room for another wounded man. One of Edmonds' men, who was helping push the raft, threatened the corpsman with his Carbine and told him to leave him there. Aboard the ship, doctors were able to save Edmonds' life. Months later, while in a naval hospital in Klamath Falls, Ore., the boy to whom Edmonds had loaned his helmet that pre-dawn morning on the transport showed up to visit him – the helmet had two dents in it where bullets had glanced off.

On the Bird's Beak PFC Ed Moore was hauling ammunition from the crippled "My Doloris" to machine gunners who had set up on the other side of the seawall. Enemy mortar shells were impacting all around the area and, while Eddie was crouched behind the seawall putting sulfanilamide powder and a bandage on a man whose kneecap had been blown off, fragments from one that exploded behind him wounded Moore in the shoulder and arm. After getting over the initial shock, he resumed carrying ammunition to the gunners. When someone suggested that he board one of the amphtracks carrying wounded back out to the ships, he refused. He had seen a number of the tractors hit by Japanese artillery and mortar fire on the reef as they left the island, and Eddie figured that, for the time being at least, he was better off where he was. Finally, at about 1445 (2:45 p.m.), five and a half hours after landing, Eddie got on a LVT-2 Buffalo with other wounded returning for treatment. Also aboard, unwounded, was a Navy Captain, who had seemingly materialized out of nowhere. Shortly after leaving the beach the Captain ordered the amphtrack crew chief to stop on a spit of coral and sand about 100 yards out. There were at least 25 Marines laying on the spit and the Captain wanted to check them for signs of life. As he got out of the tractor he said, "Nobody leave this vehicle; just keep an eye on me and if I go down get the hell out of here." Still subject to enemy fire, the Captain checked each of the fallen Marines, but they all were dead. Visibly shaken, the Captain climbed back aboard, shook his head sadly and said, "They are all gone; let's get out of here."

Correspondent Sherrod loaded into an LCVP with Marines who were supposed to constitute part of the fifth wave. They were scheduled to transfer to an amphtrack for the

Picture of western end of Betio Island, Tarawa Atoll at 1406 (2:06 p.m.), November 20,1943. Amphibious tractors had made initial landings almost five hours previously.
In the lower part of the picture is the "Bird's Beak," located at the extreme western end of Red Beach One, which primarily constituted the cove area shown. The beach along the right is Green Beach where the 1st Battalion, 6th Marines landed unopposed on the third morning.
Vehicles from right to left are T-34 Sherman tank and then Ed Moore's LVT-1, #49 ("My Doloris"), up on the seawall. Between it and the next amphtrack to the left is a log structure which housed a Japanese 13-mm machine gun nest that riddled "My Doloris" armorplated windshield on the way in. As the amphtrack drove onto the beach, Moore paused momentarily to shift gears to climb the seawall, at which time two Marines jumped out and tossed grenades into the nest, knocking it out.
On the island, clouds of smoke from the firing of Japanese weapons can be observed.
In the cove are eight amphtracks. Because they are not creating a wake, they are obviously disabled. Many more, further out and in front of Red Beaches Two and Three (not visible in this photo) are in the same condition.
In the lower left corner the dark marks on the sand spit, 75 to 100 yards from the island, are the bodies of approximately 25 dead Marines. They were wading toward the beach from either a disabled amphtrack, not in the picture, or an LCVP that had let them out at the edge of the reef some 700 yards from the beach.
US Navy photograph (Courtesy of Edward Moore)

ride to the beach, but so many tractors had been knocked out that they couldn't find one. They bobbed around as 40mm bullets peppered the water and shells burst overhead; one Marine in his boat gulped and picked six pieces of shrapnel out of his lap. Two amphtracks passed by with dead and wounded in them. Then another came along and the driver said he would take them as far as the edge of the reef but could not endanger the tractor by taking them any closer. The driver stopped at that point and Sherrod and the others jumped into neck-deep water.

No sooner had we hit the water than the Jap machine guns really opened up on us. I believe I could have reached out and touched a hundred bullets.

Because of the Navy's erroneous assumption that the tide depths would be sufficient to handle supply boats going to the beaches, the supply situation was in total chaos. This was due to the Navy's fear that Japanese fleet units based in the Marshall and Mariana Islands, particularly aircraft carriers, might come to the aid of their beleaguered troops on Betio and launch an attack on the warships. So the removal of anything of a volatile nature, such as munitions and gasoline, had a high priority. Boats of varying sizes began stacking up willy nilly in the waters out from the reef and the Marines were not getting what they needed. The only recourse was to unload at the end of the pier, which was still under enemy fire.

Protestant Chaplain W. Wyeth Willard of Forestdale, Mass. had served the 2nd Regiment on Guadalcanal. He believed in being at the scene of the action with the troops to whom he was ministering, and he landed with one of the early waves at Tarawa. At the annual reunion of the Second Marine Division Association in Dallas in 1988 Willard, then in his 84th year, told a story about a sergeant who had been assigned from the Marine Raiders to serve as his aide on Guadalcanal. The young man, Bill Culp of West Palm Beach, Flor., had joined the Marine Corps after graduating with honors from a military prep school three years before the war started. For three months he helped Willard in his spirtual ministrations and nursed him through attacks of dysentery and malaria, then he requested a transfer to a line outfit. He told Willard that his association with him had been fulfilling – in fact, after the war he intended studying for the ministry – but he was trained in the ways of war and felt it was his duty to perform in a combat role with his friends and for the Marine Corps. He was reassigned to a company commanded by Capt Maxie Williams of Waverly, Tenn. and so distinguished himself that Williams recommended that he be given a commission as a 2ndLt. Later, on the docks at Wellington, New Zealand, as the division loaded into ships that would take it into another battle, Lt Culp told Willard he had a strong premonition that he wouldn't make it through this next action. After Willard had alit on the beach at Betio, the young lieutenant was one of the first dead Marines he saw. Willard went on to tell the old Marines assembled at the reunion's memorial service on Sunday morning that he had a picture of Bill Culp in a hallway of his home and that he paused there every day to say a prayer.

The first message to get through to the *Maryland* from Shoup's command post was a chilling one: "Have landed. Unusually heavy opposition. Casualties 70 percent. Can't hold." The 1st Battalion, 8th Marines had been ordered to land on the left flank of Red Beach Three after the initial waves had landed in the amphtracks. But, like the other ships and boats in the armada, they had scurried out of range in their LCVPs when the Japs opened up with their long-range guns and had lost contact with the *Maryland*. MajGen Julian Smith assumed they had already landed, but the battalion spent the rest of the day and all through the night chugging around in a big circle. At dawn, sick from breathing diesel fumes for something like 20 hours, they were located and ordered into the fray.

Having spent a lot of time fishing in the Chesapeake Bay region, Gen Smith was familiar with the idiosyncracies of tides, and he strongly objected to attempting to land across the reef with the LCVPs. It was only due to his persistence in requesting additional amphtracks that 50 more had been rushed from San Diego, arriving only hours before the assault. But his protests were overruled by the Navy brass, which had assumed control of the operation; Smith insisted that the rejection of his protests be put in writing. He also requested that the warships move in closer to Betio so that the bombardment would be more effective, but the admiral was concerned that he might lose some ships if shells from the shore batteries penetrated their armorplate. Smith pointed out to the admiral that the only armorplate the Marines would have was "the thickness of their kahki shirts." After the debacle at Tarawa, Marine MajGen Holland M. "Howlin' Mad" Smith, commander of Marine operations in the Pacific and called "the father of modern amphibious warfare," howled so loud that, from then until the end of the war, all tactical decisions relating to amphibious landings were solely in the hands of Marine officers.

Along part of the seawall of Red Beach Two at "Terrible Tarawa" (US Marine Corps Photo)

At the end of the first day the beachhead could be measured in hundreds of yards in length and, except for a few points where minimal advances had been made, its depth stopped at the seawall. With only 1,500 troops ashore and outnumbered something like 3 to 1, the Marines expected a counterattack that night that likely would have overwhelmed them, but it never came. The naval gunfire had had *some* positive effect in that, apparently, it had wrecked the Japs' communications and rendered them incapable of effective coordination. In addition, it was determined years later that Betio's commander, Admiral Shibaski, and his staff had been killed that afternoon by a naval shell that burst over them as they moved, in the open, from one bunker to another, thereby causing tactical confusion among the surviving leadership. Setting up an operating facility in a captured bunker, Navy surgeon Lt Herman Brukardt, assisted by three corpsmen, operated on 125 men through the night, saving all but four of them. They used up four flashlights and "When our anesthetics gave out, I had to perform some painful operations, but very few of the men let out a whimper." Col Shoup ordered corpsmen to wade out onto the reef to get first aid kits off the cartridge belts of dead men. During the night some additional troops and equipment were landed, and the tenseness of the situation was relieved somewhat when the Japs yelled "Screw Babe Ruth" and laughing Marines hurled back invective on the head of the Emperor.

Larry Wade was a 19 year old seaman first class from Oklahoma City. He, a coxswain, and a motor machinist constituted the crew on LCVP No. 13 attached to the attack transport *USS Heywood*. After the war he would become a minister and serve in several pastorates for a total of 38 years before retirement, but on the first day at Tarawa he helped bring in a platoon of Marines, which had been dropped off at the end of the pier, and he had assisted in transporting wounded back to the ships. The LCVPs carried Stokes' stretchers, which were made of a latticework of steel shaped for a body and were superior to the flat, canvas-covered stretcher. On the first trip back with the boat full of seriously wounded – one even laying on the engine hatch – Larry got sick at the sight:

> *My eyes had never seen anything like this. My stomach couldn't stand it. After vomiting a few times, I kind of got used to it. Before the trip was over, I could eat my rations standing by someone who had been gut shot.*

One of Larry's passengers was a sergeant who had lost a leg at the knee. He refused to lie on a stretcher, maintaining it should be used for someone in worse condition. He had used a web belt to apply his own tourniquet and, as he stood on his good leg during the 30 to 40 minute trip out to the ship, would occasionally release the tourniquet, let his stump bleed to forestall gangrene, then twist it back again with a bayonet. When they got close to the ship, because an air raid alert had been sounded, it was underway and they were told to "stand off." But the coxswain ignored the man with the megaphone and drew alongside. Underway, and in rough seas – "We could see all the way under the ship sometimes" – the wounded were unloaded. Someone suggested to the sergeant with the stump that he should be the first to be hoisted up the side with the hooks and cables, but he said "No, let the badly wounded go first." He waited until the last.

Staff Sergeant William J. Bordelon was a native of San Antonio. Born on Christmas Day in 1920, he was just a month shy of his twenty-third birthday when he was killed the first day on Betio. Landing in the first wave on Red Beach Two, his amphtrack took a direct hit from a high velocity shell about 30 yards from the beach, killing all but four men in his tractor. Working with two fellow assault engineers, Sgt Elden Beers of Deer Park, Wash. and PFC Jack Ashworth of Los Angeles, he destroyed two Jap machine gun emplacements with dynamite and, in the process, sustained shrapnel wounds in his face and a bullet through his left arm.

Attacking a larger fortification farther inland, Bordelon destroyed it but took another bullet through the same arm. Then a fourth dynamite charge exploded prematurely in his hand as he threw it. Although now seriously wounded, he refused first aid and went to the assistance of a comrade who was wounded and hung up on barbed wire in the water just off the beach. Immediately after this, Beers' Carbine jammed as he attempted to shoot a Jap who was throwing a grenade at him. He jumped to the side and hit the "deck," but the grenade went off just before landing on the ground and Beers was severely wounded, mainly in the chest. With his one good arm, Bordelon dragged him to a narrow swale and, out of demolition, acquired a rifle grenade and started to attack another fortification. At this instant, unseen by Bordelon, a Jap came up out of a spider trap with a light machine gun; he fired, killing Bordelon instantly. In the meantime, Beers had picked up an M-1 rifle and he and Ashworth quickly shot the Jap.

At Central Catholic High School in San Antonio Bordelon had been commander of the ROTC unit. He made excellent grades and was remembered as the "most studious" in his class. He also was known for his high level of integrity and his willingness, in any situation, to do more than was expected of him. The class prophecy about him was unusually accurate: "Military first, last and always." Two of Bordelon's classmates, Cpl Charles Montague and PFC Gene Seng, also were in the assault engineers. As part of a 15-man squad, they landed in an LVT-1, called "Worried Mind," with the third wave on Red Beach One, just east of the Bird's Beak, and were met with a torrent of ordinance. The engineers swept over the first position but then were caught in crossfire from adjacent strongpoints and all were killed.

Staff Sergeant Wiliam J. Bordelon
His repeated, courageous actions on the first day helped secure the initial, tenuous beachhead.

The President of the United States takes pride in presenting the CONGRESSIONAL MEDAL OF HONOR posthumously to

STAFF SERGEANT WILLIAM J. BORDELON
UNITED STATES MARINE CORPS

for services as set forth in the following

CITATION:

For valorous and gallant conduct above and beyond the call of duty as a member of an Assault Engineer Platoon of the First Battalion, Eighteenth Marines, tactically attached to the Second Marines, Second Marine Division, in action against the Japanese-held Atoll of Tarawa in the Gilbert Islands on November 20, 1943. Landing in the assault waves under withering enemy fire which killed all but four of the men in his tractor, Staff Sergeant Bordelon hurriedly made demolition charges and personally put two pillboxes out of action. Hit by enemy machine gun fire just as a charge exploded in his hand while assaulting a third position, he courageously remained in action and, although out of demolition, provided himself with a rifle and furnished fire coverage for a group of men scaling the seawall. Disregarding his own serious condition, he unhesitatingly went to the aid of one of his demolition men, wounded and calling for help in the water, rescuing this man and another who had been hit by enemy fire while attempting to make the rescue. Still refusing first aid for himself, he again made up demolition charges and single-handedly assaulted a Japanese machine gun position but was instantly killed when caught in a final burst of fire from the enemy. Staff Sergeant Bordelon's great personal valor during a critical phase of securing the limited beachhead was a contributing factor in the ultimate occupation of the island and his heroic determination reflects the highest credit upon the United States Naval Service. He gallantly gave his life for his country.

Eddie Albert was in a small, fast boat; his job during the initial landings was to help keep the waves on an even line and to assist any amphtrack or boat that might have mechanical, or other, problems. At some point during the first night he encountered Col David Shoup, commander of the landing force, on the pier. Shoup told him the troops needed ammunition, mortar shells, plasma and drinking water immediately. He told Albert to find it and personally get it delivered to the pier. The propeller on Eddie's small boat had been damaged on the coral reef and he looked around for a replacement boat. He found it among the group of LCVPs awaiting orders to land the 1st Battalion, 8th Marines. Larry Wade became his coxswain and for several hours they shuttled supplies to the pier and brought wounded back with them to the ships.

Instead of Red Beach Three, the 1st Battalion, 8th Marines erroneously headed for Red Beach Two, in the center of the landing area. As they approached the reef, to their left was the long pier that extended from the island to just past the reef, to their right was an inter-island freighter, the *Niminoa*, which the British had run aground two years previously to keep it from falling into Japanese hands. The Japs had set up six machine gun nests on the freighter and, during the night, snipers swam out to wrecked amphtracks and, with stealth, also positioned themselves along the pier. The troops were dropped off in deep water at the edge of the reef and began their slow 700 yard wade to the beach; they were met with a fusilade of mortar, machine gun and small arms fire. One panic-stricken coxswain approaching the reef abruptly stopped his boat, tilting it, and simultaneously dropped the ramp on the front spilling more than 30 men, with heavy gear on their backs, into the water – most drowned.

Pharmacist's Mate Robert Costello, who had assisted Lt Brukardt with the surgeries the night before, paused, along with others, in his ministrations to the wounded to watch transfixed at the horror occuring on the reef. He was interviewed by Col Alexander:

> *It was terrible watching the Marines being shot down. By that time I felt our cause was hopeless and the Marines would never get on the island. ... [Then] I watched one Marine coming in carrying a heavy load and saw him get hit. He continued coming in and I saw him get hit again, and still he kept coming, and then he was hit a third time. When he reached the shore I grabbed him, saying, "You stupid S.O.B., why in hell didn't you drop that load and crouch down in the*

water so you wouldn't make such a target?" As I dressed the wounds in his arm, jaw, and shoulder, I heard him mutter, *'They said we had to get this ammo to the Marines on the beach – that they were running short – I had to bring it in.'*

> *... but man it's a long ways; you can't believe it. And the Japs were shooting at us. And by the time we got to the beach we didn't have a handful of Marines in my company.*
> -Plt/Sgt Murl Bright
> Caldwell, Ida.
> (Awarded Silver Star)

A naval officer aboard one of the American warships observed the carnage through binoculars; he wrote: "The water never seemed clear of tiny men slowly wading beachward. They kept falling, falling — singly, in groups and in rows. I wanted to cry." Sherrod's view was from the beach and he wrote that the men seemed "calm, even disdainful of death... black dots of men, holding their weapons high above their heads, moving at a snail's pace, never faltering." One Marine said he didn't know whether to stay up high and try to get through the water as quickly as possible or to occasionally go under water; he decided on the latter course:

> *They were firing short of the line I was in, and you could actually see the machine gun bullets hit the water and hear them zing over your head. So I kept a pretty good eye on where the bullets were hitting and when they got fairly close I would go under water, and I suppose I made 10 or 12 feet progress toward the island, and I would come up and get a gasp or two of air and go back under water. I suppose it took me an hour and a half or two; I really had no way of guaging time.*
> -Cpl Bill Crumpacker
> Redding, Cal.

Two-time Pulitizer Prize winning historian Samuel Eliot Morison, in his 15 volume *History of United States Naval Operations in World War II*, said "... the Japanese fire was horribly accurate; several times it dropped a shell right on a landing craft just as the ramp came down, spreading a pool of blood around the boat." The reef became an outdoor abattoir, its chalky water containing an appalling melange of severed heads and limbs, torn torsos and desperately wounded men.

> *There were a lot of wounded Marines and dead bodies floating in the water.*
>
> -S/Sgt Jack Lent
> Dallas, Tex.

The Marines along the seawall began attacking in an attempt to enlarge their miniscule beachhead and provide some relief for the Marines wading ashore. It was a real slugfest on the most elemental and savage levels with rifles, grenades, bayonets, knives, flamethrowers, explosives, mortars, automatic weapons and, later, tanks, artillery and bulldozers.

> *And the lieutenant says, 'Send the scouts out and over the seawall and let's go; let's get even with the Japs.' And I had a scout in the platoon from West Virginia named Jones. (long pause) He threw his rifle up on the seawall and over he went. And they blew him back; they blew him past where we were standing and he must have had 25 holes in him.*
>
> -Plt/Sgt Murl Bright

From his vantage point behind the seawall, Robert Sherrod observed three Marines attacking a pillbox with explosives and a flamethrower.

> *As another charge of TNT boomed inside the pillbox, causing smoke and dust to billow out, a khaki-clad figure ran out the side entrance. The*

flamethrower, waiting for him, caught him in its withering stream of intense fire. As soon as it touched him, the Jap flared up like a piece of celluloid.

When the 1st Battalion, 8th Marines began landing at dawn, Eddie Albert was busily engaged in trying to retrieve two disabled LCVPs and transfer their troops into spare boats so they could get to the island. Then he became aware of the carnage occurring on the reef. More than fifty years later the scene is still acute in his memory. In an interview with Col Alexander, that appeared in *World War II* magazine in January 1995, he remembered:

> *It was a terrible sight. The beach and the shallow water offshore were covered with dead and wounded Marines. Closer at hand, there were about 150 Marines wounded or otherwise stranded along the reef. Somehow, the Japanese had infiltrated troops out to the end of the pier and to several disabled landing craft and to the hulk of Niminoa. They weren't just snipers – they had heavy machine guns as well. Our men were being shot from all sides and we seemed helpless.*

Albert began picking up wounded and shuttling them to larger boats or out to the ships, but it was taking too much time – the tide was finally coming in and some of the men were in danger of drowning. He commandeered five more boats and tried to lead them back to the reef, but the Japanese machine gun fire was so intense he waved the others back and again went in alone. While Larry Wade fearlessly ran the boat and another sailor manned the LCVPs machine gun and helped neutralize the Japanese fire, Eddie jumped into the water and started lifting wounded men up over the partially-lowered ramp of the boat.

> *It was awful. Sometimes I think we hurt the men more by pulling them up by their broken arms or legs than if we had left them in the water. We didn't have a choice. I still don't like to think about it.*

Aboard the LCVP were half a dozen or so 55 gallon barrels of gasoline, but their delivery to the pier would have to wait. The little boat, with wounded laying on its deck and on top of the barrels was riddled by the Jap machine gunners firing incendiary rounds. The crew stamped out small fires around the barrels or scooped up spent bullets and tossed them overboard and heard them sizzle when they hit the water. They later found .60-caliber, armor-piercing rounds in the boat and Albert brought one home and gave it to his son. Through their efforts at least 100 men were rescued. One of those who came aboard was a big, well-built Marine who had lost an eye and whose face and jaw were almost shot away. But he still had enough strength to lift Lt Dean Ladd, of Spokane, Wash., up over the ramp with one arm. He and Ladd lay side-by-side on the ride out to the ship. Although the man had difficulty talking because of the nature of his wound, they conversed all the way out, but he died shortly after being hoisted up to the ship. Ladd had a serious abdominal wound and was taken immediately into surgery. Fortunately for him,

After dashboard wiring on LVT-1 #49, "My Doloris," was shot-out during initial landing on "Bird's Beak," it ws repaired that afternoon and the amphtrack was put back into service. This photo, taken immediately after the battle, shows the tide in and My Doloris butted up against the seawall at the junction of Red Beaches One and Two. The log structure behind #49 is one of many similar structures that housed Japanese machine gun nests. The vehicle in the foreground is an LVT-2, "Water Buffalo." Note the bullet holes, received in the initial landing, in the armorplate over the windshield of #49. US Marine Corps photograph (Courtesy of Edward Moore)

one of the three surgeons had been an abdominal specialist at Mayo Clinic; Ladd would survive to participate in two more amphibious landings and acquire two more wounds before returning home.

The pier had been cleared of Japs the first morning by 29 year old 1stLt William Deane Hawkins' Scout and Sniper platoon along with engineers under 1stLt Allen Leslie. Hawkins' father was from Louisiana and his mother was the daughter of a Missouri doctor, but the family was living in Fort Scott, Kan. when he was born. While living in Los Angeles, a neighbor using the Hawkins kitchen to do her washing walked out a door holding a pan of scalding water. Little three-year-old William Deane ran into her and upset the pan. He suffered severe burns on a third of his body — his arms, his back, a shoulder, a leg. One of the baby's legs was drawn and an arm was crooked and the doctors wanted to cut the muscles, but his mother wouldn't allow it. For a year she massaged his arm and leg every day for two or three hours. The muscles responded and he began learning to walk again.

The family moved to El Paso, and when Hawkins was only eight his father died. He grew up there and did well in school, skipping the fifth grade, graduating from high school at 16 and winning the state chemistry essay contest. He wanted to go to the Naval Academy to study aeronautical engineering but was turned down because of his burn scars. Later, he tried to enlist in the Army Air Corps; again, the scars kept him out.

He attended Texas School of Mines on a scholarship and studied engineering. Like most sons of the poor, he worked and held a variety of menial jobs while in school. When the Japanese attacked Pearl Harbor he was working as an engineer for a Los Angeles title insurance company. Before the war he had said, "I hate war; I don't know why the United States ought to get into it." After the attack he said, "I've got to go," and he was proud when, despite his scars, the Marines accepted him.

As he left the West Coast to go overseas with the Second Marines in June 1942, he bade farewell to a friend by saying, "I'll see you again, someday – but not in this lifetime." Only a PFC then, he was a sergeant by the time his unit assaulted Tulagi, adjacent to Guadalcanal. Because he was fearless and endowed with natural leadership abilities, only months later he was commissioned a second lieutenant. His primary job on The Canal was leading patrols behind enemy lines to gather information. Jack Lent, of Dallas, remembers him as having a "good sense of humor" and being "a lot of fun." Most people referred to him as "Hawk," but Jack usually called him "Willie." He said Hawkins was a "cowboy" and had a slight limp from a broken leg when a horse once fell on him. Jack noticed it but, apparently, few others did. Hawkins was able to go through boot camp and, after Jack had completed it and recommended it to him, Scout and Sniper School, without the limp being detected or impairing his ability to perform.

He was proud of his Scout and Sniper Platoon and his men were devoted to him. Aboard the transport the day before the landing at Tarawa, he told correspondent Sherrod:

> *You know, we're going in first. We are going to wipe every last one of the bastards off that pier and out from under that pier before they have a chance to pick off the first wave. But one man has to stay behind to care care of our equipment. I asked for volunteers. Not a man in the platoon would volunteer to stay. My men are not afraid.*

Hawk plunged pell mell into the fighting. He was wounded slightly during the initial landing and, again, on the second morning. While in the forefront of his men attacking a fortified position just as the lstBtn, 8th Marines began to land at the edge of the reef, he was severely wounded in the chest by shrapnel from a grenade, but he held his ground and continued throwing grenades into the pillbox until resistance ceased. He returned to Shoup's command post and reorganized his men for an attack on another position, refusing to be evacuated for treatment, "I came here to kill Japs; I didn't come here to be evacuated." Another lieutenant told Sherrod: "He is a madman. I'll never forget the picture of him standing on that amphtrack, riding around with a million bullets a minute whistling by his ears, just shooting Japs." Outraged by what was happening to the men crossing the reef, he led his men in attacking a series of strong points that were firing on the lstBtn, 8th Marines, "... crawling or dashing up to the pillbox, tossing in grenades, leaping up to shoot through the slits." It was only a matter of time; the third wound was a mortal one and he fell just 50 yards from where Bordelon had died the day before.

He was carried to the aid station, but Lt Brukardt could see that the wound was fatal. The axillary artery in the armpit had been severed and he had lost a lot of blood. Treatment called for immediate surgery to clamp the artery and the transfusion of large amounts of blood, but there was precious little plasma on Betio. Hawkins lived only ten minutes after being brought in and his last words to his men were, "Boys, I sure hate to leave you like this."

Col Shoup said he came as near winning a battle as any first lieutenant ever did. Gen Julian Smith named the airfield on Betio for him, unusual for a non-aviator. Smith said, "It is the least I can do in tribute to a man like that."

1stLt William D. Hawkins
*I'll see you again, someday
—but not in this lifetime.*

The President of the United States takes pride in presenting the CONGRESSIONAL MEDAL OF HONOR posthumously to

FIRST LIEUTENANT WILLIAM D. HAWKINS
UNITED STATES MARINE CORPS RESERVE

for services as set forth in the following

CITATION:

For valorous and gallant conduct above and beyond the call of duty as Commanding Officer of a Scout and Sniper Platoon attached to the Second Marines, Second Marine Division, in action against Japanese-held Tarawa in the Gilbert Islands, November 20 and 21, 1943. The first to disembark from the jeep lighter, First Lieutenant Hawkins unhesitatingly moved forward under heavy enemy fire at the end of the Betio pier, neutralizing emplacements in coverage of troops assaulting the main beach positions. Fearlessly leading his men on to join the forces fighting desperately to gain a beachhead, he repeatedly risked his life throughout the day and night to direct and lead attacks on pillboxes and installations with grenades and demolitions. At dawn on the following day, First Lieutenant Hawkins returned to the dangerous mission of clearing the limited beachhead of Japanese resistance, personally initiating an assault on a hostile position fortified by five enemy machine guns and, crawling forward in the face of withering fire, boldly fired point-blank into the loopholes and completed the destruction with grenades. Refusing to withdraw after being seriously wounded in the chest during this skirmish, First Lieutenant Hawkins steadfastly carried the fight to the enemy, destroying three more pillboxes before he was caught in a burst of Japanese shell fire and mortally wounded. His relentless fighting spirit in the face of formidable opposition and his exceptionally daring tactics were an inspiration to his comrades during the most crucial phase of the battle and reflect the highest credit upon the United States Naval Service. He gallantly gave his life for his country.

Alexander Bonnyman, Jr. was born in Atlanta. When he was an infant his family moved to Knoxville, where he grew to manhood. His father owned a large coal company and the family was well-to-do. When he completed prep school he

attended Princeton University for a year and played football for the Tigers. But college must have bored him, for he dropped out and went to work for his father's Blue Diamond Coal Co.

"Sandy," as family and friends knew him by, was a gregarious, free-spirited young man who was fun to be around. His personality and love of adventure got him into escapades that inspired others to tell stories about him. After hunting and fishing all over the West, in 1932, at age 22, he joined the Army Air Corps and was sent to flight school in San Antonio. The third time he buzzed the control tower at Kelly Field the Air Corps decided he was too exuberant for its taste, and they came to a parting of the ways. But he had been smitten by a local lass and stayed on in the Alamo City, working at small jobs, until he won her hand.

Bonnyman later acquired two copper mines in New Mexico, and when the war started he and his wife and three small daughters were living in Santa Fe. His anticipation of the United States being involved in war had been the impetus for his joining the Air Corps; now, he told his partner one of them should go into the service while the other stayed and tended to the business. Either his familial status or his employment in an industry essential to the war effort would have kept him out of the military, but Sandy felt a patriotic obligation to fight.

Bonnyman enlisted in the Marine Corps as a 31 year old private, served on Guadalcanal where he received a battlefield commission and landed at Tarawa's Red Beach Two on the first day. He was a shore party officer, responsible for channeling supplies to the troops from the beach, but the supply ships were unable to get to the beach and the narrow pier was choked with boxes and crates, so Bonnyman had nothing to do. He began helping out as best he could and, in the natural course of events, ended up at Red Beach Three where he encountered a handful of assault engineers who had penetrated about 100 feet inland from the seawall where they had been stopped cold by a large, concrete and sand-covered bunker that was holding up the advance in that entire sector of the island.

With only narrow corridors of open space along two sides of this huge, two-story pillbox, it was virtually surrounded by all sorts of debris and fallen palm trees where the Japs could secrete themselves and set up fields of fire without being seen. In addition to slits in the pillbox from which to fire at the Marines, there also were machine gunners on the top who had a wide range of vision on the flat island. All of this combined to enable the Japs to unleash a tremendous amount of firepower. 1stLt Bonnyman was unknown to the enlisted men from the 2nd Battalion, 8th Marines who had been trying to capture the pillbox, so he did not attempt to take over and give orders. He listened attentively to the methods they had been employing and what the results had been and a plan began developing in his mind. His charasmatic personality and confident demeanor had by now gained the confidence of the men and he gathered together half a dozen of them and explained how he thought the attack should be carried out. The battle was entering its third day and for at least the same period of time the men had had virtually no sleep and were exhausted, but Bonnyman inspired them for one more all out attack.

Assigning a specific task to each man and getting them into position for the attack, Bonnyman then led the charge through a hail of bullets to the base of the pillbox. They climbed up the loose, sandy slope of the two-story high structure and when they got near the top Cpl Harry Niehoff of Portland, Ore. tossed a packet of TNT up on it. The smoke and dust resulting from the explosion provided cover for the slow ascent by Cpl John Borich of Pittsburgh with 70 pound flamethrower tanks strapped to his back. Rising into a crouch, Borich pulled the trigger that ignited the "match" at the end of the nozzle and depressed the lever that released the air-pressured fuel. The flames roared over the lip of the pillbox's top and incinerated a Japanese machine gun crew. Bonnyman, Neihoff, Borich and a fourth man ran to the top and quickly annihilated the other machine gun crew. TNT charges were dropped into ventilation vents and at the entrance to a tunnel connected to the pillbox. The Japs came swarming out like angry hornets from a disturbed nest and a vicious firefight ensued with Bonnyman getting shot and killed.

Because it led to a breakthrough that helped turn the tide of the battle, the capture of the pillbox was a significant accomplishment. Niehoff and Borich were both recommended for the Silver Star. Bonnyman's memory is perpetuated through the maritime prepositioning ship *Bonnyman* and the

Alexander Bonnyman, Jr. Marine Corps League chapter in Knoxville. Heroic achievements apparently run in the family. Sandy's brother, Gordon, was an Army captain with the famous Merrill's Marauders that fought in Burma; he was severely wounded, spending many months in Army hospitals, and was awarded the Silver Star.

1stLt Alexander Bonnyman, Jr. His two days of heroism, culminating in the seizure of the heavily-garrisoned bomb-proof bunker, broke the back of the Japanese defenses. Painting, by an unknown artist, from a photograph. (Courtesy of Alexandra Bonnyman Prejean)

The President of the United States takes pride in presenting the CONGRESSIONAL MEDAL OF HONOR posthumously to

First Lieutenant Alexander Bonnyman, Jr.
United States Marine Corps Reserve

for services as set forth in the following

CITATION:

For conspicuous gallantry and intrepidity at the risk of his life above and beyond the call of duty as Executive Officer of the Second Battalion Shore Party, Eighth Marines, Second Marine Division, during the assault against Japanese-held Tarawa in the Gilbert Islands, from 20 to 22 November, 1943. Acting on his own initiative when assault troops were pinned down at the far end of Betio pier by the overwhelming fire of Japanese shore batteries, First Lieutenant Bonnyman repeatedly defied the blasting fury of the enemy bombardment to organize and lead the besieged men over the long, open pier to the beach and then, voluntarily obtaining flamethrowers and demolitions organized his pioneer shore party into assault demolitions and directed the blowing of several hostile installations before the close of D-Day. Determined to effect an opening in the enemy's strongly organized defense line the following day, he voluntarily crawled approximately forty yards forward of our lines and placed demolitions in the entrance of a large Japanese emplacement as the initial move in his planned attack against the heavily garrisoned, bombproof installation which was stubbornly resisting despite the destruction early in the action of a large number of Japanese who had been inflicting heavy casualties on our forces and holding up our advance. Withdrawing only to replenish his amunition, he led his men in a renewed assault, fearlessly exposing himself to the merciless slash of hostile fire as he stormed the formidable bastion, directed the placment of demolition charges in both entrances and seized the top of the bombproof position, flushing more than one hundred of the enemy who were instantly cut down and effecting the annihilation of approximtely one hundred and fifty troops inside the enplacement. Assailed by additional Japanese after he had gained his objective, he made a heroic stand on the edge of the structure, defending his strategic position with indomitable determination in the face of the desperate charge and killing three of the enemy before he fell, mortally wounded. By his dauntless fighting spirit, unrelenting aggressiveness and forceful leadership throughout three days of unremitting, violent battle, First Lieutenant Bonnyman had inspired his men to heroic effort, enabling them to beat off the counterattack and break the back of hostile resistance in the sector for an immediate gain of four hundred yards with no further casualties to our forces in this zone. He gallantly gave his life for his country.

It was about this time that Charles Taliaferro, who had played on Memphis Tech High's 1941 football team and had swam on its Prep League championship swimming team, landed with the 10th Marines, an artillery regiment. Their 75-mm pack howitzers were vitally important in providing supporting fire for the infantry and helping to reduce Japanese fortifications throughout the rest of the battle.

Late that morning, Capt Maxie Williams received orders to move his people across the airstrip to the south shore of the island. "It appeared to be a suicide order," he said, "absolutely no cover, terrain wide open and flat as a pancake." Their only chance, he concluded, was to stage a charge and hope to catch the enemy off guard. Jumping from their foxholes, Williams' company ran screaming like frenzied banshees toward the other side of the island. Every man made it safely across the airstrip. "Once we occupied their trenches, however," he added grimly, "it was a different story."

On the right flank of Red Beach One, Maj Mike Ryan of Galveston, Tex. had taken over the first day when the battalion commander was killed just before reaching the beach. Integrating into his battalion other Marines who had become separated from their units, he attacked and turned the Japs' flank, thereby securing the entire western end of the island and clearing Green Beach for an unopposed landing. Major William K. Jones' 1st Battalion, 6th Marines was ordered to land on Green. The outfit had been trained to land in rubber boats, which could navigate shallow water, but the outboard motors provided to propel the boats were useless in salt water; they had been designed for fresh water use only. So the Navy provided some LCVPs, with each one towing seven rubber boats. The battalion was brought to the edge of the reef and paddled and waded the rest of the way in. The boys in the battalion and some of Jones' friends in other outfits referred to him as "Admiral of the Condom Fleet." Ryan's organizational skill and aggressive maneuver, along with Bonnyman's capture of the bombproof bunker, were the battle's turning points, but much tough fighting remained as the Marines were forced to systematically destroy several hundred more fortifications defended by a tenacious enemy that fought to the death.

At 0500 on the third day four Japanese planes flew over the island and dropped a few bombs, one landed on the beach, killing one Marine and wounding seven. Later that day Eddie Albert was called ashore to help sort out the supplies that had piled up on the pier and that now were reaching the beach. That night, exhausted, he found a little slit trench and lay down in it, hoping to get some much needed rest. But it was not to be. During one burst of fire a Marine jumped into the small depression with him. He told Albert he had been a combat Marine for 38 years and this was the worst he had ever seen. About that time a howitzer was rolled up close by and blasted away through the night, so their conversation became intermittent and rest was forgotten.

> *He did one thing that amazed me. In the middle of all that fighting, he took off his trousers and folded them carefully across his chest so they would be neatly pressed in the morning. Sure enough, he was up before dawn, putting his trousers back on. Then he nudged me and motioned at the palm tree overhead. 'There's a sniper up there,' he calmly observed. 'Let's leave this area singly, but before it gets any lighter.' He went first, very casually; I waited a scary five minutes, then followed. He was the coolest man I'd ever met.*

That morning Albert learned his companion had been LtCol Evans Carlson, who had been an observer of Mao Tse Tung's guerilla tactics on the "Long March," and had commanded the Second Marine Raider Battalion.

The remaining Japanese had been driven into a pocket at the eastern end of the island and they made plans to attack the Marine line in an attempt to effect a breakthrough and wreak as much havoc as possible before they all were killed. At 1930 in the evening of the third day, 50 Japs made a probing attack, searching for a weak point in the line. After hand-to-hand fighting with Jones' 6th Marines, they were annihilated to the last man. At 2300, with grenades, light machine guns, rifles with fixed bayonets and their officers swinging swords, 100 more probed the 6th Regiment's line. They, too, fought until all were killed. Then, at 0400, about 350, screaming "Japanese drink Marines' blood," charged in a final *banzai* attack.

Although aided by supporting fire from howitzers and two destroyers close to shore, B Company, 1st Battalion, 6th Marines, wavered. The company commander went on his radio and asked for reinforcements, but he was told none were available and that he must hold. PFC Jack Stambaugh killed three attackers with his bayonet, but an officer ran him through with his samurai sword; another Marine brained the officer with his rifle butt.

Fifteen-year-old William Sam "Billy" Trero of Birmingham, Ala. was a machine gunner with B Company. Four .30 caliber light machine guns had been set up to provide crisscross fire. To keep the barrels from getting too hot, adjoining guns would alternate in firing short bursts. The gunner next to Trero, Maurice Markham of Gladewater, Tex., usually referred to him as "Willie Sam from Alabam'," but after firing a burst, Markham would holler over to Trero, "Let 'er buck Billy." Two of the other guns, including Markham's, were knocked out that night, so their remaining ammunition was carried to Trero's gun, but then the firing pin broke. Replacing the bolt containing the firing pin involved removing the back plate and other pieces, putting it all back together and cocking the bolt twice before the gun would fire again – a fairly time-consuming procedure. Just as Billy completed the necessary steps, a charging Jap loomed in the darkness about 10 feet away. Billy got off a short burst hitting him in the legs and, as the Jap reeled, his momentum carried him forward and he fell across Trero's gun. Markham, at 6'4" and 240 pounds, pounced on him and began working him over with his K-bar. The attacker, who a few seconds before would have delighted in killing his antagonists, in perfect English yelled "Mercy, Marine," to no avail, of course.

Again, the Japs fought to the last man. After daybreak, one Marine was heard to remark, "They told us we had to hold and, by God, we held." Shortly after noon, November 23, the island was officially declared secured.

Col David M. Shoup, commander of all troops ashore, was born in Tippacanoe, Ind. He grew up on a farm near a hamlet, close to Lafayette, whose name, Battle Ground, was appropriate for him. He was bull-necked and profane, usually chewed on an unlit cigar while playing an excellent game of poker and wrote poetry in his spare time. Seventeen years after Tarawa he would become the 22nd Commandant of the Marine Corps. His men were comfortable and at ease with him and his belief in and trust of them was reciprocated right down to the lowest private.

When he graduated from high school he expressed a desire to go to college. His father agreed, told him to pack his bags and drove him in the old family car to the nearest highway, where he let him out. He pressed five dollars in his son's hand and pointed up and down the highway. "There's a college in either direction, I don't suppose it makes much difference which way you go."

Shoup hitchhiked to Depauw College in Greencastle, Ind. With money earned at such mundane jobs as washing dishes in a local restaurant and the help of an Army ROTC scholarship, he paid his way through Depauw. After graduating and receiving his commission, Shoup switched from the Army to the Marine Corps.

Col David M. Shoup
His courageous and inspirational leadershiop and confidence in his men, through two days of unremitting, vicious fighting, paved the way for the ultimate victory.

The President of the United States takes pleasure in presenting the CONGRESSIONAL MEDAL OF HONOR to

COLONEL DAVID M. SHOUP
UNITED STATES MARINE CORPS

for services as set forth in the following

CITATION:

For conspicuous gallantry and intrepidity at the risk of his life above and beyond the call of duty as Commanding Officer of all Marine Corps troops in action against enemy Japanese forces on Betio Island, Tarawa Atoll, Gilbert Islands, from November 20 to 22, 1943. Although severely shocked by an exploding enemy shell soon after landing at the pier, and suffering from a serious, painful leg wound which had become infected, Colonel Shoup fearlessly exposed hirmelf to the terrific, relentless artillery, machine gun and rifle fire from hostile shore emplacemats and, rallying his hesitant troops by his own inspiring heroism, gallantly led them across the fringing reefs to charge the heavily fortified island and reinforce our hard-pressed, thinly held lines. Upon arrival on shore, he assumed command of all landed troops and, working without rest under constant, withering enemy fire during the next two days, conducted smashing attacks against unbelievably strong and fanatically defended Japanese positions despite innumerable obstacles and heavy casualties. By his brilliant leadership, daring tactics and selfless devotion to duty, Colonel Shoup was largely responsible for the final, decisive defeat of the enemy, and his indomitable fighting spirit reflects great credit upon the United States Naval Service.

Going without sleep and almost dehydrated by the oppressive equatorial heat, most of the Marines were near exhaustion by the second and third days. They had been issued reversible, camouflage dungarees (green side out/brown side out) of Army twill, a nonpourous material that tended to double in weight when wet. The heat burned and cracked the skin and a cloying powder caked the eyes and nostrils and made breathing difficult. Alexander wrote that a derelict, blackened LVT drifted ashore filled with dead Marines and one observer said he "came across a shattered Higgins boat (LCVP) drifting in the partial moonlight. The boat was nearly split in two by a shell – I can't imagine how it still floated – and it was littered with burned bodies. The most awful thing I ever saw." The surging tides scattered derelict craft and lifeless bodies throughout the lagoon and beyond, into the open sea. Capt. C. Julian Wheeler, commanding the USS *Mobile*, expressed astonishment that Betio's gruesome flotsam extended to his gunfire support station, six miles at sea. "I remember Marine and Japanese corpses floating by the ship in great numbers... It was a ghastly sight."

The heat also had begun to do its work on the unattended, bloated bodies laying everywhere. The sweet, sickly odor permeated everything. Weeks later, even after many showers and shampoos, men could still detect it.

> *Later on I talked to several pilots that came in after we had captured the airstrip. Some of them got airsick coming in on their bombing and strafing runs. They would be a thousand feet in the air and could smell the odor from the dead bodies. It was terrible.*
>
> -S /Sgt Jack Lent

It has been said that the bond that develops between fighting men who have been thrust together into the maw of battle and shared the worst horrors of war kindles a type of love that only they can fathom. Perhaps the extreme example of this is all those who have covered a hand grenade with their body to protect their comrades nearby. Sherrod said one of the most "touching things" was the willingness to lend a helping hand, "where every man wants to help every other man." He saw men, when asked for a cigarette, "bulge out the pack, proffer the last one, then pocket the empty pack so the other man would not know that he was accepting all there was." Five gallon cans for drinking water had been filled weeks before when the troops left New Zealand, but many of them were old and rusted and someone came up with the inappropriate idea of spraying the insides with white paint. The equatorial heat had caused the paint to dissolve in the water, making it undrinkable, and Sherod said:

> *Thus, the only palatable water was that which each man brought in his two canteens from his*

transport. Yet, I have seen several men give their last drink of water to a comrade, with the untrue remark, 'Oh I've got some more in my other canteen.'

Of the estimated 4,601 Japanese personnel on Betio at the battle's inception, 146 survived and were taken prisoner. Only 19 were identified as Japanese, or "probably Japanese," with the remainder classified as conscripted Korean construction laborers. True to their Bushido Code, almost all of the Japanese "Marines" had fought to the death and only eight remained alive; some of these were so incapacitated by wounds that they lacked the ability to continue fighting or commit suicide. American casualties consisted of 1,113 Marine and naval personnel killed or missing and 2,290 wounded. Four navy doctors and 85 hospital corpsmen were killed or wounded. Toward the end, some of the Japs, trapped in their pillboxes, committed suicide by strapping a big toe to the trigger of their rifle, placing the muzzle to their forehead and pulling the trigger with a kick. For a couple of days afterward, singly or in small groups, Japs slipped out of pillboxes, where many had hidden under the bodies of their own dead. They drifted through the darkness, sneaked past sentries and crept up on Marines in their foxholes. Three of them were shot on the lip of the shell hole containing the 6th Regiment's command post.

Perusing one of the battalion's roster of wounded, Col Alexander noted, at random, the following:

- Gunshot wound chest, compound fracture left arm.
- Burns, third degree, face, both hands, and forearms.
- Gunshot wound, multiple, face and right shoulder.
- Shrapnel wound, left arm, chest, face.
- Gunshot wound, left arm, chest, shoulder, right foot.
- Gunshot wound, right side of upper lip to left side of neck.
- War neurosis.
- Shrapnel wound, left arm and leg, burns both arms and face.
- Bayonet puncture, right knee.
- Gunshot wound, scrotum and right foot, concussion left eye.
- Gunshot wound, multiple, right shoulder and arm, left

knee, right thigh, left posterior chest, right anterior chest.

o Shrapnel wound, multiple, left leg; amputation traumatic left leg at thigh.

The Marine Corps does not award medals for heroism in combat whimsically, and another example of the ferocious nature of the fighting on Tarawa is evidenced by the number of medals given for an operation of slightly over three days' duration. In addition to the four Medals of Honor awarded, the Navy Cross, the second highest award for valor in combat, was bestowed on 46, while the third highest decoration, the Silver Star, was given to 248.

As Adm. Nimitz and MajGen Julian Smith and other high-ranking officers toured the island after the battle and saw the dirty, unshaven, hollow-eyed and haggard men, MajGen "Howlin' Mad" Smith observed that "they looked older than their fathers." They had survived the raging inferno, "but," he said, "it chilled their souls."

... there's blood; there's pieces and parts of people around. And you shouldn't become accustomed to that sort of thing. But after you've been through a battle like that, as you walk off there's another part of us, I guess, that takes care of a thing like that and puts it someplace else.

-PFC Carroll Strider

... we were so decimated we were evacuated immediately. And I'll never forget standing on the pier and looking out over the reef. I think every American ought to have to stand on that pier and look at the thousands of dead and wounded people, destroyed ships, amphtracks, weapons, tanks upside down — to realize that the price of freedom is not people with banners walking down streets talking about how badly they've been mistreated, but the young 19 and 20-year old Americans, who, through the centuries, have done what

Marine dead lying on the beach just after the battle. U.S. Marine Corps photograph

Of several plaques commemorating those interred in a temporary cemetery on Betio right after the battle one, by an anonymous Marine, read in part:

To you, who lie within this coral sand,
We, who remain, pay tribute to a pledge
That dying, thou shalt surely not have died in vain.
That when again bright morning dyes the sky
And waving fronds above shall touch the rain,
We give you this -- that in those times,
We will remember.

*their country asked them to do — who
destroyed Hitler and Tojo and made it possible for us to have had fifty years on this earth
without a global war.*

-2ndLt Roy Thaxton
Memphis

After the battle Eddie Albert got his boat back and
endured the grisly task of helping retrieve the dead floating in
the waters covering the reef. When he returned to the *Sheridan*
he went to sick bay and visited some of the wounded he had
rescued. One of them remembers that after being operated on
he had been left naked on a bunk. He said Eddie left and then
came back shortly with a pair of pajamas for him in one hand
and a guitar in the other; then he sat down and played and
sang for all the wounded men in the ward. Albert was recommended for a Silver Star for his heroic actions at Tarawa.

In early September 1995 a great celebration commemorating the 50th anniversary of victory over Japan was held in
Long Beach, Cal., former home of the Pacific Fleet. In a letter
to the author a week or so later, Eddie Albert said:

*It was a great experience to meet up with the
men from the 2nd Marine Division in Long
Beach. What they went through at Tarawa
nobody will ever quite know.*

The wartime manpower shortage opened up certain
jobs for certain classes of people who, during peacetime,
would never have been considered for the positions they
filled. "Woman-power" and "teen-power" helped win the war.
One of the jobs that some high school boys enjoyed — with all
that power under the hood and the lights and sirens — was
that of ambulance driver. With no skills other than knowing

how to drive a car, sixteen-year-olds jumped behind the wheel of an ambulance and zoomed off to accidents and other emergency medical calls. Red Doyle, Bill Trickett and Al Guthrie were some of those who worked in this capacity. Usually, their sojourn in the job was somewhat brief as they lost interest or went into the service.

One night Trickett and another boy picked up a woman in the latter stages of labor. They called ahead to Baptist Hospital where a phalanx of medical personnel were awaiting their arrival as they roared up to the emergency room entrance, narrowly averting, to their considerable relief, their having to assume the mantle of midwife. Al Guthrie, a definite individualistic and idiosyncratic personality who sometimes wore tennis shoes to football practice, one night made a run to the West Tennesee Mental Hospital at Bolivar to pick up a body. Accompanied by the son of the deceased, he made the 70-mile return trip to Memphis on a dark, winding two-lane highway in something like 50 minutes flat. Given the circumstances, the son was justifiably upset at what he felt was a lack of respect by Al and he rather forcefully expressed his feelings the next morning to the owners of the funeral home. Even though he was fired, Gaddy Goose, undoubtedly, thought it was hilarious.

During the summers of 1943 and 1944 Billy Buckles and Elwyn Rowan worked nights at the huge Illinois Central Railroad yards in south Memphis west of South Third Street. They would ride the streetcar to and from work. One year they worked during the school months in the spring and would catch a streetcar after classes and return home the next morning in time to clean up, eat breakfast and get over to Central High. Trains would come and go all night and as "call boys" it was their task to awaken the crews – two engineers and a brakeman – in time for them to take a train out. They bunked in a little building in the yards and got intermittent shut-eye. They would periodically be awakened by their alarm clock and then get on bicycles and peddle about a mile to the boarding house outside of the yards where the crews slept. As some of the crew members might have been out on a toot (pun intended) earlier in the evening, sometimes lengthy cajoling was necessary to rouse them sufficiently.

One summer Buckles and Ray Brown worked at a sheet

metal shop during the day and Billy then would go from there to his railroad job. Before coming to Memphis Buckles had lived for a short time in Brownsville, Tenn., 58 miles up Highway 70. "Buckin' Billy Buckles from Brownsville" had a music teacher there at Haywood County High School by the name of R. Roy Coats who, with E. F. "Sleepy" Yerby, had written the Ole Miss fight song "Forward Rebels." Under his tutelage Billy became reasonably competent on the tuba and the bass violin. The father of Vince Skillman, one of his teammates at Central, was business agent for the local musicians union (appropriately, the first such union in the country) and got him a union card. This enabled him to play the two instruments with the Memphis Symphony.

The final semester was winding down and graduation was approaching. Most were still in school but others were scattered around the country at various military bases. Phil Turner had gone through Marine boot camp, went on to advanced training without getting the customary ten days' leave to come home, and was about to be shipped overseas. Many boys were attracted to the Army Air Corps and wanted to be fighter pilots. That branch of service did have its advantages; a job like that would ordinarily keep one away from such things as muddy foxholes and cold "C" rations, off crowded ships, and out of shark-infested waters. Some, growing up watching movies about dashing, handsome pilots in *Dawn Patrol* and *A Yank in the RAF*, probably envisioned themselves in glamourous dogfights with a cigar clamped in their teeth and a scarf flowing in the breeze. Early on, the supply of pilots approximated demand and standards were raised to such high levels that most aspirants were "washed-out" of pilot training and sent somewhere else to become, such as, bombardiers, mechanics and waist gunners. If all the washed-out pilots of World War II had been laid end to end, they probably would have encircled the globe two-and-a-half times, so it certainly was no disgrace to wash-out.

It was the lot of Sam Angier, a former CBC end, to become a member of this group and he was stationed at an airfield near Madison, Wis. Sam had entered the service in February, and as the date for graduation of his class at CBC neared, class sponsor Brother Gabriel wrote a letter to Sam's commanding officer requesting that he be given leave to come home for the ceremony. This was not at a time when the war was winding down and things were lax; it was still at its height and its resolution yet uncertain.

The first Sam knew of the letter was when an irate first sergeant from the unit office looked him up in his barracks and chewed him out for wanting leave, saying there were other men more deserving of it than he was. Sam was directed to report to the CO who wanted to know who this Brother Gabriel was. When the situation was explained to him, to Sam's surprise, he was granted the leave, but it was not a popular decision with the non-commissioned officers who ran the outfit.

Leaves began at midnight on their first day, but it was customary to check out prior to that time after the completion of the work day. This was discretionary with the individual designated as "Charge of Quarters" (CQ), who ran the barracks and kept a log of those coming and going on leave and liberty. Making it as difficult on him as possible, Sam was kept busy with picky assignments until late and wasn't able to begin packing until after lights out.

As Sam started getting his gear together one of the guys in the squad bay, which housed about 50 men, turned the lights back on for him. In short order the irascible CQ was back in the squad bay from his office down the hall carrying a flashlight. He unleashed a string of profane invective and threats to all within hearing and flipped the lights back off. He was immediately denounced by a disgusted voice at one end of the dark bay which equated his actions with poultry excrement. This oft-used military term is applied in such instances – rather than horse, ape, bull or elephant dung – "because it is small-minded and ignoble and takes the trivial seriously" (*Wartime*, Fussell, P. 80). Carrying his flashlight the choleric CG charged toward the direction whence the voice had come and flashed his torch around. "Who said that?" he demanded. As soon as the words were out of his mouth a fowl-excrement reference boomed from the other end of the bay and, with long, quick strides, he hastened there and repeated his question. Succumbing to his anger and not realizing how ridiculous he appeared and that his flashlight was helping Sam to see to pack, back and forth the CQ went as Sam's buddies gleefully played him like a tennis ball. Angier made his train and arrived in time for the graduation ceremony.

A plethora of parties and dances, inspired by upcoming high school graduations and fraternity and sorority spring formals, swirled through the balmy days winding down to the end of the school year. After a big dance one night at the Continental Ballroom on the mezzanine of Hotel Peabody and when all their dates had been taken home, a group of Central boys met at the house of John Trent, whose parents were out of town. During dances at the Peabody there always were crap games in full swing in at least one of the many smaller rooms off the mezzanine and someone had brought a pair of dice with them to Trent's house. In addition to John, Rip Rowan, Billy Bolton, Milton Newton, Billy Lacy, and Howard Stringfellow, a basketball player, were in attendance, along with two or three others.

The boys were still in a partying mood and a hot crap game got underway with the customary imprecations to the cubes to turn up the right numbers and the boisterous shouts of gratification from the winners and howls of disgust from the losers. Apparently, the Trents had some neighbors who objected to the noise and didn't approve of gambling, because they reached for the phone and dialed the law. With the game at a fever pitch Bolton looked up and saw a policeman's face framed in a window. In fact, as he glanced around it seemed there was one peering in every window he could see. The alarm was sounded and boys took off in all directions. Two flew out the back door and kept going, but the others were rounded up and taken to the police sub-station on Barksdale Street just off Union Avenue.

Upon arriving at "Barksdale" the boys were booked for "gaming" and all put in the same large cell — probably the "drunk tank." After an evening of high-spirited fun the letdown was like a runaway elevator and they all were now a little tired and down at the mouth. Drawing straws to determine who would call their parents, the cops let Rowan call his brother-in-law, an attorney. Although it didn't seem that way to them, he got there fairly soon armed with coffee and dough-nuts that he passed around to everyone. He laughed at them and thought the whole situation was very amusing, but he couldn't do anything for them until morning. Then the cops let Billy Lacy call Joan Murphy, who had been his date earlier in the evening, and she came to the station with her father and Jean Burt who was spending the night with her. But Mr. Murphy's efforts to get the boys released were to no avail, in fact he almost got a ticket for parking too close to a fireplug. When Joan got home she called Lacy's mother, as he had requested, because the cops shut down all additional calls. Two or three of the boys who had *Commercial Appeal* routes and would pick up their Sunday morning papers at Poplar and Evergreen were not even permitted to call their route man-agers.

Howard Stringfellow started doing handstands and similar monkeyshines to cheer everybody up and, gradually, they began to see a little humor in the situation. Somebody found a tin cup and started raking it across the bars like a scene from *The Big House* and they all joined in with a rendi-tion of "If I Had the Wings of an Angel." Then Lacy's mother showed up and gave the cops a tongue-lashing remonstrating them for wasting their time arresting boys, for no good reason, who were about to go off and fight for their country while there were real criminals running around preying on people. She knew Lytle McKee, a cotton man who was chairman of the Shelby County Election Commission and, obviously, in the hierarchy of the Crump organization, and she called him up. Soon, word was passed down to release the boys and to destroy any documents pertaining to their arrest.

John Fox, of course, had left for the Marine Corps the morning after the Blind Game and Phil Turner entered the same branch of the service the next month. Also in January, Malcolm Baker took off for the wild blue yonder with the Army Air Force as did Sam Angier in February, the same month Jack Callicott entered the Army. Before the frost was on the pumpkin that fall, Mark Follis and Henry Bateman had gone into the Army Air Force; Slick Williams had enlisted in the Navy Air Corps; Percy Roberts, Al Huebner, Jack Nieman and Maurice Keathley were in the Army; Emmel Golden, Don Hollowell, Butch Daltroff and Billy Lacy had left for the Navy and Bill Burke and George Whitehead enrolled in that service's V-12 program, and Judd Williford, Billy Bolton, Joe Highfill, Ira Whitley, Louie Hansberger, Bill Wright and Red Doyle were in the Marine Corps. A little later Dippy Coles entered the Merchant Marine and Joe Smith, Tommy Mulroy, and Bill Roberds enlisted in the Merchant Marine Cadet program.

Gayden Drew, the standout track and football athlete at Central the year before, who had struck the first blow in the brawl behind Pig 'n Whistle, had previously been accepted in the Navy's V-12. This was a program that sent boys through an accelerated college curriculum leading to commissioning as a naval officer for duty with the fleet. However, Gayden tired of waiting in Memphis for an assignment and joined the Merchant Marine in the summer of 1943. After ninety days training he made trips aboard freighters from Gulf ports to London and Liverpool. He then was assigned to the Merchant Marine Cadet program on the old Chrysler estate at King's Point, New York. In the summer of 1944 Congress passed the "GI Bill" providing educational, housing and other benefits for veterans of the armed services, but the Merchant Marine was excluded. When Gayden learned of this he promptly quit the Merchant Marine and enlisted in the Marine Corps. He and Red Doyle would get together a year later on Okinawa.

About this time Bob Hope came to town with his entourage to put on a show at the Navy base at Millington and to sell War Bonds at a performance at Ellis Auditorium. Accompanying him were Les Brown and his "Band of Renown" featuring Doris Day and Bob's straight man, the mustachioed comedian Jerry Colonna. Dippy Coles, Sandy Kincannon and Julius Smith put their heads together and decided this was something they couldn't afford to miss. Dippy's grandfather had worked in some capacity at the auditorium for years and Dippy was familiar with its layout and operation; the boys were certainly not going to let their lack of the price of admission be a deterrent to their attending the show.

They showed up well before show time with their sleeves rolled up and businesslike expressions on their faces. Somehow they found an unguarded door and went backstage. Whenever anyone came around where they were sort of hiding out, they would put on their own show, pretending they were working. Dippy would give Sandy an order and he would pick up a curtain weight, carry it about twenty feet and set it down. Then, at the appropriate time, Julius would set his broom down and walk over and pick up the weight and move it back to its original position. This sham saw them through until show time. As Bob Hope stood in the wings waiting to go on, the boys were right next to him. At this time, true to form, Shifty Logan strolled up.

"Hi, Shifty," said Bob, "am I still a member of the Bum's Club?"

"Bob, you know you are; you have a lifetime membership in the Bum's Club."

As mentioned earlier, Gayden Drew had driven Russell Swink and Maurice "Dick" Chism to the railroad station in the middle of the Central football banquet in December 1942. Both Russell and Dick would have been back on the team the next year, and they didn't have to leave, but they were eager to get into the war; they headed for boot camp at San Diego.

During most of his three years in the Marine Corps Russell was "seagoing," being in charge of a 40-millimeter gun crew on the battleship *North Carolina*. Prior to this, and before his eighteenth birthday, he was a combat conditioning instructor.

In the late spring of 1944 a giant armada began assembling in the western Pacific for the invasion of the Mariana Islands. The *North Carolina* was anchored at Ulithi and Lamon Kelley was on one of the nearby transports that would take Marines to Guam. Lamon knew that Russell was on the big battleship and his native ability to get what he wanted garnered him a ride on a lighter over to the *North Carolina*, where he surprised the elated Swink with a visit.

The course of their conversation eventually got around to the 1942 CBC-Central game won by the latter 7 to 2. Kelley had blocked a Central punt that went out of the end zone for a safety. Later, the Brothers had driven to the Warrior two-yard line, fourth down and goal to go for the potential winning touchdown. Kelley was at center for CBC and Swink was at left guard for Central. When CBC lined up tight, Swink anticipated a quarterback sneak, although CBC quarterback Jack Salmon says he remembers calling a play with the tailback running the ball. In any event, Swink charged quick and low with his arms wide and locked onto the ankles of Kelley and right guard Al Huebner, which prohibited them carrying out their blocking assignments and, thereby, bottled up the play. Swink held on until the nearest linebacker and defensive backs came up and pushed the pile over halting the play short of the goal line. Because of the pile in the middle, the officials couldn't see Swink holding and he got away with it.

The *North Carolina* was involved in just about every major action in the Pacific and received eleven battle stars. Swink was called back in the Marine Corps during the Korean War and served another two and one-half-years.

On June 6, 1944, "D-Day," Operation Overlord was unleashed and the allies invaded Fortress Europe. Jack Hall, 1942 Central fullback and piano and vocal virtuoso who had been clobbered by Rabbit Cook in the Prep League fights at the YMCA early in 1943, had gone into the Army. One day while he was in training at Fort Jackson, S.C. an airplane flew overhead and a stick of soldiers parachuted out and landed in front of his platoon. One of them approached his group looking for volunteers for the paratroopers. When he told Hall and his compatriots that they would get to wear the type of fancy boots he had on and would receive extra pay each month, that's all Jack needed to hear. With the 82nd Airborne Division at 3:30 in the morning of D-Day Jack jumped out of one of the 822 C-47s carrying 13,000 paratroopers over German-occupied France. As he was coming down in the dark the Germans were firing their anti-aircraft guns and a piece of flak hit him in the leg. Before he reached the ground he passed out. He came to in a hospital and spent three week there. Upon release he was transferred to the 101st Airborne Division.

Nottingham, England, June 5,1944. In less than 24 hours, Jack Hall would jump into German-occupied France. (Courtesy of Dr. Jack Hall)

In early June, Phil Turner and John Fox left Maui, Hawaii with their respective outfits and headed for Saipan. Fox was an amphtrack driver for the Fifth Amphibious Corps of which Turner's Fourth Marine Division was a part. Saipan was one of the Mariana Islands, which also included Tinian and Guam, and was the first island invaded by American forces that had been held by the Japanese before the war. It was the cornerstone of Japan's Pacific defensive system and it was felt that it must be held at all costs. On June 15 8,000 Marines landed on Saipan's beaches in the first 30 minutes, then a firestorm of Japanese artillery began blasting the beaches and the ships and small boats near the island; 2,000 Marine casualties were suffered the first day.

Phil's battalion was held in reserve aboard ship and

Billy Bolton, boot camp, Parris Island, South Carolina, summer, 1944.
(Courtesy of Bill Bolton)

never got ashore. John's unit got into the battle in its latter stages. On July 7, close to 3,000 Japanese soldiers, souped up on several hours of sake swilling, made a suicidal *banzai* attack on the American lines. Overrunning some of the infantry, they charged the artillery behind the line. Charles Taliaferro, of Memphis Tech, says the 10th Marines depressed the muzzles of their 105-mm howitzers to a horizontal position and cut the timers on the shells to explode in three-tenths of a second — at about 50-yards out. Firing as fast as they could, the Marines were getting shrapnel blown back at them from their own shells and had to step behind the protective plates on each side of the gun every time they fired. When it was over the Japanese had been annihilated. When the battle began there were upwards of 30,000 Japanese troops on Saipan. When resistance ended on July 9 less than 1,000 had been taken prisoner; the rest were dead.

The Japanese high command dispatched a naval task force, including aircraft carriers, to provide relief for their besieged troops. In what became known as "The Great Marianas Turkey Shoot," planes from American carriers shot down hundreds of Japanese with relatively negligible losses of their own.

On July 21 the Marines landed on Guam, also in the Marianas. Lamon Kelley, Roy Key and Shelby Flowers, the Vicksburg boy, were there. Possibly indicative of his free spirit, Flowers went around with the sleeves cut off his dungaree jacket at the shoulder. When LtCol Sam Puller, brother of Marine legend Lewis "Chesty" Puller, was killed by a sniper, Flowers felt he should do something about it. Puller had been riding in a jeep wearing his insignia of rank, something ordinarily not done by officers in combat. Flowers took a Browning Automatic Rifle and went tromping around in the high grass and woods until he found the sniper and shot him out of a tree. Flowers was later killed on Guam. Months later Billy Bolton participated in the continuing mop up of Guam; the last known Japanese survivor surrendered in 1972, having escaped detection on the small island for 28 years.

On July 24 both John Fox and Phil Turner went in with one of the early waves when the Marines landed on Tinian, a Japanese-held island only two and one-half miles from Saipan. This was the island from which, a little over a year later, the bomber "Enola Gay" would take off on its way to drop the first atomic bomb on Hiroshima. On the fourth day, while advancing through a sugar cane field with stalks about seven feet tall, Phil was hit in the left side of his neck by a .25 caliber bullet that lodged in his shoulder. He was evacuated and subsequently transferred to a hospital in New Caledonia. From there he was sent back to Maui to prepare for the Iwo Jima landing. Fox came out of Tinian unscathed.

Jack Salmon, CBC's All-Memphis blocking back in 1942, enrolled at Notre Dame in the summer of 1943 and got an academic year under his belt before enlisting in the Navy Air Corps in March 1944. While he was at Notre Dame the coaches tried to convert Jack from a single-wing quarterback to a T-formation quarterback. That was fine except that the Fighting Irish's starter at that position was Angelo Bertelli, who won the Heisman Trophy that year; his backup was Johnny Lujack, who went on to win the same trophy in 1947.

Slick Williams also had signed up for the Navy Air Corps but, like the Army Air Corps, it seemed that the Navy had about all the pilots it needed. Prospective Navy pilots customarily were sent to college for a period of time prior to flight training under what was known as the V-5 program and that was what Jack and Slick had entered. Instead, they were shunted into the V-12 program, for line officers, and sent to Milligan College at Johnson City, Tenn.

With so many students in uniform or war work, the college programs conducted by both the Army and the Navy during World War II were the financial salvation of many colleges and universities. This was particularly true in the case of a small, private school like Milligan. In fact, in possibly the only instance of its kind, the Navy completely took over Milligan; not only were there no coeds, there were no civilian males in attendance either.

The Navy, apparently more so than the Army, believed in strong athletic programs to keep its people in good shape and to build morale and strengthen teamwork. Teams like Georgia Tech Pre-Flight, Iowa Pre-Flight, Great Lakes, Ill. and Fleet City, Cal. were some of the best in the country.

Milligan also fielded a team that Jack and Slick played on. Jack was elected a co-captain and, except for a loss to North Carolina State, Milligan went through an undefeated season playing mainly small colleges. The head coach was Chief Petty Officer Jack Tittle, older brother of Y. A. Tittle and a friend of Tulane coach Monk Simon. Tittle wanted Salmon to play ball there after the war, but Jack was committed to returning to Notre Dame. Upon completion of the season, Milligan was recognized as the titular small college national champion.

Ray Brown's father had been judge advocate for the Second Army, under Gen Ben Lear, stationed at the Fairgrounds. He later served in the same capacity for the China-Burma-India Theater of Operations, during which time he was stationed in India. Reassigned to the Pentagon, he was named Assistant Judge Advocate of the Army and Ray left Central at mid-term of his senior year to live with his family in Falls Church, Va. When he graduated from high school he decided to attend the University of Virginia.

During Ray's first year at Virginia he played end, his position at Central, but Coach Frank Murray liked his elusiveness and speed and switched him to halfback his sophomore season. From this position he led the Cavaliers in scoring in 1945 and 1946. He also participated in baseball, basketball and track.

Rip Rowan and Bill Buckles were still 17 and there was a likelihood they could get in a year of college football before entering military service. They were recruited by a number of schools and visited the campuses of Duke, Auburn, Mississippi State, Ole Miss and Louisiana State. Both of them had relatives living in Baton Rouge and favored LSU from the beginning. When they left for Tigertown, John Trent and Butch Daltroff accompanied them with full scholarships. Butch was too small to be considered college material and the coaches wanted him to be a manager, but he quit school and joined the Navy. Rowan and Buckles both started for the Bayou Bengals that year. The opening game with Alabama ended up 27 to 27, but it provided Rowan with one of the biggest thrills in his storied college career. On his first college play he took a flat pass (shades of the Blind Game) from freshman quarterback Y. A. Tittle and dashed 78 yards for a touchdown. Buckles also distinguished himself by intercepting two passes thrown by Alabama freshman tailback Harry Gilmer, who would have a great career with the Tide and go on to star with the Washington Redskins. On Billy's second interception he received a hip injury that plagued him throughout his college career.

In a 13 to 0 loss to Tennessee, which played in the Rose Bowl that year, the Vols had a player who later would become close friends with Rowan and Trent. Joe Steffy, who had played for Chattanooga Baylor Prep against Memphis Central at Crump Stadium in the tenth grade, was a guard for Tennessee. He went on to West Point where he became a teammate with Rip and John.

With an open date on the schedule and neither having ever been to New Orleans, which was only some 80 odd miles away, Buckles and Rowan decided they would mosey on down from Baton Rouge to the Crescent City and investigate its charms. So early on a Saturday morning they got a lift out to Florida Boulevard and Airline Highway and put their thumbs to work.

Buckles, Rowan, and Trent get their heads together in Tiger Stadium at LSU. (Courtesy of Bill Buckles)

Traffic was fairly light, but in about 20 minutes a huge, black four-door Chrysler went flying by and then, suddenly, squealed to a stop about a hundred feet away. The driver ground the gears in reverse and backed up. In the front seat were two young men not much older than themselves.

"Where ya goin?" the one sitting next to the driver demanded somewhat impatiently. The big car sat there idling – like the low growl of a suspicious bear – rocking slightly from side to side as if it was as eager to again get moving as the young man who had tossed out the question.

"New Orleans," replied Rowan, with just the right amount of flourish in his voice that his youthful exuberance deemed appropriate for identifying their exotic destination.

"Well hop in then, we are too."

As soon as the back door closed behind them, the driver let out the clutch and roared off. The boys had never before been in a car quite this large; it appeared to have the capacity to accommodate a squad of long-waisted Abe Lincolns, stovepipe hats and all, or a couple of Indian motorcycles with sidecars. Lickety-split the great car thundered down Airline Highway through the bayou country of south Louisiana.

After awhile Rip and Billy began to get somewhat uneasy over the speed at which they were traveling and the quiet, intense demeanor of their hosts. They exchanged knowing glances and, as they approached the little town of Sorrento, Rowan spoke up.

"How about just letting us out at this next town; we want to stop and get something to drink. We're really not in all that big of a hurry."

The boys in front chuckled to themselves. Clyde, the driver, said, "Tell 'em Ralph."

Ralph turned and faced the boys with a sardonic grin. "I've got a pistol in my hand. You said you wanted a ride to New Orleans; well you're gonna get the fastest one you've ever had. This is a hot car in more ways than one and they're lookin' for two guys, not four. So just relax and enjoy the scenery."

Envisioning being possibly involved in a wreck or caught in the midst of a gun battle, Rowan and Buckles settled back with a rigid tenseness in their bodies and got tighter grips on the plush armrests.

Twenty-five miles down the road they entered La Place. Halfway through a car swung in behind and they heard a siren. Clyde just pushed harder on the accelerator and in a few moments the sound gradually began to diminish. But another police car got behind them in New Sarpy and then another in Harahan. Kenner and Metairie were blurs. By the time they entered the New Orleans suburbs, four police cars were in the chase and their piercing, frantic wails ripping across the bayous and marshes elicited a responsive chorus of mournful howls from a substantial segment of south Louisiana's considerable hound dog population.

Clyde didn't want to get tied up in traffic downtown, where he would end up if he stayed on Airline, and knew he needed to start making some turns to lose the cops. He saw a likely intersection coming up and into it made a fully-locked, screeching, sliding left turn. He had entered a boulevard with two lanes of traffic on each side of an esplanade.

Too late he discovered he had turned north into the south-bound lanes and was hurtling into oncoming traffic with nowhere to go. With a head-on collision imminent, Clyde jerked the steering wheel sharply to the left. The behemoth bounced over the curb, flattened the decorative metal figure of a miniature Negro jockey, obliterated a row of hollyhocks and, as it came to rest with a final grinding-lurching bump, skewed the little front porch of a "folk cottage" that was the domicile of one Francois Ducharme.

Clyde and Ralph bounded from the car and quickly disappeared behind the row of little houses. With front doors standing open, the great car resembled some ear-extended bull elephant that had strayed and blundered onto the scene from a passing circus. Unhurt, Rowan and Buckles piled out the right rear door, got together on the sidewalk and, in an attempt to appear inconspicuous, strolled away with a studied nonchalance as if in no hurry to tend to some innocuous errand.

They had gone less than half a block when a police car sailed into view and slowed down. That was the cue for a slatternly woman, with a face that would scare a hant up a thornbush, to waddle off her porch, point an accusing finger at the boys and screech: "That's them!"

After being accosted by the police, the boys shakily explained what had happened and tried to identify themselves. As this was being done, a sizable crowd materialized out of nowhere. Some gawkers wandered over to the car and gaped curiously inside; others, with their feet planted wide apart and arms sanctimoniously folded across their chests, stood surveying the boys with suspicion.

Rowan had been written up in an article the previous week in the sports section of the *Times-Picavune* and, fortunately, one of the policemen recognized him from his picture that accompanied the article. They were taken down to the police station at Tulane and Broad to make a statement and then, with jokes and guffaws, were released.

For their part, Rip and Billy's dispositions had not yet reached a point where they could see any humor in the situation; the experience had dulled their expectations. They called an assistant coach in Baton Rouge and told him what had happened. After a quick lunch they caught a bus back to school. The siren call of the Vieux Carre would have to be responded to at a later date.

As an example of the urgent need to get troops to the European theater for the upcoming invasion and subsequent battles, when Jack Callicott entered the Army in early 1944 he never even went through basic training but was assigned to the 95th Infantry Division in training at Indiantown Gap, Penn. After getting overseas Jack was sitting in a foxhole somewhere on the western front one day when another soldier walked by with an armload of newspapers. He tossed Jack a copy of *Stars and Stripes*. Idling through the paper Jack got to the sports section and a headline caught his eye: "Rip Rowan Scores Touchdown on First College Run."

Boys off in the service didn't forget some of the people and places they missed the most. From around the world postcards and notes arrived at the Pig 'n Whistle addressed to Redwood, Cadillac and Preacher. These were dutifully taped to a large, slick-surfaced supporting column near the juke box for all to read.

The Japanese knew they could neither repel the Marines nor be reinforced. Knowing this, they simply killed, without hope and without meaning.

Wartime
-Paul Fussell
p. 293

On February 19, 1945 the Third, Fourth, and Fifth Marine Divisions assaulted Iwo Jima, one of the Japanese Volcano Islands. The Marines were now bringing the war close to the "Home Islands." Tokyo was only 650 miles away and the 22,000 Japanese troops on Iwo fought with a disciplined and ferocious intensity. This battle, referred to by one participant as "Hell With the Fire Out," cost more than 26,000 American casualties, of which more than 6,000 were killed. The battle also produced the most famous picture of the war, the flag-raising on Mount Suribachi at the southern end of the sulfuric island.

The Marines landed on volcanic ash and soft sand beaches that rendered most vehicles ineffective of movement and in which it was impossible to dig foxholes. The Japanese allowed the first few waves to land without opposition and then opened up with tremendous firepower from their hidden positions in the heights above the Marines. One of these weapons was a mortar that fired a 675-pound projectile, "bigger'n a damned 55-gallon oil drum." Leading from the beaches the Japanese had planted anti-tank and anti-personnel mines augmented with 500-pound bombs, naval depth charges and naval torpedo heads buried vertically beneath pressure detonators. They also booby-trapped many items that would be desirable for souvenirs such as binoculars, helmets and swords.

The Japanese hid in caves and an elaborate system of connecting tunnels seven layers deep and, as they had no intention of surrendering, had to be blasted out one way or another. The hot earth and sulfur fumes made it almost impossible to sleep on the ground or in foxholes and, too, shelling by both sides continued throughout the night.

Probably the primary reason for the seizure of Iwo Jima was to facilitate the bombing of Japan. B-29s were flying out of the Mariana Islands of Saipan, Tinian and Guam but, because of the great distances to the Home Islands and back, carried bombs only in the front bomb bay and additional fuel in the rear bomb bay. After Iwo was captured B-29s were able to carry a full bomb load and then, on the way back to the Marianas, land at Iwo for refueling. Fighter planes, with their shorter range, could also be based on Iwo Jima to provide air cover for the bombers.

Leslie Morgan, who had played on Central's 1942 team and would have played in 1943 if he hadn't been drafted right after turning 18, flew 31 missions off of Tinian and says he saw a lot of planes on their way back from their missions ditch in the ocean after running out of fuel just a few miles short of the island. Les worked from a ball turret on top of the B-29 and was in charge of all guns on the airplane. He was awarded a Purple Heart for a wound and a Distinguished Flying Cross for bravery and skill.

The B-29s initially bombed in mass formations from altitudes ranging from 30,000 to 40,000 feet, but they were losing too many planes grouped together that way. So as they approached their targets, they started making their bombing runs individually at different altitudes. They were fired on by anti-aircraft guns and harassed by Zero fighter planes. Another tactic the Japanese used was to send up Kamikaze planes that attempted to crash into the bombers; however, these were not very effective. They were, simply, manned flying bombs, which didn't even have the ability to land, so theirs was a suicide mission. The Americans called them "Great Balls of Fire." The B-29s started landing on Iwo Jima even before the five-weeks battle was over and it was estimated that this capacity to do so may have saved the lives of 25,000 U. S. airmen.

After his wound on Tinian, Phil Turner was back in action on Iwo as a machine gunner. One day he was blown about ten to fifteen feet into the air by either a satchel charge or an artillery shell. He spent three days in his battalion field hospital and then went back into the line. However, as a result of the bullet he had caught on Tinian, which had never been removed, his shoulder started swelling and he was put on a ship and operated on to remove the bullet as the ship returned to Maui.

John Fox was the driver of an amphtrack and went in with the first wave at Iwo Jima. Unlike most of the other vehicles, including tanks, that couldn't move well in the volcanic ash in and around the beach, the amphtracks had good maneuverability. John made a number of runs back out to the ships bringing in loads of supplies and carrying them as far inland as possible. The amphtrack was equipped with .30 caliber and .50 caliber machine guns and all its crew members carried .45 caliber automatic pistols in shoulder holsters. As he drove inland with another load, a mortar shell made a direct hit on his amphtrack knocking a large hole in it. Part of the shell hit John's holstered .45 knocking off the stock and denting the receiver, but that prevented the shrapnel from entering his body and, presumably, saved his life. Instead, the shrapnel continued on to enter his left upper arm causing a compound fracture of the humerus bone.

Fox was operated on aboard a ship headed for Saipan. From there he was flown on a bunk-equipped DC-3 hospital plane to Hawaii. He was put in a body cast for awhile with his arm extended and a pin in his elbow. While he was in the hospital in Hawaii the pin pulled out. When his arm started feeling strange, Fox told a nurse about it. But she didn't believe him until the blood started oozing through the cast. He was rushed to an operating room and in the process of re-setting the pin, given four pints of blood. He still carries shrapnel around in his upper left arm bone.

The Sunday edition of *The Commercial Appeal* published a column in the society pages under the byline of "Penelope Pepys" that told of all the adult social activities around town: who gave what kind of party, who was there, what the ladies wore and so on. On Wednesday mornings a version came out for the high school set by "Penny Jr.," that was more of a gossipy piece. It always was of interest to find out who was with whom at what party or what unidentified (but hinted at) young lady had said about some unidentified (but hinted at) young man. One Wednesday morning at the breakfast table Julius Smith, who had spent the night with Jack Gibson, got frustrated as Hoot leisurely read the paper.

"Come on, Gibson, we're going to be late for school."

Jack's mother smiled. "Julius, you had better just go on and go without him, he's not going to move a muscle until he has read every word of Penny Jr."

Just prior to the 40th reunion of the CBC class of 1946, Julius in Houston called Jack in Charlotte to see if he was coming. Hoot had just undergone a series of radiation treatments for cancer, was too ill to go to Memphis and would die less than six months later. Julius was not fully aware of the seriousness of his condition. One of Jack's daughters answered the phone.

"May I say who's calling?"

"Tell him it's Penny Jr. calling for an interview."

Jack came to the phone: "Julius, you son-of-a-gun, ...You know me, boy, I would come if I could."

In what came to be called the "Battle of the Bulge," on December 16, 1944 the Germans attacked American forces in the heavily-wooded, rugged plateau area of Belgium known as the Ardennes. This occurred through deep snow during the most bitter winter Europe had experienced in many years. While this brainchild of Hitler's, the scope of which was in opposition to the best judgment of his high command, was a last-gasp effort to turn the war around, it nevertheless posed a serious threat to Allied forces on the continent. Early on, the Germans had stunning success and drove deep into Belgium, but they did not have sufficient troops, equipment and fuel to sustain the attack.

On the northern half of the bulge a counter-attack at Malmedy by the U. S. 30th "Old Hickory" Division, whose core was made up of Tennesseans and which the Germans called "Roosevelt's S. S.," stymied further advances in that sector. The Germans made more substantial progress in the southern half of the bulge. On December 19 Jack Hall and his 101st Airborne Division rode trucks into Bastogne and joined some elements of the 9th and 10th Armored Divisions in setting up defensive positions. The next day, XLVII Panzer Corps, following its instructions, by-passed the town to north and south leaving the 26th Volksgrenadier Division the job of laying siege to it. With the 101st now surrounded, the Germans called on it to surrender. This prompted its commander, General James McAuliffe, to respond with his famous one-word reply, "Nuts."

As the German advance continued westward, well past Bastogne, the holdout by the 101st remained a thorn in the Germans' side. The cut-off American troops were running low on supplies of all kinds and were cold and hungry. Because of days on end of overcast skies and heavy fog, it was impossible to execute air drops. Jack Hall dug a nice foxhole and, in a pitiful attempt to fight the bitter cold, lined it with his parachute. Running out of something to eat, he joined his buddies in digging down through the snow and uprooting leeks to munch on.

Of all the American generals, George Patton sensed something was in the wind before the attack occurred. His Third Army was well to the south moving east, so he ordered his staff to prepare a contingency plan that would enable him to turn 90 degrees and move rapidly to the north if the Germans attacked when and where he thought they might.

Having been by-passed by the main attacking force and having no conception of what was going on in the rest of the world and that the Allies might actually be on the verge of losing the war, the cold and hungry "Battered Bastards of Bastogne" were under a cloud of despair. But they continued to fight and hold out and were encouraged when they began hearing Patton's guns as he approached from the south.

On December 24 the skies cleared and planes were able to drop some supplies to the beleaguered troops. Patton's advance was strongly contested by the German 5th Parachute Division and it was December 26 before advance elements managed to reach the Bastogne area through a narrow corridor only a few hundred yards wide. Suffering irreplaceable heavy losses in other sectors, shortly thereafter the Germans began a general withdrawal on all fronts. It had been a battle of immense proportions. American casualties numbered 77,000 while the Germans had suffered 82,000 killed and wounded. Casualties among the British, Canadian, and other Allied troops, were similarly high.

This was an example of the heightened intensity of the war in all theaters. Because of this, it became the norm to lower physical standards and reduce the period of time troops were trained in order to get them to the battlefronts as soon as possible. There were instances of boys being pulled out of high school as soon as they reached 18 years of age who were sent through six weeks of boot camp or basic training and then quickly shipped off to the war zones.

Henry Bateman had played a lot of football for the Central Warriors in the fall of 1943. Except for the fact that he was killed in combat, not much is known about his military service. It is believed he was a tail gunner on a bomber and was killed on his first mission over Europe.

After his Army training at Camp Fannin, Tex., Central halfback Jack Neiman went overseas in January 1945 on the former passenger liner Queen Mary that had been converted to a troopship. On April 15, only three weeks before the end of the war in Europe, his unit was driving toward Czechoslovakia and nearing the German town of Schwabach, near Nuremberg. Expecting stiff resistance in capturing Schwabach, they were approaching the town cautiously on foot when Jack momentarily turned his head to glance to the right. At that instant a rifle bullet struck him on the left side of his head in front of his ear. The bullet did not exit and is still inside at the top of his head.

The wound paralyzed Jack on his right side and he spent many months in rehabilitation learning to walk all over again. While he is still physically plagued by the effects of his wound, Jack's grit and determination have made him a regular on the golf course.

After spending some time in a naval hospital at Oakland, Cal., John Fox took a train for Memphis and spent an additional three months at the naval hospital at Millington. Released for active duty, he was stationed at the Philadelphia Navy Yard for a brief time and then sent to the Oceanside Boat Basin at Camp Pendleton, Cal. It was here where he had orig-

John Fox after recovery from his wound on Iwo Jima wearing Asiatic-Pacific campaign ribbon with three battle stars and Purple Heart. (Courtesy of John Fox)

Back in Memphis, Billy Burke and John Fox. (Courtesy of Patsy (Mrs. Bill) Burke)

inally trained on amphtracks. One day his name popped up on a list for a return to Pacific combat duty. Whoever had prepared the list was unaware he had previously been overseas and been wounded; when this was confirmed, he was taken off the list.

It was common ... throughout the (Okinawa) campaign for replacements to get hit before we even knew their names. They came up confused, frightened, and hopeful, got wounded or killed, and went right back to the rear on the route by

which they had come, shocked, bleeding, or still.

With the Old Breed: At Peleliu and Okinawa

-E. B. Sledge

p. 267

After boot camp at Parris Island, S. C. Jimmy "Red" Doyle and Gayden Drew ended up in the same anti-tank outfit at Camp Pendleton, Cal. in early 1945. One day a clerk, making up a replacement draft for overseas duty, came into the barracks and selected them for his list. They left aboard a troopship from San Diego on April 12, the day President Roosevelt died. The ship stopped at Pearl Harbor and then sailed on to Guam where it stayed for several weeks and additional troops were added to the draft. After stopping a day at Saipan for refueling, the ship landed at Okinawa, which had been invaded April 1. The battle for this island, 60 miles long and two to 20 miles in width, involved three Marine divisions and several Army divisions and resulted in Japanese losses of 109,629 killed and 7,871 captured and 39,000 American casualties. This was the last big battle of World War II and lasted until June 21. Okinawa was the site of the Japanese military academy and one of the students' tactical problems over the years had been to devise plans for the island's defense.

Doyle and Drew were assigned to "L" Company, Third Battalion, Fifth Regiment of the First Marine Division and

Gayden Drew in 1945. Before Okinawa.
(Courtesy of Gayden Drew)

ended up on the line. All during their first day they hauled weapons and ammunition through the mud to the front and then, just at dark, exhausted, dug a foxhole alongside a road that had a slightly higher elevation than their hole and provided a little more protection. Half a mile away was a hill that Marine artillery had pounded throughout the day.

The rain was constant and they sat on the edge of their water-filled foxhole under their ponchos spending a miserable night griping about their circumstances, wondering what the hell they were doing in a place like that and wishing they were back at the Pig 'n Whistle. It was customary for one man to stay awake while the other slept but, except for an occasional brief nodding off, their night was a sleepless one. Behind them the artillery fired flares periodically that lit up the countryside in front of them, but Doyle and Drew were so green they thought it was the Japs doing it.

In an adjacent foxhole they noticed that after one man had gone to sleep the other one also was dozing. Red and Gayden didn't want an infiltrator sneaking up on them, so they occasionally pelted the dozer with rocks and tossed in a few words of remonstrance to keep him awake. In the hole on the other side of them they found a guy with an ample supply of cigarettes, so for something to do and to help keep them awake they bummed butts and puffed through the night under cover of the ponchos. At daylight they learned that the guy at whom they had been tossing rocks was a sergeant and the source of their smokes was a lieutenant. The former was somewhat hacked at their antics during the night and assigned Doyle to a detail (the Marines have a term for it) going to the rear about a mile and hauling more ammo through the mud to the line.

The platoon to which Doyle and Drew were assigned had been on Okinawa since the inception of the battle six or seven weeks before. Under wartime tables of organization a Marine rifle platoon had a complement of 43 men; when Red and Gayden joined theirs it had only 12 or 13 men left from its original members and at least seven lieutenants, platoon leaders, had been killed or wounded to a degree sufficient to put them out of action. The platoon was divided into three squads that, in turn, were divided into three fire teams of four men each. One of the fire team members was equipped with a Browning Automatic Rifle while the other three carried the M-1 rifle.

About noon the order came down for a general advance all along the line toward the hill brimming with Japanese defenders. Red and Gayden's platoon was on the extreme right flank of the First Division with the Sixth Division adjacent to it. Approximately 35,000 men stood up and began moving forward. Doyle and Drew moved out with their fire team advancing across open farmland crisscrossed with shallow drainage ditches and pockmarked with shell holes. With Red in the lead they sprinted from one depression to another seeking maximum cover. Flame-throwing "Zippo" tanks clanked across the fields and artillery sent shells screaming into the hill. Japanese artillery responded in kind and a shell landed nearby. A small fragment hit Doyle in the side putting him on the ground and knocking the breath out of him. Crawling into a shell hole he examined his side and saw that it was scratched but not even bleeding, but it later became infected. Then another member of the fire team jumped into the hole and said to Doyle, "Your buddy got hit pretty bad back there." About this time the Japanese began opening up with their Nambu machine guns. Red ran back to try to locate Gayden and then reported to the lieutenant that Drew was lying out there wounded.

Gayden had been hit by a .25 or .31 caliber rifle bullet that had entered his left shoulder and traveled down into his chest severing an artery. He dropped down and wedged himself in a ditch about a foot wide and a little over a foot deep. He bled profusely at first (Doyle said he had a bloody splotch on his dungaree jacket the size of a football), but it stopped rather quickly. Somehow, possibly from the heat of the bullet, the artery had been cauterized. Other members of the platoon threw smoke grenades and under cover of these Doyle ran back out into the fields calling Gayden's name; he located him he helped him back to the line. When Gayden responded in the affirmative to the lieutenant's question as to whether he could make it back to the battalion aid station, he got up on his feet but almost passed out. They then put him on a stretcher and, under fire, Doyle and three others carried him back to where he could receive medical attention.

Gayden was sent to a naval hospital on Guam where

his attending doctor was a LtCmdr Miles Standish. The latter took some mercurochrome and marked on Gayden's chest where the bullet had lodged; it was under the third rib near the heart and a lung. Gayden wanted him to remove it but Standish demurred. He felt it would be too hard to get to and it would be better to leave it in. He claimed that shrapnel moves around but a protective tissue builds up around a bullet; he went on to say he still had three bullets in him from World War I. Gayden later was sent to a hospital on the West Coast and then to Pensacola. A knee injury incurred in the eleventh grade and again in the twelfth grade had been aggravated by his military service and the bone was pulling apart. The knee was operated on at Pensacola and shortly thereafter Gayden was discharged.

On Okinawa Red ran into his brother Gene, the CBC halfback who had suffered the concussion in the 1941 South Side game. Gene had been out in the Pacific for three years and had fought with the First Division in the jungles of Cape Gloucester, New Britain and at the bloody ridges and caves of Peleliu. He now was in graves registration and was able to get Red transferred into his unit. Red later spent 10 months in China, primarily at Tientsin on the coast, and contracted yellow jaundice there.

While Doyle and Drew were receiving their baptisms of fire, Billy Bolton, who had backed-up Rowan at fullback, also was fighting his way across Okinawa. One day as his squad was moving along a railroad track, they came under fire from Japanese knee mortars, devices that hurl hand grenades long distances. They dropped down in a shallow ditch alongside the track and, during a momentary lull, Billy raised up in an attempt to see where the fire was coming from. As he reached to put one hand on the track, he was startled to see, at eye level, an inscription on a plate bolting together two sections of track: "Made by Pidgeon-Thomas Iron Co., Memphis, Tenn."

Later, when his fire team entered a cave to flush out some enemy troops, he was shot at virtual point-blank range by a Japanese soldier hiding behind a big rock. Billy was hit by a dum dum, which is a soft-nosed bullet that expands upon contact. It hit his left shoulder bone and splintered down into his chest. Although this bullet was outlawed by the Geneva Convention, the Japs used them throughout the war. For many years small fragments of the bullet would occasionally work their way to the surface of his skin.

While home on leave, Slick Williams and Billy Buckles get together for some partying at the Claridge Hotel's Balinese Room.

Because of his musical talents, after the end of the war in Europe Jack Hall was transferred into special services and sent to Berlin. He worked as a disc jockey with the Armed Forces Radio Network and played piano and sang with the "82nd Airborne Jumpmaster Band," a snazzy group that wore white parachute lines for laces in their jump boots. There were a lot of different Army units represented in and around Berlin and the band would visit them and put on concerts almost nightly.

Marlene Dietrich's mother was ill and living in Berlin and Marlene came there to be with her. For a month or so she performed almost nightly with Jack's band. The Army made up a uniform for her and she would roll up to the site of the concert in a car bearing MaiGen Maxwell Taylor's two stars on the license plate. Each unit, of course, had its own distinctive patch. Someone would acquire the pertinent one on the eve of a concert and make a garter out of it that Marlene would wear high on her thigh. Toward the end of her performance she would launch into her trademark "See what the boys in the back room are having; tell 'em I'm having the same." Then she

Berlin, 1945. Top row, second from left: Jack Hall snuggles up to Marlene.
(Courtesy of Dr. Jack Hall)

would put her foot up on a box and, as she sang "Lily Marlene," would slowly raise her skirt until the garter bearing the unit's patch was exposed. The din of the resulting cheers and whistles was almost enough to put the Russians on full alert.

Just when he thought he couldn't get any better duty, Jack was designated for some "R and R" and sent to the fashionable resort town of Biarritz, France on the Bay of Biscay at the foot of the Pyrenees Mountains. The government had sent a large group of American college professors over and Jack and his cohorts spent mornings going to class and their afternoons trying to learn how to ski.

The Army sent Percy Roberts to California for awhile where he ran into Jack Salmon in San Francisco. In their explorations of the city they ran across a Pig 'n Whistle in the downtown area, so it wasn't a drive-in and, except for the name, bore little resemblance to the one back home. However, they couldn't resist sending a card to Redwood telling him about it.

Later, while in Miami, Percy learned that Slick Williams was in the area when he read in a copy of *The Commercial Appeal* that Slick's mother had visited him there. One day Percy was sitting at a soda fountain chowing down on a banana split and watching a flood of people, primarily sailors, streaming by on the sidewalk. Suddenly, his eagle eye spotted Slick strolling along. After excitedly chasing him down and exchanging "I don't believe its," the two would meet at Walgreen's at First and Flagler about every other night and go out on the town. The Air Force had commandered a number of hotels along Miami Beach reserved for pilots and crewmen coming back on R and R from overseas, so when Percy and Slick didn't want to go back to their bases they would slip into one of these posh establishments, surreptitiously make their way around until they found an empty room, and spend the night. On VJ (Victory over Japan) night, like most young people in the Western World, they roamed around watching all the crazy things people were doing and stayed up all night. Somewhere along the way, while wearing his white Navy pants, Slick inadvertently sat down in some tar. Because they had spent all their money during the evening, the next morning Percy hocked his CBC class ring for $5 and they spent $4.50 on breakfast.

After the Japanese surrender, Ira Whitley, who had become a football manager at Central after an injury and had gone through boot camp with Red Doyle, moved into Japan with Marine occupying forces. While on liberty one day he walked into a curio shop looking for a memento to send home to Memphis. Although not fluent, the sales girl could speak some English and Ira learned she had attended UCLA before the war. After awhile she said "I'll bet you are from the South?"

"That's right," Ira replied, "I'm from Memphis."

Apparently the girl had taken a political science course at UCLA, for she promptly said, "Oh, then you must know Boss Crump."

Over in Germany Central tackle Maurice Keathley, 19 years old, had received a commission as a second lieutenant, "Because I was big." He was assigned as a prison officer guarding the Nazi war criminals scheduled for trial at Nuremberg. While he was sent back home before the trials were concluded, he was there long enough to become familiar with the faces of Goering, Hess, Kitel, and all the others.

After the 1944 football season down at LSU Billy Buckles entered the Army in December and John Trent went into the Army Air Corps shortly thereafter. Rowan had an appointment to West Point and he entered the academy in the summer of 1945. That fall Rowan played behind Heisman Trophy winner Doc Blanchard at fullback. Also in that backfield were Glenn Davis, who would win the same trophy in 1946, All-American quarterback Arnold Tucker, and Shorty McWilliams, who would return to stardom at Mississippi State the next year. Joe Steffy, the Chattanooga Baylor and Tennessee guard also joined the West Point team that year and the following year John Trent received an appointment.

The 1943 Central tenth graders were now seniors and they returned to Arkansas to again play their old nemesis, Little Rock Central. Little Rock had pulled that 7 to 6 upset in 1943 when Memphis had beaten them in every category but the final score, having four passes intercepted and losing seven fumbles. In their game in Memphis in 1944 Little Rock's big, fast fullback John Hoffman, future Chicago Bear, had carried the brunt of the attack leading his team to a 7 to 0 win. This time the Warriors were determined to come out the winner.

Both teams went after it hammer and tongs and it was a rough game that got out of control. Memphis had fifteen 15 yard penalties slapped on them and three of their touchdowns were called back. An arm of one of Little Rock's ends was broken, their fullback lost some teeth and others hobbled off the field for various reasons. Then, at about the start of the fourth quarter, Memphis tackle Harley Jeffery was in a pass protection stance when Little Rock tackle Fred Williams, who later would star for Arkansas and the Chicago Bears, rushed the passer. Harley came up with a mighty forearm and his elbow inadvertently caught Williams in the mouth and knocked out four of his front teeth. Because the two were somewhat isolated when this occurred, everybody in the stadium saw it and it almost caused a riot. Little Rock won again, this time 18 to 12.

After the game Williams' father and two big brothers came to the Central dressing room looking for Harley, but they were fended off by Coach Ruffner Murray, who might have decked one of them before police sealed off the area. The Warriors had planned to spend the night, but the cops told them not to go back to the hotel. Their bus was driven onto the field and, under police guard, they made their way to it and, after pulling away under a barrage of rocks, drove straight back to Memphis. The trainer later went to the hotel to retrieve their wallets and watches they had left in their rooms.

The Little Rock newspaper was indignant and referred to the Memphians as "gangsters." Little Rock Central was so beat up and demoralized that they lost their next three games. A delegation from the Memphis Central student government went to Little Rock to meet with their counterparts in an effort to smooth things over.

The reason for it is not known, but no Blind Game was held in 1944; however, it was renewed in 1945 and would continue annually through 1970. The 1945 game was the only one involving an out-of-town team, as Tech played Knoxville High, the same school that had been picked over Central as the state champion in 1943. Tech won 20 to 0, but the score was not indicative of just how badly Knoxville was beaten. Tech had a big, tough team and a number of the Knoxville boys were, as they say, "shaken up." The Knoxville sportswriters were disappointed and embarrassed by the severity of the thrashing their boys received and, of course, they didn't particularly like anything about Memphis anyway, so in the writeups of the game they used extremely derogatory adjectives in describing the character and style of play of the Tech boys. Jimmy Crawford, later a three-time All-Southeastern Conference guard at Ole Miss, was out of the Tech lineup with a broken leg. But he was very much into the game. He didn't let his cast restrain him as he patrolled the Tech sideline like a caged tiger, exhorting his teammates.

During his two years in the Marine Corps Bill Wright was always just behind the combat at Saipan, Guam and Okinawa. He was assigned to the Sixth Marine Division and ended up in China after the war. Like Red Doyle, he contracted yellow jaundice there, but he had a more severe case and spent almost six months in a hospital.

The toll of war cannot be fully expressed simply by listing those killed and wounded; the scope of its insidious impact on those involved in its prosecution, and even those considered bystanders, can never be fully comprehended. Those who recently have had a mild malarial recurrence to remind them of their days on Guadalcanal or New Guinea, those who were told it was safe to swim in the nearby waters after the atomic test at Bikini Atoll, those who were slowly debilitated and destroyed by Agent Orange infused in Vietnam and those with the mysterious ailments developed during Desert Storm are all casualties who, to some degree or other, have had their lives affected adversely.

For his football prowess at Central High, Bill Wright had a scholarship to the University of Alabama. When he entered the Marine Corps he weighed about 185 pounds. During his bout with yellow jaundice he dropped to 155 and stayed there. When he got home in the summer of 1946, the coaches at Alabama recommended that he attend a junior college for awhile to get back in shape, so Bill enrolled at Copiah-Lincoln at Wesson, Miss. Here, for two years, he played football, basketball, baseball, and broad-jumped in track. But he never was able to get back up to his "playing weight" and he never went to Alabama.

Although there certainly were others, those not previously mentioned who are known to have gone into military service before the official end of World War II, December 31, 1946, were: John Ross in the Coast Guard, Tommy Welsh, Leon Shahun, John Walt, David Steffan, Ralph Giles, Mike Tansey, Joe Crim, Bill Durbin and (with a big contingent from Central's 1944 team in January, 1945) Ralph Baker and Babe Welch in the Army, Bill Dulweber and Vance Cartwright in the Marine Corps, Bill Trickett, George Sneed, Don Hollowell and Guthrie Castle in the Navy, Joe Gold and Minor Tait in the Air Force, and Basil Crone and Arvin James in the Merchant Marine.

Billy Bolton was back from Okinawa with his shoulder in a cast and home on leave. One day as he and his father were walking past the cotton offices along Front Street, they spotted Mr. Crump across the way. The Boss waved at Billy's father and called him by name and then, although Billy had met him only once at the Blind Game two years previously, he said, "Hi, Billy, good to see you." Then Mr. Crump did something that struck Billy as strange. Leaning over on his cane he took his hat off and set it on top of the cane as he stood there looking at them from across the street. Presumably, this was a salute to Billy for his military service.

During Ray Brown's first two years at Virginia his Cavalier team had a pretty good record, winning 13 games while losing only three and tying two. The team entered the 1946 season with high expectations and dispatched Hampden-Sydney 71 to 0 in the opening game. The next game with Virginia Poly was hotly-contested and ended up 21 to 21. During this game Ray returned a VPI punt about 60 yards for a touchdown. The next day Ray read in the *Richmond Times-*

Four former Central High players at Virginia in 1946. Left to right: Jimmy Dickerson, reserve guard, Gene Barbour (transfer from Baylor), reserve back, Buck Pennel (transfer from Ole Miss), reserve back, and starter Ray Brown, who scored eleven touchdowns in 1945. (Courtesy of Ray Brown)

Ray Brown returns a VPI punt for a Virginia touchdown. (Courtesy of Ray Brown)

406

Dispatch that a Richmond resident, L. Gleason Giannini, who was listening to the game on the radio, got so excited when Ray ran the punt back that he ran to tell his wife and tripped and fell down some stairs breaking his arm. Considerate fellow that he is, Ray promptly wrote him a letter of commiseration. Later in the season, Ray made another long touchdown run from a fake punt formation. While at a dance that night he got a telegram from Giannini: "What do you want me to do, break my neck?" These events set the stage for a friendship of sorts and the Cavalier fan and his wife later went up to Charlottesville to visit Ray at school.

Further distinguishing the Central High Class of 1944, in the summer of 1947 Miss Memphis, Barbara Walker, was crowned Miss America in Atlantic City. After fulfilling her responsibilities in that capacity, to her credit she eschewed the glitter and bright light opportunities that ordinarily accompany such a role and settled back down in Memphis to marry her med-student fiance. She lived on Harrison Street

Barbara Walker, Central High Class of 1944, Miss America, 1947. (Courtesy of Barbara Walker (Mrs. John) Hummel)

and, in recognition of her achievement, the city re-named it Barbara Drive.

As the 1947 season approached for the "Black Knights" at West Point on the Hudson, Coach Earl "Red" Blaik had only three returning starters and was facing tougher competition. The three previous years had produced a record of 27 wins, no losses and one tie. The tie was a scoreless one with Notre Dame in 1946 after Army had beaten the Fighting Irish 59 to 0 and 48 to 0 the two previous years. Gone were such All-Americans as Doc Blanchard, Glenn Davis and Arnold Tucker in the backfield and Tex Coulter, Barney Poole, and Hank Foldberg on the line. The three returning starters were Rowan at fullback, Goble Bryant at tackle and Joe Steffy at guard, who had been elected captain.

The quality of football played those first few years after World War II is recognized as probably the historical zenith of college football. The professional teams were about half in number what they are today and their games were some years away from being universally televised; writeups of their games were usually relegated to the inside pages of the sports sections. This resulted in greater publicity and support for college teams in their particular geographic locality. Too, in most cases the teams were loaded with mature talent. Some had played before the war and, after several years in service, returned for a couple of more years of college ball. Others had played service football after coming out of high school and were ready to step into starring roles. For example, Charlie "Choo Choo" Justice, the great North Carolina halfback had played three years in the Navy after high school and then played four years at Chapel Hill after entering as a 22 year-old freshman and, because four years of his college football were considered service-connected and didn't count against his eligibility, Barney Poole played eight years at Ole Miss, North Carolina Pre-Flight, West Point and, again, at Ole Miss.

The great backs of that era are legion: Chunkin' Charlie Conerly of Ole Miss, Y. A. Tittle of LSU, Travis Tidwell

408

Army's Empty Helmets

For three years the U.S. Military Academy at West Point has dominated college football. Lead by Glenn Davis, Felix "Doc" Blanchard and Arnold Tucker, the greatest backfield combination of all time, the cadets won 27 games, tied one, lost none. But last week, as practice began at West Point, Coach Earl "Red" Blaik (right) ruefully started to build a new team with three regulars--Tackle Goble Bryant, Halfback Elwyn Rowan, Guard Joe Steffy--and eight empty helmets and 16 empty shoes for this year's 52-man squad to fill. (John Trent in back row, fourth from right.) (Time/Life photo)

of Auburn, Harry Gilmer of Alabama, Bob Chappius of Michigan, Doak Walker and Kyle Rote of SMU, Bobby Layne of Texas, Charlie Trippi of Georgia, Buddy Young of Illinois, Clyde "Smackover" Scott of Arkansas, Johnny Lujack of Notre Dame, Ray Evans of Kansas and Lynn Chadnois of Michigan State, to mention just a few. And then there were linemen such as Dick Huffman of Tennessee, Weldon Humble of Rice, Bob Gain of Kentucky, Leo Nomellini of Minnesota, Heisman Trophy winner Leon Hart and Jim Martin, ends at Notre Dame, George Connor and Moose Fischer of Notre Dame, Art Donovan and Ernie Stautner of Boston College and Charles "Concrete Charlie" Bednarik of Pennsyvania.

Under Coach Frank Leahy, Notre Dame won the national championship in 1947. Army traveled to South Bend for their seventh game of the season. They had won four, played a scoreless tie with Illinois and, in a major upset, lost to Columbia 21 to 20, a game in which Rip Rowan had an 85-yard touchdown gallop.

Terry Brennan took the opening kickoff for the Irish and returned it 90 yards for a touchdown. Eight minutes later the Ramblers scored again and it was 13 to 0. Then Army put on a 50 yard drive that ultimately petered out. In the second quarter Rowan punted out of bounds on the Notre Dame 14, but the Irish put on a drive that carried to the Cadet 11. Three runs lost ten yards and a five yard penalty moved the ball back to the 26. A pass to Martin in the end zone misfired.

Army quarterback Arnold Galiffa hit Rowan with a pass to the 36 and then threw to John Trent for a six-yard gain. But Army was stopped there and on a low snap the punter was forced to run and was brought down on the Cadet 44. Army held and the Irish punted out of bounds on the 16. Rowan then reeled off a 20-yard gain, but the play was called back for a roughness penalty. Rip then ran for 14 more yards, but it was short of a first down due to the penalty. Galiffa was stopped on a quarterback draw and the Cadets punted on third down.

The kick was returned by Coutre to the Notre Dame 37.

Three runs were just short of a first down and the Irish went for it on fourth down, however Brennan fumbled and Galiffa recovered on the Notre Dame 47. Winfield Scott got in the clear inside the 25 but Galiffa's pass to him was a whisker too long. Lujack knocked down another pass and then Rowan picked up eight yards through the middle. With time running out in the first half Galiffa threw again, but it was intercepted by Lujack.

In the opening minutes of the third quarter Notre Dame partially blocked an Army punt and took over at the Cadets' 45. The Irish moved to the 29 but were held there. An exchange of punts gave the ball to Army on its own 11. Rowan lost six yards and Army punted again to midfield. Mixing runs and passes Lujack moved the team downfield to score and the Irish had gone ahead 20 to 0.

The Cadets began a drive at their 44 that continued on into the fourth quarter. Rowan carried to the Notre Dame 13 and Bobby Jack Stuart circled end to the five. Rip smashed to the one and then scored on the next play. Joe Steffy kicked the extra point and it was Notre Dame 20 Army 7. After Army's kickoff into the end zone, Notre Dame took over on the 20 and drove for its fourth touchdown. There were no more significant drives during the remainder of the game and the Irish chalked up a 27 to 7 win.

Rowan had played a sterling game against the best team in the country. In his 16 rushes he had gained 83 yards, reputedly setting a record for rushing by an individual opponent in Notre Dame Stadium that stood for something like 25 years. One of his two passes was completed for 13 yards and he also did some of the punting, caught a pass, and played linebacker. Notre Dame coach Frank Leahy was sufficiently impressed by his performance to name Rowan as the fullback on his All-America team. Rip's old teammate at Central, John Trent, only a sophomore in eligibility, started at end for the Cadets. And Joe Steffy shone as he outplayed the bigger and highly-publicized Notre Dame interior linemen.

The same day of the Notre Dame-Army clash, Ray Brown and Virginia were dropping a 19 to 7 game to Pennsylvania at Franklin Field in Philadelphia. This was when the Quakers still turned out competitive teams. That year it was led by Bednarik at center and linebacker who played both offense and defense, a feat he continued during a long career in the professional ranks with the Philadelphia Eagles. Ray says he is the best he ever played against. The following week Army also met Penn at Franklin Field with the game ending 7 to 7. Penn won its seven other games that season by decisive margins.

Two weeks later the Cadets returned to Philadelphia, this time before a throng of 101,500 people, to complete their season against Navy. The Midshipmen came out full of fire, determined to upset the West Pointers and gain some measure of satisfaction for an otherwise disappointing season.

Twenty-eight hundred Midshipmen marched onto the field followed by the 2,200-member Corps of Cadets, then the combined bands played for the singing of the National Anthem. Included in the crowd were President Harry Truman, who tossed the coin for the captains to call before the game, and tons of military brass including Generals Dwight Eisenhower and Omar Bradley, Admirals Chester Nimitz and "Bull" Halsey along with presidential cabinet members and Supreme Court justices. Also in attendance, but with a better seat than all the bigwigs, was former CBC center and linebacker Julius Smith. He was in the Army stationed at nearby Fort Dix, N. J. A special section was set aside for "purple heart veterans," and a sergeant from the base, with whom Julius was friendly, suggested he come along with them on the bus. Actually, the sergeant didn't believe Julius' claim that he knew Rowan and Trent and wanted him to be there so the claim could be disproved and he could win a bet with him. A bench was added like the ones the Army team was sitting on and Julius sat next to assistant coach Vince Lombardi throughout the game.

Nov. 8, 1947. Virginia's Ray Brown reels off nice gain against Penn at Franklin Field. (Courtesy of Ray Brown)

One week later, in a strikingly similar photo, Army's Rip Rowan breaks into secondary against Penn at Franklin Field. No. 60 is "Concrete Charlie" Bednarik. (Bettman Archives)

Navy returned the kickoff to their 34 and made eleven yards on the first play. Three runs moved it to the Army 38 and then Bill Yoeman broke through from linebacker and dropped the quarterback for an eleven-yard loss. Navy was able to move the ball to the Army 30 but lost it on downs at that point. After the Cadets couldn't move they punted and Navy returned the ball to its 38. The Sailors picked up two first downs to get to Army's 41, but a five-yard penalty put them back on the 46. Then came one of those plays that analysts like to describe as "turning points." Carrying on a fullback dive, Middie Bill Hawkins fumbled when clobbered by Joe Steffy and Goble Bryant recovered on the Army 45. Hawkins was knocked unconscious and left the game for good; the loss of his talents was a severe blow to Navy.

Army moved the ball to midfield and then a roughness penalty put it on the Navy 35. Stuart picked up three yards, then Rowan faked a pass and ran around end for nine for a first down at the 23. A couple of more plays put the ball on the 18. Rowan then got a direct snap from center through the quarterback's legs. Quarterback Galiffa turned around to fake a handoff, the halfbacks crossed in front of Rowan as he bent over, and then Rip raised up and tossed a pass down the middle to Bill Kellum, who had played at LSU in 1943; Kellum careened into the end zone for a touchdown.

Navy returned the kickoff to its 33 yard line and moved on past midfield until Galiffa intercepted a pass on his three and returned it to the 36 as the first quarter ended. After a fake to Rowan up the middle, Winfield Scott cleared around right end for 26 yards to the Navy 38. Bobby Jack Stuart broke loose for a long gain but fumbled with Navy recovering on its eight-yard line. A penalty on Army for roughness put the ball on the 23.

Navy then moved quickly through the air and had a first down on the Army 12. But the Middies were pushed back to the 20 and on fourth down a completed pass carried only to the eight and Army took over. On the next play Rowan broke over left tackle and, after getting a good block from Kellum and faking-out another man, turned on his speed and had clear sailing 92 yards down the sideline for a touchdown. It was the longest run from scrimmage in the history of the Army-Navy series.

Navy's offense was shut down for the rest of the second quarter. Their final effort ended when Army intercepted a pass at midfield. The Cadets moved the ball to the Navy 29 and then Scott was dumped for an 11-yard loss. Rowan's attempted punt was blocked and Navy's Art Markel picked it up and ran it to Army's 33 just before the first half ended.

Early in the third quarter Navy received two big penalties that gave Army the ball on the Middies' 22-yard line. But Galiffa fumbled and Navy recovered. Navy moved to their 42 but a failed pass on fourth down gave the Cadets the ball back at that point. Stuart, Scott and Rowan carried it to the Navy 15 but the Midshipmen held. On fourth down Mackmull missed a field goal attempt.

With the ball on their 20 Navy's quarterback flipped a lateral to halfback Myron Gerber who attempted a pass back across the field into the flat. But John Trent had quickly diagnosed the play and was in good position when the ball came his way. He grabbed it out of the air and raced across the goal line for Army's third touchdown. The fourth quarter was colorless as Navy couldn't move the ball and Army, too, never again threatened. Army won 21 to 0.

With his 148 yards rushing in 18 carries, Rowan was the outstanding player on the field. He also completed two passes out of three for 26 yards and a touchdown. A player from Central High had had a hand in all three touchdowns: Rowan's touchdown pass to Kellum, his 92-yard dash, and Trent's interception return. And left-footed kicker Joe Steffy from Chattanooga had booted the three extra points.

After the game Julius Smith won his bet with the skeptical sergeant. He didn't see Rowan but he did run into Trent on the sidelines. Trent's elation at winning the game so decisively and scoring a touchdown, to boot, and then his surprise at seeing Julius caused him to grab Smith in a low bear hug and throw him up in the air. When Julius told him about the doubting sergeant Trent noticed a kicking tee on the ground; he went over and picked it up and said, "Here, give this to him, maybe that will convince him." He invited Julius to go out and hoist a few with him and Rowan, but Julius felt it was their big moment to savor with their teammates and he didn't want to intrude.

That year Joe Steffy was awarded the Outland Trophy

as the nation's top collegiate lineman. At a get-together of former Army players years later he asked Coach Red Blaik what had been his biggest thrill in his long football career. Blaik replied, "Watching Rip Rowan run 92 yards against Navy."

A year or so before, probably because he knew two Memphis boys would be playing with the Cadets, Mr. Crump had written Memphis' Senator Kenneth McKellar asking him to use his influence in trying to get the 1947 Army-Navy game in Memphis. But the academies had a contract with the Philadelphia Municipal Stadium through that year, plus its seating capacity was almost four times that of Crump Stadium. It was a nice thought but not a practical one.

The skeptical sergeant was the kind of guy who could get you in trouble if you hung around him long enough. He and Julius were in special services and their duties were not particularly demanding. The lieutenant in charge of their section had bought a new car and he asked, or directed, the sergeant to get his old one ready for him to sell by having some of his peons wash and clean it over the weekend.

None of the guys in the section had a car and the sergeant saw this as a good opportunity to get away for the weekend and have a big time. He selected Asbury Park, a resort town only about 35 miles away as the locale for their romp. It was a place where a fellow could meet girls, go to the beach, meet girls, gamble, and meet girls.

With the sergeant behind the wheel, Julius seated next to him and two of their compatriots in the back seat, they left Fort Dix in the lieutenant's old car. But it was a slow trip. Bars were frequent along their route and the sergeant gave the impression of wanting to help keep them all in business so they would still be there the next time he was in the vicinity. By the time they were within five or ten miles of their destination he was so gassed and his driving so erratic that he gave in to Julius' insistence that he let him drive.

As they began entering Asbury Park on a six-lane highway, they came up on a string of cars stopped at a traffic light. Julius took his foot off the accelerator and started to gently apply the brake. Nothing happened! He pushed it to the floor but the car maintained its speed. He jerked on the emergency brake and it came off in his hand. The boys in the back seat were becoming a little apprehensive. A nervous voice suggested "You had better stop!"

"I don't have any brakes."

"Try the hand brake."

Julius handed it over the back seat, "Here, you try it." They were almost to the intersection, with traffic stopped both ways. The light changed, but it was too late to do them any good. Julius swung the wheel to the left and zoomed across the fronts of the cars facing him, that had just started moving, and entered a side street. The boys in the back clapped and cheered. The noise roused the sergeant from his slumped stupor and he raised up and grinned inanely like a hillside possum.

As soon as Julius turned into the street the first thing he noticed was a big wooden sign with letters saying "Dead End." The next thing he noticed was the steep down-grade. Like on a rollercoaster, down they went gathering momentum – what to do? what to do? as Julius' knuckles whitened akin to a snake's belly. At the end of the street two houses faced him on a steep rise. The car reached the bottom, dipped, and then soared up the long driveway of the house on the right. Just before they were in imminent danger of crashing into the house, Julius jerked the steering wheel to the left, cut across the front yard, cut across the front yard of the next house, and jerked the wheel again in an attempt to line up with the downward slope of the driveway. He got the left side wheels partially on it, but the right ones hit a little drainage ditch at the bottom and the car caromed and bounced out into the street heading back up the slope. The car finally stopped and, after a momentary exhalation of breath, the boys in the back seat clapped and cheered. They got out and put the jack under a tire.

The lieutenant assembled the section. He announced that the army was weeding-out all the dunderheads with low IQs, who had been handling the kitchen police jobs, and now they were short-handed over at the mess hall. To help take up the slack, the section was going to have to supply a man for awhile. Then he asked where his car was. The other guys that had made the trip were up for promotions and a foul-up could keep them from getting it. Recognizing this, Julius stepped forward and said it was his idea to take the car and that he had driven it to Asbury Park. Without embellishments, he told him that the brakes had gone out and because it was a weekend they weren't able to get it repaired.

Receiving "company punishment," for the next three days Julius labored in the sweltering, frenetic atmosphere of the mess hall from before dawn to midnight. He had had his eye, for awhile, on a very attractive WAC lieutenant a few years older than him. Although it wasn't kosher for commissioned and enlisted to date, her demeanor toward him indicated encouragement. Coming out a mess hall door one day carrying a big two-handled bucket of slop, his hairy belly exposed beneath his cut off T-shirt and sweat pouring down his face, he encountered the object of his interest. Her seeing him in such a demeaning situation and untidy appearance promptly put the skids to any potential romantic entanglement.

By coincidence, Dippy Coles had relatives living in Asbury Park. With money acquired from his voyages with the Merchant Marine he bought a new Buick convertible and decided to drive up to Asbury Park to visit his kinsmen and also see Julius. Because Smith was in a small loosely-run unit, for a couple of weeks they were able to spend a lot of time together. Usually, Julius would go back to the base and sign in, check right back out, and someone would cover for him. Sometimes he could handle it by phone.

The boys started trying to figure out how they could meet some girls. They decided the ones with whom they wanted to become acquainted were daughters of families that had membership in the most exclusive country club in that part of New Jersey. They couldn't just march in the door and introduce themselves, so they concluded that the situation called for a dramatic attention-getting stunt.

The club was situated on the ocean, so they acquired a worthless little boat of some sort and paddled over near the club in view of people on the shore. When they had drawn even with a group of girls congregated around a swimming pool, they started rocking the boat side to side and slopped water into it until if filled up and sank. Obviously, having no other recourse, they were forced to swim and wade in to the club property. Soon, they were conversing and getting acquainted with a bevy of attractive young ladies who were curious and solicitous of their welfare.

From that point on they came in the front door of the club as guests. As most of the local boys were in summer school at college somewhere or off in the service, the enterprising and resourceful pair were never without dates. Once, when Julius had to stay at Fort Dix for a couple of days the girls, not having been told he was in the Army, inquired as to his whereabouts; Dippy informed them that Mr. Smith had to make a brief trip to Kentucky to check on his thoroughbred horses that were training for an important race.

Percy Roberts
1951 Memphis State Tigers' captain.
(Courtesy of Percy Roberts)

In 1947 Ralph Hatley left CBC and assumed duties as head football coach at Memphis State College, now the University of Memphis. That year, and for the next several years, a number of his former pupils at CBC played for him: Lamon Kelley, Percy Roberts, Dippy Coles, Harry Costello, Hall Crawford, Jack Gibson, Julius Smith, Richard Mercer from his 1946 team and, also, George Sneed from Central. Percy had been in the Marine Corps Reserve and was called to active duty in 1950 for the Korean War; he returned in time to captain the 1951 team.

After discharge from the Navy, Slick Williams attended the spring 1946 semester at LSU and then transferred to his father's old school, North Carolina State, where he was on the football team. He came back to Memphis and obtained his bachelor's degree from Memphis State; he went on to earn a law degree from Southern Law University in Memphis. During the football seasons of 1945, 1947, and 1948 he helped coach the Central High team.

When Harley Jeffery graduated from Central in 1946 he accepted a football scholarship from Purdue University, but he first had given some consideration to going to college at Clemson. Central's coach, Ruffner Murray, was a friend of Clemson's colorful coach Frank Howard and he all but promised Howard that Harley would play for the Tigers. Then one day someone called Harley from Clemson inquiring about his uniform size. Harley thought it was a little strange that someone would be asking about sizes for a football uniform and wondered what kind of league they played in over there. As the conversation progressed he learned that the caller was talking about a military uniform. It was only then that Harley found out that Clemson was, at that time, a military school and, of course, had no girls in attendance. That's all he needed to know to nix that idea. Apparently, Ruffner Murray had extolled Harley's football potential to Howard and Harley doesn't think Murray ever forgave him for not going to Clemson.

At Purdue Harley was one of two freshmen to make the varsity. He was moved from tackle to end and played second string ahead of two guys who had lettered at Wisconsin and Illinois before the war. For the next three years he was a starter. Probably because they both are in Indiana, Purdue almost always plays Notre Dame tough. In 1948 the Boilermakers went into South Bend and almost pulled a huge upset, losing 28 to 27. Playing both offense and defense, it was probably Harley's best game ever. Notre Dame made only two yards around his end all day and he caught a pass for Purdue's final touchdown. That catch was chosen "the play of the week" in college football. In that pre-television age, it was shown in newsreels in theaters across the country.

Harley Jeffery as a freshman end at Purdue, 1946 .
(Courtesy of Harley Jeffery)

Against Minnesota that same year Harley went charging down the field on a punt hoping to drop the returner as soon as he caught the ball and took a step. Harley was the first Boilermaker down the field, arrived at just the right moment to make the tackle, and had the guy in his sights ready to blast him. Then, before 65,000 spectators, this third-string Gopher back juked to the side and Harley had nothing but air to grab before he hit the dirt. The guy made a nice return of the punt and Purdue's end coach was livid. Hank Foldberg, All-American end on Army's great wartime teams, jerked Harley out of the game. He grabbed his jersey up by his shoulder pads and shook him.

"That was a stupid mistake," he thundered, "who ever taught you how to play end?"

"You did, Coach," Harley deadpanned, and quickly took a seat on the bench.

Harley also boxed at Purdue and was the campus heavyweight champ with eleven wins and no losses. "Boom Boom," as he was called, won eight decisions and had three TKOs. On his squad at Purdue were three whose names became well-known in the football world. Abe Gibron became an All-Pro performer, John McKay coached Southern California during an era when it had some of its greatest teams, and Hank Stram, whom Harley used to tutor in English literature, coached the Kansas City Chiefs when they upset the Minnesota Vikings in Super Bowl IV. In another illustration of wonders never ceasing, in 1953 Harley served as line coach at CBC.

After Ray Brown graduated from Virginia, Davidson head coach Charley Jamerson asked him to be his backfield coach. Jamerson had coached those terrific Memphis Tech teams around 1940 and then had gone to North Carolina to serve as end coach for Carl Snavely. Ray was in the unusual position of coaching two former Tech standouts, Bert Anderton and Carl Pahl, who had played several years before he had in high school and had started college after the war.

Davidson opened the 1949 season against Army in Michie Stadium at West Point. Ray had seen John Trent briefly before the game and kidded him about how they were going to run around his end. Brown was working the phones in the press box that day and on Davidson's first offensive play he called a quick pitchout that caught Trent flat-footed and went around his end for ten yards. Trent looked up at Ray in the press box, laughed, and shook his fist at him. Army won 47 to 7.

Robert Jeffrey, who had played behind Billy Buckles at center in 1943 and then went on to make All-Memphis the next year, played at Mississippi State in 1945. He spent two years in the Army after that with part of the time on occupation duty in Korea with the infantry. After his discharge Bob went back to State and participated in football and track for three more years.

Jim Laney, who started at guard for Central in 1943 and was a co-captain in 1944, played football at Yale for a year. Like Jeffrey, he entered the Army for two years and spent some time in Korea in counter-intelligence. He returned to Yale to play more football and get his degree, but, as noted in a later section of this book, he also would have occasions to return to Korea.

Others off the two 1943 squads who played football in college were Don Malmo, who played a year at Purdue and then at Washington and Lee, Bobby Ladd at Union University, Jim Doyle at Southern California and Lou Sampson at Notre Dame. Billy Buckles came back and played two more years at LSU and then, when Coach Bernie Moore left, played his last year at Oklahoma City University. While in service Buckles played on a team hastily assembled by the Eleventh Air Force to play an impromptu game with another service team in the Hula Bowl in Honolulu. A group at Southwestern at Memphis included Judd Williford, Vance Cartwright, Ted Hay, Jack Hall, Bill Durbin, Bill Roberds and George Bland; Frank Halford played at Vanderbilt. Judd also played basketball and baseball. Tommy Welsh played baseball at Vanderbilt, Bobby Ladd played golf at Memphis State, as did Herbie Abraham at Tulane. Billy Bolton played tennis at Mississippi State and Don Crone played baseball at Christian Brothers College.

Hoagy Carmichael wrote a song entitled "Memphis In June" extolling the city's weather and flora during that month, with the last line saying "For there's nothing quite like Memphis in June." It's easy to agree with him, for it seems that Memphis in June, or June in Memphis, is a month of bright sunshine, low humidity, and blossoms providing a plethora of options for lazy, buzzing bees – seemingly an ideal time for any and all outdoor recreational pursuits. But when Memphis decided to put on its biggest community activity of the year – the Cotton Carnival – involving four or five parades, a carnival midway, an air show, and multitudinous garden parties, it selected mid-May, a time when the weather is still subject to sudden storms. Maybe the time was related to a symbolic thing like just having completed planting the year's cotton crop, or maybe it was because the weather was not quite as warm as it would be in June, or because it would not interfere with summer vacations. In any event, there always seemed to be some activities that got rained on that week.

Fortunately, however, in 1948 the Maid of Cotton parade

was held on a day of clear skies and warm yet comfortable temperatures. With a score of beautifully-decorated floats interspersed with a dozen or so high school bands, some from as far away as Texas, it was launched from Ellis Auditorium and rolled and trumpeted its way down Main to Beale and then back up Second Street without any known discordant aspects. But there was one element in the parade that was somewhat out of place.

Julius Smith, Percy Roberts, Sandy Kincannon and Dippy Coles decided they would like to be a part of the fun and pageantry. They hand-lettered two signs that said "Queen Amen" (Ah-Men) and taped them to each side of Dippy's snappy convertible. Queen Amen was Fifi Riddick,who later would become Mrs. Merrick "Dippy" Coles. Rustling up some bed sheets they drove downtown to the Fun Shop to buy masks. After donning their sheets and masks and satisfying each other as to the appropriateness of their costumes, they headed toward the auditorium to find a place in the parade. Wearing a veil covering the lower part of her face, Queen Amen sat up on the back of the open convertible. Unwittingly, they had selected an apt name for their queen, as there had been four kings bearing the name Amenhotep in the Egypt of antiquity.

As they approached a barrier guarded by a policeman at Third Street, Sandy proclaimed in authoritative and stentorian tones, "Make way for Queen Amen." They were quickly let through and Kincannon's repeated pronouncement also provided entre through the barrier at Second Street. Fortunately, for the success of their ruse, the parade was well underway when they arrived.

A policeman asked, "What number are you?"

"Number 31," replied Percy, picking a number at random.

"Well move in right over there," he told Dippy.

As Dippy drove slowly down Main Street between a float and a band, Percy, Julius and Sandy ran alongside playing the fool with the crowd lining the route. With a hideous rubber mask covering his face, Julius would purposely seek out the biggest, ugliest women he could find and throw his arms around them and kiss them on the cheek as they squealed in mock terror. When someone asked Sandy what secret society they were in, he told the inquirer "It's so secret we don't even tell each other."

They got away with their charade and no one ever challenged their right to be in the parade. But as they passed the reviewing stand set up in Court Square, questions undoubtedly passed through the minds of Cotton Carnival officials.

Although he was probably not the only one around town to pull the stunt, Percy Roberts was more apt to do it than anyone else. Occasionally, he would have a date with an out-of-town girl not that familiar with Memphis. Shortly after picking her up they would be riding along and Percy would suddenly exclaim, "Doggone it, I left my wallet at home," or he might say, "I don't particularly like this tie I've got on, if you don't mind I'm going to run by the house and change it."

The revelation always came when they were in the vicinity of Clarence Saunders' Pink Palace that had been turned into the Memphis Museum. Percy would wheel into the grounds of the estate and up the long driveway to park in the front near a corner of the mansion and would walk around to a side entrance, where a light was always left on. In a few minutes he would be back in the car with the flabbergasted girl and say, "Whew, I'm glad I thought of that."

In 1948 and 1949 Red Blaik guided the Army football team through two more successful seasons. Rowan and Steffy were seniors in the fall of 1948 but had used up their eligibility because of their playing one year at LSU and Tennessee, respectively, so they served as student assistant coaches. By the time of the last game against Navy in 1948, the Cadets had won eight games with no losses and no ties, including a 26 to 21 win over Illinois, a 49 to 7 rout of VPI and a 43 to 0 victory over Stanford. In one of the better games of their long series, the Middies tied the soldiers 21 to 21. In 1949 John Trent served as captain of Army's undefeated team that rolled through a nine-game schedule with victories over Penn State 42 to 7, Michigan 21 to 7 (national champions the year before) and Navy 38 to 0. The Cadets more than made up for Columbia's 1947 upset by pulverizing the Lions 63 to 6. Notre Dame, however, was voted as national champion. During Rowan and Trent's combined five-year tenure, 1945 through 1949, Army won 40 games, lost two and tied four.

Elwyn Phillips Rowan
West Point, Class of 1949
Lettered four years in football (All-American, 1947; coach, 1948). Lettered two years in track. "Rip is one of the best-liked men at the Academy. No one who comes in contact with him can resist his natural joviality and keen wit." (Courtesy of U.S. Military Academy)

Five-star General Henry H. "Hap" Arnold, who had commanded the U. S. Air Force throughout World War II, died January 15, 1950 and a huge military funeral was held in his honor in Washington, D.C. On a cold, gray day all military personnel in all service branches in the vicinity of Washington participated in a solemn funeral parade down Pennsylvania Avenue from the Capitol Building to Arlington National Cemetery. Also attending were the cadets and midshipmen from the service academies.

Billy Buckles was a second lieutenant assigned to the Air Force's Office of Special Investigations and was attending a nine-month school in Washington receiving the same type training as FBI agents. Buckles knew that John Trent would be in town and that the cadets would have come in on a train from West Point, so after the funeral he went to Union Station to look for him. When he arrived only a few cadets were milling around outside waiting for the buses that would bring the rest of the corps. Trent was on the first bus and they promptly got together.

Buckles was living in the Carroll Arms Hotel within walking distance of the station. It was still daylight and, as

Coach Earl "Red" Blaik and Captain
John Trent
(Courtesy of U.S. Military Academy)

the cadets had free time until early that evening, they walked to Buckles' hotel where they had a nice, long visit in the lounge. Trent told him that he had ordered a black Ford that he had always wanted and that Rowan, who would be preceding him to his post-graduation assignment at Fort Benning, Ga., would drive it down there from West Point for him. Accompanied by his roommate, who was a major, Buckles took Trent to the finest restaurant in Washington and spent about a third of his monthly salary as a lieutenant treating him to a steak dinner. As they got back to the hotel it was getting dark and a light snow began to fall, and Trent said he needed to get on back to the station. The major had imbied rather heavily during the afternoon and Buckles told John that as soon as he got the major back to their room and settled in he would walk on over to the station.

When Buckles entered Union Station's concourse the cadets were all in formation by companies ready to march to their respective cars on the special train. It was almost as if they were awaiting his arrival. He was immediately approached by a cadet officer and two enlisted men who asked if he would permit them to serve as his escort. That's when he realized that something was up. Trent, wearing his saber and standing at the back of the column with the regimental staff, had arranged for the entire Corps of Cadets to pass in review in honor of lowly 2ndLt William Buckles. This was a ceremony ordinarily reserved for high ranking officers and dignitaries.

After Billy's escort had led him to the entrance to the gangway leading to the train and had posted themselves on either side of him, the order to "pass in review" rang out and the Corps began its march. As the front of each unit came abreast of Buckles, the guidon bearer snapped the pennant to a horizontal position, the cadet officer popped a salute and those in the ranks did "eyes right," as did Trent (with a grin) and the staff when they passed by. After all the units had marched by the point of review, Buckles' escort requested permission to be relieved and they rejoined their comrades. The thrill of the experience, as well as the underlying amusement inherent in the situation, overcame any embarassment Billy might have felt and he thoroughly enjoyed the recognition as well as taking pride in his old team-mate's ingenuity and prestige in being able to pull it off.

At the train they laughed about it and then John pulled off his gray gloves and scarf and handed them to Buckles. "Here, keep these to remember the time the Cadet Corps passed for your review." Billy accepted them and still has them. It was the last time that he and Trent would see each other.

BOOK FIVE

Requiem for the Halcyon days

(Over the hills and far away)

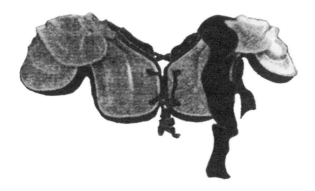

Every phrase and every sentence is an end and a beginning,
Every poem an epitaph. And any action
Is a step to the block, to the fire, down the sea's throat
Or to an illegible stone: and that is where we start.
We die with the dying:
See, they depart, and we go with them.
We are born with the dead:
See, they return, and bring us with them.

-Little Gidding
T.S. Elliot

It originally was intended that the story of the Blind Game be told in a magazine article. Early on, however, it was determined that a "before" was needed and an "after" would satisfy curiosity. The before part would provide the setting – the background necessary for the reader to appreciate the essence of the city and how it influenced the character of the young participants in the story; hence, the biographical sketches illuminating the nature of those who shaped the community. The after part would tell something about the lives of the football players subsequent to their high school years. It then was apparent that this enlarged story could only fit between the covers of a book; it was too lengthy to chop up and layer among advertisements in a magazine.

On April 8, 1950 Joe Steffy got married and John Trent served as his best man. Steffy and Rowan, of course, had graduated the year before and had stayed on as coaches at West Point. Now Trent received his diploma and commission and all three were assigned to Fort Benning. On June 25 the North Koreans invaded South Korea and a war was on that would last a little over three years and kill almost as many Americans as died in ten years in Vietnam. Although fifteen other member countries of the United Nations sent token forces to Korea, the Americans shouldered the brunt of the fighting.

The war did not go well in the early days. The soldiers of the Republic of Korea and their American support troops were overwhelmed and quickly driven back and Seoul, the capital city, was abandoned. U.S. Army troops were brought in from Japan, but they were poorly-trained occupation forces and had inadequate firepower. The North Koreans' big Russian tanks cut them to pieces and they were pushed into a small perimeter around the port of Pusan in the southeastern corner of the Korean Peninsula. The First Marine Provisional Brigade was rushed from Camp Pendleton, Cal. to avert a Korean Dunkirk.

In 1950 Tommy Mulroy and Phil Turner had each bought residential lots at Walnut Grove and Shady Grove Roads for $1,700. They had made down payments and were paying on them each month. When Tommy told Phil that the pay from his National Guard drills with the 196th Field Artillery was making the payments on his lot, Phil decided to also join the Guard. However, he was receiving disability pay due to his World War II wounds and, although Phil was not aware of it, this was not permitted under National Guard regulations. When this was discovered, someone was supposed to process his papers for discharge and he stopped attending the drills. Then the Korean War came along, "someone" had neglected to attend to his paper processing, and Phil was still on the rolls. One day in August the newspaper reported that the 196th had been ordered to active duty and that its members should report to the National Guard Armory on Central Avenue that morning, which was a Sunday. Presuming he no longer was a part of the unit, Phil decided that afternoon, because it was such a nice sunny day, that it was a good time for him to get the lawnmower out and cut the grass. He donned a pair of shorts and was about halfway through his chore when a jeep drove up in his driveway. It contained two dour military policemen wanting to know why he hadn't reported and that he had better come with them pronto. He changed clothes and they gave him a free ride to the armory.

Phil, Tommy Mulroy and Sandy Kincannon spent a week or so at the armory operating out of tents during the day and going home in the evening. Then they shipped out on Labor Day for Fort Carson, Colo. where they received additional training. The 196th left for Korea in January 1951, went into action in April and came back to the states the following December.

This type thing was happening all across the country. National Guard and organized reserve units, as well as inactive reservists, were promptly called to active duty to buttress the regular forces. Once again, less than nine years after Pearl Harbor, the U. S. found itself undermanned and ill-equipped to contend with what was deemed to be a military threat. As the scope of the debacle widened, President Truman's politically-appointed crony resigned as Secretary of Defense.

Down at Fort Benning Trent and Steffy were ordered to Korea. Rowan's wife, Pat, was expecting their first child and the Army had a rule prohibiting sending a man overseas whose wife was pregnant. John and Joe left on a train from Fort Benning on August 23 bound for the West Coast. (This was the same day the author's organized Marine Reserve unit left Houston's Southern Pacific station headed for Camp Pendleton, Cal.; 200 strong they marched down a ramp to a waiting train as a local Air Force base band played "The Marines' Hymn"). Arriving in Japan on a troopship, Trent and Steffy spent a couple of weeks there drawing cold-weather clothing and equipment and receiving additional troops to bring their units up to full strength.

He's a good guy.
(frequently overheard in high school)

He was really a nice person.
-Patsy (Mrs. Bill) Burke
1993

I guess of all the people who were a part of the Central High School athletic family, the one I remember most and the one who I admired most and the one who set the best example for his peers was John Trent. Even at that age, as I remember it, he had an unconscious mystique about him that made him a leader and an example for the rest of us. It certainly was nothing that he purposely did and I am not sure whether he ever realized the high esteem that everyone that was associated with him had for him.

-Jerry Hanover
Letter to author, 1993

We were living in Oklahoma City and had gone to Memphis on a visit and were riding around in this station wagon. We had just had our first child and the baby and I were sitting in the back. Everytime we stopped John Trent would jump out of the front seat and open the back door and help me and the baby out and be so solicitous. I fell in love with him right then.

-Mildred "Midge" (Mrs. Bill) Buckles
1993

John Charles Trent
West Point, Class of 1950

Lettered four years in football (captain 1949) two years in lacrosse and one in basketball.
(Courtesy of U.S. Military Academy)

On November 12, 1950 John Trent and Joe Steffy participated in an unopposed amphibious landing at Wonsan, on the east coast of North Korea; they moved out from there with the Army's 15th Infantry Regiment to a hill where a perimeter defense was set up. From this elevation they could see the city, five miles behind, and the harbor where a large hospital ship was berthed after 3,000 Russian-laid mines had been cleared out. To their front were barren, snow-covered hills – and uncertainty.

Approximately fifty miles to the northwest, the First Marine Division, representing the bulk of X Corps, and the Eighth Army were moving northward on crude, high-mountain roads in parallel lines on each side of the Chosin Reservoir toward Manchuria.

After the highly successful Marine amphibious landing at Inchon in mid-September had outflanked the North Korean Army and led to the recapture of the South Korean capital of Seoul, the combat effectiveness of the enemy had been greatly diminished. The Eighth Army broke out of the Pusan Perimeter and when the North Koreans realized their supply lines had been cut by the Marines they became demoralized and began a withdrawal on all fronts. Although Chinese Army units had forcefully attacked United Nations troops in North Korea on October 25, they had broken off contact and withdrawn to the north on November 6. Douglas MacArthur's headquarters in Tokyo and the Joint Chiefs of Staff in Washington didn't quite know what to make of the Chinese intervention and what their ultimate intent was; in any event, they miscalculated. Toward the end of the month upwards of 300,000 Chinese troops, essentially traveling at night, wearing white uniforms to blend with the snow, and carrying much of their gear on Manchurian ponies, slipped undetected across the Yalu River and attacked Marine and Army forces at multiple points on both sides of the Chosin Reservoir.

In the meantime, the fighting had a desultory nature. Roving bands of North Korean soldiers would ambush a train here or attack a position there, so the fluidity of the battlefront led to considerable speculation about the intent of the enemy.

Riding the knifing winds birthed in the tempestous arctic climate of Siberia and sweeping across the Manchurian plain, winter roared into North Korea turning it into a gigantic, perpetual icebox from which there was no escape or surcease. It flowed over the desolate mountains, filled the gorges with snow, glazed the rocks and froze the waters. After rising to possibly 10 or 20 degrees in the shortened daylight, at dark the temperature plunged rapidly to 20 to 30 degrees below zero before dawn.

Winter in North Korea is a wet and penetrating cold. It dominates and makes every human action subject to its whims. In his attempt to adjust, man is forced to rethink his normal ways of doing things. Flesh freezes, rations freeze, weapons freeze – the Carbine becomes a useless stick; if the M-1 is oiled it freezes, so graphite must be used instead; fired artillery pieces take half a minute easing back into position from the recoil; water-cooled machine guns must be filled with anti-freeze, or fired periodically. With the frost level at a depth of fourteen inches, brittle entrenching tools break on the iron-like ground. Blood oozing from wounds freezes before it clots, plasma is useless and doctors and corpsmen thaw syrettes of morphine in their mouths. LtCmdr Chester M. Lessenden, regimental surgeon of the Seventh Marines told Keyes Beech of the *Chicago Daily News*:

> *Everything was frozen. Plasma froze and the bottles broke. We couldn't use plasma because it wouldn't go into solution and the tubes would clog up with particles. We couldn't change dressings because we had to work with gloves on to keep our hands from freezing. We couldn't cut a man's clothes off to get to a wound because he would freeze to death.*

Men abate their thirst with snow after their canteens have frozen and burst. Snow is melted and boiled in pots on wood stoves and added to powdered coffee, but it must be drunk quickly before it freezes. "C" rations containing meat may be tossed into the pots to thaw, but only the outside becomes edible leaving a core of frozen food within. A famished man will impatiently devour it, frequently resulting in enteritis or diarrhea.

A friend of the author who went ashore at Inchon on September 21, six days after the original landing, standing 6'3" and weighing 200 pounds, was down to 155 pounds when he was evacuated for the second time, due to frostbitten feet, on November 25.

Clothes are worn in layers: heavy underwear, a sweater and trousers, a field jacket and, over all, a parka that makes it difficult to see side to side. Bulky mittens with inserts for trigger fingers and two or three pairs or socks encased in boots or rubberized shoe-pacs complete the ensemble – but it's never enough to make one comfortable. If a man sweats too much he will freeze to death in his own sweat, and particular care must be given to hands and feet to prevent frostbite that could result in the loss of fingers and toes. If a hand touches metal it can freeze to it; the only recourse being to jerk the hand away leaving skin behind and resulting in a bloody palm.

Such were the conditions encountered by Lieutenants John Trent and Joe Steffy when they set up their perimeter on the hill out from Wonsan. Below the hill in front of Trent's Third Platoon, Company E, passed an ordinary country road; Steffy's Second Platoon, Company E, was emplaced on the other side of the hill. They situated their men so as to establish proper fields of fire and to guard against infiltrators or flank attack. Regimental headquarters warned that enemy activity had been detected in the area and to be on the alert. Having never before been in a potential combat situation and only newly–arrived in this strange and hostile land, all were on edge.

Aware of the Asian propensity for night attack and exhibiting those qualities that had earned him the captaincy of the football team and made him so highly regarded by all who knew him, at one o'clock in the morning of the third day of their arrival, Trent told his platoon sergeant he was going out to check on his men located in their various positions around the perimeter. He wanted to ensure they were awake and alert, keeping sufficiently warm to avert frostbite, and adequately prepared for whatever they might encounter.

Thirty or so minutes later a group of old Korean men,

who had been visiting a bar in a nearby hamlet, came walking noisily down the road, jabbering and yelling. Unaware of their identity and thinking they were about to be attacked, some of the green troops opened fire. There then ensued a general firing all along the line that went on for some minutes. There was an indication that, in turn, incoming fire was received, but this was never proved nor disproved.

About three o'clock Lt. Steffy received a call on his radio from Trent's platoon sergeant. The cold affected the transmission adversely, but Steffy could make out that Trent had been gone for two hours and couldn't be located.

"Lt Steffy, this is Sergeant Walker."

"Roger, sergeant."

"Lt Trent went out two hours ago to check on the men, and he hasn't come back. I sent a runner out 20 minutes ago to look for him, but he couldn't find him. I'm worried that something might have happened to him – maybe during all that firing."

A wave of dread more icy than the Korean night swept over Steffy. "Did the runner check with the men in each position?"

"Yes sir."

"Unless you think it appropriate to continue the search, sit tight and I will be over there as soon as it gets light."

As the rays of dawn began creeping in from the Pacific to permit enough light to move about, Steffy went to company headquarters to report on the situation and to inform the CO that he was going to look for Trent. The battalion surgeon happened to be there and he accompanied Steffy as they trudged through the snow around the hill to Trent's platoon.

With the sergeant leading the way, they set out on their search. It didn't take long to find him. He lay prone at the bottom of a 20-foot bluff. Kneeling down, Steffy gently turned him over – and knew immediately. The surgeon examined him and determined that he had been shot once, precisely through the heart; death had been instantaneous.

The resultant investigation of the circumstances precipitating the firing and the origin of the fatal bullet was inconclusive. The image of his close friend on that clear, blustery, frigid morning in a faraway land remains indelibly imprinted in Joe Steffy's memory. Forty-five years later he says, "I've never gotten it out of my mind. I think about Korea and John Trent every day ... every day!"

Although the war was less than five months old and gathering momentum, 16 other Memphians had already been killed in Korea. Tom Lombardo, Army's 1944 football captain, had been killed in late September. Lombardo had been a member of the St. Louis Soldan High team that played Memphis Tech in 1940. It took almost ten days for word of Trent's death to filter back to Memphis and the rest of the country. Then, on its editorial page, *The Commercial Appeal* spoke of him thusly:

Lieut. John C. Trent

News that Second Lieut. JOHN C. TRENT had been killed in action in Korea was recieved with genuine regret in all America and wherever the flag of this Nation flies today. Everywhere people admire good sportsmanship coupled with unusual athletic ability JOHN TRENT'S name had become familiar because of his football prowess. As these same people learned more of him, they mingled respect and affection in equal parts with their admiration because of his other sterling qualities.

Here in Memphis, where JOHN TRENT was born and grew to young manhood, grief for his death is keenest. Memphians knew, even more than others, his modesty and fine character, the courage with which he met all his problems, and his refusal to take the easy way. He was respected here and an object of community pride that was never for one moment misplaced or betrayed. His death on the threshold of a career of bright promise has increased our understanding of the willingness of our boys and young men to risk and give their lives, as others from our community have done before him, so that decency, freedom, justice, and right shall prevail.

As previously noted, Jim Laney, who started at guard on Central High's 1943 team and was a co-captain of the 1944 team, had spent a year at Yale and then gone into the Army for two years with some of his service in Korea before the war. He returned to Yale for his degree in 1950, took a Bachelor of Divinity in 1954 and was ordained a Methodist minister. He earned a PhD in 1965. All three of his degrees at Yale were bestowed with honors. He was a member of Omicron Delta Kappa, national leadership fraternity, and Phi Beta Kappa.

Laney taught at Vanderbilt and Emory and served as president of the latter institution from 1977 to 1993. From 1959 to 1964 he taught at Yonsei University in Korea. He has been a director of the Coca-Cola Company and is a trustee emeritus of the Henry Luce Foundation. Laney has served on the Executive Committee of the Yale University Council and as chairman, Harvard Overseas Committee for the Divinity School. At the request of his many friends in the Republic of Korea, he was appointed U. S. Ambassador to that nation in 1993.

A former high school fraternity brother, he told the author in 1993 that the gymnasium at Eighth Army headquarters in Seoul was named in honor of John Trent. When he assumed his duties there he had pictures made of the gym and forwarded them for inclusion in this book.

Trent Gymnasium

*Eighth Army
Headquarters,
Seoul, Korea*

*(Courtesy of
Ambassador James
T. Laney)*

Another Memphian in Korea during the war was Maurice Keathley, Central tackle in 1943. Coming back to Memphis from Nuremberg after World War II, Maurice had remained in the Army Reserve and was called back to active duty shortly after the war started. While he was a lieutenant and executive officer of an infantry company in April 1951, he was placed in command of the company when it went into the line to relieve another one that had been attacked and overrun by the Chinese the night before. Preceded by an artillery barrage, the Chinese attacked Keathley's position in the middle of the night. The Americans had searchlights that they shone on low clouds that reflected the beams back to illuminate the area. During the attack Maurice was hit by shrapnel, but he directed his men in such manner that the attack was repelled with minimum American losses. He was awarded a Silver Star for his skill and fortitude under fire and a Purple Heart for his wound. Maurice retired from the Army Reserve in 1966 as a lieutenant colonel.

Former Central end Bill Roberds had graduated from the U. S. Merchant Marine Academy and later earned a degree in economics from Southwestern at Memphis. He, too, was called back in October 1950 for almost two years of active duty and served in Korea with the rank of ensign on an LST.

Other players and managers off the CBC and Central teams who served during the Korean War era were Don Crone, Charlie Reagin and Kenneth McCarver in the Air Force, Percy Roberts in the Marine Corps, and Tony Evangelisti, John Nash, Lou Sampson, Arvin James, Jimmy Foley, Bill Rainer, Bobby Ladd, Herbie Abraham and Ted Hay, all in the Army.

A month or so after his death in Korea, John Trent's body was shipped home to Memphis and he was buried in Forest Hill Cemetery. Serving as pallbearers were Rip Rowan, Slick Williams, Bill Buckles, Butch Daltroff, Leslie Morgan and Commodore Ferguson, who was married to Trent's sister.

I certainly want his
memory to last.
-Joe Steffy
1993

In 1952 Slick and Betty Williams' first child was born. He was named John Trent Williams.

Billy Bolton graduated from Mississippi State with a degree in agricultural economics. His career in agribusiness and commodity brokerage took him to over 40 countries, principally as an independent consultant for the World Bank and the U. S. State Department. When he and his wife Joyce, sister of Churchill Roberts, were raising their three children, they lived in seven different countries in Central and South America. While at a dinner theater with some other ladies in San Jose, Costa Rica in 1952, Joyce ran into former Central coach Cecil Glass. He was teaching Spanish at the Lincoln School for North Americans. It seems that Glass was attracted to towns with the name of Memphis. Years later he operated a motel in Memphis, Tex., a small town in the Panhandle, and died there.

Two of those most prominent in the promotion and playing of the Blind Game were touched by illness and death in the fall of 1954. While serving at Fort Benning after a two-year tour in Germany, Elwyn Rowan contracted a mild case of polio. It affected his right arm and left leg, leaving the latter a little thinner than the right one but not really impairing his mobility.

Around the same time, on Saturday, October 16, E. H. Crump died at age 80. Dictated by his work ethic and innate desire for order and efficiency in all things, the strenuous pace he had set for himself throughout his life and the burdens of responsibility for the cares of the rest of the world that he had willingly assumed, ultimately were too much for his heart to sustain.

In Sunday's edition of the *New York Times* an article tracing his career began at the bottom of page one and continued on an inside page for almost three columns. On Monday's editorial page, under the heading "He Liked To Run Things," were the following comments:

> In one sense Edward Hull Crump of Memphis, who died Saturday at the age of 80, was a typical old-fashioned political boss. He seemed to have Shelby County completely under his control, and when votes were needed, he could ordinarily deliver them in the desired spots and numbers. This was done by organizational methods that the layman finds it difficult to understand. Indeed, there is a science to it. It has its traditions and customs, just as do the legalized forms of political government. Mr. Crump did it well, though sometimes he miscalculated, as when he tangled with Estes Kehauver in 1948.
>
> But Mr. Crump was more than a typical boss. He was unique: a man with a sense of the dramatic, who wore his white hair long in his later years, dressed like a fashion plate and had, as his published photographs show an inmitable smile. The Crump smile, when applied to a person or a situation that Mr. Crump approved of was genial, self-satisfied and philosophical. He seemed to know all about the human race, to feel a little sorry for it and to be convinced that it needed a strong hand, such as his own. And he did like to run things his way.
>
> He gave Memphis what he and many others considered to be good government. Fire risks were reduced, the crime rate dropped, pains were taken to promote traffic safety and the city's administration was said to be efficient. Mr.

Crump was proud of all this. He wondered why some people objected to it. He did not suffer from a sense of guilt, for he was not charged with personal corruption. Some citizens of Memphis thought it a good idea to deal with Mr. Crump's insurance agency, but nobody said it was not an excellent agency.

So Mr. Crump passes. The political scenery becomes a little drabber. He will probably not be replaced. Bosses these days come in less colorful form.

The Commercial Appeal's political cartoonist Cal Alley's tribute to Mr. Crump.

Indeed, Crump was not replaced, and the local political scenery definitely became more drab and less colorful. The shadow of his influence affecting the way things had been done lingered awhile but, like all things, eventually paled. However, the legacy of the man endures in the sustaining public improvements and social programs that he was so instrumental in effecting and that changed the squalid, brawling city on the bluff into the Place of Good Abode. Many have wondered what might have been the outcome of some of the city's main crises that occurred after his death had he been there to provide his usual imaginative and forceful leadership.

Ralph Hatley had a successful tenure as head football coach at Memphis State through the 1957 season. He then turned that duty over to Billy "Spook" Murphy, who had been one of his assistants since first coming to the school. For the next 15 years Hatley served as chairman of the Department of Health and Physical Education at Memphis State and retired in 1977. In 1965 the Memphis Chapter of the National Football Foundation Hall of Fame gave him its Distinguished American Award. Hatley is a member of Christian Brothers High School Hall of Fame, Memphis State University Hall of Fame, Jackson and Madison County Sports Hall of Fame and the Tennessee Sports Hall of Fame.

After military service and college Judd Williford entered the insurance business. By 1960 he had become sufficiently successful to be named to that industry's "Million Dollar Roundtable," the designation of achievement that had been the brainchild of Lester Rosen at a meeting at Hotel Peabody back in the 1930s. That same year Judd attended a convention in Hawaii with others from around the country who also had earned membership in that group.

One of the functions was a cocktail party held late one afternoon on the verandah of the Hawaiian Village Hotel. A short distance from the verandah, on the emerald lawn facing Mamala Bay, was a flagpole topped with an American flag lazily fluttering in the soft breeze of the dying day. As the sun slowly disappeared into the western Pacific, two hotel employees began lowering the flag. Another employee, a Hawaiian girl off to the side, began singing "Taps" as the ensign was deliberately and respectfully retired for the day.

The party had peaked to a jocular crescendo, but as those on the verandah became aware of the simple ceremony on the lawn, laughter stopped, voices hushed in mid-sentence and all turned to face the colors. The effect of something that was an ordinary, daily rite had been magnified and elevated by the beauty of the setting in this tropical paradise from which so many, including Judd, had departed 15 to 20 years before to fight in defense of that flag on islands scattered across the serene and vast expanse of the ocean they were facing. As the singer's emotional, yet measured, voice caressed the words, each reveler stood erect with his own thoughts, some, undoubtedly, thinking of friends or relatives lost or one's own wounds suffered and endured on those far-away islands, once hellish and now peaceful.

The next day Judd attended a Memorial Day parade that wound through downtown Honolulu and he experienced a reinforcement of what the flag, and being a part of the United States for less than a year, meant to the people who resided in this new state. As the color guard came into view murmurings began in the crowd: "Here comes the flag." When the colors approached, all removed their hats and stood at attention until the flag had passed.

Judd was quite impressed by what he had observed in Hawaii on consecutive days and he doubted that the same depth of sincere devotion and respect for the "Red, White and Blue" would be evidenced under similar circumstances back home. An idea began to take shape in his mind. Williford was a member of the Phoenix Club, a Memphis organization of men under 35 years of age whose aim was to provide recreational opportunities and guidance for under-privileged boys. When he got back to Memphis he told the club he would like to present a program to the group. He recounted what he had experienced in Hawaii and challenged the membership to try to rekindle a patriotic fervor on the local scene and "put the flag back into the hands of Americans." He suggested that they could sell flags and use the profits to finance the establishment of boys' clubs throughout the city.

Judd made 16 speeches to various organizations and the Phoenix Club members started contacting businesses to encourage them to display the flag. It seemed that nobody had one, but there was a good response to the idea. Ultimately, businesses up and down Main Street and those situated along Union, Madison and Poplar avenues from Main all the way out to Parkway had them on display.

The club had portable, concrete receptacles made up in which to put the flagpoles, and at 2 a.m. on a Monday the club members started setting out the stands and flags at all the businesses that had been enlisted in the program. This was when the bulk of retail and business activity was still concentrated in the downtown area and as people drove in to work that morning and returned home that afternoon they passed a continuous, awesome display of uniform-sized flags waving in the breeze. The effect was so dramatic that some thought war had been declared. The program continued indefinitely for a long time, until businesses started moving out into other sections of the city.

The flag idea spread to other cities. When Judd told a group at a meeting in Chattanooga what had been accomplished in Memphis, he received an order for 100 flags. Orders came in from other locales and the Phoenix Club began its first club with 14 boys and a budget of $14,000 meeting in the basement of Calvary Episcopal Church. The program has grown to now include 3,500 boys with a budget of $1.5 million and clubs at five locations in the city.

After graduation from Southwestern, Vance Cartwright, the little Central boxer and scatback who refused to wear hip and thigh pads, went on to dental school. He later pursued graduate work in that field that qualified him to become an instructor in the University of Tennessee School of Dentistry at Memphis. When he was at Central High, it had been the practice to give footballs to individual senior players for games in which they had particularly distinguished themselves. Back in 1945 Vance had scored both touchdowns in a 14 to 0 win over Treadwell and he had really wanted a ball for that game; however, guard Herbie Abraham got it. Later in the season Vance received one for the Catholic High game, which Central won by a big score.

In the late 1970s Vance became ill with heart disease and a by-pass operation did not alleviate his condition sufficiently to forestall his death a year or so later. As Christmas neared in the year before Vance's death, Herbie got to thinking about their playing days together and how much Vance had wanted that Treadwell game ball. Herbie rummaged around his house and found the ball and sat down with it in a comfortable chair; he took a pen and retraced the faded, thirty-some-odd-years-old signatures of all the members of the 1945 team. When he was satisfied with the results, he gift-wrapped the ball and, one day when Vance was away from home, took it by the latter's house and left it with Vance's wife, who sneaked it under the tree on Christmas Eve.

After leaving the Army Rip Rowan became associated with the John F. Everett Co., a manufacturers' representative. He and his family lived in North Carolina for eight years but, ultimately, came back to Memphis and Rowan became president of the company. In the mid-1980s Rowan developed cancer. He underwent treatment and it was thought he was improving. In June 1985, accompanied by his wife Pat, he made a business trip to Orlando. While they were there Elwyn got sick again and they promptly flew back to Memphis. After going to his doctor and having tests run he was told the cancer had developed in his liver and he had only a couple of months to live. Because it would dull his faculties, Elwyn refused to take medication for his suffering. He died only eight days later.

CBC tailback George "Bubba" Whitehead was that rare type of person with a sunny disposition and accommodating nature who was liked by everyone. An example of his interest in people and willingness to help them was the time in the early 1980s when a neighbor decided to spend his vacation painting the exterior of his house. With no Tom Sawyer-like cajolery from the neighbor regarding the charms of painting, George simply walked down the street and started helping him with his chore. Whitehead was essentially retired, and when the neighbor's vacation time was up and he had to return to work, George continued the painting until it was complete.

George had owned a small grocery store on Burnham Street off North Watkins in Frayser. He had sold it to another party, but in August 1987 when the new owner became ill, George agreed to operate it for him until he was able to return to work. The store was in a quiet, isolated area between a service station and a city library. They were both closed late one night and George was in the store alone when an unknown party or parties came in and held him up and stole his car. Precisely what transpired is not known, but George was shot and killed and the perpetrator has never been apprehended.

Former CBC end Sam Angier heard about it the next day. Remembering George with respect and affection, Sam was anguished and distraught at the cruel manner in which George had lost his life and been wrenched from those who loved him. That night, Sam put the following words on paper:

An Elegy
To George Whitehead

The whistle's stilled the game is o'er
Now gone the cheering throng,
And he that ran now runs no more
Among the quick and strong.

Though he was felled by robber's blast
And pitched upon the floor,
He'll chide not chance for chance is passed
To others to deplore.

For ransom then was cruelly given
By the intruder at the door,
Whose bullet swift has sharply riven
The light that went before.

So raise once more the pennant high
And to God above implore,
He'll heed the keen of widow's cry
For him that fate foreswore.

Having always been interested in art, when Sandy Kincannon went to Korea with the 196th Field Artillery he carried an extra bag containing his art supplies. Whenever he had a lengthy respite out in the field, he would break out his materials and paint something that interested him. One day as he was looking in a mirror doing a self-portrait, a Midwestern farm boy in his unit aimlessly wandered up. "What are you doing?" he asked inanely. Sandy had difficulty abiding ignorance. "What does it look like?" he retorted. "Heck," said the boy, "I've got a cousin who can draw better'n that and he's never even had a lesson." Sandy was good-natured and usually had a quip for every occasion, but that comment so disgusted him that he abruptly packed up his materials for the day.

Sandy had an extensive record collection that was heavy on Benny Goodman. If he heard only two or three notes from any Goodman rendition, he probably could identify the song and where the notes fell within it. He earned a master's degree in fine arts from Iowa State and became director of the Memphis Academy of Art at Brooks Memorial Art Gallery in Overton Park. In front of the building one day in 1965 he was stricken with a fatal heart attack. Not long thereafter, Percy Roberts and some other friends of Sandy established a scholarship in his name at the Academy.

BOOK SIX

Keeping the Flame alive

Think where man's glory most begins and ends,
And say my glory was I had such friends.

> – The Municipal Gallery Revisited
> Wiliam Butler Yeats

Almost without exception, the boys on the CBC and Central football teams of 1943 developed into useful and productive citizens. Most fulfilled their military obligation to their country, advanced their education as appropriate to their calling, and made significant contributions to the businesses or professions they entered. Some raised quite large families and, in contrast to today's high divorce rate, a very high percentage are still married to the girl who originally captured their heart. One with four great-grandchildren says of his wife, "She is still making me happy..." They have a sailboat for Caribbean cruising. "We are taking off, just the two of us – no kids, no worries. We'll lie on several lonely beaches we have found and plan another 47 years together. Someday is here!"

The boys of '43 have confronted life's travails, to which most of us are subjected, and met them with the same grit and stoicism as when they endured two-a-day practices every August. They are such straight-arrow types as to be almost dull – there are no Richard Halliburtons or Machine Gun Kellys in the group – but they constitute the type of glue that helps hold civilization together.

Listed below, in alphabetical order, are the living members of the two squads showing their educational attainments, primary life occupation, and their current city of residence.

CBC

Sam Angier. End. BA, Vanderbilt. Active. Insurance agent. Memphis.

R. Gilbert Bratton. End. Attended CBC (college). Retired. Electrician. Memphis.

Bob Burke. Tackle. Retired. Owner of heavy equipment business. Pensacola Beach, Florida.

Harry Costello. Wingback. Active. Painting contractor. Memphis.

J. Basil Crone. End. Active. Electrical sales. Memphis.

Don Crone. Manager. CBC (college); Univ. of Tenn. Active. Children's dentist. Memphis.

Hall Crawford ('42 team). End. Memphis State. Semi-retired. Attorney. Memphis.

Bill Dulweber. Tackle. BS, Univ. of Tenn. Retired. Mechanical engineer. Longview, Texas.

Tony Evangelisti. Manager. Retired. Grocery merchant. Memphis.

Jim Foley. Blocking back. Retired. Cotton business. Memphis.

Mark Follis. Tackle. BS, Univ. of Illinois. Retired. Architect. Memphis.

John Fox. Tackle. Active. Owner of heavy equipment business. Memphis.

Jim "Red" Doyle. End. BS, Univ. of Sou. Calif. Active. Real estate development. Houston, Texas.

Joe Gold. Fullback. Attended Southwestern; Memphis State; Detroit Inst. of Tech. Retired. Industrial Engineer. South Gate, Michigan.

Arvin James. Tackle. BA, Vanderbilt. Retired. Radio broadcaster and writer. Bastrop, Louisiana.

Tom James. Guard. BA and JD, Vanderbilt. Active. Attorney. Memphis.

Charles "Billy" Leppert. Blocking back. Active. Sales of food and food service equipment. Memphis.

Kenneth McCarver. Halfback. Attended St. Ambrose College. Retired. Electrician. Memphis.

Tom Mulroy. Blocking back. Retired. Cotton, home building and investments. Memphis.

John Nash. Guard. MD, Univ. of Tenn. Active. Surgeon. Memphis.

Charles Reagin. Guard. BS, Memphis State. Retired. Accountant. Daphne, Alabama.

Percy Roberts. Guard. BS, Memphis State. Active. Shelby County Health Dept. Memphis.

John Ross. Tailback. BS, Arkansas A&M. Retired. Forester. Forrest City, Arkansas.

Jack Salmon ('42 team). Blocking back. BA, Notre Dame. Active. Manufacturers rep. Dallas, Texas.

Louis Sampson. Tackle. BS, Notre Dame. Retired. Stock broker. Memphis.

John Schaffler. End. Attended Vanderbilt; LLb, Memphis State. Active. Television advertising sales. Memphis.

Leon Shahun. End. BA, VMI. Retired. Memphis.

Julius Smith. Center. Attended Memphis State; LLb Southern Law Univ. Active. Real estate. Houston, Texas.

David Steffan. Fullback. Active. Owner of kitchen cabinet company. Houston, Texas.

Mike Tansey. Guard. Retired. Production director, American Snuff Co. Memphis.

John Walt. Center and blocking back. BS, Memphis State; JD, Vanderbilt. Retired. Attorney. Memphis.

Tom Welsh. Tackle. BA, Vanderbilt. Active. Wood products. Memphis.

CENTRAL

Herbert Abraham. Guard. BS, Tulane. Active. President of food manufacturing company. Memphis.

Ralph Baker. Guard. BS, Univ. of Tenn. Retired. Traffic manager. Shelby, Alabama.

Malcolm Baker. Tackle. BS, Univ. of Tenn. Retired. Industrial managment and director of corporate wage administration. Richmond, Virginia.

Bill Bolton. Fullback. BS, Miss. State. Retired. International agribusiness and brokerage. Memphis.

Ray Brown. End. BA, Univ. of Virginia. Active. President of mortgage insurance company. New Orleans.

Bill Buckles. Center. MBA, Louisiana State Univ. Retired. Marine surveyor and consultant. Mandeville, Louisiana.

Jack Callicott. Halfback. Attended Washington and Lee Univ. Retired. Television advertising sales. Memphis.

Guthrie Castle. Halfback. Attended Wheaton Coll. Retired. Furniture and upholstery business. Hardy, Arkansas.

Joe Crim. Center. Attended Wm. R. Moore School of Tech. Retired. Troubleshooter for General Motors. Jacksonville, Florida.

Gayden Drew ('42 team). End. Attended Southwestern. Retired. Owner of waste disposal company. Memphis.

Bill Durbin ('44 team). Quarterback. BA, Southwestern. Active. Computer consultant. Dallas, Texas.

Emmel Golden. Tackle. BS, Univ. of Tenn. Active. Cotton linter dealer. Memphis.

Jack Halford. End. Active. Dentist. Memphis.

Jack Hall ('42 team). Fullback. Attended Southwestern; PhD, Vanderbilt. Retired. Anthropologist. Miami, Florida.

Jerry Hanover. Manager. BS, Cornell. Active. Senior VP, Belz Enterprises. Memphis.

Louis Hansberger. Quarterback. BS, North Carolina State. Retired. Textile industry. Milledgeville, Georgia.

Ted Hay. Halfback. BS, Southwestern; MS, Austin Peay. Retired. Teacher. Clarksville, Tenn.

Joe Highfill. Guard/Tackle. BS, Oklahoma A&M. Retired. Agricultural lending. Decaturville, Tenn.

Don Hollowell. Guard. Attended Union (Tenn.), Memphis State and Univ. of Tenn. Active. Real estate. Covington, Louisiana.

Harley Jeffery. Tackle. BS, Purdue. Retired. Sales executive, paperboard packaging. Atlanta.

Robert Jeffrey. Center. BS, Miss. State. Retired. Advertising and sales director, produce marketing. Memphis.

Maurice Keathley. Tackle. Retired. Owner of wholesale baked goods company. Hot Springs, Arkansas.

Bob Ladd. Halfback. Attended Union (Tenn.) and Memphis State. Retired. Owner of golf course equipment company. Memphis.

Jim Laney. Guard. PhD, Yale. Active. Former university president; U. S. Ambassador to South Korea. Seoul, Korea.

Don Malmo. Halfback. BS, Washington and Lee; LLb, Vanderbilt. Active. Attorney and investment banker. Memphis.

Leslie Morgan. ('42 team). End. Attended Louisiana State and Davidson. Semi-retired. Owner of auto parts store. Memphis.

Joe Powell. Guard. Little Rock, Arkansas.

Bill Rainer. Tackle. Attended Memphis College of Art. Retired. Illustrator for Dept. of the Navy. Memphis.

Jack Nieman. Halfback. Attended Univ. of Tenn. and Memphis State. Retired. Memphis.

Bill Roberds. End. BA, Southwestern. Retired. Stock broker. Memphis.

George Sneed. Fullback. Attended Vanderbilt; BS, Memphis State. Active. Insurance and real estate. Memphis.

Addison Soltau. End. BS, Wheaton College; MS, Calvin Theological Seminary; PhD, Concordia Seminary. Active. Minister. Pompano Beach, Florida.

Russell Swink ('42 team). Guard. Attended Univ. of Tenn. Retired. Cotton business and U. S. Postal Service. Memphis.

Minor Tait. Tackle. BS, Memphis State; LLb, Southern Law Univ. Active. Attorney. Memphis.

Bill Trickett. Quarterback. BS, Univ. of Tenn. Active. Owner of auto dealership. Nashville.

John "Babe" Welsh. Halfback. Retired. Memphis.

Ira Whitley. Manager. Attended Memphis State and Southern Law Univ. Retired. Auto parts sales. Millington,Tenn.

William "Slick" Williams. Halfback. Attended Louisiana State Univ., North Carolina State; BS, Memphis State; LLb, Southern Law Univ. Semi-retired. Senior criminal court judge, State of Tenn. Memphis.

Judd Williford. Halfback. BA, Southwestern. Active. Owner of insurance agency. Memphis.

Bill Wright. Halfback. Attended Copiah-Lincoln Jr. Coll. Retired. Boat business. Memphis.

The foregoing academic accomplishments should dispel the time-worn cliche – surely now badly out-of- date – of the "dumb jock," and, beyond this, it is appropriate also to present a representative sampling of the achievements of a few of the group to better illustrate what they have done with their lives.

Percy Roberts has been honored by and held leadership positions in a number of organizations; just a few of these are CBC Hall of Fame, Memphis State Athletic Hall of Fame, President of United Service Organizations (USO), President of Highland Hundred (Memphis State booster club), President of Memphis chapter, National Football Foundation and Hall of Fame and board member of the Liberty Bowl.

Harley Jeffery conceived and developed a new paperboard packaging material while serving as vice-president and general sales manager of a national company in this field. Bill Trickett has served as president of his local chamber of commerce. David Steffan provided the kitchen cabinets and counter tops for former President George Bush's new home in Houston.

Since retiring as an attorney, John Walt has made trips to China as a missionary. After earning his PhD in English from Vanderbilt, Jack Hall went to Greece on a Fulbright fellowship. He spent ten years there and became involved in archeology, which evolved into anthropology. He is now retired as former chairman, Department of Anthropology, University of Miami.

In his 40-year career with the wholesale grocery company Malone and Hyde, Robert Jeffrey was advertising director for 10 divisions and sales manager of the Memphis division; in 1968 he was named National Merchandiser of the Year. In 1965 Arvin James was selected by the Mississippi Wildlife Federation as the broadcaster and/or columnist of the year.

Before his retirement Maurice Keathley was president of the Tennessee Bakers Association and a vice-president of Optimist International. Tom Welsh has served as president of the International Hardwood Products Association and the Forest Products Traffic Association; in conjunction with his business, he has made approximately 50 trips to the Orient. As a minister, Addison Soltau spent 17 years in Japan as a missionary; he currently is Minister of Missions for "Evangelism Explosion."

William "Slick" Williams has served as assistant attorney general for Shelby County and, also, as Shelby County Attorney; he has been president of the Tennessee Judicial Conference and in 1969 became a state Criminal Court judge. Over the years he has served his profession in a number of capacities as chairman of various committees working to improve the judicial system. He retired in 1990, but in 1991 was designated and commissioned as Senior Judge by the Tennessee Supreme Court, being assigned to preside over the Shelby County Drug Court, created to dispose of the large backlog of pending drug cases in Shelby County. In 1951, his first full year in the real estate business, Julius Smith was named "Salesman of the Year" by the Real Estate Board of Memphis. Since moving to Houston in 1963, he has served several terms as a director of the Real Estate Board of Texas.

Don Malmo is a senior partner in the largest law firm in Tennessee and also heads up an investment banking house with 75 employees.

As research began for this book in the summer of 1993, the idea of a reunion of the two teams began to form in the author's mind. Coincidentally, it was about this time that Criminal Court Judge Bernie Weinman, a colleague of Slick Williams, happened to attend an estate sale at 2044 Walker

Avenue, John Trent's former home. It is not known who was conducting the sale, but among the conglomerate impedimenta customarily found at such events, Weinman happened across various athletic letters that had been awarded to Trent in junior high, high school and college. Knowing of Slick's close friendship with John, Weinman bought the letters and delivered them to Slick, who gave some of them to his son, John Trent's namesake. When he had finished his playing days at Central, Trent, for a token payment, passed his green and gold reversable letter jacket – wool on one side and satin on the other – with his name sewn into it, on to Harley Jeffrey, who was just coming out of the tenth grade. After his senior season Harley, in turn, sold it to Bob Beard, likewise in the tenth grade at that time.

The author felt that a reunion of the two opposing teams, who had butted heads in a significant sports event, was appropriate. There had never been any serious animosity between the two schools and, as previously noted, opposing players later went into combat with each other and participated in each others' weddings. With the 50th anniversary of the Blind Game coming up in a few months, it was then or never. True, some of the major participants in the game such as Al Huebner, Bill Burke, Joe Smith, George Whitehead and Dippy Coles for CBC and Rip Rowan, John Trent and Butch Daltroff for Central, had passed on, but enough major players were available to justify proceeding with the idea. After initially contacting Tommy Mulroy of CBC and Slick Williams of Central, co-captains in 1943, and laboriously acquiring names and addresses, the author sent letters to those who could be located at that time. The response was generally positive and provided the incentive to continue with the project. Others were located and the list of those indicating their intent to attend grew. As plans solidified, three more mailings were sent out.

On December 3, 1993 44 former players, evenly divided between the two teams, assembled at Memphis' University Club to partake of a delicious spread and enjoy three hours of camaraderie, a remembrance of things past and, in some cases, being brought up to date on events of the previous half century. It had been exactly 50 years since the two teams had played the inaugral Blind Game only a few blocks away at

Crump Stadium and, again, it was on a Friday night.

Considering the mobility of contemporary life, a surprising number of the players still reside in Memphis. Julius Smith and David Steffan were in from Houston, Bill Buckles and Ray Brown from New Orleans, Harley Jeffery from Atlanta, Bill Trickett from Nashville, Bill Dulweber from Longview, Tex. and Joe Highfill from Decaturville, Tenn. Twenty-three players and three coaches were deceased and 11 players could not be located. Also in attendance were CBC's Coach Ralph Hatley and Brother John Michael from Chicago, who had been assistant athletic coordinator at CBC in 1943. Special guests were Henry Reynolds, sportswriter who had covered the Prep League for *The Commercial Appeal* in 1943, in from Heber Springs, Ark. and Frank White, who had been the primary force behind the Lions Clubs' reinstitution of the Blind Game in 1991 after a 21 year hiatus. When it was learned that it was Bill Wright's birthday, he was presented a small cake and roundly serenaded by all. Richard Langford, CBC '46, videotaped the festivities and Tom Gilbert, Central '44, who had helped with publicity, were also present.

Plans had been made to assemble the squads the next morning for a picture session at Crump Stadium, but several days of rain rendered this impractical and the idea was dropped. In the chilly, misty rain on Saturday morning Bill Buckles and Slick Williams drove out to Memorial Park Cemetery on Poplar. They located the graves of Elwyn "Rip" Rowan and Louis "Butch" Daltroff, placed a flower on each, and stood for a moment in mute solemnity with their own prayers and thoughts of their friends and memories of those days of their youth, which seemed really not all that long ago.

That evening the group assembled with their wives and dates at Heffernan Hall, on the Christian Brothers High School campus on Walnut Grove Road. An excellent dinner was catered by Mike Garibaldi and songs popular during the 1940s were played by the Memphis Doctors Band, led by plastic surgeon Dr. Charles White. Bill Wright again demonstrated why he was considered Central's best dancer in 1943.

Sunday morning was a time to remember and honor those coaches and teammates who had passed away. The memorial service was conducted by Monsignor Paul W. Clunan who, as a newly-ordained priest, had attended the

Blind Game, and his long-time friend, Reverend George Comes, a retired Methodist minister who was a Central High senior in the fall of 1943. The hymns, sung by all, were selected and led by Maurice Keathley, who played tackle on Central's team and had been a part-time minister of music for Baptist churches for 30 years. Barbara Walker Hummel, Miss America of 1947 and another '44 Central grad, sang and was accompanied on the piano by Joan Gilbert, a cousin of Tom Gilbert. In appreciation for having put the reunion together, the author was presented a beautiful plaque.

On the basis of many comments, it seemed apparent that everyone enjoyed the reunion and appreciated the opportunity to get together and socialize with teammates and gridiron foes whom, in some instances, they had not seen since high school. The degree of good feeling that pervaded could be sensed as well as observed. Widows of several of the players, such as Pat Campbell Rowan, Patsy Hart Burke and Louise Wright Cotter, attended with former teammates of their deceased husbands.

As president of the Downtown Lions Club, attorney and former state senator Frank White began in 1991 to consider how to unite the 17 local clubs to become more effective in raising money for their programs funding eye glasses, leader dogs and other operations for the sight- and hearing-impaired. He thought back to his youth when he had attended some of the early blind games in the 1940s and how much he had enjoyed them and their attendant hoopla. The various Lions clubs operate pretty much independently, and White thought they ought to get together to renew the game that had been discontinued after the last one in 1970.

However, things had changed over the years. A bowl game, per se, was no longer practical because a playoff system had been instituted leading to state champions in different divisions, based on sizes of the schools, that required leading teams to play on into December, so the only practical approach was to sponsor a couple of playoff games. Through White's energetic efforts the first sponsorship in 1991 raised over $25,000. It was far short of the Lions' goal, but sufficient to encourage them to continue with the idea. After a couple of more years of sponsorship, however, it became apparent people's sporting tastes had changed. High school football no longer captured the interest of the fan as it had years before. With the television networks saturated with all manner of sporting events, the rise of Memphis State into a higher lever of competition and the local introduction of professional teams in several sports, fan allegiance became too splintered to continue support of high school football. Attendance at games these days is comprised largely of family members and friends of the players.

After three years of disappointing financial results, the Lions stopped sponsoring the playoff games. So, the resurrection of the Blind Game died aborning. With simply playoff teams participating, rather than two teams vying for "king of the mountain" like CBC and Central featuring such players as Huebner and Burke and Rowan and Buckles, the interest just wasn't there. More to the point, Mr. Crump wasn't around to insure that the stadium was full. In 1994, at the request of Memphis State, the Lions sponsored a football game pitting Tennessee and Kentucky high school all-stars. In 1995 the Lions got behind a celebrity golf tournament co-sponsored by Sam's Town casino and hotel in North Mississippi that fared much better financially than had the football games.

Because of the spying incident, the original Blind Game was probably the most unusual event in Memphis' sports history. As previously noted, it occurred during an era which constituted a watershed in the economic, political and social development of Memphis and, being a product of its time, can never be replicated. To some who played and today survive, it was just another ball game. Most, however, without any particular attempt at analyzation, sense it was more than that. To them it was an event that spotlighted interesting personalities and focused on the interaction between the students of two different schools while occurring at a time of wartime stress and when Memphis was yet of a size and stage of its development to physically, architecturally, economically and socially embody remnants of its early character and be a special place in which to grow up.

Slick and Betty Williams and Ray Brown

Maurice Keathley and Louise and Carmen Keathley

Judd Williford and Bill Trickett

Basil and Beverly Crone; Mike and Charlotte Tansey

Tommy Mulory, John Fox, and John "Sleepy" Ross

Ralph and Virginia Hatley

Jack Callicott, Hall Crawford, and Mike and Charlotte Tansey

Joe Highfill and Midge and Bill Buckles

Bobby Jeffrey, Violet Whitehead, and Harley Jeffery

Bill Bolton and Jack Nieman

Photgraphs Courtesy of Bob Ladd

In Memoriam

CBC	Central
Gene Berretta	Paul Barton
George Bland	Henry Bateman
Bill Burke	Vance Cartwright
Ed Clasgens	Louis "Butch" Daltroff
Merrick "Dippy" Coles	Cecil Glass (coach)
Barney Costello*	David "Buddy" Halle
Tommy Cotter	Louis Jones
Leo Davis (coach)	Ed Larkin (manager)
Jimmy Foley*	Buddy Malmo
Jack "Hoot" Gibson	Charles Bobo Meriweather
Ralph Giles*	Churchill Roberts (coach)
Albert Heubner	Elwyn "Rip" Rowan
Herbert "Bertie" Huebner	Vince Skillman
John "Sleepy" Ross*	John Trent
Joe Smith	
Phil Turner*	
George "Bubba" Whitehead	

*Deceased since the 1993 reunion

AFTERWORD

CBC Fight Song
(to tune of Texas A&M "Aggie War Hymn")

Hulla Ballu, Kaneck Kaneck
Hulla Ballu, Kaneck Kaneck

All Hail to dear Old Memphis CBC
Rally around with all your might, Rah, Rah, Rah
Drive on old Purple 'n Gold to Victory
You are the boys who show the fight, fight, fight, fight

That loyal Brothers' spirit thrills us all
And makes us yell and yell and yell
So, let's fight for the Purple Wave of CBC
We're gonna beat you all to
Chicka-bo-rick, Chicka-bo-rick
Smash 'em, crash 'em, CBC

Central Fight Song

Come on you Warriors; up on your toes
Give your best to Old Central

Break down all barriers; up at your foes
We are with you in glory or defeat

So let us fight to keep our banners high
Carry onward to Victory

Rah for the Green
Rah for the Gold
Central High School

Ralph Hatley's First Assistant

As previously mentioned, Ralph Hutley's first assistant at CBC was Andrew "Pop" Calhoun, who had been a star football player at Memphis State College. He joined the Army Air Corps early in the war and was trained to fly the P47 Thunderbolt fighter plane. He was killed while flying a mission in continuing support of the Normandy invasion, just a few weeks after that momentous event.

Not long before he was killed, Calhoun's wife, Theresa, had given birth to Andrew, Jr. and her husband received pictures of his son prior to his fatal flight. On June 21, 1944 Pop wrote Theresa that he had flown 160 combat hours in 50 missions, plus 106 sorties over enemy lines, and had been awarded the Air Medal with 10 Oak Leaf Clusters. He was killed the next day.

Five years later Theresa Calhoun met and married another airman, who had been a bombardier on B24s. In addition to Andy, Jr., they raised three children of their own. Over the years she never learned the circumstances of Pop Calhoun's death – until 1996. She received a telephone call from Quentin Aanenson, who had flown with Pop and had produced a film history of their unit; he told her to expect a letter from a Frenchman who would provide details of that last flight.

The letter from Remy Chuinard said he had found the crash site near the village of La Roserie and obtained details from eyewitnesses. Calhoun was flying in the third position in a flight of 12 Thunderbolts on a low-level bombing mission when they were attacked from above by German fighters. "Calhoun cannot escape or regain altitude. Hit, he will attempt to jump just as his plane crashes on the bank of a cowpath next to [the village of] La Roserie."

Chuinard's proposal to put up a plaque honoring Pop Calhoun was approved by the village council and, during appropriate ceremonies on the 1996 anniversary of V-E Day, the plaque was attached to La Roserie's World War I monument and Chuinard made a speech: "...He had died, simply for the freedom of a country that wasn't his."

After receiving Remy Chuinard't letter, Theresa and Andy, Jr. immediately made plans to visit the little French town that had clarified the circumstances of her first husband's death and recognized the sacrifices made in its behalf by the Calhoun family 52 years before.

Wherefore Art Thou Pig 'n Whistle?

In November 1944 the Pig 'n Whistle had its own reunion. Of course, the original Pig had ceased to function as a restaurant in 1966 and the building was torn down in February 1994, but the name is carried on at restaurants on Winchester Road and on Bartlett Road. The hold that the old Pig 'n Whistle had on people is illustrated by a story related to the author by the manager of the Bartlett location.

A lady came into the restaurant with some friends and, while they were standing in the reception area waiting to be seated, she noticed a picture of the original Pig on the wall. As she gazed up at it, she surrendered unashamedly to her emotions and tears began trickling down her cheeks. She told Phil, the manager, that she had met her deceased husband there, they had their first date there, he proposed there and they went there frequently after they were married. She really missed the homey old place with its lovable employees and all the sweet memories it evoked.

Mike Mosteller, one of the new owners, issued a public call for all Mid-Southerners to "Come Home to the Pig" on Sunday, November 20 at the restaurant on Winchester. About 20 former employees were tracked down and most showed up, along with some of their relatives. Altogether, 200 or more people arrived to look at a collection of old photographs, menus from the World War II era, original drinking glasses and old matchbooks. Representatives of local government spoke and November 20 was proclaimed "Pig 'n Whistle Day." A plaque was presented to Estelle Hood Hornsby, honoring her father Herbert Hood, Jr., the original owner, and a scholarship in the culinary arts was established in his name at the local State Technical Institute.

Old-time employees were inducted into a "Pig 'n Whistle Hall of Fame" and their names were inscribed, and old pictures were hung, on a wall built to preserve the Pig's history. Barbecue sandwiches, at the old price of 40 cents, were to be served from 5 to 6 p.m., but the time was extended to about four hours and more than 700 were sold at that price at each of the two locations.

Tarawa Revisited

It's quite obvious to the reader that the Battle of Tarawa had nothing to do with a *Showdown in Memphis*. However, this book is primarily a slice of life of the early 1940s and, to more fully portray the era, the author felt it was incumbent to describe one World War II battle in some detail. Because of its relative simplicity vis-à-vis tactics, its limited geographic scope, its short duration and its ferocity, Tarawa was chosen – it had the elements that made it ideal for ease of description by the writer and comprehension by the reader. For those who read this book and were living during the war, but are not really aware of its down-and-dirty aspects, and for those who were then not yet born and have little knowledge of its ramifications, the author wanted to broaden their perspective, albeit to a limited extent, of the background and character of the people who fought it, the depth of sacrifice necessary to win it and the bestial nature of those who started it and with whom we had to contend.

During the approximate eight months that the Second Marine Division spent in New Zealand recovering from wounds and tropical fevers incurred on Guadalcanal and training for Tarawa, a strong and lasting bond developed with the people of this island country. Even today, individually and in small groups, Second Division veterans return to "Kiwiland" to visit with old friends. The New Zealanders' initial favorable response to the Marines sprang from their gratitude for having been saved from the Japanese juggernaut that had swept through southeast Asia. If the Japanese had not been dislodged from Guadalcanal and the Solomon Islands by the First Marine Division and elements of the Second and, later, Army troops and the Third Marine Division, their next move would probably have been an invasion of New Zealand.

At regular social events held at recreational clubs, the Marines learned to drink warm beer, eat fish and chips and crumpets, and balance a tea cup on one knee; they also taught the girls how to jitterbug. The local boys and men of military age were away from home on other warfronts and, in the natural course of events, romances, many leading to marriage, developed between the Marines and New Zealand girls.

Almost 600 marriages resulted and many of these young women were widowed by Tarawa; some children, born afterward of course, never knew their fathers. Just like they were their own, for weeks after the battle New Zealand newspapers listed the names of Marine casualties as they became available, the name of a Wellington street was changed to commemorate those who had fought at Tarawa, and the division's colors have hung in St. Paul's Cathedral for fifty years.

Many families, in some cases with their own sons away at war, welcomed the Americans into their homes and "adopted" them for the length of their stay in that beautiful country. Bill Bordelon, who would be killed the first day on Betio and be awarded the Medal of Honor posthumously, was one who, with several of his buddies, regularly spent weekends with a local family. The couple was almost his parents' ages and they had two school-age daughters. They all became very close and shortly before the Division shipped out to Tarawa Bordelon confided in the mother. He wasn't aware of the cause, but he told her that he had recently been experiencing dizzy spells; he hadn't turned in to sick bay because he was afraid the doctors would find something wrong with him and he would let his buddies down by not being able to participate in the upcoming operation. Although at that time none of the troops knew where the next battle would be, he also told her, reluctantly but straightforwardly, that he felt strongly that he would not survive it. All of this was revealed in letters written by the woman to Bordelon's mother after his death.

What inspired Bordelon's premonition? Do all those going into combat sense it, but not verbalize it, or does the Grim Reaper convey an extra-sensory message to those on his list? William Deane Hawkins probably knew it. He said "I hate war," but he enlisted when duty called. When he shipped out overseas he told a friend "I'll see you someday, but not in this lifetime," and when wounded on Betio he said "I didn't come here to be evacuated." Bill Culp knew it when he confessed his feelings to Chaplain Willard on the Wellington docks. And Eddie Moore's best friend Claire Goldtrap knew it.

We had just made our second practice landing on Efete in the New Hebrides Islands on 9 November 1943 and had a couple of hours to kill before loading our LVTs (Alligators) on our respective ships, Goldy's on the USS Thuran and mine the USS LaSalle.

I ran across Goldy sitting under a coconut tree reading a comic book (we called them "funny books" in those days), his favorite pastime. We made a couple of minutes of small talk when suddenly Goldy looked directly into my eyes and very firmly and convincingly told me he wasn't going to make it through the upcoming operation – the battle for Tarawa.

I couldn't believe what I was hearing and told him to knock it off! – everything was going to be all right; I just couldn't seem to convince him otherwise.

Cpl Goldtrap was, of course, killed just after driving his tractor onto Betio, not far down the beach from where Eddie landed his. One wonders what goes through the minds of those entering a battle certain of impending death – when will it come, today? tomorrow?; what will be the cause, an artillery shell? machine gun bullets?; what will it be like, sudden and quick? will I suffer much?; will there be enough of me left to ship home? will I be buried at sea? – and what gives those people the strength and motivation to continue carrying out their routine duties with stoicism and not shirk in the clamor of battle?

After spending some time in a naval hospital on the West Coast, Eddie Moore got convalescent leave and entrained home to Dallas; he could stay as long as it took for his wounds to heal, as determined by the Navy doctor at the local recruiting station. On January 10, two days after arriving home and seven weeks after Tarawa, he answered the doorbell at his parents' home and was handed a Western Union telegram. Addressed to his mother from the Commandant of the Marine Corps, it read:

Deeply regret to inform you that your son Private First Class Edward J. Moore USMCR has been wounded in action in the performance of his duty and service of his country. I realize your great anxiety but nature of wounds not reported and delay in receipt of details must be expected. You will be promptly furnished any additional information received. To prevent possible aid to our enemies do not divulge the name of his ship or station.

Eddie spent about three weeks at home. He could have stayed longer, but after where he had been and what he had

Eddie Moore at 17; shortly after boot camp in 1941. The medal on the left is for qualifying as a sharpshooter with a Springfield .03 rifle. On the right, each bar represents simple qualification with a particular ancillary weapon, e.g. bayonet.

seen Dallas was boring and he wanted to get back to Marine Corps life; he requested a return to active duty. While in Dallas, though, he was assigned to duties in connection with the war's Fourth War Bond Drive. At the nearby Lockheed aircraft plant he appeared with comedian Red Skelton and Capt Lowell May on a small stage in a big hanger before 2,000 war workers. May was an Army Air Corps bomber pilot whose radio response to an inquiry from his base in Italy about the condition of his damaged plane, "Earthquake McGoon," as he returned from a raid, inspired the popular song "Coming in on a Wing and a Prayer."

Later, in conjunction with the war bond drive, Moore and May appeared on a national radio hookup from Dallas station KRLD. Among others appearing with them, were Mrs. Mark Clark, wife of the general commanding American forces in Italy, Mrs. Richard Bong, wife of the Air Corps fighter ace who had shot down 40 Japanese aircraft and the actor Victor Mature, who introduced Eddie and interviewed him about his experiences at Tarawa. The broadcast was scheduled for 8 p.m. and that afternoon everyone assembled to rehearse their parts; Eddie describes what transpired:

> *Victor Mature was one of those Hollywood celebs who always seemed to receive accelerated promotions and was a slick-sleeved U. S. Coast Guard chief petty officer. We had gone through the script three or four times working out the kinks and checking the time element when all of a sudden Mature threw his three-page, cardboard-backed script into the air and loudly exclaimed "I can't say this" (introduction of me). "Can't say what, Mr. Mature?" the producer asked, stunned.*

> *Mature:*   *I can't say Private (me a PFC) Moore is from the 'fightingest force in the world,' the United States Marine Corps.*

> *Producer:*   *Why not Mr. Mature?*

> *Mature:*   *Because the Coast Guard ship I'm assigned to is the 'fightingest force in the world.'*

> *At this point the producer and script writers asked me if it would be all right to modify the original wording and just introduce me as being from the 'fighting U. S. Marines.' Of course, I consented.*

We started rehearsal again and had gone through the new script a couple of more times and everyone was real pleased, thinking everything was going smoothly, when all of a sudden and out of a clear blue sky I threw my three-page script all the way to the high-ceilinged overhead and shouted "I can't say this!!"
The producer, with jaw sagging in disbelief, said "Gee, Eddie, what's wrong?"

Moore: *Well, look, Mr. Producer (not knowing his name and caring less) on three or four occasions you have me saying 'yes, sir' to Mature (I spoke his name with derision).*

Producer: *What's wrong with that Eddie?*

Moore: *I don't have to say 'sir' to Mature because he's just another enlisted man like I am. In the Marine Corps, 'the fightingest force in the world,' enlisted men don't call each other sir.*

Eddie Moore would later leave the West Coast in the same overseas draft that took Red Doyle and Gayden Drew to Okinawa. Staying in the Corps, he participated in the Korean War and retired as a master sergeant and, along the way, wrote and published a book of poetry entitled *Spirit of America*. After over seven years in the reserve, his request for return to active duty was approved and, at age 44 and the father of six children, Eddie went to Vietnam as a combat correspondent "to show the young dissenting factor in America that to serve one's country in a time of need is not as difficult to do as certain elements may lead them to believe."

Eddie named the first of his four daughters after the nun whose picture he carried throughout the war. And, although he has lived in San Diego since his retirement and she is retired – but still spry and active – in Dallas, he keeps in touch with Sister Teresa on a regular basis.

The Navy named a destroyer after Bill Bordelon and on April 9, 1994 the new Navy-Marine Reserve Training Center in San Antonio was dedicated and named in his honor. For more than 50 years his body had lain in a grave in a military cemetery at Honolulu known as "The Punchbowl," where many dead from World War II Pacific battles are buried. In 1995, through efforts initiated by a San Antonio newspaper reporter and the Bordelon family, his remains were exhumed and returned home. For the first time in 50 years and for only the fifth time in history such an event had occurred, on November 19, 1995 his casket lay in state in the chapel of the Alamo, Texas' historic shrine. The public was invited to pay its respects and, between 6 and 10 p.m., 2,600 people filed through the chapel to view his flag-draped casket – flanked by two Marine honor guards – his Medal of Honor, and pictures of Bordelon and the destroyer named for him.

The next morning, the fifty-second anniversary of his death, a memorial mass was said at the historic Mission San Jose, where he had served as an altar boy. Assisted by nine other priests, Rev George Montague conducted the mass. He was the younger brother of Charles Montague, Bordelon's classmate who also died that first day at Tarawa. The funeral procession traveled to Veterans Memorial Plaza where a short ceremony was held to re-name a street in his honor and to announce plans to erect a monument to all those from San Antonio who had been awarded the Medal of Honor; it featured local dignitaries and a U. S. Senator and was attended by a group of Bordelon's old shipmates from the Second Marine Division. Re-interment was in the Fort Sam Houston National Cemetery.

A group of Tarawa veterans returned to the atoll in 1983 to observe the 40th anniversary of the battle. No longer a British protectorate, Betio is part of the independent island nation of Kiribati. The long pier was gone, but the bombproof bunker, pockmarked with indentations from naval shells, was still intact, along with some of the Japanese coastal defense guns, and the wreckage of amphtracks and Sherman tanks still dotted the reef. Accompanied by a Marine band from

Hawaii, they came back in 1988 to dedicate the new monument to those who perished there. They went again, probably for the last time, in 1993 to recognize the battle's 50th anniversary.

On these return visits the former Marines have been welcomed warmly by the natives, who view them as their friends and liberators. Some still remember the inhumane treatment they received during the two years of Japanese occupation; during that time the natives fled to other islets of the atoll or neighboring islands in the Gilberts. The Marines met one of a group of nuns who just escaped beheading by traveling down to the end of the atoll on the eve of the battle. The old veterans were invited into a large hut where they were treated to a feast and entertained by native children singing and performing their indigenous dances.

Tarawa is little changed from the World War II era and living conditions are still quite primitive. On their visit in 1988 some of the Marines learned that a Catholic mission school was in need of a generator. Eddie Owen of Dallas raised the necessary money for it and after writing at least eight letters to the nun he had spoken with – apparently the mail service to Tarawa is not very reliable – finally got a response. Sister Alice said a group in Australia had supplied the generator and asked permission to apply the funds to help construct a dormitory. During the return visit in 1993 the nuns invited Eddie and some of his friends and their wives to an elaborate tea and showed them the dormitory their funds had help construct. And some of them are still assisting with donations – even after 50 years, the Marines are still helping the natives of Tarawa.

ABOUT THE AUTHOR

A native Memphian and CBC graduate, Tom Hammond played quarterback at the University of Houston. His master's degree in city planning is from the University of Tennessee.

He and his wife, Barbara, the parents of four grown children, live in Dallas.

Hammond wrote and produced the World War II audio tape series, "Remember With Me." His next book, due out in late 1997, is a biography of Bill Trero, at 14 the youngest combat Marine of World War II and, later, a professional boxer. Hammond is also working on a novel focusing on the homefront during World War II tentatively entitled *Friends Such as These*, scheduled for publication in 1998.

A NOTE ABOUT THE TYPESTYLE

In examining a large number of typefaces for potential usage, typesetter Britt Winn ran across one called "Memphis." Its name and pleasing readability made it a given that it would be the typeface in which this book would be set.